THE DEVELOPMENT OF THE ITALIAN
SCHOOLS OF PAINTING

PRINTED IN THE NETHERLANDS

MADONNA (1370)
By Barnaba da Modena, Gallery, Turin.

Photo Alinari.

THE DEVELOPMENT
OF THE
Italian Schools of Painting

BY

RAIMOND VAN MARLE

Doctor of the Faculty of Letters of the University of Paris

VOLUME IV

With 4 collotype plates and 254 illustrations

THE HAGUE
MARTINUS NIJHOFF
1924

759.5
M
V.4

TABLE OF CONTENTS.

Chapter I: Venice and the neighbouring regions 1
Chapter II: The Painters of Padua, Verona and Treviso . 110
Chapter III: Painting in Lombardy and Piedmont . . . 209
Chapter IV: The Painters of Rimini 279
Chapter V: The Painters of Modena 355
Chapter VI: The School of Bologna 394
Chapter VII: Painting in Ferrara and other little centers in
             Emilia 482
Additions and corrections 509
Indices 511

N.B. The terms "right" and "left" are used from the standpoint of the spectator unless the contrary be stated.

CHAPTER I.

VENICE AND THE NEIGHBOURING REGIONS (¹).

If, in writing the history of the minor Italian schools of the 14th century, we begin with that of Venice, it is because, as in the past, the City of the Lagunes took rather an unusual place in the development of painting. We must admit, however, that it was not a very distinguished one. Venetian painting, more than that of any other region, remained under the domination of the Byzantine tradition. The geographical situation of the city suffices to explain this persistence, and the specimens of art that we find along the Dalmatian coast are abundant proof of the route by which the Byzantine style reached Venice. Nevertheless if the city had possessed any painters of exceptional talent, it is very probable that the Oriental domination would have disappeared long before the 15th century; but the Venetian artists, although skilful in technique and very capable, had little individuality. However we cannot deny the presence of characteristics peculiar to the Italian national art in almost all the pictorial productions of Venice, and the struggle which took place between the Byzantine and the Western elements in the rest of Italy more than a hundred years before, is manifest in Venetian painting of the 14th century. The Occidental form of art, however, had acquired a different aspect. Whereas in the 13th century, we called the current manner of painting during the transition stage,

---

(¹) *Zanetti*, Della pittura veneziana e delle opere pubbliche de veneziani maestri, Venezia, 1771. *B. Cecchetti,* Saggia, Arch. Venet., XXXIII, 1886. *Caffi*, Pittore veneziani dall 1300. Arch. Venet., XXXV, 1888, p. 57. *Flat*, Les premiers Venitiens, Paris, 1899. *P. Molmenti*, I primi pittori veneziani, Rassegna d'Arte, 1903, p. 129. *L. Venturi*, Le origini della pittura veneziana, Venice, 1906. *L. Testi*, La storia della pittura veneziana, I, Bergamo, 1909.

the Italo-Byzantine style, in Venice during the 14th, we have to give it another name and that which I think best describes it is Gothico-Byzantine. It is however a Gothic element peculiar to Venice and very different to the Northern Gothic.

There are also some Venetian productions of the 14th century which are entirely Byzantine, at least there is no trace of Gothicism in them. These are not any older than the others; on the contrary the most striking example, that of the mosaics in the Baptistery of S. Marco, dates from about 1350, while some of the panels are still later. There was not a great number of painters at the end of the 13th or beginning of the 14th century. It is true, however, that as early as 1271, Venice had already a corporation of painters (¹) and although this is the oldest with which we meet in Italy, it seems to have been composed uniquely of painter-decorators (²).

Paintings in Venice of about the year 1300 are the frescoes in the church of the SS. Apostoli which I have already dealt with in the first volume of this work, the crucifix on the altar in the Chapter room of S. Marco, and in the church of St. Agnese, a panel from a box belonging to the Blessed Juliet which was adorned in 1297 with a figure of the saint herself and with those of SS. Cataldus and Blasius (³). Executed about the same time and very much after the same manner, is a panel in a room over the sacristy of the school of S. Giovanni Evangelista. It comes from the Badoer Hospital and represents the Virgin as Orante with the Child Jesus blessing between SS. John the Baptist, Peter, John the Evangelist and another figure which has now disappeared. The picture is signed: *"Franciscus Pinsis ocp"*, which might very well be the signature of a certain "Francesco pittore a S. Croce" who is mentioned in a deed of 1291 (⁴).

These panels however are of little importance as they do not possess any local individuality. The first typically Venetian painting which is of some artistic value is found in the church of S. Donato at Murano; it represents a large figure of this saint in

---

(¹) *G. Monticolo*, Il capitolare dei pittori a Venezia, Nuov. Arch. Veneto, I, p. 321. *L. Testi*, op. cit., p. 137.
(²) This is the opinion held by *L. Venturi*, op. cit., p. 15.
(³) *P. Molmenti*, Rassegna d'Arte, 1903.
(⁴) *L. Testi*, op. cit., p. 171.

Fig. 1. Venetian School, Relief of St. Donato, 1310. S. Donato, Murano.
Photo Alinari.

low relief and coloured and two miniature painted figures of the donors (fig. 1).

Below to the left we read: *"Corando MCCCX indicion VIII in tempo de lo nobele homo miser Donato memo honora do Podesta de Muran facta fo quest ancôna de miser San Donado"*.

The importance of this panel lies in the extreme fineness of the execution, especially of the two small kneeling figures, but they alone are not sufficient for us to be able to recognize a local style. This work has been attributed to a certain Bartolomeo Nasôn (¹) or Cà Naxon but it has now been ascertained that no such artist ever existed (²); though at Murano in 1325, there was a painter of the name of Bartolomeo di S. Stefano (³).

Among the pictures now dispersed but of which we find mention in old descriptions of Venice (⁴), there was one of the Saviour and the Virgin in the "Scuola della Nunziata dei Servi" bearing the date 1314. Of another work of 1321, originally in the little church of S. Sebastiano of Venice, there remains one panel, the back of a box, which is preserved in the Cathedral of Dignano in Istria. On it the Blessed Leo Bembo and two of his miracles were represented and below the inscription: "*MCCCXXI fatu fecit hoc opus*".

The names of several artists of the first quarter of the 14th century are found in documents (⁵) but of these we do not possess any works. The few dated pictures that we have already mentioned do not really belong to the Venetian school of which Maestro Paolo is the most important figure, if not the veritable founder.

The characteristcs of the Gothico-Byzantine school are the outcome of an intermingling of Gothic forms and design with the general conception and technique of Byzantine art. The elongated forms show but rarely the hardness of outline and rigidity of the folds of drapery of genuine Byzantine productions but display a truly Gothic elegance, while the long folds of the drapery seem to foreshadow that typical and almost international form of drapery which we find at the beginning of the 15th century. On the other hand the solemnity of the images, the dark colour of the faces

---

(¹) *V. Zanetti*, Guida storica di Murano, 1866.

(²) *L. Testi*, op. cit., p. 149.

(³) *R. Fulin*, Cinque testamenti di pittori ignoti del sec. XIV, Archivio Veneto, XII, p. 130.

(⁴) *L. Testi*, op. cit., p. 151.

(⁵) *Idem*, p. 103 note 4 and p. 131.

— sometimes quite brown — with marked effects of chiaroscuro, the black hair and the types of the figures in general as well as the magnificence of the textures, frequently threaded with gold, all connect this school with the Byzantine tradition.

The Gothico-Byzantine style seems to have made its appearance in Venetian painting shortly after 1330. The earliest dated work is the altar-piece of the Death of the Virgin at Vicenza; it is a production of Maestro Paolo's and shows the date 1333 in the inscription. A polyptych at Piove di Sacco is probably of the year 1334 and the panel which adorns the tomb of Francesco Dandolo in the church della Salute of about 1340.

There is one panel still somewhat earlier; it dates from 1324 and represents the Coronation of the Virgin with eight angels behind the back of the throne (fig. 2).

I only know this picture from the photograph from which I judge that it was to be found once upon a time in Venice, but I have never come across the original in any church or collection, nor is it mentioned by any author who has written on the Venetian school of this period. It is not unusual to find false signatures and dates on old Venetian pictures and it would be very important to find this picture again in order to establish the authenticity of its signature; for if genuine we should have in this panel the oldest dated monument of the Venetian school.

The earliest date that we have concerning Maestro Paolo is that of 1333 which we find inscribed on his panel at Vicenza (¹). About the middle of the 17th century Count Gualdo possessed a picture of the Death of St. Francis which was signed: *"Paulus Venetiis fecit hoc opus 1333"* (²) but is has disappeared.

Towards the year 1335 Maestro Paolo, together with his brother Marco who made the windows of the Frari church, executed some designs for tapestries. In 1341 and 1346 he is mentioned as inhabitant of the S. Luca quarter and in April 1345, he, with his sons Luca and Giovanni, signed the painted cover of the "Pala d'Oro" in S. Marco. The following year he was paid twenty ducats for an altar-piece for the S. Niccolo chapel of the

---

(¹) The dates for this painter which have been published by divers authors have been united together by *L. Testi*, op. cit , p. 187.

(²) *Idem*, p. 192.

Fig. 2. Venetian School, the Coronation of the Virgin, 1323.

Photo Naya.

Palace of the Doges but this picture was destroyed by fire in 1483.

The Madonna signed by Maestro Paolo at Carpineta (near Cesena) dates from 1347; of the year 1358 we possess two other works signed by the master and his son Giovanni, the one at

Sigmaringen representing the Coronation of the Virgin, the other an allegorical picture at Stuttgart. As Marco — probably another son — is mentioned in September 1362 as "del fu Maestro Paolo pittore" we can assume that his father must have died before this date.

The authentic works of this painter are then only five in number, three of which were executed with the assistance of his sons.

The Death of the Virgin between SS. Francis and Antony of Padua of 1333 comes originally from the church of S. Francesco at Vicenza and after having passed through various hands, it is now to be found in the Gallery of that town (previously no. 28 now no. 157, fig. 3). This picture is probably only part of a more important polyptych. The frame is modern and the eight figures of the predella as well as the eight others in the three pinnacles are of a later date ([1]).

The composition of the central panel is traditional; the Virgin is stretched on her bier with the Apostles and numerous angels grouped behind her; in the centre the Saviour is depicted with the small personification of His Mother's soul in His arms. Higher up He is seen carrying it to heaven. Each of the two lateral saints is represented on a separate panel; one holds an open book, the other a closed one. Below the couch of the Virgin we read: "*MCCCXXXIII Paulus de Veneciis pinxit hoc opus*".

From this work we see at a glance that Paolo was greatly dominated by the Byzantine tradition; this is specially obvious in the schematic composition, the solemn and rather rigid attitudes, the types, the technique of the drawing, the colour of the faces and the gold weaving in the robe of the Saviour. There are certain Gothic elements in the construction of the figures, especially those of the lateral saints, and in the drapery, as may be observed in the figures of SS. Peter and Paul who can be recognized at the head and feet of the Virgin. But in the whole group of Gothico-Byzantine paintings, this, I think, is the one in which the Oriental influence is most pronounced.

I believe we should ascribe to this early stage in the evolution of Maestro Paolo a Coronation of the Virgin in the Brera Gallery (no. 227, plate I) which for a long time was attributed to Lorenzo

---

([1]) I should think even later than Battista da Vicenza to whom Signor *Testi* hesitatingly attributes them.

Fig. 3. Maestro Paolo, the Death of the Virgin and saints, 1333. Gallery, Vicenza. Photo Ist. Art. Graf.

Veneziano. Messrs. Malaguzzi Valeri and Testi hesitatingly adhere to this attribution ([1]); Cavalcaselle and Signor L. Venturi contradict it ([2]), but no one has as yet ever connected this picture with Maestro Paolo.

([1]) *F. Malaguzzi-Valeri*, Catalogo della R. Pinacoteca di Brera, Bergamo, 1908, p. 132. *Testi*, op. cit., p. 228.

([2]) *L. Venturi*, op. cit., p. 28; on account of certain non-Venetian details in the composition Signor Venturi is of opinion that the picture could not have

Nevertheless, comparing this panel with those of the Death of the Virgin and Coronation of the Madonna of 1358 at Sigmaringen, it seems to me possible that Maestro Paolo might have been the author of this work which is the finest of the group of Gothico-Byzantine paintings.

If this be so, the Brera picture must be of slightly later date than the Death of the Virgin at Vicenza, because the line of the folds is more Gothic. In the Coronation at Sigmaringen the Oriental peculiarities are less marked — perhaps due to his having collaborated with his son — but neither the proportions nor the types and form of the faces have changed. The angels in all three works are very alike.

It has been suggested that some small pictures which surround another panel of the Coronation of the Virgin in the Gallery of Venice (no. 21) formed part of the same polyptych as the Coronation in the Brera, in other words the central part (the panel in Milan) has been substituted for another representation of the same subject which is signed by a certain "plebanus" Stefano who will be discussed further on.

I certainly think that these small paintings (fig. 4), twenty in number [1] are from the same hand as the Coronation in the Brera and consequently are works of Maestro Paolo's. The execution is much finer than that of the panel of 1333 and is very analogous to that of the second row of scenes on the cover of the Pala d'Oro; on the whole, however, the style is more Byzantine and the Gothic features rare. In any case this manner of painting does not resemble that of Lorenzo Veneziano to whose school these panels have been ascribed [2].

In attributing these pictures to Maestro Paolo we have to

been made until towards the end of the 14th century. This is a question with which I shall deal later on.

[1] Apart from the figures of two prophets, these panels represent on the highest row, Pentecost, St. Francis receiving St. Clare, St. Francis breaking with his father, the stigmatization of St. Francis, his death and the Last Judgment. These pictures are smaller than the others and are separated one from another by figures of the four Evangelists. The second row shows the Infant Christ in the manger adored by the Magi, the Baptism, the Calvary and the Crucifixion, and the third the Last Supper, the Kiss of Judas, Noli me tangere and the Ascension.

[2] L. *Serra*, Catalogo delle R.R. Gallerie di Venezia, Venice, 1914, p. 14.

admit that a considerable change took place in the artist's manner. This change seems actually to have occurred already in the painting with which he adorned the cover of the altar of S. Marco in 1344 (fig. 5) where there is clear evidence of it; but we should not forget that the artist was assisted by his sons and, furthermore, that the panel was entirely repainted in 1847. This

Fig. 4. Maestro Paolo and a Venetian Master of the 2nd half of the 14th century, polyptych. Accademia, Venice.
Photo Anderson.

panel is divided into fourteen divisions the upper seven of which contain half-length figures; the central one shows that of the dead Christ with the Cross behind Him, on the left are depicted SS. George, Mark and the Virgin and on the right SS. John the Evan-

---

(1) Note 1 of p. 11. The incidents illustrated are: St. Peter crowning St. Mark pope, St. Mark healing the wound in the hand of the shoemaker Anianus, the saint in prison conversing with the Saviour, St. Mark thrown to the ground and beaten by soldiers, the body of the holy Evangelist being brought to Venice, the relics worshipped in the basilica and the sick and maimed around the saint's tomb begging to be cured.

gelist, Peter and Nicholas. The lower row is composed of seven scenes from the life of St. Mark (¹).

The conjecture that the original aspect of the panel was fairly Byzantine is supported by the actual appearance of SS. Gregory, Peter and Nicholas. The elongated proportions and the drapery of St. John the Evangelist rather belong to the Gothic tradition. It is much more difficult to imagine what the scenes on the second row must have been before the restoration which has greatly changed the details, leaving, however, the composition

(¹) See note on p. 10.

Fig. 5. Maestro Paolo and his Sons, Cover of the Pala d'Oro, 1344. S. Marco, Venice.

and the architecture probably much as they were. Below the first panel on the left the date: "*MCCCXLV M̄S Āplis Die XXII*" is inscribed and on the second picture from the right we read: "*Mgr. Paulus c̄u Luca et, Johe Filiis suis pinxerut hoc opus*".

In his Madonna in the church of Carpineta near Cesena, Maestro Paolo created a type which was to be widely disseminated in Venice (¹). The Virgin sits on rather an elaborate throne over the back of which appear six angels; she holds the Child standing on her knee. The appearance of the Madonna is not dissimilar to that in the Coronation of the Brera and in the picture at Sigmaringen; the faces in particular are alike and the same amount of Byzantinism is present in all three. Below in the centre of the panel of Carpineta the artist has signed: "*Paulus De Veneciis pinxit MCCCXLVII*".

The attitudes of the principal figures in the Coronation of the Virgin in the Museum of Sigmaringen (fig. 6) (²) which it appears came originally from Ravenna, are identical with those in the panel of the Brera. The fall of the draperies and the form of the crowns are also remarkably alike in these two works. Since the cloaks are entirely repainted we cannot exclude the possibility that they too originally showed an ornamental design. This ornamentation, however, is visible on the revers of the cloaks which leads one to think that the outer surfaces were not also adorned in this manner for the revers in the panel of the Brera are plain, and Maestro Paolo then probably imagined these cloaks plain on one side and figured on the other. In both cases the sun and the moon are depicted at the feet of the Saviour and the Virgin but only the feet of the former are visible. Again in both we see an angel at either side holding a little organ of Gothic design, and a large group of angels playing on musical instruments behind the throne; the thrones, however, in no way resemble; the motif in the border of the back of the one in Sigmaringen is borrowed from Arabic characters.

Although Venetian painting of the Trecento abounds in Coronations of the Virgin, there is not another instance of such a

---

(¹) *F. Harck*, Quadri italiani nelle gallerie privati di Germania, Arch. Stor. dell' Arte, 1893, p. 388.

(²) *G. Gigli*, Per un quadro di Paolo di Venezia, Rassegna d'Arte, 1908, p. 182. L. *Testi*, op. cit., pp. 534—535.

Fig. 6. Maestro Paolo, the Coronation of the Virgin, 1347. Gallery, Sigmaringen.

striking resemblance. It is, however, very clear that in the latter the artist is less inspired by the Byzantine style; this is evident in the technique of the faces which besides are much less dark, and in the generally less austere spirit of the whole work. The signature at the foot of the picture runs: *"MCCCLVIII Paulus cum Johaninus eiu filiu piserut hoc op"*.

It is quite probable that the change in this artist's style is due to the collaboration of his son Giovannino but perhaps a certain evolution towards an Occidental supremacy took place in Maestro Paolo's own art. All the same I cannot admit that Paolo, the same year that he executed the Coronation of Sigmaringen also painted the panel at Stuttgart and as this work is again signed by the father and the son, I think the latter must have executed the greater part of it.

The picture illustrates the legend of Ottavianus Augustus whom, on account of his great beauty, the senators desired to include among the divinities adored in the sacred chants, but Octavian, on consulting the sibyl Tiburtina, is shown an image of the Virgin and Child in a circle of gold (¹). The principal part of the composition is a medallion of the Madonna. Below on either side, the background is filled in with elaborate architecture; in the centre a fountain, supported by three nude figures, shows the inscription: "Fons acque in liquorum dei versus est; qua Christus di Maria Virgine natus est". The building on the right is the temple from which the heathens flee, while within the statues fall over and break; the building on the left is the palace of Octavian who is seen looking up at the vision shown him by the sibyl. The signature is inscribed on the fountain, it runs: *"MCCCLVIII Paulus cum filio ...."*. Cavalcaselle believed the picture to be by Maestro Paolo but doubted the authenticity of the signature which seems to be quite genuine. I must admit that if I were not certain of the signature, it would not have been difficult to convince me that the picture was by another artist. The Virgin and Child have but little in common with Paolo's

---

(¹) Leggenda Aurea, cap. VI, La Nativité de N.S. Jésus Christ. *A. Graf*, Roma nelle memorie e nelle immaginazione del Medio-Evo (Ristampa), Turin, 1915, p.247. *Loeser*, I quadri italiani della Galleria di Stoccarda, L'Arte, 1899, p. 172. *Testi*, op. cit., p. 198. *L. Venturi*, op. cit., p. 21, *A. Venturi*, Una rappresentazione della leggenda Augusto, Ausonia, I, 1906, p. 93.

other works; there is no trace of Byzantinism to be found in them and there can be no doubt that this part was left entirely to the son. The architecture too is very different, so also the fountain which suggests to our minds the reminiscences of classical art so frequently met with in Giotto's works. Only the small figures in the lower part of the picture show a fairly strong resemblance to what we find in Maestro Paolo's other works; the technique of the faces is especially Byzantine.

Signor Testi finds that Signor Moschetti exaggerates the importance of Maestro Paolo when he says that it is to him we owe the start and early perfection of Venetian art. This, however, to a certain extent is almost incontestable. The only question which might arise is whether there did not exist other artists just as important as Paolo but whose names have not come down to us.

This does not seem probable. Maestro Paolo was almost certainly the first painter of that period in Venice, and we have already seen that the oldest certain dated work of that school of Venetian painting which we call the Gothico-Byzantine, is from his hand. Besides this, the entire school whose members apart from Caterino and Donato, are anonymous, is chiefly inspired by Maestro Paolo, and that it owes its existence and characteristics largely to him is consequently almost certain. The rather harsh judgment of Cavalcaselle, Molmenti (¹) and other lovers of the Venetian school of the 15th century is easily explained by the wide difference in tendency and in artistic manifestation which existed between these early artists of the Lagunes and the geniuses of the Renaissance; but once we admire the primitive productions of other schools there is no reason why we should not appreciate those of Maestro Paolo and his group of followers.

It is obvious that the Venetian, more than any other school of the Trecento, was dominated by the Byzantine tradition, and to what extent Maestro Paolo himself tried to free it from this yoke is difficult to say. The authentic works dated and executed entirely by the master's own hand are only two in number, the Death of the Virgin of 1333 and the Madonna at Carpineta of 1347. In comparing them, we cannot admit any diminution of the Byzantine influence; perhaps he made no attempt to reduce it.

(¹) P. *Molmenti*, La peinture vénitienne, trans. by M. J. de Crozals, Florence, 1904, p. 8, says "Maître Paul est informe".

On the other hand, it would be unjust to pretend that his works do not contain other elements, because in the structure of the bodies and the drapery there are traces of a thoroughly Northern Gothicism which probably reached Venice directly from the North, from Germany, in fact.

In some of the small scenes on the lid of the Pala d'Oro and the altar-piece (no. 21) in the Gallery of Venice, there are certain details which are reminiscent of Giotto. Besides, when Maestro Paolo executed them, Giotto's frescoes at Padua, almost at the gates of Venice, were already thirty or forty years old; naturally Maestro Paolo knew them and considering Giotto's universal fame had probably studied them. From here no doubt originate the interiors seen in section such as we find in the small scenes of the panels in S. Marco and the Gallery. They are conceived in exactly the same way as in the works of the great Florentine, for the buildings in which the events should take place form the background. We can no doubt also ascribe to a Giottesque influence, the tragic action which is rendered in a manner very superior to what one would expect from an artist purely inspired by the Byzantines. Signor L. Venturi thinks that the panel in the Venice Gallery must have been executed towards the end of the 14th century on account of the presence of certain details which he believes were only introduced into the Venetian school at this moment. Among them he quotes the Giottesque iconography of the scenes from the life of St. Francis. But before agreeing with this, we must first of all prove that Giotto really introduced important innovations in the representations of the legend of St. Francis — and this seems very doubtful if we compare his frescoes in the Upper Church at Assisi with the 13th century series in the nave of the Lower Church and if we consider with what fidelity to old iconographical traditions Giotto depicted scenes from the Evangel — and secondly, if this be so, a reason should be given why these images remained unknown in Venice until almost a century after Giotto represented them at Assisi.

Therefore, I see no reason to suppose that the altar-piece in the Accademia of Venice should be posterior to the date of Maestro Paolo's activity, and I am of opinion that we are right in ascribing it to this artist. As in all his other works, here too, we find certain Gothic elements intermingling with a Byzantine foundation, and as in the panels with small scenes, a Giottesque influence can be observed in the composition.

Maestro Paolo's numerous pupils must remain anonymous; the only disciple mentioned in the documents is called Niccolo da Zara([1]) and none of his works are known.

The oldest painting which shows some connection with Paolo's art is — apart from the Coronation of the Virgin of 1324, which is probably earlier but only known from the photograph — a panel in the sacristy of the church of Piove di Sacco (province of Padua).

Pinton, who was the first to publish it([2]), states that the inscription ran: "*Mag. Paulinus 1332 pic. d. Veneci*", but this signature has since disappeared and as the chapel which it adorns was built only in 1334, there must be some mistake, more especially as it is difficult to believe that it can be a work from the master's own hand. It represents the enthroned Virgin with two small devotees at her feet and at the sides SS. Clare, James Minor, Martin, Thomas, Ursula and Francis. Of the pinnacles, there only remain the Virgin and angel of the Annunciation and a bust of the dead Christ between two small figures of saints. These latter panels are considerably repainted and the others much damaged. The Virgin, however, possesses a certain charm and seems of finer execution than the other figures. The colours are Byzantine but the long elegant figures seem to be modelled on Gothic proportions.

Chronologically we now come to the picture in the form of a lunette which originally adorned the tomb of Doge Francesco Dandolo in one of the sacristies of Sta. Maria della Salute, Venice (fig. 7)([3]).

The Virgin sits on rather a low seat, the background being formed by a curtain held up by four angels. The Child Christ blesses the Doge who kneels on the left apparently presented by St. Francis who seems full of solicitude for his protégé. The Virgin turns towards the Doge's wife who kneels on the right and behind whom stands the protecting figure of St. Elizabeth, forming a pendant to St. Francis on the other side. This is a

---

([1]) R. *Fulin,* op. cit.

([2]) Nuovo Arch. Veneto, 1891, vol. I, p. 77.

([3]) There is a project to reconstruct this tomb in the Frari church, v. Venezia studi di arte e storia e cura della Direzione dei museo Correr, Milan, Rome, 1920, p. 270.

Fig. 7. Venetian School, Madonna, saint and adorers, 1339. Sta. Maria della Salute, Venice.

Photo Alinari.

composition which persisted in Venice for several hundred years. The death of Francesco Dandolo which occurred in 1339 enables us to date this picture with precision. The spirit of the work is slightly less Byzantine than that of Paolo's own productions, nevertheless the type of the angels and the technique of the faces, with their hard design and marked contrast of light and brown shadows, closely connects this artist with the founder of the school, as do also the decorative details.

I think this picture, as well as the previous one, shows a fairly strong resemblance to a small group of four paintings, three of which Signor Testi has already classified together. They are a Madonna in the Louvre, a polyptych at Chioggia and an altar-piece in the Cathedral of Pirano in Istria, and to them I think should be added a polyptych in the Museum of Lecce (Apulia).

At the foot of the central panel of the polyptych (fig. 8) in the Oratory of S. Martino at Chioggia, we find the date: "*MCCCXLVIIII MS JULI...*"(¹). This altar-piece no longer possesses its original form, the various panels having been dismounted and reunited in quite another manner, while others, of more recent date have been added. The principal figure is the Virgin holding the Child Jesus on her knee; He is in the act of receiving a banner surmounted by a cross from one of the two figures of a confraternity who kneel below. The lateral panels show the images of SS. Peter, who carries a staff instead of his traditional keys, John the Baptist, John the Evangelist and Paul. The half-length figures in the predella are those of the Magdalene, SS. Dominic, Martin, Agnes and Julian. Over the central panel there is a sculpture of later date of St. Martin on horseback and the beggar, and at either side four scenes from the life of the titular saint (fig. 9). Still higher we see the Saviour on the Cross between the Virgin and St. John and over it the bust of an Evangelist; between this part and two other scenes from the life of St. Martin which are depicted at either side, there are two figures of angels dating from the 16th century.

The connection between this artist and Maestro Paolo is obvious. It is not only the type of the Madonna that is analogous, but we find here the same Byzantine spirit and similar colours

---

(¹) *L. Testi*, op. cit., p. 202, from the few remaining fragments, completes the inscription *fu fatta quest opera.*

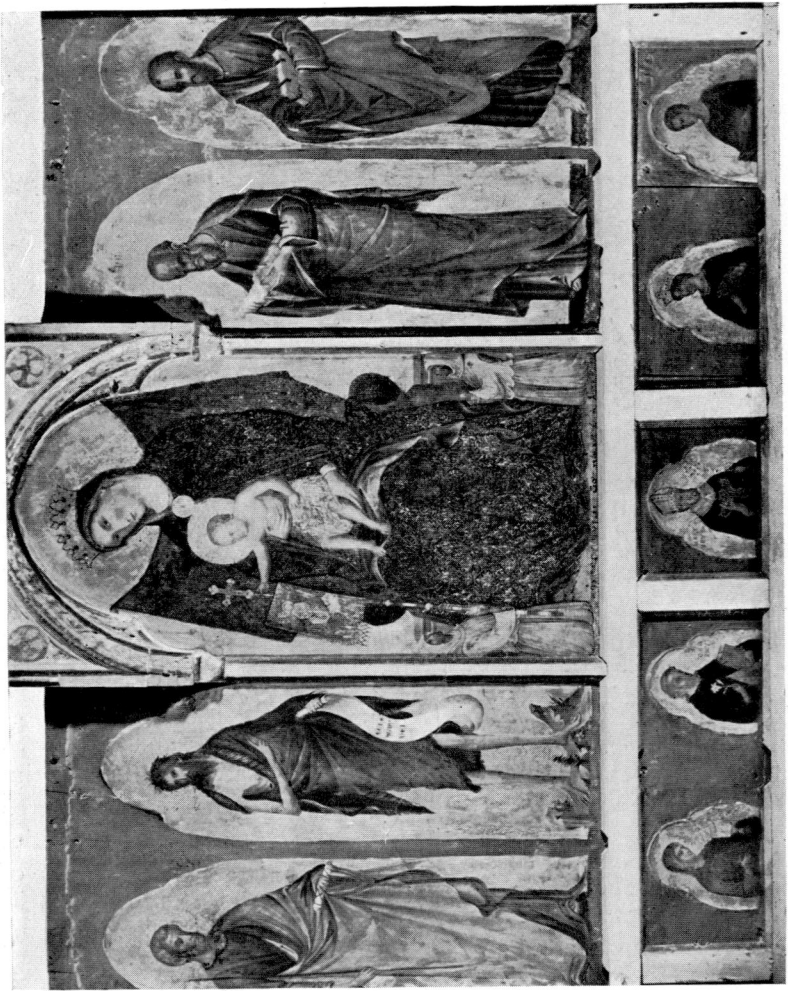

Fig. 8. The Master of the Pirano altar-piece, polyptych. Oratory of S. Martino, Chioggia.   Photo Alinari.

and technique. The differences between this painter and Maestro Paolo consist in the exaggerated length of the figures at either side of the Virgin, the vivacity of the Infant Christ, which is quite a characteristic of this master, and the poorness of composition and architecture which, however, in one instance (the saint lying on his couch) corresponds in form with what we found in one

Fig. 9. The Master of the Pirano altar-piece, polyptych. Oratory of
S. Martino, Chioggia.   Photo Alinari.

of Maestro Paolo's works. All the same, it can be said that in general the compositions of the Master of Chioggio are more Oriental than Maestro Paolo's.

The chief feature which induces us to associate the panel on Francesco Dandolo's tomb and the polyptych at Chioggia is the animation of the Infant Christ; the same is the case for the polyptych at Piove di Sacco which shows, besides, the same attenuated proportions of the figures. The resemblance is much less marked

Fig. 10. The Master of the Pirano altar-piece, Madonna. Louvre.
Photo Braun.

between this last polyptych and the one at Lecce; the form and decoration of the frame are also somewhat different. The greater part of the frame of the picture at Chioggia is missing, but from the few remaining pieces and the traces of it on the panels, one can suppose that it was very similar to that surrounding the panel at Lecce. The polyptych in the sacristy at Pirano has a slightly different frame and one in a good state of preservation (¹). Here again the centre is formed by a figure of the Virgin seated on a throne behind which two angels hold a curtain. The agitated Child is held in His Mother's arms and at either side are four very elongated figures of saints.

Comparing the Madonna of this polyptych with the one in the Louvre (no. 1541, fig. 10), which is there attributed to Stefano Veneziano, it is very evident that they are by one and the same artist. The chief points of difference are the absence of the angels in the background and a slight change in the attitude of the Child, Who, however, has the same lively appearance. In the right-hand lower corner we see the date *"MCCCLIII M O T"* (October). This panel originally formed the central part of a triptych the wing sof which were sent to the Museums of Toulouse and Ajaccio in 1876; they showed St. Antony with St. Bartholomew and the Baptist with St. Francis (²).

A point which differentiates the Madonna of the polyptych at Lecce (fig. 11) from the other images is the absence of the Virgin's crown, and in this the picture resembles the altar-piece at Piove di Sacco (³). The Madonna at Lecce is depicted nursing the Child Who seems very intent on his little task. Again four saints are seen at either side and as in the polyptych at Chioggia their names are inscribed above; at Pirano the inscriptions were below. Above each lateral panel is a smaller one containing a bust of a saint; the one over the Madonna is missing. The marked resem-

---

(¹) *Caprin*, L'Istria nobilissima, Part II, p. 58. *The Same*, L'Istria e la Dalmazia, Bergamo, p. 36.

(²) S. *de Ricci*, Description raisonnée des peintures du Louvre, I, Paris, 1913, p. 146. *H. Rachon*, Le musée de Toulouse, Toulouse, 1906, p. 38. *P. Perdrizet et R. Jean*, La Galerie Campana et les musées français, Bordeaux, 1907, p. 32. *Cavalcaselle* read the date as 1354.

(³) This polyptych has been attributed to Jacobello del Fiore: *O. Valentini*, Di un polittico di Jacobello del Floro esistente in Lecce, Bolletino d'Arte del Ministero della Pubbl. Istr., July 1913. *M. Salmi*, L'Arte, 1919, p. 162.

Fig. 11. The Master of the Pirano altar-piece, polyptych. Museum, Lecce.
Photo Minist. del. Pubbl. Istr.

blance which exists between the lateral figures of this polyptych — especially the two nearest the Virgin — and those at Pirano, not only in their attenuated from but also in their hard ascetic aspect, is sufficient to confirm our supposition that they are from the same hand.

Although a certain number of individual characteristics, among them the attenuation of his figures, reveals the "Master of Chioggia's" independence, the most important factor in his painting is the influence of Maestro Paolo, whose most faithful pupil we can certainly consider him to be. There are few details which differentiate his art from that of Byzantium, but the vivacity of the Child Jesus is one so opposed to the Oriental spirit that in this alone the "Master of Chioggia" is slightly more Italian than Maestro Paolo with whom he was almost contemporary. I see no reason for dating the polyptych of Pirano as late as 1372, as Signor Testi has done ([1]).

The most important of the other works which manifest a connection with Maestro Paolo's art is the triptych in the Museum of Trieste, which Signor L. Venturi has already judiciously classified among the works which reflect this master's influence (figs. 12, 13 and 14) ([2]).

The principal part of this picture is divided into six rows, each of six scenes, thirty-three of them illustrating the history of the Saviour from the Annunciation to the Ascension, the other three the death of the Virgin, the death of St. Clare and St. Francis receiving the stigmata. It is curious to note that between the Calvary and the Crucifixion, the head of the Redeemer represented against a cloth is symbolic of St. Veronica having wiped His face and the miracle which resulted thereof. On the inner surface of each of the wings there are three divisions, slightly larger than the central ones, showing figures of saints. Apart from the isolated images, we find the representation of an event, perhaps the confirmation of the order of the Poor Clares. A saint is depicted on the outer surface of each of the wings of the triptych. The picture comes from the convent of the Poor Clares.

The author of this beautiful work was even more dominated

([1]) L. *Testi*, op. cit., p. 234.
([2]) G. *Caprin*, Il Trecento a Trieste, Trieste, 1897. *The same*, Trieste, Bergamo, 1907, p. 50.

Fig. 12. Venetian School, Scenes from the Life of Christ, 1st half of the 14th century. Museo Civico, Trieste.

Photo Alinari.

by the Byzantine style than Maestro Paolo himself. The compositions, types, attitudes, expressions and gestures are reminiscent before all of the miniaturists whose productions we find in Greek manuscripts of the 11th and 12th centuries. This is especially the case for the thirty-six scenes of the central panel among which we also observe traces of Giottesque backgrounds and architecture similar to what we found in some of Maestro

Fig. 13. Venetian School, Scenes from the Life of Christ, 1st half of the 14th century. Museo Civico, Trieste.   Photo Alinari.

Paolo's works. In the larger figures it is clear that we are dealing with a Venetian interpretation of Byzantine art.

There can be no doubt that Donato tried to imitate Maestro Paolo's art, but as the only work of his that has come down to us was executed in collaboration with Caterino, we shall discuss him together with this latter artist whose paintings belong to the transition manner.

Fig. 14. Venetian School, Saints, 1st half of the 14th century. Museo Civico, Trieste.

Photo Alinari.

Among the anonymous works of the school of Maestro Paolo, a panel of the Coronation of the Virgin in the author's collection might still be mentioned (fig. 15). The composition is unusual, because not only are the figures in inverse order to the usual arrangement but rather a fantastic image of God the Father, placing a hand on each of the nimbi of the Saviour and the Virgin, is depicted behind. The folds of the draperies fall in fine Gothic lines and the decorative details are minutely executed. In different churches in Venice we find some other works which can be classed with this Coronation of the Virgin; they are a polyptych, (repainted in 1756) of the Virgin with saints, in the sacristy of S. Silvestro; a Madonna in prayer in which Paolo's influence is faint, in the sacristy of S. Trovaro; a similar panel in S. Francesco alla Vigna; an image of the Saviour in S. Samuele; and at Murano a polyptych of the Death of the Virgin and saints.

With this same group can be included two panels, each showing two figures of saints, in the Correr Museum [1]; a very fine little panel of a polyptych representing St. Catherine, from the Earl of Southesk's collection, which is exposed in the Edinburgh Picture Gallery where it was ascribed to Bartolo di Fredi; fourteen isolated figures from a polyptych — the Madonna and saints — in the Museum of Poitiers (nos. 186 and 187) of a coarser execution and slightly later date, and a fairly large number of half-length figures of the Virgin that belong to different private collectors. The Venetian "Madonari" continued for some hundreds of years to reproduce the same image [2].

---

[1] *L. Testi*, op cit., pp. 159 and 167, classifies with this group a panel of the Virgin and Child between the Baptist and St. James Major with a half-length figure of the dead Saviour above, in the Accademia of Venice (no. 6). It is however the production of a late artist of the second half of the 15th century who worked largely after the Byzantine manner.

[2] The following productions of this current might still be mentioned: two figures of Evangelists in the Storeroom of the Vatican Gallery (nos. 163-164), executed rather after the manner of Maestro Paolo; a polyptych in the same place (no. 122) showing the Virgin and six saints all separately framed, the work of a provincial artist; four fine half-length figures of saints that I saw for sale in Rome a short time ago; they closely approach Maestro Paolo's manner but the drapery is more Gothic; while a few years ago an art-dealer in Paris had a panel with three half-length figures of saints, two of whom held a book, the third bestowing a blessing after the Greek manner, a good early Venetian production, showing a strong Byzantine influence.

Fig 15. School of Maestro Paolo, the Coronation of the Virgin. The Author's Collection.

Fig. 16. The Baptism of the Lord and prophets, mosaic, 13421—355. The Baptistery, S. Marco, Venice.

Photo Alinari.

Before passing to that group of painters which occupies the transition period between the Gothico-Byzantine and a newer form of art, I should like to mention a few works in which the Gothic or Western element is almost entirely absent, and which, from their appearance might make us think that they were produced in Byzantium itself.

The tendency towards this more purely Oriental style of painting seems to have coincided with the execution of the mosaics in the baptistery adjoining the basilica of S. Marco which were made between 1342 and 1355 by order of Doge Andrea Dandolo who governed the city during these years ([1]).

The dome of the baptistery is adorned with an image of the Redeemer, Who sends His Apostles forth to preach and baptize in the different parts of the world; the four Doctors of the Church are depicted on the pendentives, and at the sides of the windows, seven scenes from the life of St. John the Baptist (fig. 16) and the Crucifixion, in which the kneeling figures of the Doge as donor, his chancellor Caresini and an unidentified person are represented. In that part which serves as entrance to the chapel we see, above, Christ surrounded by prophets and, on the walls, Herod sending forth the Wise Men, the Adoration of the Magi, the Flight into Egypt and the Massacre of the Innocents (fig. 17).

Of all the works of this group, these mosaics are the most purely Byzantine. With the exception of the Latin inscriptions, there is nothing whatsoever in this decoration to reveal its Occidental origin, and what is particularly strange is that the artists do not manifest a familiarity with the austere and primitive form of Byzantine art but with that rather decadent manner of which the weakness of form, exaggerated rigidity and abundance of detail characterize the contemporary productions of this art in the Orient. Therefore I see no reason to believe, as many do, that these mosaics were executed by Venetian artists. Even admitting that the Venetians had a thoroughly Byzantine training, I find it hardly possible to accept this hypothesis.

I do acknowledge, however, that the mosaics of the St. Isidore chapel in the North transept, although an imitation of Byzantine productions, possess certain Italian peculiarites. It was also Doge Andrea Dandolo who ordered the ornamentation of this chapel, whither he had transported the relics of the saint which had been discovered in 1342. I am not of M. Diehl's opinion that

---

[1] *P. Saccardo*, Les mosaïques de St. Marc à Venise, Venice, 1897, p. 136.

this chapel is "entirely decorated in the Giottesque style" (¹), but it is nevertheless true that in comparing these mosaics with those of the Baptistery, we observe that the compositions are more natural and more dramatic, the backgrounds more elaborate and the forms and expressions less hard. The scenes here illustrate incidents from the life of the saint, the transporting of his relics first to Venice and then to this chapel.

(¹) *Ch. Diehl*, Manuel d'Art byzantin, Paris, 1910, p. 510.

Fig. 17. The Flight into Egypt and the Massacre of the Innocents, mosaic, 1342–1355. The Baptistery, S. Marco, Venice.

Fig. 18. Veneto-Byzantine School, St. Andrew, 2nd half of the 14th century. Correr Museum, Venice. Photo Ist. Art. Graf.

This return to mosaic decoration in Venice seems to have influenced the painters to imitate the technique of that art. It is difficult, however, to date with any precision the productions in which this archaism is voluntary. The most characteristic works of this tendency are two half-length figures of SS. John the

Evangelist and Andrew (fig. 18) in the Correr Museum (nos. 7 and 8)([1]) of which the former bears the false signature: "*Giovanni de Venetia fece MCCLXXXI*". The curious contours and delineation of each feature in the faces provide us with sufficient proof that the painter imitated mosaics, but on the other hand these two panels show so much difference to the other pictorial productions of the Trecento in Venice that we can certainly not base on them alone the argument that all Venetian primitive painting derives from mosaics. Executed much in the same manner as the two saints in the Correr Museum is a head of St. Mark in the Brera Gallery, Milan; it is dated *MCCCLIV*, but on account of certain details which seem to reveal a knowledge of 15th century painting, Signor L. Venturi thinks that possibly a C is missing ([2]).

The influence of the mosaic technique is more evident in two figures of saints — SS. Andrew and John the Baptist — in the National Gallery, Rome, probably to be transferred to that in the Palazzo Venezia (fig. 19), although the elongated forms indicate a certain familiarity with the art of the "Master of Chioggia" or of Lorenzo Veneziano, who will be dealt with later on, and to whom this work has been wrongly attributed.

Another little group is formed by those paintings which, although not in any way imitating the mosaics, show none of those Gothic effects which characterize the works of Maestro Paolo and his followers. These paintings then are thoroughly Byzantine and can only be distinguished from Italo-Byzantine productions of the previous century by a more advanced stage of evolution of some of the details of this category; we can make a sub-division which would comprise those panels in which the figures are large and amply draped and the proportions and attitudes majestic.

A Crucifixion in the Correr Museum (no. 10) shows these peculiarities; the Virgin and St. John are depicted under the Cross and SS. Andrew, Augustine, Catherine and Nicholas at the sides. Two other panels of this group are found in the Ravenna Museum; one is a Crucifixion, similar in composition to the previous one, the other a representation of the Trinity amidst ten figures of saints. Not long ago I saw at a Parisian art-dealer's, three

---

([1]) As this chapter was written before the Correr Museum was transferred to its new site, the numbers here mentioned are those of the old catalogue.

([2]) *L. Venturi*, op. cit., p. 50.

Fig. 19. Veneto-Byzantine School, SS. Andrew and John the Baptist, 2nd half of the 14th century. National Gallery, Rome.

Photo Anderson.

panels in this manner; one of them which represented the Last Judgment has lately been acquired by the Museum of Worcester U.S.A. (¹). Here the Saviour in glory, surrounded by angels, the Virgin and St. John, stretches forth His hand towards the saved

Fig. 20. Byzantine School executed in Venice, Saints, 1st half of the 14th century.

while below the wicked are depicted. The other two showed each four figures of saints (fig. 20).

A certain number of paintings reveal only the peculiarities of Byzantine works and the fact that they are Venetian in origin can but faintly be discerned in some unimportant details. The name of one of the artists of such works is known to us through

(¹) It was published as a 13th century painting from Central Italy by R. Hennicker-Steaton, An Italo-Byzantine panel, Art in America, 1924, p. 76.

a signed picture. It is Gulielmus whose panel in the church of Sta. Maria at Castelnuovo, near Recanati, in The Marches, shows the Virgin enthroned in the centre, her crown supported by two little angels while two miniature devotees kneel at her feet; two saints, one above the other, are depicted at the sides, they are SS. John the Baptist, Antony, Andrew and Christopher (¹). At the foot of the throne we read: "*MCCCLXXXII del Mexe De Março a di vi fe far S. Andrea de Choluço citadin de Venexia questo lavorier Gulielmus pinxit*".

A panel showing the same composition is preserved in the church of S. Niccolo at Piove di Sacco (prov. of Padua); the saints here are the Baptist, SS. Martin, Nicholas and Francis. A fragment of the signature is still visible, it runs: "... *ielmù de Veneci pinxit hoc opus*". The quality of the painting is slightly superior to that of the one at Castelnuovo (²) which is rather a vulgar work and one not easily distinguished from the panels contemporaneously executed in Greece; the types of the Virgin and Child as well as of the saints, the design and the colour belong to the decadence of Byzantine art. For this reason it seems to me inexact to classify Gulielmus as a retrograde Venetian artist; never before in Venice was any painter so absolutely Byzantine. Artists of the name of Guglielmus are mentioned in Venetian documents of 1352, 1364 and 1367 (³). A Venetian painting of a slightly less Byzantine aspect is a triptych in the Gallery of Parma (no. 458) showing in the centre, above, the Crucifixion with a fairly large gathering under the Cross, and below, a half-length figure of the Virgin with the Child, while in the wings are depicted the Annunciation, the Assumption of Mary Magdalene and some figures of saints. It is not a work of very great importance and dates probably from about 1360 or 1370.

Five little panels in the Gallery of Pesaro are of much finer quality; they represent Joachim driven from the Temple, the Meeting at the Golden Gate, the Nativity of the Virgin, the Presentation of the Virgin in the Temple and her Marriage (⁴). The

---

(¹) *Colasanti*, L'Arte, X, 1907, p. 409.

(²) *Testi*, op cit., p. 177.

(³) *Testi*, op cit., p. 178.

(⁴) *L. Serra*, in his guide to the Museum of Pesaro (1920), p. 12, apparently considers them to be Italian works of the beginning of the 14th century.

fineness of the technique of these panels is reminiscent of Duccio's art but they are more Byzantine in style; even the inscriptions are in Greek. Had it not been for one or two details which betray the artist's Occidental temperament, one might almost have believed them to have been executed by a Greek miniaturist. In the composition of the Meeting at the Golden Gate, he seems to follow Giotto and expresses the same tenderness between husband and wife as did the great Florentine; this manifestation of affection does not at all conform to the austere spirit of the Byzantine school. These little pictures were no doubt executed in the first half, probably the second quarter, of the 14th century. A panel of St. Jerome with the lion in the National Gallery, London (no 3543), is a slightly later production of the same current.

D'Agincourt[1] and Rosini[2] both reproduce pictures which seem to have been Venetian productions made under a strong Byzantine influence, but from the plates we are unable to make any critical comparison.

In the history of Venetian painting, Lorenzo does not actually belong to the transition, but he seems to me to have been the painter whose influence brought about the change which occured in the greater part of the Venetian school after the death of Maestro Paolo; this change consisting in the gradual disappearance of the Byzantine elements.

The data we have concerning Lorenzo are chiefly to be found in the inscriptions of his various works. The earliest of these has disappeared; it was the inscription "*MCCCLVI hoc opus Laurentius pinxit*" on a picture which Maffei, the historian of Verona, in his "Verona Illustrata", tells us belonged to him and we can have complete confidence in the statement of this talented writer. Signed works, dating from 1357 and 1359, are found in the Gallery of Venice. A Madonna of 1361 is conserved in the Museum of Padua, and a polyptych of 1366 in the Cathedral of Vicenza.

The Correr Museum possesses a signed panel of 1369 (1370);

[1] *G. B. L. G. Seroux d'Agincourt*, Storia dell' Arte dimostrata coi monumenti (trans. from French), Prato, 1826 etc., Pittura, pls. LXXXV, LXXXVI, LXXXVIII.

[2] *G. Rosini*, Storia della pittura italiana, Pisa, 1839 etc., pl. CXII.

the date 1371 is inscribed at the foot of an unsigned panel in the Accademia of Venice; two figures of saints from a polyptych in the same collection also show this date, and lastly the Madonna in the Louvre bears the date 1372.

Fig. 21. Gulielmus, Madonna and saints, 1382. Sta. Maria at Castelnuovo, Recanati.   Photo Minist. del. Pubbl. Istr.

To these dates which we find or once found on the artist's works, we can add some others which, however, are less certain. Malvasia in his "Felsina Pittrice" informs us that in 1345 Lorenzo painted in the cloister of S. Domenico at Bologna in a competition with Vitale, the well-known painter of that town([1]), and that he

---

([1]) *Filippini*, Rassegna d'Arte, 1912, p. 105, quoting the edition of 1868, I, p. 27, confirms this statement. In the one of 1841 this competition is not clearly mentioned.

signed a fresco of Daniel in the lion's den in the Oratory of Mezzaratta: "*Laurentius pictor 1360*" ([1]).

According to a manuscript of the 17th century containing records of the church of S. Giacomo at Bologna, Lorenzo painted a panel for the high-altar of this church in 1368; the picture remained there until 1491 when it was transported to the "scuola della Madonna di Consolazione"; in 1616 it hung in the Chapter house and in 1636 the various pieces which had been taken apart were placed in the S. Lorenzo chapel ([2]). In 1362 Facino di Giovanni di Lucca, a merchant at Bologna, left 175 lire for the execution of an altar-piece ([3]), and doubtless it is this picture with which we are now dealing. Whether the fragments of a polyptych that we still find in this church can be identified with this altar-piece is another question and one to which we shall return later.

Lanzi mentions another of Lorenzo's works which also dated from 1368; it once belonged to the Hercolani family in Bologna and was signed: "*Manu Laurentii de Venetiis*" ([4]). And lastly we have some documentary evidence; one act of 1365 mentions a Lorenzo son of "Nicolo pittore", another of 1371 refers to a painter called Lorenzo while a third of 1379 records that a "*Lorenzo pentor di Santa Marina*" contributed 400 imperial lire for the expenses of the war with Chioggia. It is possible of course that these documents do not refer to the same artist ([5]). There exists also the possibility that all the evidence of the activity of Lorenzo at Bologna need not necessarily concern our artist,

---

([1]) *Brunaldo*, Minervalia Bononiensia, Bologna, 1641, p. 239 (*Filippini*, loc. cit.) A guide to Bologna of 1592 reports that these frescoes were signed "Laurentius F.". Testi, op. cit., p. 179; *Lanzi*, The History of Painting in Italy, (trans. by Th. Roscoe) II, London, 1847, p. 71, tells us that the signature ran "Laorentius P.", that the date of their execution must have been about 1370 and that the style of the painting was non-Giottesque. Malvasia, however, who wrote a century before Lanzi, informs us that already in his time the frescoes were entirely ruined.

([2]) *Filippini*, op. cit.

([3]) *F. Malaguzzi Valeri*, La chiesa e il portico di San Giacomo a Bologna, Arch. Stor. dell' arte, VII, 1894, p. 318.

([4]) *Lanzi*, op. cit., p. 79.

([5]) *Testi*, op. cit., pp. 210 and 179; it seems very unlikely especially with regard to the entry of 1371.

for the city of Bologna might also have possessed a painter of that name.

The first dated work then of Lorenzo Veneziano's is the altar-piece with the Annunciation in the centre, in the Accademia of Venice (no. 10). It is dated 1357, but comparing it with some of the master's other works, the style points to an earlier period in Lorenzo's career, one in which he was more inspired by the artist whom I believe to have been his master and who was not Maestro Paolo, as is frequently thought, but the anonymous painter whose works we found at Chioggia, Pirano, Lecce and in the Louvre. We discover in Lorenzo's pictures the same elongated proportions and the same ascetic types of old men as we saw in this master's productions. I do not exclude the possibility that this earlier period, at least a large part of it, passed at Bologna; let us not forget that according to Malvasia, Lorenzo painted there in 1345 and he must certainly have been active some time before 1357 to acquire such familiarity with the art of the Master of Chioggia whose dated works are from 1348 and 1354.

The paintings which show Lorenzo entirely under the influence of this artist are the detached panels of a polyptych in the church of S. Giacomo, Bologna, and two half-length figures of saints in the Gallery of this town. The works which we find by him at San Severino, in The Marches, may be of a slightly later date but all the same are previous to the polyptych of 1357 in the Accademia of Venice.

I grant that it would simplify matters to identify the panels that we now find in S. Giacomo, Bologna, with the work that Lorenzo executed for this church in 1368, but their appearance is so very different from the paintings we know the artist to have executed at this slightly later period that I am convinced that not one of the panels in S. Giacomo belongs to it. They and the works at San Severino are the outcome of a manner which is transitional between that of the Master of Chioggia and that followed by Lorenzo himself in 1357. The altar-piece that Lorenzo painted in 1368, therefore, must have been another, perhaps the picture cited by Lanzi as belonging to the Hercolani family, which showed the same date.

We can conclude then that Lorenzo worked on two different

occasions for the church of S. Giacomo, once early in his career, of which activity there still exists evidence, and the second time in 1368. We find not infrequently that artists were recalled to work for persons who had already employed them and we can only infer from this that their first services gave full satisfaction.

What remains of Lorenzo's polyptych in the church of S. Giacomo is now preserved in the Sta. Croce chapel, or that of the Cari family, behind the choir, united to a Coronation of the Virgin and other panels by the Bolognese painter, Giovanni di Paolo. There are six panels of full-length figures of saints, a row of nine smaller panels, three of which represent scenes and the other six, half-length figures of saints, and below, six middle-sized panels, two of which show St Martin dividing his coat with the beggar and St. George killing the dragon, while the other four are adorned with half-length figures of saints. No doubt this polyptych resembled the one now in the Cathedral of Vicenza, for here too the various parts show the same diversity of size.

Two figures in the Bologna Gallery of SS. Antony Abbot and Bartholomew (figs. 22 and 23) which have been cut at the level of the knees, probably once belonged to a similar polyptych. The names are inscribed in the same way but the execution here is perhaps somewhat finer.

The little Gallery of San Severino, in The Marches, also contains some panels from a polyptych by Lorenzo (no. 5) ([1]) which were previously attributed to Allegretto Nuzi. The original altarpiece must have been more important for there remain eight full-length figures of saints and below them six half-length figures. Some of the former are considerably damaged.

These three groups of panels, each of them proof of the existence of an important polyptych, were very likely executed in the first stage of the artist's career and reveal to us the aspect of his earliest manner. In none of them do we find much evidence of a Byzantine influence with the exception perhaps of the hard ascetic appearance of some of his figures and in that the connection is not always very distinct. The types are not Oriental,

---

([1]) v. *E. Aleandri*, La pinacoteca di San Severino Marche, Le Gallerie nazionali italiane, III, p. 136. *G. Bernardini*, Le Gallerie comunale dell' Umbria, Roma, 1906, p. 77. Rassegna Marchigiana, 1923, p. 460.

Fig. 22. Lorenzo Veneziano, St. Antony. Gallery, Bologna.

Photo Minist. del. Pubbl. Istr.

the colours still less; the dark brown shadows, the rigidity and conventional design of the features and of the hands have all disappeared; the expressions are quite animated. The drapery

Fig. 23. Lorenzo Veneziano, St. Bartholomew. Gallery, Bologna.
Photo Minist. del. Pubbl. Istr.

and general line of the figures are markedly Gothic, and it is this style that dominates Lorenzo in his earliest productions.

The attenuated forms which Lorenzo borrowed from the Master of Chioggia and which are so evident in the different panels at Bologna, are less marked in the work at San Severino, and still less, although not entirely gone, in the first dated work,

Fig. 24. Lorenzo Veneziano, polytych, 1357. Accademia, Venice.
Photo Anderson.

the altar-piece in the Gallery of Venice (no. 10), originally in the church of S. Antonio al Castello (figs. 24 and 25). The central panel of this work is occupied by a representation of the Annunciation: before the enthroned Virgin kneels the angel Gabriel while from above God the Father sends forth the Holy Ghost in the form of a dove; a miniature figure of the donor, Domenico Leo, kneels in adoration at the foot of the throne. At either side

---

(¹) The actual position of these saints is reversed, those on the right should be on the left and vice versa.

Fig. 25. Detail of fig. 24.

Photo Anderson.

there are two pairs of full-length figures of saints and below each of the five principal panels, there is a medallion containing a bust; they are of a holy anchorite and the four Evangelists. Above each of the lateral figures there is a half-length figure of a saint, but the central part here has disappeared; and is replaced by a panel of the Almighty executed by Benedetto Diana in 1525. The larger pilasters, six above and six below, are adorned with three small figures of saints.

The date, 1357, which is still legible, forms part of a long inscription. The latter which is difficult to decipher and interpret is not the original; it runs: "*MCCCLVII Hec tabella fca fuit et hic affissa p̄ Laurecius pictoresq caninus scultores itpe regis ven, viri Dn̄i fris Goti d' Abba Tīb D R̄. Lot p. iois* ([1]) *et funto monis isti. Hanc tuis . . . . . s abne* ([2]) *triunphato orbis Dominicus lion ego nunc supplx arte pre politam Dono pa bellam*".

Cicogna, after giving a fac-simile of the date ([3]), persists in contradicting the old authors, such as Zanetti and Zucchini, who read the date as 1358, and believes that the year inscribed on the picture is that of 1367. Signor Testi is inclined to accept this version with which he finds the manner of painting corresponds, but I think the contrary opinion is much more likely to be correct, because, not only do we find in this picture the characteristic proportions that Lorenzo borrowed from the Master of Chioggia but the figures of the Annunciation in the centre resemble much more those of the Marriage of St. Catherine of 1359 than the artist's productions of about ten years later. The Virgin and the celestial messenger are rather different from the other figures. They are less conventionally Gothic and larger of form, reminding us to a certain extent of the art of Central Italy and above all of Sienese painting.

This new tendency is still more manifest in the mystic marriage

---

([1]) This is as it has been transcribed by *L. Serra*, Catalogo delle RR. Gallerie di Venezia, p. 8. *Cicogna*, Iscrizione veneziane reccolte ed illustrate, I, p.185, gives a slightly different version; Thus the last words *Goti d' Abba* etc. have been read by this authority as *Goti d. Flot p. ois* etc.

([2]) Instead of *Abne* Cicogna gives *Agne* which seems to me more probably the correct reading.

([3]) *Cicogna*, loc. cit.

Fig 26. Lorenzo Veneziano, Madonna, saints and angels, 1358.
Accademia, Venice.

of St. Catherine in the Accademia of Venice (no. 650, fig. 26) (¹), in which the Virgin seated in glory slightly bends towards the Child, Who, looking up at His Mother, passes the ring on to the finger of St. Catherine. The latter stands on the left, accompanied by another figure; on the other side a kneeling angel plays a little organ, another standing figure conceals those behind in a similar manner as its pendant. Eight musical angels surround the Virgin's aureole; at her feet the sun and moon are depicted. Below we see the signature: "*MCCCLVIIII al XX......e Fevraro fo fatta sta. ancona p. man de Loreço pentor in Venexia*".

Although we can reproach the painter with a certain lack of finesse in the forms and the faces which are of a slightly more vulgar type than in the previous picture, the Sienese influence is still more marked; this is most evident in the somewhat sentimental attitude of the Virgin and the appearance of the two saints on the left whom one might compare with the SS. Agnes and Catherine of Alexandria by Pietro Lorenzetti in the Gallery of Siena (nos. 578 and 579) (²). This influence, however, is not very profound and although there is no trace of Byzantinism, the artist is before all thoroughly Venetian.

Belonging no doubt to the same period is the beautiful altarpiece, originally in the monastery of Sta. Maria della Celestina, which has recently been transferred from the Imperial Museum (no. 41) of Vienna to the Accademia of Venice (fig. 27). Here the Virgin is seated on a very elaborate throne, the back of which is adorned with statuettes; she is surrounded by numerous angels and under her feet the moon is depicted. Eight full-length figures of saints arranged in two rows, comprise the rest of the polyptych. There is an empty space below the central panel; it might have been occupied by another panel or the central part might originally have been on a lower level. The execution is finer than that of the marriage of St. Catherine or of the polyptych of 1357; the reliefs especially are very subtly rendered and the general spirit of the work quite Italian. The type of the Christ, however, is the same as in the previous picture and in some of

---

(¹) *Cantalamessa*, Le Gallerie Nazionali, V, p. 42.

(²) v. vol. II, fig. 223. Signor *Testi* finds that these figures betray a Giottesque influence.

the figures of saints, particularly the upper pair on the left, there are reminiscences of the master's Bolognese manner (¹).

The chief interest of the Madonna by Lorenzo in the Pinacoteca of Padua (no. 383) lies in the signature: "*MCCCLXI die XVII mēsis Septembri Laurenci^{us}. D. Veneciis pinxit*", which is

Fig. 27. Lorenzo Veneziano, polyptych. Accademia, Venice.
Photo Alinari.

inscribed at the foot of the panel. The Virgin is depicted offering a pomegranate to the Infant Christ, but the painting is so damaged and restored and the colours so faded that it is of no significance for our knowledge of the artist. There is however, a rather marked Gothic line in the folds of the draperies.

(¹) Signor *Testi* is a little doubtful about this picture being a work of Lorenzo's (op. cit., p. 230) but to me it seems fairly obvious.

The polyptych of 1366 in the Cathedral of Vicenza is perhaps the only one of Lorenzo's works that has retained its original appearance. Besides the central panel which shows a representation of the Death of the Virgin, there are three full-length figures on either side and above each a half-length figure of a male or female saint; the Crucifixion, with the Virgin, St. John and two little angels between two figures of saints, is depicted over the central panel. Five of the pinnacles contain busts of saints, the others being formed by carved ornaments. The predella is composed of fifteen small panels, twelve of which show half-length figures, and the three in the centre, the Adoration of the Magi, the Virgin and Child between St. Joseph and the three Wise Men.

The composition of the Death of the Virgin is an unusual one because the Saviour carrying away the soul of His Mother is not depicted behind the bier but above in a mandorla surrounded by angels. A small adorer kneels at the feet of either of the saints adjacent to the central panel; the one on the left whose name, "*Messer Tommaso*" is inscribed, was probably the donor. Below the central panel we read: "*MCCCLXVI mense Decemb. Laurentius pinxit*".

The various figures of this altar-piece are particularly beautiful and the execution very fine. These two details closely connect it with the picture from Vienna but here there is practically no trace of what we called his Bolognese manner. The image of the Baptist which has generally shown the most characteristics of the master's early ascetic manner reveals here that Lorenzo followed another schema, one in which the elegance was not diminished, but on the contrary, the form and attitude of the figures have become even more graceful.

The panel of 1370 in the Correr Museum, Venice, representing the Saviour giving the keys to St. Peter shows again that resemblance to Lorenzetti's art which we observed in some of Lorenzo's earlier works. This is very noticeable in the general composition, which reminds us of that of the mystic wedding of St. Catherine; in both cases there is a large central figure which might almost be said to be framed in the smaller surrounding ones. The proportions are large, the plastic effects very pronounced and the figures finer and more animated than those in the panel of 1357.

Fig. 28. Lorenzo Veneziano, SS. Peter and Paul, 1371. Accademia, Venice.
Photo Anderson.

In its general aspect, however, the picture bears more resemblance to this latter work than to the polyptych of 1366 at Vicenza, the grace and elegance of the latter being somewhat less marked. The signature is "*MCCCLXVIIII mense Januari Laurencū pinxit*".

Of the year 1371 we have two works from the hand of Lorenzo; one, comprising two panels, represents SS. Peter and Mark and is now in the Accademia of Venice (nos. 5 and 5a, fig. 28);

the other in the same Gallery shows the Annunciation between four figures of saints (no. 9).

The two figures of saints, which come from the "Ufficio della Zecca" or "della Seta" (¹), are beautiful images, full of expression and executed in a purely Italian manner without any Byzantine elements. The Gothicism is very marked in the drapery which has here acquired another aspect, one approaching the flowery Gothic style. Under the feet of the saints the signature reads: "*MCCCLXXI mēse Noveb Laurēci pinxit hoc o.p̄.*".

Two panels very similar in appearance and of about the same date are to be found in the Berlin Museum (²) whence they came from the Cheney collection (³). The saints represented here are SS. Mark and John the Baptist; the former has a curious, ugly face. The Gothicism is less marked, which might indicate that these panels are slightly earlier than those in Venice.

A beautiful picture in the Gallery of Pesaro which has sometimes been ascribed to the school of Allegretto Nuzi belongs, I think to this period in Lorenzo's career (⁴). It depicts St. Ambrosius in full episcopal vestments sitting on a very simple throne. The fineness of execution, the chiaroscuro effects, as well as the type and expression point to this rather late stage in the artist's development.

In the second work of 1371 we observe a Gothicism more florid, almost manneristic, which is not very pleasing (fig. 29). In the centre the Virgin sitting on a monumental throne, inclines towards the angel who kneels before her, while from above the Almighty sends down the Holy Ghost and a small figure of Christ carrying the Cross. Two figures of saints stand on either side but as the frame is modern, it is possible that the picture is not complete.

The forms are unpleasant, even sometimes ugly, the central

(¹) *Testi*, op. cit., p. 224.
(²) *Crowe and Cavalcaselle*, ed. *Langton Douglas*, III, p. 270 note 3.
(³) This collection was sold in London in 1905 v. L'Arte, 1905, p. 286.
(⁴) G. *Vaccai*, Pesaro, Bergamo, 1909, p. 109. L. *Serra*, in his guide to this Museum, more rightly ascribes this picture to the Venetian school of the 14th century; in the Rassegna Marchegiana, 1923, p. 332, this picture was attributed to Lorenzo's school.

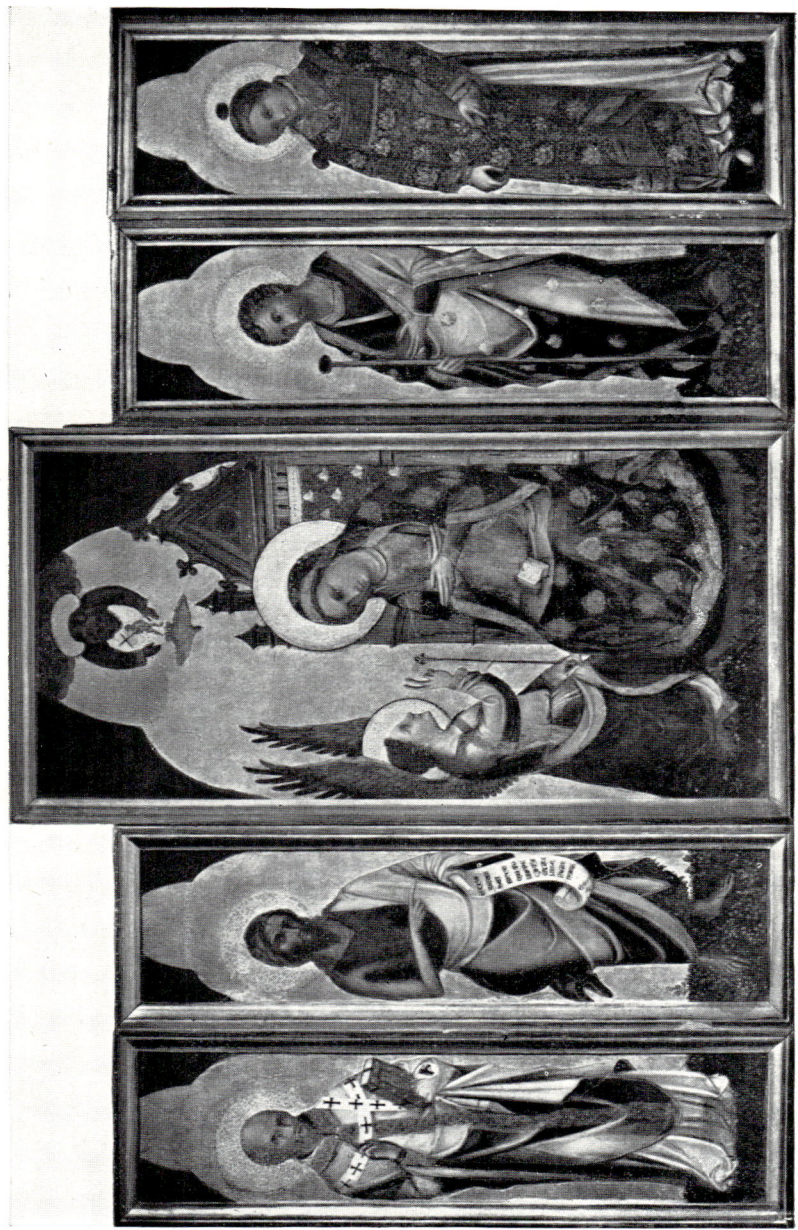

Fig 29. Lorenzo Veneziano, Annunciation and saints, 1371. Accademia, Venice. Photo Anderson.

figures are very heavy, the two adjacent saints are of a markedly conventional design, while all show a hardness of outline, a rigidity of attitude and an exuberance of Gothicism. The fact that all the saints are placed in flowery fields is an innovation. Perhaps the restorations which this polyptych has undergone have helped to give it its present disagreeable aspect. The picture comes from the "Scuola di S. Giovanni Evangelista" and was given to the Accademia by the collector Molin. The signature I think has been repainted but what we now see is probably a faithful copy of the original; it runs: "*MCCCLXXI Laureci pinsit*".

A much more pleasing work is the Madonna from the Campana collection, now in the Louvre (Room VII, no number); it is a painting of the year 1372 and the last we possess from the master's hand. The Virgin, with slightly inclined head, is seated on a monumental throne under an architectural baldaquin; she holds a rose which the Child, standing on her knee, grasps in His little hand. None of the shortcomings of the previous picture is evident here; on the contrary the Gothic elements are fairly pure, the forms charming and the expressions very sweet. The signature is inscribed in the usual place and reads: "*MCCCLXXII Mese Setebris Laureci d Venetis pisit*" ([1]).

Among the works attributed to Lorenzo there is an enthroned Madonna with two little angels in the church of S. Zaccaria that Signor Testi believes to be by the master ([2]), but it is so overpainted in the manner of the Vivarini that it is impossible to say with certainty.

Signor L. Venturi ranks four figures of saints in the Martinengo Gallery at Brescia (no. 12) among Lorenzo's finest productions and although I do not share his enthusiasm about them, I think that the attribution is correct; Signor Testi however is of opinion

---

([1]) *P. Perdrizet et R. Jean,* La galerie Campana et les musées français, Bordeaux, 1907, p. 33, must confound this picture with a wing of a triptych of 1354 by the Master of Chioggia of which the central panel of the Madonna is now in the Louvre, when they inform us that this painting of Lorenzo's was sent in 1876 to the Museum of Ajaccio where, according to a letter written by the director, it was no longer to be found.

([2]) *Testi,* op. cit., p. 226 *L. Venturi,* L'Arte, 1909, p. 84.

that they belong to the school of Brescia but were executed under a strong Venetian influence (¹).

Lorenzo Veneziano occupies a very special place in the school of painting of his native town. Of the two conventional styles, the Gothic and the Byzantine, which constituted the chief characteristics of this school, it was the former which dominated our master. It is true that the appearance and curious proportions of his early works reveal his close connection with the Master of Chioggia who himself was a faithful follower of Maestro Paolo, but the resemblance to the works of this master, who was under a strong Byzantine influence, is quite external in Lorenzo's painting and I think that the opinion of writers of former generations, such as Lanzi and Cavalcaselle, that Lorenzo belongs to the group of "Byzantinized" artists, is wrong. I do not think that Lorenzo was a really great painter; he was too much dominated by the conventionality of the Gothic style, but it is certainly to him that we owe the introduction of a new form of Venetian painting, one free of all Byzantine influence, and, as I have already remarked, showing some connection to the contemporary productions of Central Italy, especially those of the town of Siena.

Not only Lorenzo's drawing but also his colours are independent of Byzantine art. There is no trace of these dull tints with dark brown shadows and the marked contrast of light and shade which seem to have been acquired from mosaics and which in any case, characterize Byzantine painting. Lorenzo's colours are very bright and the tints sometimes even lighter than in contemporary Tuscan works. This may perhaps be due to a Northern, that is to say German, influence. The shading is finely graduated and shows no resemblance to the Byzantine technique.

Thus, Lorenzo was the artist who revolutionized Venetian painting, for he abandoned the Byzantine style which, until then, had constituted its principal basis. After Lorenzo, there existed quite a little group of painters who seem to have been inspired

---

(¹) *Testi*, op cit., p. 230, believes four saints in the Correr Museum (nos. 15 and 22) by the same hand but to me this seems improbable.

by his art; in their works Byzantinism has almost disappeared and the Gothic style is predominant (¹).

Contemporaneous with the adherents of Lorenzo, there existed certain painters in whose art the Gothico-Byzantine manner, as it was interpreted by Maestro Paolo, had acquired a more purely Italian form. Before going further we shall discuss this group of artists and their productions.

Signor Testi is of opinion that Guariento had a considerable influence on most of the painters who were active in the second half of the 14th century, especially on Stefano Pievan di S. Agnese, Jacobello Alberegno and Jacobello di Bonomo. I do not deny that Guariento may have exercised a certain influence during his sojourn in Venice, but I find that in the art of this painter, who started his artistic career at Padua, the Giottesque elements are very much more important than in any Venetian painting of the 14th century. The preponderating influence of the Florentine school in Guariento's painting can only be explained by his Paduan origin and it is for this reason that I consider him and Semitocolo to be the founders of the Paduan school with which they will be discussed later on.

The correspondence of style that Signor Testi observes between certain Venetian painters and Guariento actually does exist but this is rather the result of the fact that in both cases many of the earlier Venetian characteristics have been replaced by those purely Italian. I have just mentioned how it came about that these were introduced into Guariento's art. As for the Venetian painters, the Byzantine style which had prevailed in the City of the Lagunes longer than in any other artistic centre began at last to give way to an Italian form of art. It is only natural that this art, which was current throughout the rest of Italy, should sooner or later replace in Venice the conventional

(¹) Among Lorenzo's school works I should like to mention in the Correr Museum, II, 6, six figures of saints; II, 9. St. Peter with a devotee and St. John the Baptist; VII, 12, a small panel showing four scenes with the false signature, "*M. Simon f. 1396*"; VII, 15 and 22, four saints; Walters collection, Baltimore, triptych, the Madonna seated on the ground in the centre with the Crucifixion above and two saints and the Annunciation in the wings; *B. Berenson*, Venetian Painting in America, London, p. 3, ascribes this panel to about 1400 but judging from the illustration, I would not place it later than about 1375.

Byzantinism which had elsewhere been abandoned since the beginning of the 14th century. That Venice was so backward in following this example is in part due to its uninterrupted intercourse with Byzantium and in part to its distinctive political life, which isolated it in a very special way from the rest of the Peninsula.

It may seem strange to place the Coronation of the Virgin of 1372 by Caterino and Donato in the Querini-Stampalia Gallery among the works of the transition, but taking into consideration the career of the former of these artists, there is no doubt that he played an important part in the realization of this transformation.

From the documents, it is very clear that there existed two artists of the name of Caterino; the one, Caterino di Maestro Andrea, a sculptor mentioned in 1394 and deceased before 1430, who was in no way connected with the painter of the same name [1]. The latter is mentioned for the first time in 1362; we then find him acting as a witness in 1367, during which year we know that he executed, in collaboration with Donato di San Vitale, a cross for the church of St. Agnese for which they together received one hundred gold ducats. At this period he inhabited the S. Angiolo quarter. In 1372 the same two painters signed the above mentioned Coronation of the Virgin; a large polyptych painted by Caterino in 1374 was once found in S. Georgio Maggiore, while the following year he executed the Coronation of the Virgin, now in the Accademia of Venice. Our artist is mentioned for the last time in 1382 when he lived in the quarter of S. Luca.

There are eight references between 1344 and 1382 concerning an artist or artists of the name of Donato. Considering the lapse of time between the first and the last of these data and considering that the document of 1344 and another of 1353 speak of the artist as an inhabitant of the S. Luca quarter while those after

---

[1] The facts concerning Caterino and Donato previously published by other authors have been collected by *Testi*, op. cit., p. 236 et. seq. This writer contradicts *Ludwig* who erroneously states (Archiv. Beitr. zur Gesch. der Venezian Malerei, Jahrb. der K. Preus. Kunstsamml., 1903) that Caterino is first mentioned in 1365. We possess no data for this year and *Ludwig* must have wrongly read the inscription on the Coronation of the Virgin of 1375.

1367 inform us that he lived in that of S. Vitale, Ludwig ([1]) has already propounded the hypothesis that we must herein be dealing with two different artists.

From the documents of 1344 and 1353 we gather but little information; they simply mention the artist, the former including him in the membership of the "Scuola grande delle carita". Another document of 1371, without mentioning the quarter that the artist inhabited, offers us the same information; it no doubt refers to the same artist. The Donato who received payment for a work executed together with Caterino in 1367 is he of S. Vitale, and is naturally the same man who with Caterino signed the Coronation of the Virgin in 1372. His name appears in notarial acts of 1374 and 1382, the same address being given; he must have died before 1388 for in that year there is mention of his widow.

Previously there existed a carved and painted polyptych in the church of S. Giorgio Maggiore, showing the inscription: "*Bonincontrus Abba... H... Christus sit MCCCLXXXIII nel mexe di Decembrio Katarinus pinxit hoc opus*". Because the name of the sculptor is not mentioned, Testi infers that Caterino should be held responsible for the entire work but the preciseness of the word "pinxit" seems to contradict this hypothesis: the artist would never have omitted mention of the plastic part of the work or would at least have employed a term of a more general significance. A similar inscription is found on a wooden relief of 1394 in the Correr Museum which was sculptured by the other Caterino and painted by Bartolomeo di M. Paolo, an artist about whom we know nothing except that his father was still alive in 1389 which excludes the possibility of his being a son of the famous Maestro Paolo ([2]), and again on a cross of 1404 at Verucchio, sculptured by the same Caterino and painted by Nicholas di Pietro with whom we shall deal later on.

The Coronation of the Virgin in the Quirini-Stampalia collection (fig. 30) excuted by Caterino and Donato, is scarcely less Byzantine than Maestro Paolo's own works. The Saviour and the Virgin are seated on an elaborate throne with a richly ornamented

---

([1]) *Ludwig*, op. cit., p. 29.
([2]) *Testi*, op. cit., p. 249.

Fig. 30. Caterino and Donato, the Coronation of the Virgin, 1372. Querini-Stampalia Gallery, Venice.   Photo Naya.

back; a large group of angels is massed behind while three others kneel at the feet of the principal figures, the central angel holding a small organ; two small medallions between them contain the signature which reads: "*MCCCLXXII m$\overline{x}$e Agusti Donatû et Catarinu' picxit"*.

The types of all the figures, the colouring especially of the faces, and the draperies of gold-threaded material give to this picture a markedly Byzantine appearance.

Comparing this work with those that Caterino painted alone, we discover that the great artistic qualities of the panel of 1372 as well as the Oriental tendencies are due to the hand of Donato.

The composition and attitudes of Caterino's Coronation of of the Virgin of 1375 in the Accademia of Venice (no. 16) show a good deal of correspondence to what we found in the previous picture.

However, the grouping is more simple, the angels below are absent and those above much less numerous while neither type, technique, nor drapery has a Byzantine character; the faces, above all, are here thoroughly Italian, bearing a resemblance sooner to the Florentine than to the Sienese manner of painting. But the general aspect of the work is rather vulgar. The signature which is inscribed below the feet of the principal figures runs: "*MCCCLXXV $\overline{d}$ mexe $\overline{d}$ Março Chatarinu' pinxit"*.

Another Coronation of the Virgin in the same Gallery (no. 702) ([1]) is of finer quality. The number of escorting angels is still further diminished and the throne has been given quite a western form (fig. 31). The central figures vary but little, they are however more animated and more graceful of form. This picture is the central panel of a triptych, the wings of which are adorned with the figures of SS. Lucy and Nicholas of Tolentino. Again the work retains but few Byzantine characteristics.

The other work signed by Caterino shows strongly the influence of Lorenzo Veneziano, the absence of which in his other productions is rather curious. It is a polyptych which previously belonged to the art-dealer Piccoli in Venice but now forms part of the Walters collection, Baltimore ([2]). The centre is occupied

---

([1]) This picture was bought from Signor T. Mezzoli in 1902: *Paoletti*, L'Arte, 1902, p. 126.

([2]) *Testi*, op. cit., p. 242. B. *Berenson*, Venetian Painting in America, p. 2.

by a figure of the Virgin holding the Child naked on her knee; a miniature adorer kneels below. Two saints are depicted at either side; they are St. Antony Abbot and the Baptist, St. Clare and

Fig 31. Caterino, the Coronation of the Virgin and saints. Accademia, Venice.   Photo Naya.

St. James. Above each of these there is a half-length figure of a saint and over the central panel the Crucifixion, with the Virgin and St. John between two saints, is represented in the same way as in Lorenzo's polyptych in Venice. In the more elongated proportions, the Gothicism of the draperies, and the types, especially that of St. Antony, there is a resemblance to Lorenzo's style that no one can deny. This connection shows more affinity with the manner Lorenzo followed at the beginning of his career, when he was still inspired by the Master of Chioggia, and of which the altar-piece of 1357 was the last production, so that we must certainly be dealing here with a youthful work of Caterino's. We cannot pass without mentioning the remarkable resemblance which exists between the St. Christopher of this polyptych and the one signed by Giovanni da Bologna in the Museum of Padua, but instead of explaining this by an influence of the latter artist on Caterino, we should rather think of the fact that both were inspired by Lorenzo, as has just been demonstrated for Caterino and as we shall find later on to be also the case for Giovanni da Bologna. The polyptych at Baltimore is signed: "*Chatarinu' de Venecii pinxit*".

No trace remains of a picture by Caterino representing the Virgin with the Twelve Apostles and a lion in the background which Cavalcaselle mentions as probably coming from the Corpus Domini and to be found in his time in the Lichtenstein collection, Vienna [1].

The chief interest of Caterino's art is that it leads the way to purely Italian forms. It seems improbable that he himself was ever dominated by the Byzantine influence; the only picture which betrays an adherence to this style is the Coronation of 1372 which he executed together with Donato. In the altar-piece of the Walters collection we see that he was inspired by the art of Lorenzo who was not a follower of the Byzantine school. The hieratic spirit and stiff attitudes of Caterino's figures link him with the Gothico-Byzantine artists of previous generations but the purely Italian element in his painting is much more important.

A Coronation of the Virgin in the Accademia of Venice (no. 23) shows the false signature: "*Nicolo Semitecolo MCCCLII*" (fig. 32).

The composition is the same as in Caterino's works, only the type of the Virgin is somewhat different and she does not gesticulate with the right hand as was invariably the case in Caterino's panels, as well as in the one which he executed in collaboration with Donato. The type of the angels is slightly more Byzantine, but, apart from these minor details, this painting strongly resem-

---

[1] L. *Venturi*, op. cit., p. 34. *Testi*, op. cit., p. 245.

VENICE AND THE NEIGHBOURING REGIONS. 65

Fig. 32 Manner of Caterino, the Coronation of the Virgin. Accademia, Venice.
Photo Ist. Art. Graf.

bles Caterino's compositions and may be considered a production of his studio.

Another panel in this Gallery (no. 4) can be ascribed to the same hand (fig. 33). The false signature: "*M. Smion 1394*", which is seen below to the left, has occasionally caused it to be attributed to Smion da Cusighe with whom we shall deal further on. This picture comprises four scenes arranged in two rows; above they represent the Descent of the Holy Ghost and the Ascension, and below the Entombment and the Resurrection. These representations offer a curious mixture of Florentine style and dramatic force with reminiscences of Byzantine types and technique; the execution is not very fine but the picture is interesting on account of the action which is depicted.

Stefano "plebano" or "pievan di S. Agnese" is rather a vague figure in the history of Venetian painting. The only two pictures bearing his name which have come down to us, seem to be by two very different artists so that they cannot be looked upon as authentic, while another work which the painter executed for the monastery of S. Alvise and which showed the inscription: "*MCCCLXXXIIII P. Stefanus Plebanus S. Agnetis pinxit*" ([1]), has disappeared. Cavalcaselle only added to the confusion by attributing to this artist the Madonna of 1353, which is by the Master of Chioggio and is now in the Louvre.

One of the pictures on which Stefano's signature appears is conserved in the Correr Museum (XV, no. 21); it shows the crowned Virgin, seated on a finely designed throne, holding in her left arm the Infant Christ to Whom she offers a rose (fig. 34). The rich decoration of the throne and the garments of the two figures betray the artist's adherence to the Venetian tradition but the faces show no trace of Byzantinism, revealing rather a Giottesque inspiration ([2]). The Virgin's robe describes a Gothic line, but the picture as a whole is not very beautiful. The signature inscribed below on the left runs: "*MCCCLXVIII Adi XI Avosto Stef Pleb. Sce. Agn. P.*", but its authenticity has always been doubted for paleographical reasons and, further, because at that date there was no "plebanus" or parish priest of the name of Stefano at the church of St. Agnese ([3]).

([1]) *Cicogna*, Iscriz. Venet., V, p. 507.
([2]) *Cavalcaselle* and *L. Venturi* have already remarked on the absence of Guariento's influence. *M. Testi*, op. cit., p. 304 note 6, finds that a comparison between this picture and the Madonna in the Museum of Padua provides us with sufficient proof of the contrary. I do not agree with him and am of opinion that the resemblance which does exist arises from the fact that both were influenced by Giotto's school.
([3]) *Testi*, loc. cit.

Fig. 33. Manner of Caterino, the Descent of the Holy Ghost and three other scenes. Accademia, Venice.

Photo Ist. Art. Graf.

Nor was there any priest of that name in the year 1381, the date found on the other panel signed by Stefano. It is a Coronation of the Virgin which forms the centre piece of the altar-piece (no. 21) in the Accademia of Venice. The surrounding panels originally belonged to the Coronation of the Virgin in the Brera, Milan (no. 227), which, as we saw, may have been painted by Maestro Paolo([1]). The attitudes of the principal figures as well as the grouping of the angels makes us classify Stefano's Coronation with those of Caterino. There is nothing in this picture, apart from its composition, which is reminiscent of Byzantium or even of Venice. Types, technique and above all the sentiment of the work seem purely Tuscan, showing a close connection especially to the Sienese school, and it would be very easy to believe that this is only a free copy, made by a foreign artist, of the picture now in Milan. The signature which is inscribed on either side at the foot of the panel reads: "*MCCCLXXXI Stefan Pleban Sc̄e Agnet pinxit*", but there are but few who believe in the authenticity of this inscription.

A certain number of other works reveal the influence that Central Italian art had on this emancipated school of Venetian painting; some of them also show false signatures. Belonging to this group, is a small altar-piece in the Accademia, representing in the centre, the Virgin nursing the Child, over which we see the Crucifixion between the Virgin and St. John with the figures of the Baptist and St. Jerome at the sides, and still higher the Madonna and angel of the Annunciation. Although of rather coarse workmanship, this picture is none the less very characteristic of the effect that the Giottesque tradition had on Venetian artists of this period. It bears the false signature: "*Antonius Ven . . . . 1368*".

In the Correr Museum there is a large panel depicting the dead Saviour upright in His tomb between the Virgin and St. John with two little angels above; the inscription: "*Angelus pinxit*" is again a counterfeit ([2]). The tragic spirit of this picture and the appearance of the Saviour, of St. John and of the angels obviously show a Florentine influence; the image of the Virgin, however, as well as the colour, and technique of light and shade, recalls the old Venetian style. Caterino's manner of painting, together with

---

([1]) v. p. 9.
([2]) *Caffi*, Pittori veneziani nel milletrecento, Arch. Ven.. Vol. 35, p. 60, believed that this may have been Angelo Tedaldo whose will dates from 1324 but Signor *Testi*, op. cit., p. 171, has demonstrated the improbability of this hypothesis.

Fig. 34. Venetian School, Madonna, 2nd half of the 14th century.
Correr Museum, Venice.   Photo Alinari.

many Tuscan elements, is evident in a Coronation of the Virgin in the Correr Museum (VII, no. 16). The picture dates from about 1400; it shows the false signature: "*Alvise Vivarin*".

One of the painters who, although belonging to the Venetian school, nevertheless advanced this union with the art of Central Italy, was Zanino, or Giovannino di Pietro, mentioned as witnessing a deed in 1407 ([1]). We find in the Gallery of Rieti, Umbria, a picture by this artist, signed: "*hoc opus depinxit Zanin n' petri -bitato r(abitator) Veeciis i ctrata (incontrata) tati appoliaris*"([2]).

It is a triptych showing in the centre a representation of the Crucifixion: Our Lord is depicted between the two thieves and a large crowd of agitated figures stand below; among them the fainting Virgin is tended by her faithful companions, Mary Magdalene grasps the foot of the Cross and several Jews converse together while numerous angels fly around the central crucifix. Three kneeling saints holding crosses and long inscriptions are seen in either of the wings. The outer surface of the lateral panels is adorned with some scenes in grisaille from the life of St. Francis. The dramatic action of the central scene, the gestures and somewhat convulsed expressions do not seem to belong to the Venetian school, nor does the soft warm colouring with its tender tints of blue and green. Some faint traces of rigidity in the drawing are the only features which vaguely remind us of Byzantine art.

In another work which we find in Venice in the Correr Museum (no. 3), Zanino is more faithful to the Venetian school (fig. 35). The subject is again the Crucifixion; Christ is represented alone without the thieves but the crowd of people below the Cross is just as numerous as in the previous picture and the action in no way less dramatic. The Christ is depicted dead although the executioners have not yet finished nailing Him to the Cross. Between the panel and the fine Gothic frame there is a border of twenty-eight busts of saints and prophets, each one holding an inscription. No one has previously thought of attributing the

---

([1]) *G. Ludwig*, Archival. Beitr. zur Gesch. der Venez. Kunst, herausgeg. von Bode, Gronau. u. v. Hadeln, Berlin, 1911, p. 106. *Testi*, op. cit., II, p. 89.

([2]) *U. Gnoli*, La pinacoteca di Rieti, Bolletino d'Arte del Ministero della Pubblica Istruzione, 1911, p. 328.

Fig. 35. Zanino di Pietro, the Crucifixion. Correr Museum, Venice.

Photo Ist. Art. Graf.

panel in the Correr Museum to the artist who executed the picture in the Rieti Museum; none the less this is likely to be the case, only in the former the Byzantine influence is more evident, the colour as well as the rigid archaic design both being due to a faint persistence of the eastern tradition. We can suppose, therefore, that Zanino started his career in Venice and that the panel we still find in this city is a production of this early period; later, he, like many another Venetian painter, felt the influence of Tuscan art. He probably painted the picture now at Rieti some considerable time after he had left his native town. In 1407, which must have been towards the end of his career, we find him back in Venice. His art reveals him as a true artist of the Trecento (¹).

One of the most purely Italian works in Venice is the mosaic of 1382 that adorns the tomb of Michele Morosini in the church of SS. Giovanni e Paolo (fig. 36). I do not see, however, in what way this monument provides us with an argument in support of the theory of Agnolo Gaddi's presence in Venice, for the style of this work, although Tuscan, is very different to that of this Florentine master. In the centre the Saviour is depicted nailed to the cross over which hover two angels; below we see on the left the Archangel Michael and the Virgin and on the right the two SS. John with the kneeling figures of the doge and his wife between either pair. The cartoon of this mosaic might very well be Florentine but by a much less able artist than Agnolo Gaddi. The figure of the Baptist alone recalls the Byzantine school, but it may be accounted for by the traditional asceticism with which this saint is usually portrayed.

The last of the Venetian Trecento artists, Niccolo di Pietro, manifests in his works his entire independence of the Gothico-Byzantine style. We possess three dated works, of the years 1394, 1404 and 1409, while mention is made of him in records of 1414, 1416, 1419 and 1430 (²). From the inscriptions on the authentic works we know that his house was situated on the

---

(¹) I suppose that the Crucifixion with the fainting Madonna in the collection of the Historical Society, New York, must be executed in much this manner. It is attributed to Taddeo Gaddi but Mr. *Berenson,* op. cit., p. 4, is of opinion that it is a Venetian work of purely Italian style.

(²) The documentary evidence has been collected by *Testi,* op. cit., p. 329.

Fig. 36. The Crucifixion, mosaic, 1382. SS. Giovanni e Paolo, Venice.
Photo Alinari

"Ponto del Paradiso" and that he was made chevalier in or before 1404 but not yet in 1394. These facts explain why he is mentioned in the documents as "*Niccolo Paradiso depentor*" or again as "*D. Nicholay militis pictoris*". It is possible that Niccolo di Santi who made his will in 1365 was the grand-father of our artist whose father, Pietro di Niccolo, was also a painter ([1]).

He has sometimes been confounded with Semitecolo who was also called Niccolo di Pietro, but the mistake is only too evident.

The earliest dated work is the Madonna of 1394 in the Accademia of Venice (no. 19, fig. 37). The Virgin sitting on an elaborate throne holds the Child with her left hand and with her right indicates the small adorer who kneels at her feet. Two angelic musicians stand on the pilasters of the throne; higher, on the back of it are the tiny figures of the Annunciation while over the Virgin's head is a group of five angels, the three middle ones playing on musical instruments, those at the extremes supporting the curtain which forms the background to the principal figure. I have been unable to trace the origin of this picture which formerly was in the Manfrin collection and was given to the Accademia by Francis Joseph I.

The group of angels in this picture is vaguely reminiscent of those we find in the works of the Gothico-Byzantine artists, including Caterino, but, apart from this, the panel might easily be taken for the production of a provincial adherent of the Florentine school. The artist has given much care to the decorative details but, apart from that, the principal interest of the picture is that it is one of the few purely Italian works executed in Venice before the 15th century. The signature is inscribed at either side of the base of the throne and runs: "*Hoc opus fecit fier Dūs Vulcia Belgarçone civis Yadriensis MCCCLXXXXIIII Nicholas filius Mgrī Petri pictoris de Veneciis pinxit hoc opus qui moratur in chapite pontis Paradixi*".

The great shortcoming of this picture is the absolute lack of expression in the faces of the two principal figures; the forms, although a little heavy, are fairly natural, the drawing is skilful

---

([1]) *Frulin*, Cinque testamenti di pittori ignoti *J. Bernardi*, Arte e Storia, 1886, 12th June. *Testi*, op. cit., pp, 133 and 330.

Fig. 37. Niccolo di Pietro, Madonna, 1394. Accademia, Venice.

Photo Filippini.

and the effects of light and shade, especially in the figures of the angels, quite remarkable. The image of the donor is without doubt an excellent portrait. The colouring too is more Tuscan than Venetian.

The work of 1404 is a small cross carved by the second Caterino who, as we saw, was a sculptor, and painted by Niccolo di Pietro. It is preserved in the church of S. Agostino at Verucchio in the province of Forli([1]). At the extremities of the cross on which the Saviour is depicted the symbols of the Evangelists are seen. The image of the Christ is similar to those we find in late Giottesque works, in fact the whole cross belongs to that tradition. The colours, as in the previous work, are borrowed from the Central Italian school of painting. The signature at the foot of the cross is: *"MCCCCIIII Nicholau Paradixi Miles De Venecis pinxit Chatarinu Sci Luce incixit"*.

Lastly there is a work by Niccolo di Pietro in the church of Sta. Maria dei Miracoli. It is a fragment of a triptych that Niccolo executed in 1409 for the sum of 14 lire 15 sous and that was destined to adorn a tabernacle in the Calle al Canton.

In 1480 the Madonna, the only part remaining, became the object of special veneration and in 1489 it was transferred to the altar of the church, then newly constructed, where it has remained until our day ([2]). It was no doubt at this same moment that the picture was entirely repainted; nothing whatsoever of the original work remains visible.

Maffi informs us that a picture in the church of S. Pietro in Castello in Verona showed the signature: *"Nichalaus filius Magistri Petri pictor pinxit hoc opus Veneciis"* but knowing nothing more about the picture ([3]) I, in accordance with Signor L. Venturi, am unable to see how this fact in any way provides us with a proof, or even with an argument in favour of Signor Testi's hypothesis that the Venetian school at that time already influenced the artists of Verona ([4]). On the other hand I do not agree with Signor L. Venturi in finding in the Madonna of

---

([1]) *Testi*, op. cit., I, p. 340, II, p. 730.
([2]) *Boni*, Archiv. Venet., XXXIII, p. 241. *Testi*, op. cit., I, p. 340.
([3]) *L. Venturi*, L'Arte, 1909, p. 80.
([4]) *Testi*, op. cit., p. 335.

1394 — the only one of Niccolo's works that furnishes us with some knowledge of his art — those Rhenish elements, which, a little later, were of such importance in the formation of Veronese art and from the presence of which we should have to infer that this artistic centre also exercised an influence on Niccolo di Pietro. The individuality of this artist is in no way problematic; he comes at the end of that long struggle which lasted in Venice throughout the 14th century and of which we have been able to follow the different stages. Once free of the Byzantine yoke, the Venetian painters had no choice but to adhere to the Italian manner which at that time was most forcibly expressed in Central Italy. The art of the modest Niccolo di Pietro and its resemblance to that of Tuscan masters can only be considered the outcome of these circumstances; it would be impossible to say exactly from which artist he acquired his manner [1].

Whilst the evolution of the Gothico-Byzantine into a purely Italian form was continued by one group of Venetian artists, another followed quite a different direction; of the old formula so wide-spread in Venice, the second element — the Byzantine — was abandoned, the first — the Gothic — alone being respected. We have already remarked that Lorenzo was the first who worked after this manner and it was probably he who founded this little school. One of the earliest and most important artists, who, to a certain extent, can be identified with this group, was Nicoletto Semitecolo, but I find it better, for reasons which I shall explain when dealing with this artist, to classify him with the painters of the school of Padua.

Giovanni da Bologna [2], whom Lanzi, Cavalcaselle and recently, Signor F. Filippini [3] place among the Bolognese

---

[1] I do not agree with Signor *L. Venturi* that the St. Lawrence in the Accademia of Venice (no. 20) is by the hand of Niccolo di Pietro. In Cavalcaselle's time there existed a picture of Christ in the A. delle Rovere collection with the signature *"Nicola pisit"* or *"Nichola pixit"* but nothing else is known about it, v. *Testi*, op. cit., p. 344.

[2] *A. Moschetti*, Giovanni da Bologna, trecentisto veneziano, Rassegna d'Arte, 1903. p. 36.

[3] *F. Filippini*, Giovanni da Bologna, pittore trecentisto, Rassegna d'Arte, 1908, p. 103 and *B. C. K.* in Thieme Becker's Künstler Lexikon, XIV, p. 112, both affirm that he received his artistic training in Bologna.

artists, came under the direct influence of Lorenzo. The last of these writers has found mention of a painter of this name at Bologna in 1359, 1365, 1371, 1380 and 1387, but the name is such a common one that these records cannot be considered of great importance. What is much more significant is this author's demonstration of points of contact between the Venetian and Bolognese schools of painting in the 14th century; according to Signor Filippini, Giovanni da Bologna's art is an outcome of this combination. I hold a slightly different opinion. There are obviously certain Bolognese traits in some Venetian paintings of the 14th century but I cannot admit the presence of any Venetian characteristics in the Bolognese school. Bologna then was probably the artistic centre which most influenced Venice at the moment of the transition from the old Gothico-Byzantine manner to a more Italianized form of art. The few paintings which Lorenzo Veneziano left in Bologna had no influence on the artists of that town; also Signor Filippini is mistaken in finding in the type of the Madonna of Humility — seated on the ground — a Bolognese element in Giovanni's art. We find this type in Caterino's polyptych, now in the Walters collection, which, of this master's works, is the one that most closely resembles Lorenzo's art and it is quite possible that both Caterino and Giovanni borrowed this iconographical type from Lorenzo. In other regions of Italy, however, the Madonna of Humility was known before this time.

It is of course quite possible that Giovanni da Bologna became acquainted with Lorenzo when the latter worked in Bologna, but the Bolognese artist also went to Venice where he is mentioned as: "*Johannes de Bononia pictor in contrata Santi Luce de Venetiis 1389*" ([1]); besides this, one of his three signed pictures comes from the "Collegio dei Mercanti" in Venice and is dated 1377.

This last work is a panel representing St. Christopher carrying the Child Christ on his shoulder. Lanzi mentioned it as being in the "Scuola di Mercanti" at Sta. Maria dell' Orto but Cavalcaselle and other writers thought that it had been lost; Signor Moschetti, however, discovered it in the store-room of the Padua

---

([1]) *Testi*, op. cit., p. 297.

Fig. 38. Giovanni da Bologna, St. Christopher. Museum, Padua.

Photo Ist. Art. Graf.

Gallery where it now hangs (no. 348, fig. 38). The technique of this painting is perhaps finer than that of any of the master's other productions. I have already drawn attention to the resemblance between this figure and the image of St. Christopher in Caterino's polyptych in the Walters collection but the execution is different. Here the general line of the figure as well as the drapery, part of which floats behind, is Gothic. Above we read: "*Xpoforus Merchantorum*", and lower down on the rocks: "*Joanes de Bononia pinxit*". We know the date from an entry in the "Mariegola dei Mercanti" (¹).

The picture in which Lorenzo's influence is most evident, is the Madonna of Humility in the Accademia of Venice (no. 17), a work which has been considerably restored and repainted. The principal figure is that of the Virgin sitting in a flowery field, nursing the Child (fig. 39); the kneeling figures of the Annunciation are depicted in the spandrels, while below kneel the white-cowled members of a religious confraternity. The figures at either side, depicted one above the other, are SS. John the Baptist and Peter on the left, and SS. John the Evangelist and Paul on the right. In the centre below we read: "*Çuane da Bologna pense*". It is especially in the four lateral figures of saints that this artist's connection with Lorenzo is apparent. A certain evolution in the Gothicism of the folds of the drapery, which are more ample, can even be noted. The appearance of these saints can but confirm the opinion held by Messrs. Moschetti and L. and A. Venturi that the artist's master or at least his source of inspiration was Lorenzo and not Caterino, as Signor Testi believes. Still I do not exclude some slight influence of the Bolognese artists, Lippo Dalmasio and Vitale.

The same remarks apply to Giovanni da Bologna's third signed work which, some years ago, was acquired by the Brera Gallery, Milan (²). It is again a representation of the Madonna of Humility, nursing the Child. It shows some variation on the usual composition, for here the Virgin is seated on a rainbow; from either side approaches a group of angels who in some ways, although not

---

(¹) *Testi*, loc. cit.

(²) *Filippini*, op. cit. G. *Modigliani*, A Picture by Giovanni da Bologna in the Brera, The Burlington Magazine, April 1911.

in style, have much in common with the angels we find behind the Madonna's throne in older Venetian painting. The picture is signed: "*Jovanes de Bologna pinxit*". I do not think that Signor

Fig. 39. Giovanni da Bologna, Madonna, saints and members of a Confraternity in adoration. Accademia, Venice.

Photo Naya.

Filippini is right in saying that this work, more than the one in Venice, reveals the Bolognese characteristics of Giovanni's art; if, on the one hand, the figures show a less strong resemblance to those of Lorenzo Veneziano, on the other hand, the groups of angels are of a purely Venetian inspiration. Besides, Giovanni has painted a Coronation of the Virgin surrounded by angelic musicians, a subject thoroughly Venetian. This picture, which seems to have been signed: "*Joanes pictor de Bologna*" ([1]), belonged, in Cavalcaselle's day, to Michelangelo Gualandi. In the small museum of S. Stefano in Bologna, there exists a picture of this subject with four lateral saints which is signed by Giovanni di Canelo or Zanello but the inscription is almost illegible. This inferior picture has sometimes been ascribed to Giovanni da Bologna with whom Cavalcaselle, who deciphered only the first two words of the signature, seems also to have associated it ([2]).

The only picture which, I think, can be attributed to Giovanni da Bologna is a Pietà in the Booymans Museum of Rotterdam (no. 179), where formerly it was ascribed to Simone Martini. This panel which nowadays is oval in shape, shows, against a gold background, the Virgin holding the dead Christ on her knees. The type of the Virgin, as well as the style of the painting, in which the Gothic elements are not absent, makes me inclined to believe that in all probability this is a work by Giovanni da Bologna.

From what has previously been said while treating the different works of this artist, it must be clear that in my opinion Giovanni was, before all, Venetian, and as we saw in some of the figures of the Madonna of Humility, inspired by Lorenzo; certain peculiarities, however, such as the round heads of his Madonnas, make it probable that at least a part of his artistic education was acquired in Bologna. We find no trace of Byzantinism in any of his works.

A picture in the Accademia of Venice (no. 14) shows much affinity with Giovanni da Bologna's art ([3]). It is a panel divided into four parts, the principal of which is adorned with a figure of the Virgin seated on the ground gazing at the Child asleep on her knee (fig. 40). Above, we see the dead Saviour upright in His tomb between the half-length figures of the Virgin and St. John, while the lateral panels show the figures of St. James Major and St. Francis.

([1]) *Crowe and Cavalcaselle*, ed. L. Douglas, III, p. 202, note 4.

([2]) *Crowe and Cavalcaselle*, ed. loc. cit.

([3]) This painting in my opinion shows no resemblance to the art of Maestro Paolo to whom it has been attributed. L. *Testi*, op. cit., p. 200, believes it to be by a pupil or imitator of this master of the second half of the 14th century.

VENICE AND THE NEIGHBOURING REGIONS. 83

Fig. 40 Manner of Giovanni da Bologna, Accademia, Venice.
Photo Anderson.

The image of the Virgin, in the Gothicism of the draperies and their ornamentation, is quite Venetian but the other figures, especially those of the Pietà, show that force of design and exaggeration of dramatic effects characteristic of the Bolognese school. The picture, which has been very much restored, comes from the church of S. Francesco alla Vigna or that of S. Gregorio.

Fig. 41. Jacobello Alberengo (?), a holy bishop. Gallery, Ferrara.
Photo Minist. del. Pubbl. Istr.

Lorenzo's influence is to a certain extent also to be found in the work of Jacobello Alberengo about whom the documents only inform us that he died in 1397 (¹). The Accademia of Venice possesses a signed work by this master (no. 25) representing, in the centre, the Saviour on the Cross between the Virgin and St. John and at the sides SS. Jerome and Gregory, each carrying the model of a church. The picture is signed: "*Jacobus Alberengo pixit*"; Cavalcaselle doubted the authenticity of this signature but it seems very likely it is genuine, since, as Signor Testi remarks, it already existed in Lanzi's day when the document mentioning his name was as yet undiscovered; it is difficult to see how his name would otherwise have been sufficiently well known to be forged. This picture is also considerably repainted.

Jacobello Alberengo in all likelihood also executed four panels, each of four saints, in the Gallery of

(¹) *Testi*, op. cit., p. 319.

Ferrara (Room XIII, nos. 180—183, figs. 41 and 42). We find here the same long rigid forms, the same hardness of outline and very similar types. The resemblance to Lorenzo Veneziano's works is more evident than in the panel in the Accademia of Venice; the Gothic effect of some of the figures, such for example as that of the Baptist, might be traced to the same source.

Signor Venturi (¹) associates with this artist's name a Virgin and Child between the Baptist and St. Jerome in the Accademia of Venice and a Presentation in the Temple in the Lazzaroni collection, Paris, which is unknown to me.

Jacobello Alberengo is one of the less important artists who came under Lorenzo's influence; still he possessed a certain dramatic sense, as will be noticed in the Crucifixion scene of the panel in Venice, which seems to be of Tuscan origin.

In the only signed work that we have by Jacobello Bonomo, Lorenzo's influence is very strong. Apart from this picture which dates

(¹) *L. Venturi*, op. cit., p. 49.

Fig. 42. Jacobello Alberengo (?), St. John the Baptist. Gallery, Ferrara.
Photo Minist. del. Pubbl. Istr.

from 1385, there exists an official deed in Venice, which mentions him in 1384 (¹).

The authentic work is a large polyptych with a very beautiful frame of Venetian style; it was originally at S. Arcangelo di Romagna, but some years ago, after several vain attempts, it was finally acquired by the Accademia of Venice (²).

In the centre is depicted the Virgin seated, holding the Child in her arms; to either side there are three figures of saints, above each of which is a half-length figure, while over the central panel we see the Crucifixion with the Virgin and St. John and two saints. With the exception of the centre, the general plan of this altar-piece is similar to that of Lorenzo's picture at Vicenza. Not only do the elongated proportions correspond to those of Lorenzo's figures but some of the types — St. Peter's for example — seem to have been copied from this master. In all probability Jacobello Bonomo learned his art from Lorenzo. The signature which is inscribed at the foot of the middle panel runs: *"MCCCLXXXV Jachobelus de Bonomo venetus pinxit hoc opus"*.

Two works showing a very close connection in style to the above altar-piece are found more or less in the same region. They are six figures of saints at the sides of a sculptured Madonna at Pesaro; and a Coronation of the Virgin, with again six lateral panels of saints, in the church of S. Angelo at Fermo. I think, however, that all three works are from different hands. The altar-piece of Pesaro, which now hangs in the Gallery of the town was originally in the church of S. Francesco whence it was transported to that of S. Ubaldo. Cavalcaselle, Morelli (³) and Cantalamessa (⁴) ascribe it to Jacobello del Fiore, Signor G. Cagnola to Jacobello Bonomo (⁵). I do not quite agree with the

---

(¹) *P. Paoletti*, Raccolta dei documenti inediti per servire alla storia della pittura veneziana nei secoli XV e XVI, Padua, 1895, p. 5. *The same*, Un ancona di Jacobello Bonomo, Rassegna d'Arte, 1903, p. 65. A Venetian record of 1355 mentioning "Nobilibus viris Ser Jacobello Bonomo" has certainly nothing to do with our painter. *Testi*, op. cit., p. 322.

(²) v. *Testi*, op. cit., p. 322, note 4 and vol. II, p. 732.

(³) Gallerie Nazionali italiane, II, p. 245.

(⁴) *Cantalamessa*, Nuova Antelogia, 1892, p. 407.

(⁵) *G. Cagnola*, Rassegna d'Arte, 1903, p. 159. *G. Vaccaj*, Pesaro, Bergamo, 1909, p. 92, attributes it to the school of Jacobello del Fiore. *Testi*, op. cit., p. 326, gives it to neither one nor the other.

latter, for the elongated proportions that we saw Jacobello Bonomo had borrowed from Lorenzo, are here absent; on the other hand the line of the draperies is more markedly Gothic and I think that the picture in question is of later date than the one from S. Arcangelo di Romagna but not so late as to be contemporary with Jacobello del Fiore's activity. I believe, therefore, that the panel at Pesaro must have been executed towards the year 1400. I even do not exclude the possibility that it may be a production of a later manner in Jacobello Bonomo's career.

What prevents me from admitting that the polyptych at Fermo (fig. 43) might be by Jacobello Bonomo is that we find here a much more marked Gothicism than in the signed work. The principal panels of this altar-piece are preserved in the church of S. Angelo at Fermo but it is not entire, the upper and lower parts having disappeared. In the centre we see the Coronation of the Virgin and to either side three full-length figures of saints. These panels have been attributed to Bonomo by Signor Colasanti[1], but Signor Testi is of the opinion that they are from the hand of Caterino[2]. The latter, I think, is far from the truth, for the figures here have quite a different appearance to those of any of this master's other works. It is true, however, that the composition of the central group is identical with that of Caterino's Coronations and behind the throne we see a similar group of angels. Gothicism is very pronounced and the forms remind us of Lorenzo Veneziano's second manner but the resemblance to his productions is not strong enough to admit the presence of this master's direct influence.

Gothicism is less evident in two other pictures of the Venetian school. One of these is also found at Fermo, preserved in the collection of paintings adjoining the Library. The principal subject is again the Coronation of the Virgin but here portrayed in a different manner, for the Virgin is depicted kneeling before the

---

[1] *A. Colasanti*, Per la storia dell' arte delle Marche, L'Arte, X, 1907, p. 410. Two panels, each of two figures, in the Correr Museum (VII 15—22) that I have mentioned among the school productions of Lorenzo are also attributed to Jacobello Bonomo. To him was equally ascribed a triptych at the Gozzadini sale (Bologna 1906) which I do not know but which Signor *Testi*, op. cit., p. 328, judges to be Venetian but inferior to Bonomo's works.

[2] *L. Testi*, op. cit., p. 329.

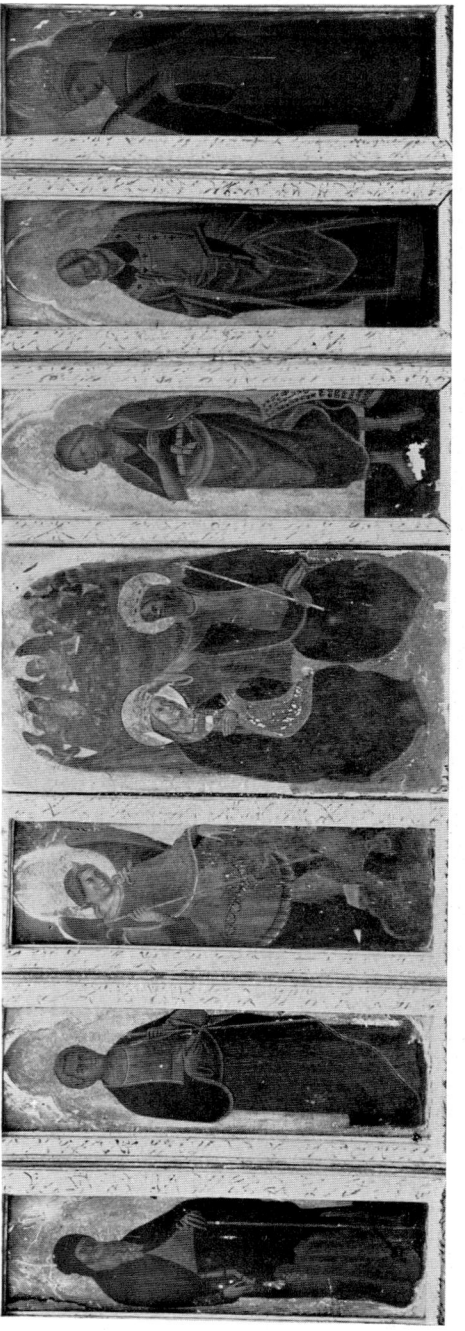

Fig. 43. School of Jacobello Bonomo, the Coronation of the Virgin and saints. S. Angelo, Fermo.
Photo Minist. del. Pubbl. Istr.

Saviour, and behind them appears God the Father from Whose mouth descends the Holy Ghost. This last detail is not unknown in the Venetian school in which this composition abounds. Another Venetian element is the group of angels behind the monumental throne. The small female figure of the donor is seen kneeling below on the right. The rest of this picture comprises five panels with figures of saints. It is beyond doubt that in these pictures, and especially in the technique of the faces, there are certain Bolognese peculiarities; nevertheless I do not believe that this is a work by Andrea da Bologna ([1]) but con-

---

([1]) *A. Colasanti*, loc. cit., attributes the picture to this artist. Before him *C. Astolfi*, with a good deal of hesitation had given it to the same master, L'Arte, V, 1902, p. 193.

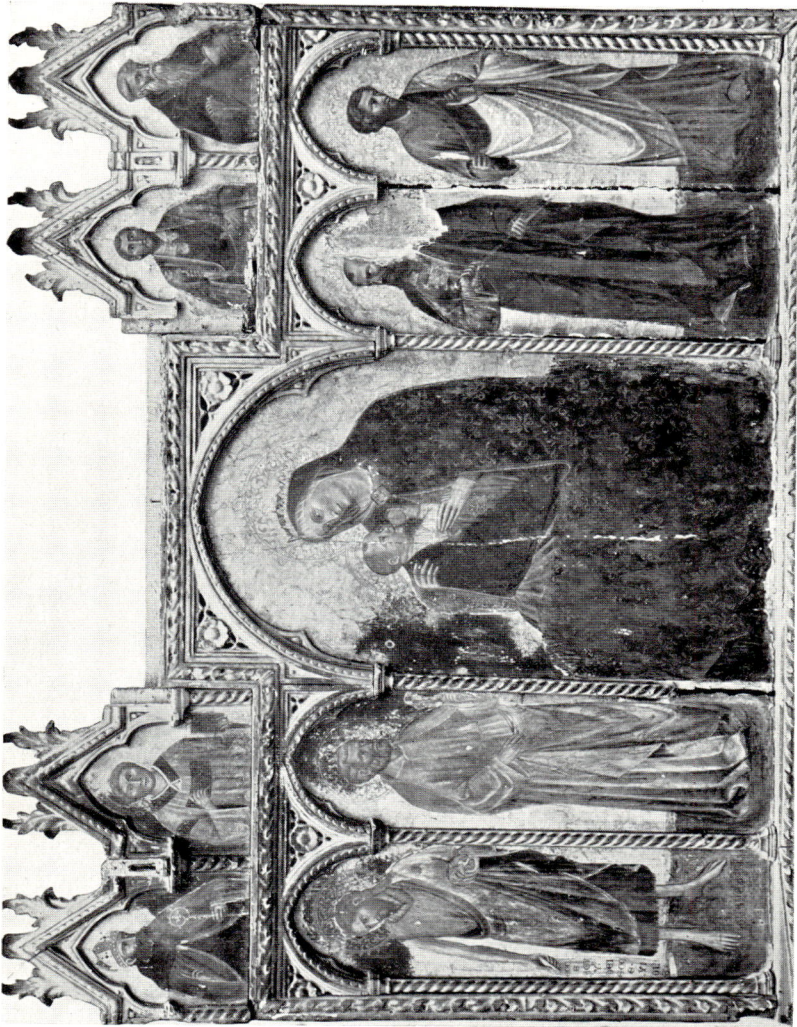

Fig. 44. Venetian School, polyptych, end of the 14th century. Sta. Maria a Mare, Torre di Palme (Fermo). Photo Minist. del. Pubbl. Istr.

sider it rather to be a production of a local artist, one who was influenced by the numerous Venetian works in the region and who was more or less familiar with the Bolognese school of painting([1]).

([1]) A panel, representing, the Arrival of the Magi, in the Accademia of Venice (no. 12), there hesitatingly attributed to the Bolognese school, is executed in the same manner.

The second picture, in which the Gothic element is less evident, is a polyptych in the church of Sta. Maria a Mare, at Torre di Palme, which has sometimes been attributed to Jacobello Bonomo (¹) but which in my opinion is in no way characteristic of this master's art (fig. 44). The centre is occupied by a figure of the Madonna of Humility nursing the Child; to either side there are two full-length figures of saints and above each a half-length figure.

The panel over the Madonna is missing. Not only the shape of the frame but also the ornamentation of the Virgin's robe and the Gothic line of the drapery affirms the Venetian origin of this work. The lateral figures are harder in design and of a more rigid form but in this strikingly resemble the saints at the sides of the panel of the Virgin and the Pietà in the Accademia of Venice (no. 14), there attributed to Maestro Paolo, but executed sooner after the manner of Giovanni da Bologna.

In concluding I should like to recapitulate the outstanding features of the somewhat complicated school of Venetian painting during the 14th century.

From its very foundation, Venetian painting can be differentiated from the mosaic art by the presence of a Gothic element which characterizes the Venetian primitive pictures as productions of a local school under Byzantine influence, but in essence Occidental. It is true, however, that certain paintings executed even in the second half of the 14th century can only be considered as imitation of mosaics which at that moment in Venice were particularly Oriental in appearance, but these works are sporadic and indeed no such form of art is found in Byzantium itself.

The principal figures of the Gothico-Byzantine manner are Maestro Paolo and the Master of Chioggia, but shortly after the year 1350, Venice, half a century after the other centres, follows the general example and replaces the Byzantine formula by an Italian national art, the models of which seem to have been Tuscan, taken no doubt from Giotto's series of frescoes at Padua, just outside the gates of the city. I do not think that the Paduan artist,

---

(¹) *L. Testi*, op. cit., p. 326, with some uncertainty.

Guariento, took a very active part in this metamorphosis; he may have contributed without, however, leaving any direct pupils. In the work of Lorenzo, active from 1356 onward, the Gothic factors are alone conserved, while, almost contemporary, another current, by a slow process of evolution, dissociates itself from both the Gothic and the Byzantine formulae. In this change the painter Caterino was an important figure These two directions of Venetian art continued until the 15th century, but while the second movement finished with Niccolo di Pietro by freeing itself from archaic elements, as did all other Italian schools about the year 1400, the painters who were influenced by Lorenzo retained, at that time, many traces of Gothicism.

To this chapter in which we are dealing with 14th century painting in Venice, there are still some words to add regarding the miniatures of that period, likewise a short account of the spread of Venetian art to surrounding regions.

Many Venetian miniatures of the 14th century manifest, as did the painting, the persistence of the Byzantine influence.

Purely Oriental in appearance is a miniature adorning the register of the S. Teodoro school in the Correr Museum, and dating probably from the beginning of the 14th century. Not only does the subject — the Saviour enthroned between the Virgin and St. John — correspond to the Greek Deesis, but the figures are typical productions of the school of Byzantine miniatures.

In a miniature, executed by Cristoforo Cortese between 1360 and 1390, which illuminates the register of the Sta. Caterina dei Sacchi confraternity and which is again preserved in the Correr Museum, a strong Byzantine influence is evident in the design, in spite of the purely Italian composition.

Many of the miniatures found in Dalmatia belong to the Byzantine style. In the church of S. Francesco at Zara, there are some liturgical books of the end of the 13th century with remarkably fine illuminations of markedly Byzantine appearance (¹), while two antiphonaries in the same building are illustrated with

---

(¹) Beschreibendes Verzeichnis der Illum. Handschr. in Österreich, herausg. von *F. Wickhoff u M. Dvořák*, VI (Dalmatiën), Leipzig, 1917, p. 15—34. *A. Dudan,* La Dalmazia nell' arte italiana, I, Milan, 1922, p. 399.

miniatures which, although somewhat more Italianized, also show a strong Oriental influence (¹). Another example is found in the Paravia Library of the same town, in the register of the "scuola S. Giovanni" of Venice which is written in Venetian dialect and again dates from the beginning of the 14th century. The Italian elements here are only very faintly discernable (²).

At Sebenico the Franciscan monastery possesses an antiphonary with miniatures resembling those of the 14th century in the church of S. Francesco at Zara but rather inferior in composition (³). We also find some miniatures, which are probably Venetian but much less markedly Byzantine, in the Duomo of Gemona in Friuli (⁴).

During this time there were miniatures of quite an Italian appearance executed in Venice. This change of technique on the part of the miniaturists took place long before there was any trace of it in other branches of painting, and it may very well be that these artists largely contributed to the introduction of Central Italian art into the City of the Lagunes.

In a choir book with a portrait of Doge Marino Zorzi (1311—1312), now preserved in the Correr Museum, there is even as early as that date no trace of Byzantinism; nor is there in the illuminations of the register of the "Pelizzeri d' ovra vera" of about 1324.

The Bolognese school of miniatures was the school which dominated the Venetian artists and this influence was felt by the miniaturists long before there is trace of it in other painting. In the illustrations which adorn the "Promissione" of the Doges Francesco and Andrea Dandolo (1329 and 1343), now kept in the State Archives, we observe the strong but unrefined technique and pronounced shades characteristic of the Bolognese school. Another example of this manner is the decoration of the antiphonary of Sta. Maria della Carita (1365) in the Marciana Library.

During this time however the Byzantine current did not entirely disappear from the art of miniature making, as is demonstrated

---

(¹) In Beschreibendes Verzeichnis, pp. 34, 38 and 39, attributed, without any reason I think, to the Bolognese school.
(²) *Idem*, p. 55.
(³) *Idem*, p. 69, again considered as belonging to the Bolognese style.
(⁴) G. *Bragato*, Da Gemona a Venzone, Bergamo, 1913, p. 58.

Fig. 45. Veneto-Byzantine, St. Peter, later years of the 14th century. Sta. Maria, Zara.

Photo Minist. del. Pubbl. Istr.

by the above mentioned illuminations executed by Cristoforo Cortese.

Signor Testi [1] gives us some names of Venetian miniaturists and cites many more examples of this art in the 14th century but all the material he has gathered together only tends to prove, that, apart from the works belonging to the Byzantine manner, Venice had not a definite individual school of miniature of its own.

The paintings that are found along the *Dalmatian Coast,* just as much as the miniatures, force us to believe that this region was even more under the influence of the Byzantine tradition than Venice itself [2]. Apart from a crucifix, by the Sienese artist, Bartolo di Maestro Fredi, at Zara [3], there is little in this district but paintings of quite a Byzantine aspect, or in which an Oriental influence is very marked.

A work of a thoroughly Greek appearance is a panel painted back and front in the church of Sta. Maria at Zara. On one side we see the Virgin and Child with a small kneeling adorer and the figures of the Annunciation above, and on the other St. Peter standing and holding the keys (fig. 45). The inscription is in Latin and the painted ornamental frame sooner belongs to the Italian style but the forms and technique are purely Byzantine. The picture seems to date from the later years of the 14th century [4].

A crucifix in the church of S. Crisogono in the same town (fig. 46) is probably of a slightly later date [5]; here we find some Italian — one might almost say Florentine — elements intermingling with those of Greek origin. Besides the Christ, we see, on the lateral extremities, the Virgin and St. John and above the half-length figure of an angel. The Byzantine influence is especially evident in the schematic manner of execution.

The abbey of Teon on the island of Pasman possesses a crucifix showing the same figures but dating from the end of the 14th century. Here all trace of a Byzantine influence is absent; the refined technique and sweetness of expression might lead us to believe that the artist had come under a Sienese influence.

[1] *Testi,* op. cit., p. 494 et seq.
[2] *Dudan,* op. cit., p. 368.
[3] v. vol. II, p. 504 note 1.
[4] *Idem,* op. cit., p. 371, dates it from the end of the 13th century.
[5] *Idem,* loc. cit., ascribes it to the 13th century.

The Cathedral at Arbe contains a panel of the Madonna enthroned, holding the Child with a figure of the donor kneeling below, a work considerably restored but no doubt dating from the 14th century.

A polyptych in the same church, in which the principal scene is the Crucifixion (fig. 47), abounds in Greek elements although the Latin inscriptions

and the expressive dramatic figures betray its Occidental origin.

Of an even more markedly Byzantine technique is a crucifix in the Ognissanti church at Curzola (fig. 48). The symbols of the four Evangelists adorn the extremities of the cross. The Latin inscription is the only western detail in this work.

Two polyptychs, one in the same church, the other in that of the Concezione in the same town, have certainly been executed by the same hand and between the 14th and 15th centuries. The first shows in the centre, the Pietà, the second the Madonna; both representations have two saints at either side, but only of the first have the terminals been preserved. These works are executed in a fairly advanced Gothic style but reminiscences of the

Fig. 46. Crucifix, end of the 14th century. S. Crisogono, Zara.
Photo Minist. del. Pubbl. Istr.

art of Lorenzo Veneziano and of Alberengo are still manifest.

Fig. 47. Crucifixion, end of the 14th century. Cathedral, Arbe.

Photo Minist. del. Pubbl. Istr.

Polyptychs at Sebenico and Zara probably date from the 15th century but are executed in the same style as the productions of past generations (¹). The Franciscan monks at Zara seem to have in their possession several panels belonging to the 14th

---

(¹) *Dudan*, op. cit., p. 372.

Fig. 48. Crucifix, end of the 14th century. Ognissanti, Curzola (Dalmatia).
Photo Minist. del. Pubbl. Istr.

century; among them, Signori Dudan and Smirich discovered a polyptych representing the Madonna and six saints which, from the description (¹), in all probability corresponds to the altar-pieces of similar composition, so many of which were executed

---

(¹) *Dudan*, op. cit., pp. 371 and 448.

in Venice. What we find in Dalmatia now is only a small part of what there originally was. During the Austrian rule the town of Zara alone lost more than sixty of its pictures (¹). As for the names of artists which have come down to us: there was a certain Joannes Clericopulo, evidently a Greek, who in 1314 signed a picture in the church of S. Demetrio at Zara, representing the Apostles, while in the same town a Magister Nicolao de Jadra was active in 1317 (²).

The city of *Trieste*, situated between these regions and Venice, contains, apart from the large altar-piece of thirty-six divisions belonging to the Venetian school, that I have already mentioned, some beautiful frescoes of the 14th century which can in no way be associated with this artistic current. I have already mentioned them among the productions of the school of Simone Martini, for they really are to all appearances purely Sienese works (³). These mural paintings adorn the five arcades of the choir of the Cathedral; four of them contain each two scenes illustrating the life of St. Justin, to whom the building is dedicated, while in the fifth the saint is depicted holding a model of the church.

The artist was certainly not one of Simone's good pupils; far from it. The design is sometimes not very skilful and the colouring a little hard but the general appearance of the figures, their elegance and sentiment betray the painter's knowledge of the art of this great Sienese master.

Apart from these frescoes we have already noted a Sienese influence on some of the Venetian artists as well as the presence of a work by Bartolo di Fredi at Zara.

At *Aquileia*, some fresco fragments have recently been discovered and restored in the Basilica and in the Baptistery of the Pagans. They show the Lord enthroned between saints, figures of saints and miracles of St. Nicholas, and are local productions of little importance, dating from the 14th century (⁴).

(¹) *Sabalich*, Le pitture antiche di Zara, 1912 and 1920.
(²) *Dudan*, op. cit., pp. 371 and 372. For pictures of the 14th century at Ragusa and Zara now dispersed, v. *Dadan*, op. cit., I, pp. 107 and 128.
(³) v. Vol. II, p. 248 note 1.
(⁴) *A. Morassi*, Bolletino d'Arte del Minist. della Pubbl. Istr., 1924, p. 419, ascribes some of these to the 13th and 15th centuries.

Fig. 49. Simone da Cusighe, polyptych, 1389. Accademia, Venice.

Photo Anderson.

To the north of Venice we find at *Treviso* some frescoes by Tommaso da Modena and his followers which will be dealt with later on.

In speaking of 14th century painters, Rosini (¹) mentions a certain Martinello at *Bassano,* without, however, being able to attribute a single work to him.

In *Friuli* there can still be discovered some traces of pictorial activity. The village of Cusighe, near Belluno, possessed an artist of the name of Simone who has left some frescoes and an altar-piece in the parish church. These frescoes, judged by Lanzi as being "very tolerably executed", no longer exist. They were signed: "*Simon pinxit*" (²). The same painter was paid 440 lire for an altar-piece for the Cathedral of Belluno; in 1400 he assisted at the opening ceremony of the large reliquary of this Cathedral and died before 1416 (³).

There is a polyptych by this artist in the Accademia of Venice (no. 18); it comes from the Pagani family of Belluno and was originally in the church of S. Bartolommeo in Salce near the town (fig. 49). The central figure is that of the crowned Virgin with an image of Jesus seated on a rainbow within an aureole against her breast; her wide-spread mantle seems to protect the figures of a confraternity that kneel in adoration at her feet. At either side of the Madonna four scenes from St. Bartholomew's legend are depicted. Below the inscription runs: "$M.IIJLXXXXIIIJ$ $indi\bar{c}$ IJ die XX $Augusti$ $act\bar{u}$ $fuit$ $h.op....$ $onesto$ $viro$ d^o p^o $\overset{o}{X}$ $foro$ $cap\overline{ll}$ $\overset{i}{S}$ $B\overline{athi}$. $Simon\ fecit$". The most Venetian part of this work of art is the frame; the figures of

---

(¹) *Rosini*, Storia della Pittura italiana, II, Pisa, 1841, p. 145.

(²) *L. Lanzi*, The History of Painting in Italy, transl. by Th. Roscoe, II, London, 1847, p. 80.

(³) *Crowe and Cavalcaselle*, ed. L.Douglas, III, p. 259, give these documents and mention as a work by Simone da Cusighe — also called dal Peron — an altar-piece with scenes from the lives of SS. Martin and John the Baptist, a work in part repainted which was in his day transported from the church of St. Martin at Belluno to the Baptistery. They also cite a panel of St. Antony enthroned amidst saints, frescoes in the church of Sala and a panel of the Virgin between saints at Orez which, as far as I know, have been lost sight of.

Fig. 50. Consecration of the Cathedral of Venzone, 1338. Cathedral, Venzone.
Photo Ist. Art. Graf.

the small scenes might easily be taken for the work of a provincial Tuscan painter. The type of the Madonna resembles those we find later on in Vivarini's paintings.

In this region there are remains of two series of frescoes, both important in that they belong to the Giottesque school and display no trace of a Venetian influence. The first of these is found in the Abbey of Sesto (Friuli) where the fragments of what can never have been an important mural decoration include representations of the Saviour on the Cross, angels and saints in heaven and the Ascension, all of which are thoroughly Florentine in appearance (¹). The second Giottesque work comprises some figures of sibyls adorning what was no doubt once the Palazzo del Capitano della Giustizia at Cortina d'Ampezzo (*Cadore*) (²).

Lanzi informs us as well that the façade of the Cathedral of Gemona was adorned with frescoes and that under a scene of a martyrdom, the work was signed: "*MCCCXXXII Magister Nicolaus pintor me fecit*" (³). Rosini and Maniago, however, tell us that the decoration comprised scenes from the life of St. Christopher and that the inscription was: "*1331 magister Nicolaus pintor refecit hoc opus sub Johane Camerario quondam Petri Merisori*" (⁴).

The façade of the hospital at Gemona is adorned with a fresco of the half-length figure of the Saviour, naked and bleeding but not dead, between the Virgin and St. John. It is a work of a certain merit but very Tuscan in appearance (⁵).

In the Cathedral of Venzone, near Gemona, a fresco of some importance represents the consecration of the church which took place in 1338 (fig. 50). The composition is divided into two parts; above we see a row of bishops of which the central and principal figure is that of the patriarch Bertrand; angels are depicted hovering over their heads; below are represented the choristers with the "camerario" Bartolommeo Sclusano and other persons who were present at the ceremony. On the left there is a

---

(¹) *A. De Carlo* in L'Illustrazione Italiana, XXXI, 1904, p. 335.

(²) *Tolomei*, Le sibile Giotteschi a Cortina d'Ampezzo, Arch. per l'Alto Adige, III, 1908, fasc. I.

(³) *Lanzi*, loc. cit.

(⁴) *Rosini*, loc. cit. and p. 159. *Maniago*, Storia delle Belle Arte Friulane, Venezia, 1829, p. 117. *Crowe and Cavalcaselle*, op. cit., p. 258 note 3, mention two documents of 1334 and 1337 in the archives of Udine concerning this artist and others regarding his family.

(⁵) *G. Bragato*, op. cit., p. 78.

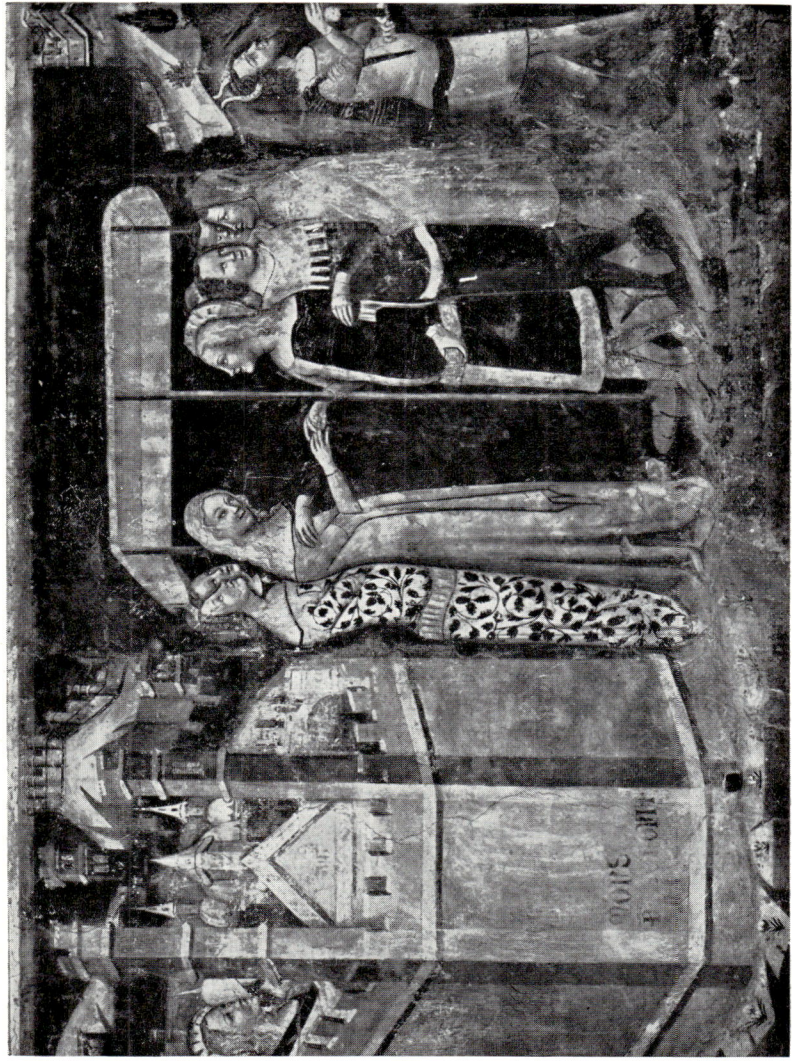

Fig. 51. Scene from the legend of St. Julian, 2nd half of the 14th century. Cathedral, Trento.

Photo Alinari.

large somewhat isolated figure of a saint. In Lanzi's day these frescoes were attributed to Magister Nicolaus who worked at Gemona in 1332, but Maniago is of opinion that they were probably executed by a certain *Giovanni guondam ser Viano*, a Venetian painter whom we find at Venzone in 1359. As is usually the case with the older historians of art, Maniago has made use of the only name he had at his disposal. But a glance at the picture is all that is required, for there were no artists in the middle of the 14th century in Venice who worked in this purely Italian manner with such strange observation of facial details, characteristic above all of Sienese artists. On the same wall and belonging to to the same current, but older, since they are in part covered by the fresco of the consecration, we find some fragments of other paintings; among them are a head of a holy bishop and St. Martin dividing his coat with the beggar.

A short distance from Venzone, in the little church of S. Giacomo, a damaged fresco of the Saviour between the Twelve Apostles, although a very mediocre work, is one of the few in this district in which a Venetian influence is manifest; the modest provincial master who worked here must have seen some of Lorenzo Veneziano's paintings ([1]).

The "Tempietto" at Cividale contains, besides the mediaeval frescoes, a row of saints of the 14th century. These figures are the production of a very rustic artist who, however, seems to have been more familiar with the Giottesque style than with the Venetian school.

The Gallery of Udine contains an unimportant detached fresco of the 14th century representing two figures of saints. A Madonna of Byzantine appearance in the Virgin's chapel of Sta. Maria delle Grazie probably belongs to the same period.

In the apsidal vault of the Cathedral of Grado an important fresco executed in a Tuscan style shows the Lord in a mandorla between the four symbols of the Evangelists, the Virgin, the Baptist and two other saints.

In *Trento*, besides the frescoes in the tower of the Eagle in the castle "del Buon Consiglio" which are of a later period, we find in the left transept of the Cathedral some mural paintings,

---

([1]) *Crowe and Cavalcaselle*, op. cit., p. 259, mention other frescoes at Venzone, of which I can no longer find any trace, in the chapel del Pio Instituto of the Cathedral, in the church of Sta. Lucia (the Saviour with the symbols of the Evangelists and the Church Fathers) and in the church of S. Antonio Abbate (scenes from the New Testament of 1405).

illustrating the life of St. Julian (fig. 51). These representations, in which the contemporary costumes are an outstanding feature, show in my opinion a German influence; the types, the expressions and gestures of the figures, their form and proportions

Fig. 52. Battista da Vicenza, polyptych. 1404. Pinacoteca, Vicenza.
Photo Ist. Art. Graf.

which seem to have been inspired by Gothic sculptures, are sufficient indication of this origin. This decoration displays a very close connection with the profane paintings with which many German castles were adorned during the second half of the 14th century. There are still some other frescoes of the 14th century in the same church. Hard by the foregoing we find represented the Nativity, the Decapitation of St. John the Baptist and the Trinity, and in the right transept some other mural decoration; all are rather mediocre works of purely Italian style (¹).

At *Vicenza*, to the other side of Padua, we find an adherent of the Venetian school in Battista da Vicenza (²) who is known to us by two signed works, the one of 1404 in the Gallery of the town (no. 17), the other of 1408 in the church of S. Giorgio, near Velo d'Astico in the heights of Asiago.

The first of these works comes from the church of S. Agostino (³); it is a large polyptych (fig. 52) quite after the style of Lorenzo Veneziano who left one of very similar model in the Cathedral of this town. Here the centre is occupied by the enthroned Virgin, fondly clasping the Child Jesus in her arms. To either side there are three full-length figures of saints, above each of which is depicted a three-quarter length figure, while the Crucifixion, which we generally find over the central panel, is here replaced by the dead Christ upright in His tomb with a small figure of a saint at either side; the medallion which forms the pinnacle encloses a bust of the Almighty.

The predella, flanked on either side by the coat of arms of the Chiericati family, comprises six small images of saints and in the middle John the Baptist and two angels. The inscription which is seen below runs: "*Opus factum Vincencie comissione magnifici Ludovici de Chierigatis. An MCCCC quarto XII indicione*". This painting, which was originally on wood, has been transferred on to linen. Lorenzo Veneziano's influence is manifest not only in the building up of the picture but also in the figures; for we can discover many elements in the proportions and general aspect of the persons depicted here that remind us of this master's art.

Velo d'Astico was destroyed during the great European War and I have not been able to discover the fate of the polyptych originally in the church of S. Giorgio on the outskirts of this village. It is smaller in size than that described above, for at either side of the Madonna there are but two figures of saints;

(¹) There exists a document which proves the presence of a painter called Bettino da Verona at Trento in 1387, Repert. für Kunstw., XXVI, p. 22.

(²) *Crowe and Cavalcaselle*, op. cit., p. 247. *Moschetti*, Battista da Vicenza, in Thieme-Becker, Künstler Lexikon, III, p. 49.

(³) *G. Pettinà*, Vicenza, Bergamo, 1912, p. 76.

Fig. 53. Battista da Vicenza (?). Saints. Kaiser Friedrich Museum, Berlin.
Photo Hanfstaengel.

the central panel above, here shows us the Christ on the Cross between the Virgin and St. John. The donor and his wife are depicted kneeling in separate lateral panels; the name of the former is given in the inscription on the predella:*"Hoc opus fecit fieri Bonencontrus q̄dam domini Andree de Pione de Vello de mese Setembris MCCCC octavo"*. This work closely resembles the foregoing.

I do not share the opinion held by Cavalcaselle and Signor Moschetti, that the frescoes found in this church are from the same hand. The vaults are adorned with the figures of the Saviour and the four Evangelists and the walls with representations of the Crucifixion, St. George slaying the dragon, the Nativity, the Pietà and the Resurrection. As Signor Moschetti himself remarks, explaining, however, the difference by an evolution on the part of the artist, these scenes are clearly inspired by the Giottesque painters of Padua; the Crucifixion is a copy of Altichiero's composition in the church of S. Antonio in Padua, while the colours and design have changed in the same degree.

I agree with Cavalcaselle in attributing to Battista da Vicenza a Madonna in the Gallery of the artist's native town (no. 23), as well as four panels with scenes from the life of St. Sylvester (nos. 13—16), while less typical of the master, although very possibly by him, are two predella panels and three pinnacles, all showing figures of saints, and very likely forming parts of the same polyptych; in the Gallery of Vicenza (nos. 18—22) they are catalogued as works by Battista da Vicenza. Quite in the master's manner but even of a more inferior execution than usual, are ten figures of saints, no doubt from one large altarpiece, in the Museum of Berlin (fig. 53). Battista da Vicenza was a provincial adherent of a good tradition but not an artist of great merit.

We cannot leave Vicenza without mentioning the frescoes in the church of Sta. Corona, which, in the chapel to the right of the choir, adorn the tombs of Mario and Giovanni di Thiene, deceased in 1344 and 1415, but probably both frescoes were executed about the latter date. Each of the paintings shows us the Madonna seated on a monumental throne, the one with two saints and a kneeling knight, the other with three saints and a devotee. They betray a stylistic relation with the paintings of

VENICE AND THE NEIGHBOURING REGIONS.

Padua and more especially with those of Verona and really belong to the group of early 15th century Gothic productions.

This little ramble in the regions around Venice makes it fairly clear that the Venetian school was not very wide spread[1]. Firstly, few works of art seem to have been exported from Venice, for of this very productive school we only found some examples at Vicenza, Bologna and Trieste and in slightly greater number in The Marches, even as far distant as Lecce.

It is very doubtful if the Dalmatian paintings executed in the Venetian manner are the outcome of a Venetian influence; it is more than probable that they are the result of common circumstances producing in two separate districts a similar form of art.

We find no trace of an adhesion to the Venetian school except in the frescoes of S. Giacomo, near Venzone, and in the art of Battista da Vicenza. This painter, although of little merit, was the only member of another centre who, in any way, contributed to the spreading of the Venetian style. In all the other regions around the City of the Lagunes we find nothing but productions of a purely Italian art [2].

---

[1] There is mention however of a Guarnerius de Venitiis who in 1369 was active in Rome for Pope Urban V; *Crowe and Cavalcaselle*, op. cit., II, p.187².

[2] While this chapter was in the press I have read the interesting book by *F. Gilles de la Tourette*, L'Orient et les peintres de Venise, Paris, 1924, who, in a pleasant form, gives in the first fifty pages a very clever and original review of Venetian painting in the 14th century.

CHAPTER II.

THE PAINTERS OF PADUA, VERONA AND TREVISO.

There are certain peculiarities which unite the painters of Padua, Verona and Treviso. Almost all were independent of the Venetian school and influenced by the Giottesque manner and produced "tableaux de genre", not of very great narrative power but full of details taken from everyday life. Their art was rather a popular one, not without some resemblance to certain frescoes executed on the other side of the Alps.

The artistic connection between Padua and Verona did not make its appearance until after the activity of Altichiero and Avanzo.

Guariento, an artist of the generation after Giotto's, was an important figure in the history of painting of Padua [1].

We come across him for the first time in 1338, just thirty years after Giotto's activity in Padua, and if Giotto, who died in 1337, did not return to that town, it is not likely that this local artist ever met the great Florentine. There is no reason to believe, then, that Giotto was Guariento's master, but he was of course perfectly familiar with the frescoes in the Arena chapel. A document of 1350 in speaking of "Guariento quondam Arpi" informs us as to his father's name. There are various records concerning him between 1347 and 1365, while from 1365 until 1368 he painted the Coronation of the Virgin in the Hall of the Big Council in the Palazzo Ducale, Venice; his death must have occurred before September 1370, for at that time he is spoken of as deceased. In a document of 1378 there is still question of "quondam Guariento".

---

[1] *L. Menin*, Sulle pitture del Guariento, Padua, 1826. *N. Petrucci*, Biogafia degli artisti padovani, Padua, 1858. *A. Schiavon* Guariento, Arch. Venet., XXXV, I, 1883. *A. Moschetti*, Il Museo Civico di Padova, Padua, 1903. *L. Fiocco*, Guariento in Thieme-Becker, Künstler Lexikon, Vol. XV, p. 172.

The "Anonimo Morelliano" — whose real name was Marcantonio Michiel — informs us that the Cappella Maggiore of the Eremitani was painted by Guariento, "a Paduan, called by some, a Veronese". This author has the same doubt as to the origin of

Fig. 54. Guariento, Madonna. Gallery, Padua.
Photo Alinari

Avanzo. The "Anonimo", on Campagnola's authority [1], speaks of the collaboration of Avanzo and Guariento in the decoration of the Palazzo del Capitano del Popolo at Padua and attributes to the latter artist the twelve Cesars and the scenes from their lives. He again repeats, after Campagnola, that Guariento

---

[1] Gerolamo Campagnola was a savant and notary in Padua and the father of the painter-engraver, Giulio Campagnola who was born in 1482.

decorated the Cappella Maggiore of the church of S. Agostino[1].

Vasari, who upheld Guariento as an artist of some repute, called him Guariero; to the list of works given by the "Anonimo", he added only the frescoes in the first cloister of the Eremitani church.

The oldest of Guariento's works that have come down to us are very probably the panels from the ceiling of the chapel in the Palazzo del Capitano del Popolo. This chapel was destroyed in 1769 and the decoration, in large part, is now conserved in the Museum of Padua; the rest has been lost. Of the Old Testament scenes we find: (1) God the Father with Adam and Eve, (2) Isaac's sacrifice, (3) the destruction of Sodom, (4) the angel visiting Abraham, (5) the young men in the furnace, (6) Judith and Holofernes and (7) Joseph sold by his brethren. There are besides some curiously shaped fragments, semi-circular, hexagonal or octagonal, the most important of which are a half-length figure of the Virgin (fig. 54) and images of the four Evangelists. A panel of the Saviour is of smaller dimensions.

Then there are a great many panels of angels belonging to the different hierarchies, some isolated, some grouped, the most curious of which is a representation of the "celestial militia" (fig. 55). In all, there are twenty-nine panels. These remains of a painted ceiling form a link between the Paduan school — in which Guariento's other works are included — and the Venetian painters of the 14^{the} century. In the hieratic spirit of the work, the somewhat rigid drawing, the juxtaposition of light and shade and the richness of the costumes, there is evident a Byzantine influence, in opposition to which the types, faces and expressions are all purely Italian and obvious derivatives of Giotto's art.

The decoration of the choir of the Eremitani church that the "Anonimo" mentions is probably of slightly later date. It is a fairly extensive work but I do not think that it is all from the same hand. Of the monochrome figures below, for example, there is only one — the Saviour with the crown of thorns — that is of a quality equal to the master's; the technique is good and the figure full of feeling. The other representations, Christ carrying the Cross, the Saviour and the Holy Women, the Descent into Hell and the

---

[1] *Th. Frimmel*, Der Anonimo Morelliano (Marcanton Michiel) Quellenschr. zur Kunstgesch. etc., Neue Folge, I, Wien, 1888, pp. 26, 34 and 36.

Resurrection are all rather inferior works and must have been left to an assistant.

Not much more skilfully executed are the pictures of the seven

Fig. 55. Guariento, the Celestial Militia. Gallery, Padua.

Photo Alinari.

ages of man (¹). The moon is represented with two children playing, Minerva with two adolescents, Venus with a young man holding a sword and a young wife; Jupiter protects a man and women of riper age; the couple accompanying Mars devote themselves to material well-fare; when the same two are depicted

(¹) *Rosini*, op. cit., II, p. 211.

Fig. 56. Guariento, the Saviour. Eremitani Church, Padua.
Photo Anderson

with Mercury, the man is seen studying, the woman making herself a necklace; Saturn is represented with an aged woman warming herself and a sick old man.

The frescoes on the walls illustrating the story of SS. Augustine and Monica were so much repainted in 1589 that their actual appearance only allows us to say that they really did belong to the original decoration. The vaults are adorned with figures of the Saviour and the Apostles, the former in a mandorla carried by angels and surrounded by others, the latter seated on monumental thrones (fig. 56). Lower down some angels are represented holding a Cross, a motif no doubt borrowed from a composition of the Last Judgment. The rest of the painting comprises a row of saints and various medallions.

Fig. 57. Guariento, Crucifix. Museum, Bassano.
Photo Alinari.

Although the monochrome figures below are of rather inferior execution, those above belong to a much higher standard of work. It is true that some traces of Byzantinism persist, but the drawing is fine, the faces almost all beautiful and their expressions full of feeling and inspiration. The Giottesque influence however has not yet prevailed over the Venetian and I think therefore that there is only a short interval between this decoration and the panels now in the Gallery.

At Bassano we find a signed work of Guariento's (fig. 57). It is a crucifix, similar in design to those that Giotto and his Florentine adherents painted, an example of which by the great master himself adorns the Arena chapel. It was no doubt the prototype of the numerous crosses that are to be found in the various towns of this region. In Guariento's, the Saviour is depicted nailed to the Cross, the knees slightly bent, the head inclined; the busts of the Saviour, the Virgin and St. John occupy the upper and lateral extremities. The foot of the Cross is embedded in a rocky eminence to one side of which the female donor kneels in prayer while to the other is painted her coat of arms. On the lower extremity of the crucifix the name of the artist: "*Guarientu' pinxit*" is inscribed and lower down: "*Emulatrix Bona' Maria Bwolinoru Helenā inventrix crucis et clavor*". *Sancxit hanc ip̄s pietate Bassān et orēt p. la xp̄m Dō Dor*". (Dominum Dominorum). As Signor L. Venturi remarks, this crucifix is more Giottesque, and for that reason probably of later date than the paintings in Padua. The type of the Saviour and the anatomical presentment especially cannot be conceived without Giotto's precedent. The drawing of the features of the surrounding figures is rather vigorous and still retains something of the Byzantine archaism.

A fresco very characteristic of our artist will be found in an annex of the S. Francesco monastery at Bassano; it represents the Virgin worshipped by a knight in armour with SS. Antony of Padua, Sigismund and Andrew, and is surrounded by a beautiful frieze. There is here a second fresco of the Virgin which in its original state must have been as fine a work as the former, but it has suffered much from restoration. Two Apostles are depicted to the sides of the principal figure [1].

We now come to the fresco that Guariento, shortly before his death, painted in the Hall of the Big Council in the Palazzo Ducale, Venice [2]. This room was decorated by order of the Doge Mario Cornaro who was in office from 1365 until 1367, for Muratori has handed down to us the inscription which existed before Tintoretto covered the composition with a representation of Paradise: "*Marcus Cornarius Dux et Milles fecit fieri hoc opus*". Sansovino, in his description of Venice of 1577, mentions Guariento's work in this room but was mistaken in saying that before this artist painted in colours, there was a monochrome decoration. The

---

[1] *F. Roberti*, Reparazione di un affresco del Guariento, Arte e Storia, XIII, 1894, p. 114. *G. Fogolari*, Affreschi del Guariento a Bassano, L'Arte, 1905, p. 122.

[2] *Rosini*, op. cit., II, p. 210. *A. Moschetti*, Il paradiso del Guariento nel Palazzo Ducale di Venezia, L'Arte, VII, 1904, p. 396. Cronaca dei restauri etc. dell' ufficio Regionale etc., Venezia, 1912, p. 23.

fact that the construction of this part of the palace was not finished until 1362 makes it highly improbable that it was decorated on two different occasions before 1367. The fresco which was discovered in 1903 has been so much spoiled by the fire that destroyed the decoration of this hall, that several have thought it a monochrome painting, but this is not so, it was a fresco in colours most of which, however, have perished. The large fragments that still remain show us the Virgin on an imposing architectural throne (¹) being crowned by the Saviour; a large number of figures arranged in regular groups are placed around the central images; they are mostly angels of the different hierarchies with a row of seated Apostles. Above in the background more Gothic arches are depicted. Guariento in the execution of this enormous fresco shows himself as an even more faithful follower of the Giottesque style than in the crucifix at Bassano. However, he never entirely got rid of a certain archaism, but of the Gothico-Byzantine formula he only retained the Gothic elements, which, united with the Giottesque, result in a Gothico-Giottesque manner.

There is a number of works of the school of Guariento which prove that in his day this artist was the centre of a group of painters. In Padua we find evidence of this in the church of the Eremitani, where over the entry hangs a crucifix resembling that at Bassano; it has even been attributed to Guariento himself but I prefer to class it as the work of a pupil. On the right wall, near the choir, there are three detached fragments of fresco painting, the most important of which represents the Coronation of the Virgin. It is the work of an artist slightly more influenced by the Venetian school than Guariento ever was.

Above the door of the "Salone" of Padua there is a fresco of the same subject which is also reminiscent of the master's manner (²).

(¹) These monumental Gothic thrones which are frequently found in Veronese works, are met with as early as the middle of the 14th century in Bohemian painting e.g. the Annunciations at Hohenfurth and in the Museum of Prague (*F. Burger*, Die Deutsche Malerei, I, Berlin, 1913, pls. X—XI) and the Madonna from Glatz in the Berlin Museum (*Dehio*, Geschichte der Deutsche Kunst, II, Berlin-Leipzig, 1921, p. 415).

(²) *A. Venturi*, op. cit., V, p. 927, gives this painting to Guariento.

At Bassano a rather damaged fresco of the Annunciation on the façade of S. Francesco and a series of frescoes illustrating the legend of St. Antony, but of which only a part now remains, in one of the rooms in the monastery school, seem to me to be school productions and even somewhat feeble ones. In the former the Virgin is seen sitting on a throne with a canopy, a lectern is placed close by; the angel kneels opposite her while above in the centre a half-length figure of the Almighty appears in a medallion and a little naked figure of the Infant Christ flies towards the Madonna. Traces of a knight, kneeling in adoration are still visible.

A Madonna between two saints and two angels on the exterior of the Cathedral and a crucifix inside the same building both belong to Guariento's school; the latter is of about the same quality and might even be from the same hand as the fresco in S. Francesco. A painting of the marriage of St. Catherine in the Gallery only faintly recalls this manner; it is a later work but one in which the large architectural throne is depicted.

Much finer and more closely resembling the master's works is a crucifix on the entry wall of S. Zeno in Verona (fig. 58).

This panel is all the more important because, belonging without any doubt to Guariento's school, it forms a link between Padua and Verona before the appearance of Altichiero and Avanzo. Maffei in speaking of this cross informs us that there were similar ones in the Crocifisso church and in St. Anastasia.

I think that Guariento has been judged a little below his real artistic value, generally being considered only a mediocre Giottesque painter. He was not only that. At an early stage in his career Guariento may have been a member of the Venetian Gothico-Byzantine tradition, although in the earliest work we have by him — the twenty-nine panels in the Museum of Padua — evidence of this is somewhat feeble, the Gothic factor alone being conserved; with this he united the peculiarities which resulted from Giotto's influence. Guariento was then an artist

---

(¹) *G. Fogolari*, op. cit., p. 142. *O. Sirén* ascribes a picture of St. Ursula and her companions in the Steinmayer collection to Guariento (Burlington Magazine, 1921, p. 169) but it is probably a Venetian work and seems to me of considerably later date.

THE PAINTERS OF PADUA, VERONA AND TREVISO. 119

of the transition, a Gothico-Giottesque, as was also Semitecolo shortly after. The union of these two manners was very natural in Padua, a town just outside the gates of Venice and within whose walls Giotto left the most important series of frescoes we have from his hand.

Besides the little nucleus of anonymous painters that gathered around Guariento and Semitecolo with whom we shall deal presently, we

Fig. 58. School of Guariento, Crucifix. S. Zeno, Verona.
Photo Lotze.

discover that the influence of Guariento's art was fairly persistent. The strongly outlined faces of Altichiero's figures as well as some of his types are reminiscent of Guariento's art, while the Coronation of the Virgin and the form of the throne in the chapel of S. Giorgio in Padua seem to have been inspired by Guariento's Paradise in Venice. This composition seems to have influenced Vivarini and other artists of the 15th century, at least in as far as the choice of a subject is concerned. I will even say that in the severity of drawing Crivelli shows in his features, there is a resemblance to certain of Guariento's figures, such for instance as those in the panels in Padua or — even more marked — those in the Bassano crucifix.

From a document of 1370. recording a difference between the town of Venice and Guariento's heirs, we gather that the painter had not been faithful to the conditions stipulated in the contract for the fresco of the Council Room, not having kept two assistants. We are also informed that his heirs were poor, so the assumption is that he must have been likewise, yet he was an esteemed artist and, out of economy, had advised the use of "azure d'Allemagne" instead of ultra-marine [1].

The incorporation of Nicoletto Semitecolo into the Paduan school does not solely depend on the fact that the only work we have by him is to be found in the town of Padua, but that his style forces us to associate him closely with Guariento.

The authentic documents concerning him prove that in 1353 he was in Venice where, together with his father, Donato, also a painter, he acted as witness [2]; that in 1367 he signed the panel in Padua and that in 1370 he had returned to Venice where he signed some paintings that Sansovino called "Storica dello Volto Santo" in the Centurione chapel near Sta. Maria dei Servi; the inscription was: *"MCCCLXX x Decembrio Nicolo Semitecolo"* [3].

Some other works on account of the signature have been attributed to Semitecolo; they date from 1351, 1371 and 1400; the first is preserved in the Accademia of Venice (no. 23), the other two in the Correr Museum, but the signatures of 1351 and 1400 have been considered apocryphal, while the panel of 1371, signed: *"Nicolo Veneto"*, has nothing to do with our artist. In 1362 mention is made of a Nicolo Semitecolo, a priest, but it is not certain, hardly even probable, that it is the same person. Besides, there existed in Venice a patrician family of this name.

The only paintings by Nicoletto Semitecolo which have reached us are the six panels in the Chapter-house Library in Padua; they represent the Trinity, the Madonna and four scenes from the life of St. Sebastian; of the last four panels, the first shows the signature: *"Nicholeto Simitecholo Da Venexia inpese"* and the last the date: *"MCCCLXVII Adi XV Decembri"*.

In the Trinity the extended hands of the Almighty are covered

---

[1] L. *Venturi*, op. cit., p. 43.
[2] *Testi*, op. cit., p. 307 note 4. *Ludwig* in Jahrb. der K. Preus. Kunstsamml., 1903, p. 28, dates this document by mistake from 1352.
[3] *Cicogna*, op. cit., I, p. 97.

by those of Christ Who, seen in half-length figure, alive and with open eyes, constitutes a very curious exception to iconographical observances.

Fig. 59. Semitecolo, St. Sebastian before his Judge. Biblioteca Capitolare, Padua.

Photo Agostini.

The Virgin is represented seated on the ground, nursing the Child Christ; the background is formed by three circles traced in the gold setting. In both pictures we are struck by the extreme sadness of the expressions, especially that on the face of the Virgin.

The first of the four scenes from the life of St. Sebastian shows us the saint before the judges, Diocletian and Maximus who are seated in a hall, one end of which is adorned with a statuette of a pagan god; a little dog plays at the emperors' feet (fig. 59). The saint turns from his judges towards a woman who kneels behind; close by stand two other holy martyrs and further behind a group of soldiers.

In the scene of his martyrdom, the naked saint is attached to a stake while from right and left soldiers shoot arrows at him, the emperors looking on from a balcony (fig. 60).

The following picture shows us how the saint is cudgelled to death; the emperors are still present but the background has changed. Lastly we see the saint entombed by his faithful friends (fig. 61). Here the background is formed by two large buildings, the interiors of which are seen by the simple means of the suppression of a wall. These panels may have been painted at both sides because at the back of the picture of the martyrdom traces of two figures and the name Daniel still remain visible.

I do not think that we possess any other works by this artist[1] about whom there is a considerable diversity of opinion. As colourist but not as designer Lanzi connected him with Giotto; Signor L. Venturi looks upon him as a pupil of Maestro Paolo's, while Cavalcaselle finds him little different from other Venetian artists, noting all the same his affinity with Guariento, as does also Signor Testi, who lays much stress on this point. Personally I find few Venetian elements in his painting, which reveals on the other hand much in common with Guariento's art, and still more perhaps with Giotto's, since Byzantinism is almost entirely absent. There is a certain amount of Gothicism, but Semitecolo's paintings belong, before all, to a popular narrative form of art, as did Giotto's before him. Action is highly important and is represented full of tragedy and realism, expressed with great vigour. The proportions of his figures are different and in this Semitecolo is very much inferior to Giotto and his immediate

---

[1] The frescoes in the Oratorio dei Lucchesi have been attributed to him without any reason, v. *Testi*, op. cit., p. 316. *Berenson*, Venetian Painting in America, p. 4, speaks of a Madonna in the Platt collection, Englewood, which he judges to be rather in Semitecolo's manner.

followers. Highly important however is his study of architecture and perspective. If it be true that Maestro Paolo and his sons, in the painted cover of the Pala d'Oro and the panel of Stuttgart, manifest a certain interest in architectural surroundings and background, their effort is only a rudimentary introduction to what Semitecolo achieved. In the first and fourth scenes from the

Fig. 60. Semitecolo, the Martyrdom of St. Sebastian. Biblioteca Capitolare, Padua.

Photo Agostini.

life of St. Sebastian, the perspective of the buildings gives a very real sense of depth to the site of the event; the latter especially reveals the artist's taste for architectural studies, for here two separate edifices are depicted at different angles. It is true that the manner in which he represents these buildings in the background, while the incidents really take place in their interior, is somewhat archaic, but an archaism sometimes met with in Giotto's works.

It seems to me beyond doubt, however, that Altichiero and Avanzo, in whose paintings architecture plays such an important part, were inspired on this point by Semitecolo. He, therefore, cannot be assigned an entirely insignificant part in the progress of art, having created, as it were, the most important element in the school of painting of Padua.

Apart from the productions of the schools of Florence and Siena, the paintings of Altichiero ([1]) and Avanzo ([2]) are the most beautiful of the Trecento. Unfortunately we possess but little information concerning them, although the conjectures which can be made are, if not genuine, not far from the truth.

The principal works of both artists are found in Padua; they are the frescoes in the chapel of S. Felice in the basilica of S. Antonio, and those in the chapel of S. Giorgio near by and attached to this church.

Altichiero came from Verona. Gerolamo Campagnola in a letter to the philosopher Leonico Timeo, informs us that he was born at Zevio ([3]), a little village near the town, where another important artist, Stefano da Zevio, was also born; Moschini tells us that his father's name was Domenico ([4]). Documents of 1369, 1379, 1382 and 1384, in which he is mentioned as "Altecherio pintore condam ser Dominici de Ferabobus Verone" or some such simular name, confirm his Veronese origin and his father's name ([5]).

Whether or not Altichiero really belonged to the artistic centre of Verona is a question to which we shall return later, but the fact remains that he has always been designated as Veronese. Before Vasari, Michele Savonarola (circa 1440), Biondo da Forli

---

([1]) *P. Schubring*, Altichiero u seine Schule, Leipzig, 1898, p. 142. *The Same*, in Thieme-Becker, Künstler Lexikon, I.

([2]) *Schubring*, Altichiero, passim. *The Same*, in Thieme-Becker, Künstler Lexikon, II, p. 270. *Gerola*, Alcuni considerazione intorno Avanzo, Padua, 1909.

([3]) v. *Vasari* ed. *Milanesi*, III, p. 385, notes 1—2 and p. 634, notes 1 and 4.

([4]) *G. Moschini*, Della origine etc. della pittura padovana, Padua, 1826, p. 9.

([5]) These documents which were in part published by *Gonzati* and *Moschini* have been collated by *G. Gerola*, Madonna Verona, II, 1908, p. 150.

(circa 1450) and Marin Sanudo (1483) have all done so ([1]). It has been thought that Altichiero was synonymous with Alighieri and that the painter must have been related to Dante whose family went and settled in Verona.

As was the case for many other painters of Northern Italy,

Fig. 61. Semitecolo, the Entombment of St. Sebastian. Biblioteca Capitolare, Padua.
Photo Agostini.

Vasari gathered most of his information concerning Altichiero from Campagnola's letter. He tells us that he was an habitual visitor at the palace of the Scala, the ruling family in Verona, at whose court gathered an important intellectual centre. He decorated a hall in their palace with scenes from the wars of Jerusalem in which he depicted the portraits of illustrious con-

---

([1]) Quoted by *Schubring,* op. cit., p. 142.

temporaries such as Petrarch and members of the Scala family (¹). The order was probably given by Can Signorio who, about 1364, added a large reception room to the Scala palace. Sanudo, towards the end of the 15th century, sang the praises of the paintings found here, but at the beginning of the 18th century, no trace of them was left (²). Avanzo helped Altichiero in this enterprise and accompanied him to Padua where he adorned the chapel of S. Giorgio with frescoes. Here Vasari in his account makes two mistakes: firstly in stating that the decoration of the chapel was ordered by the Carrara, and secondly in mentioning that a third painter of the name of "*Sebeto*" also collaborated in this work; but it was no other than Altichiero himself whom Campagnola qualifies as from "Zebato", the Latin form of Zevio, as Lanzi has already remarked.

It seems nevertheless to have been Francis I of Carrara, who was instrumental in bringing Altichiero and Avanzo to Padua, for he called them there to decorate his palace. According to Savonarola the paintings represented Jugurtha taken prisoner and the triumph of Marius after Petrarch's "de viris illustribus" (³). From a payment made to Altichiero for the frescoes in the S. Felice chapel we know that he worked there in 1379. Vasari tells us that the "three" artists returned to Verona where they executed some marriage scenes for Count Serenghi (⁴).

The arrival of Altichiero in Padua must have taken place at the very latest about 1370, for Dotto, whose tomb he adorned, died that year, while the fresco on the sepulchre of Federigo Lavelongo in the church of S. Antonio must date from 1373;

(¹) *J. von Schlosser*, in the Jahrbuch der Kunstsamml. d. Allerh. Kaiserh., XVI, p. 145, believes that certain paintings of Cangrande, Mastino and Cansignorio, which originally adorned the corridor between the Pitti and the Uffizi Galleries but were afterwards transferred to the collection of the Archduke Ferdinand of Austria, might have been copies of these frescoes.

(²) *Vasari* ed. *Milanesi*, p. 633, notes 2—3.

(³) *J. von Schlosser*, op. cit., believes the miniatures in a Petrarch in the Darmstadt Library are inspired by these frescoes, but considers them of much later date and showing familiarity with Pisanello's art.

(⁴) *Milanesi* thinks this must be a mistake and that the name was Serego. This is probably more exact, as a family of this name which I believe is of Veronese origin, still exist's.

even if we cannot be sure that the latter is by Altichiero himself, it was at least executed by an artist directly inspired by him. It has often been falsely affirmed that Altichiero's name figures in the matriculation list of the painters' corporation of 1382, a roll which was only begun in 1441 ([1]). We find it, however, in a Paduan document of the 29th September 1384 ([2]). In 1390 he must have returned to Verona again, for the fresco on the tomb of Federigo Cavallo, who died that year, in the church of Sta. Anastasia, is without any doubt by him ([3]).

As for Avanzo, it has been repeatedly demonstrated that Vasari and, before him, Savonarola were both mistaken in identifying him with Jacopo Avanzi of Bologna with whom he has nothing in common. Nor has he anything in common with Jacopo da Verona who, in 1397, worked in the church of S. Michele in Padua ([4]) and, as we shall see later, in connection with his signature, it is not even certain that he was called Jacopo. If Vasari's version be true, we have already come across him working in collaboration with Altichiero in the Scala palace and the same author informs us that according to Campagnola he painted above these frescoes two "triumphs" which were admired by Mantegna.

The "Anonimo Morelliano" states that Avanzo was the author of the frescoes in Padua that Savonarola gives to Altichiero ([5]) and that together with Guariento he adorned the chapel in the

---

([1]) *Testi*, op. cit., I, p. 285 note.

([2]) A. *Gloria*, Monumenti del' Universita di Padova, II, p. 176.

([3]) Signor *Gerola* has already observed that Signor *Testi*, in mentioning the document of 1377 referring to the painter, repeats a printer's error appearing in Selvatico's book; the document is that of 1379. Signor *Testi* erroneously cites Altichiero as taking part in the contract that Avanzo made in 1372.

([4]) I. *Biadego*, Il pittore Jacopo da Verona e i dipinti di S. Felice, S. Giorgio e S. Michele a Padova, Treviso, 1906.

([5]) The "Anonimo" gives rather a detailed description and tells us that according to Campagnola the frescoes in the Room of the Giants, representing the capture of Jugurtha and the triumph of Marius on the left, were by Avanzo, and those of the Cesars and their exploits on the right by Guariento, while Andrea Rizzo believes them to be by Altichiero and Ottaviano Bressano. Among the figures were the portraits of Petrarch and Lombardo. The nobles of Padua were depicted on a little well or fountain (?). The

palace of the Capitano del Popolo, parts of which — those by Guariento — are preserved in the Gallery of Padua. The "Anonimo Morelliano" ascribes to Avanzo part of the mural decoration in the S. Felice chapel and admires his work there even more than Altichiero's. The same authority calls him a Paduan and Altichiero a Veronese (¹). The name of Avanzo is frequently cited in these pages (²).

The document of 1379, to which I have previously referred, makes it almost certain that it is to Altichiero we owe the greater part of the frescoes in the S. Felice chapel, the second to the right in the basilica of S. Antonio. As we are elsewhere informed that he was the chief artist in Padua, we can take it for granted that he is the author of the best of the frescoes while the inferior examples can be qualified as school productions.

In 1372, Bonifazio Lupi, Marquis of Soragna, born at Padua and podesta of Florence, made the contract with the architect Andriolo, a Venetian, for the construction of the chapel. An inscription on the façade shows the date 1376. Bonifazio died in 1389 and was buried in this chapel. The accounts concerning the construction cover the years 1372—1382 (³), but the only entry

---

"Anonimo" further continues the description: "In the last small room towards the chancellor's house at the upper end of the room of Thebe are the frescoes in chiaroscuro, representing the feats of arms of the Carrara's, the battle arrays etc., from the hand of.... The room of Thebe which contains the history of Thebe is from the hand of.... by whom seems also to have been the history of the Spoleteani in the Council Room of Venice which has since been overpainted by Titian. He was good at portraying horses but in the rest was not successful". *Th. Frimmel*, Der Anonimo Morelliano, p. 34.

(¹) In speaking of the S. Felice chapel, the "Anonimo" is rather hesitating and says it was painted by "Jacopo Davanzo, Padoan ouver Veronese, ouver come dicono alcuni bolognese e da Altichiero Veronese" but when dealing with the fresco in the chapel of S. Giorgio he tells us that it was "depinta da Jacomo Davanzo padoano e da Altichiero Veronese come scrive il Campagnola" and he again calls him Paduan in connection with the decoration of the chapel in the Palace of the Capitano del Popolo, v. *Th. Frimmel*, op. cit., pp. 6, 34 and 36.

(²) *Biadego*, op. cit., reproduces many other examples.

(³) *Gonzati*, La Basilica di S. Antonio di Padua, I—II, Padua, 1852, doc. CII. They are also found in *Gualandi*, Memorie etc. risguardanti le Belle Arte, VI, Bologna, 1845, p. 135.

THE PAINTERS OF PADUA, VERONA AND TREVISO.

in connection with the mural decoration is the one in which it is mentioned that Altichiero is paid 792 ducats for paintings that he executed in the chapel and the sacristy (¹). From the manner in which the document is worded, we can conclude that it refers to the settlement of everything owing to the painter at that moment, but on the other hand, as this record, together with one about the payment of sculpture, comes after the list of expenses for the construction, and as before the next entry concerning the amount spent on liturgical instruments, the scribe has left nine pages unused, it is easy to imagine that they were left for similar expenditures and that consequently the decoration was not yet finished when Altichiero received the recorded payment.

This, however, is not of great importance; much more so is the fact that the document enables us to place Altichiero's activity here about the year 1379. The frescoes were restored in 1771 (²).

The chapel of S. Felice, which was originially dedicated to St. James as may be gathered from the inscription on the façade and the subject of the frescoes, gives one the impression that it is a separate sanctuary although it is annexed to the church of S. Antonio. It has a façade of five arches, adorned above with five statues in Gothic tabernacles, very like that of a church. The vault is decorated with twelve medallions, four containing the symbols of the Evangelists, four the figures of prophets and four the Fathers of the Church. These figures are depicted in quite a new manner, in profile and seen in motion instead of the archaic motionless images represented full face. In the groins of the vault as well as in the borders separating the two rows of frescoes, half-length figures of saints are portrayed. On the left wall are seen the separate figures of the Annunciation, each in a little tabernacle.

Eight lunettes in the upper part of the chapel are occupied with the story of St. James according to the Golden Legend.

(¹) *Gualandi*, op. cit , p. 145: Ancora dado al maestro Altichiero per ogni raxon chaveva a fare con Mess. Bonifatio cussi nel depingere la cappella de San Antonio como per la sacrestia como appare nel libro del ... ducati settecento nonantadui, d. VIIc. LXXXXII.

(²) *Bondini*, in his Guide to Padua, relates that these frescoes "furono bellamente restaurate" in 1771 by Francesco Zannoni and Antonio Tentori.

In the first, three different moments are united: the Magician Hermogenes sending forth his disciple to dispute with St. James, the disputation itself and Hermogenes ordering the demons to bring him St. James and his disciple.

The three incidents are united as if forming one scene in a large building seen in section and composed of a central nave, behind which we see the apse, and two lateral aisles. The second lunette shows St. James ordering the demons in his town to bring him Hermogenes who is so surprised at this power greater than his own that he is converted and baptised. The architectural background of this scene resembles that of the previous fresco but is even more complicated. The baptism takes place in the interior of a building.

The third scene is different because in it we see the walls of a city towards which St. James is being led prisoner. Groups of excited people, children and noblemen in beautiful costumes are represented. The priests are depicted kneeling in adoration before the saint. To the right we see the decapitation of St. James and Hermogenes, the one having already taken place, the other awaiting his turn.

The fourth scene shows us the transport of the saint's body to Spain, the vessel miraculously guided by an angel; two of the faithful followers asking the Countess Lupa, who is seen entering her castle, for a piece of ground in which to bury St. James. They are made prisoner but in the fifth lunette we see them being set free by an angel, the countess witnessing the miracle from the heights of the castle.

Until now architecture has been given an important part in the portrayal of this narrative, but in the sixth scene it is replaced by a landscape; here is illustrated the story of the two knights who are sent forth to capture the escaped prisoners, and while crossing a bridge it gives way and they fall into the river and are drowned. Then follows, in the seventh picture, the miracle of the savage bulls which become quiet and submissive on being yoked to the hearse in which the saint's body is being conveyed. This incident takes place in the court-yard of the castle and again there is a great display of architecture which seems here of finer execution than in the other paintings. In the eighth scene a building divides the baptism of the countess, whom the miracle has converted, from the ceremony of the consecration of the castle to the veneration of the saint, which event takes place amidst a large assembly of people.

Besides these eight scenes from the life of the saint, three other incidents, not recorded in the Golden Legend, are illustrated.

Fig. 62. Altichiero, the Battle of Clavigo. The Chapel of S. Felice, S. Antonio, Padua.

Photo Anderson.

They adorn the left wall of the chapel and represent Ranieri I of Asturias in a dream receiving a message from St. James to desist from the barbarous habit of delivering each year one hundred young girls to the Arabs; the monarch enthroned communicating the vision to his assembled councillors and finally the Arabs defeated in battle outside the walls of the city of Clavigo (fig. 62). In this last scene the buildings of the town form a beautiful background to the calm and in some cases rather

132   THE PAINTERS OF PADUA, VERONA AND TREVISO.

Fig. 63. Altichiero, part of the Crucifixion. The Chapel of S. Felice, S. Antonio, Padua.

Photo Anderson.

motionless warriors, over whom hovers the protecting figure of the saint (¹).

(¹) The order of events in the legendary version is slightly different but obviously the painter imagined the story as he has depicted it in these frescoes.

Fig. 64. Altichiero, part of the Crucifixion. The Chapel of S. Felice, S. Antonio, Padua.

Photo Anderson.

On the wall opposite the entrance the Crucifixion (figs. 63 and 64) is represented but the altar is placed so near the wall that the centre of the composition is hidden from view. The Saviour on the Cross is surrounded by ten angels flying in the air; two soldiers, one raising the sponge towards Christ, stand at the side of the Cross, at the foot of which kneel two women. A group of soldiers and gesticulating Jews are placed on the right while from the opposite side approach three persons, probably father, mother and son, and doubtless the donor and his family. Further away to the left we see a large group of people, among them the fainting Virgin tended by her faithful friends, and some women weeping and gesticulating in a very realistic manner.

There is a great coming and going of people who seem to question one another most naturally. Some mounted soldiers are depicted behind and the background is formed by a beautiful cluster of buildings, very like that in the foregoing battle scene. On the other side there are fewer people. Here the principal group is composed of the soldiers gambling for Christ's clothes; some other figures mounted and on foot are represented behind while a crenellated castle is seen on a mountain to the right of the background. The two tombs on this same wall are adorned, the one — the founder's — with a picture of the Resurrection, the other with the Pietà.

On the right wall near the windows the Virgin in majesty is represented, seated on a very ornate throne adorned with figures of angels, between SS. James and Catherine who present the donor and his wife, kneeling beside their respective protectors. This fresco is very damaged while the figure of St. Christopher that formed its pendant has entirely disappeared.

Schubring ([1]) believes that the decoration of this chapel was executed by four different artists, the first of whom he holds responsible for the first four and sixth lunettes and perhaps the design of the other three which, however, he is of opinion were painted by a second artist; the third artist executed the Battle of Clavigo and the fourth the Crucifixion, the scenes in which King Ranieri figures and the last mentioned votive fresco.

I see no reason for admitting the co-operation of so many artists in the execution of the dozen or so frescoes that adorn this chapel. I think that there were only two, a master and an assistant, and that the former painted the Crucifixion, the story of King Ranieri, including the Battle of Clavigo, the votive Madonna and the frescoes above the tombs which consequently were prepared before the death of the persons for whom they were intended. It is true that the battle-scene is somewhat different from the others but I

([1]) *Schubring*, op. cit., p. 36.

attribute this to the retouching which it has undergone and which has deprived it of its original character without giving it another. And we have only to compare the architecture in the background of this picture with that depicted on the left of the Crucifixion to convince ourselves that the two works are by but one artist. The lunettes and accessory figures in the vaults and elsewhere were left to the helper whose brush-strokes are a little heavier and whose figures, although not lacking spirit, are somewhat more vulgar. With the exception of the fourth and sixth lunettes, this subordinate artist was left quite free in his architectural depictions.

The principal painter was doubtless Altichiero whom we shall find active in the chapel of S. Giorgio, but the second artist cannot be identified with Avanzo who has left us a signed work in this same chapel and thus disposes of the hypothesis that Avanzo collaborated with Altichiero in the decoration of the S. Felice chapel.

The construction of the chapel of S. Giorgio was also ordered by a member of the Soragna family. According to an inscription on the façade, it was founded in 1377 by Raimundino, the brother of Bonifazio, but, as may be gathered from a commemorative stone inside the chapel, he died two years later. In 1384 his brother obtained permission to complete the work. At Raimundino's death, the construction was already finished because an enormous architectural monument, which for a long time was thought to be the tomb of St. Antony, was erected in the interior. The frescoes were at one time white-washed and were not brought to light until 1837 [1].

It is quite possible that the mural decoration was not started until after the founder's death. If such be the case, it must have been Bonifazio Lupi who asked the same painter who had worked for him on the previous occasion, to undertake the adornment of this chapel; this time, however, he brought another collaborator.

The plan of the decoration is as follows: the chapel is divided broadwise into three vaults each one containing five medallions

---

[1] *E. Foerster*, Die Wandgemälde der S. Georgenkapelle in Padua, Kunstblatt, 1838 and Berlin, 1841.

now almost effaced; one can still distinguish the symbols of the Evangelists, prophets, the Fathers of the Church and in the centre the Almighty, the Redeemer and the Virgin. A frieze of forty-four medallions divides the vaults from the walls, while a number of half-length figures surrounds the windows. Two rows of paintings, each of four divisions, occupy the lateral walls. On the left, above, we see two scenes from the life of St. George while a votive painting, the donor and his family kneeling before the Virgin, occupies the two other compartments; below all four scenes illustrate other incidents from the legend of St. George. The frescoes on the opposite wall show, above, scenes from the life of St. Catherine and below, from that of St. Lucy. On the entrance wall we see high up the Annunciation, at a lower level the Adoration of the Shepherds and the Adoration of the Magi, and below, already separated by the upper part of the door-way, the Flight into Egypt and the Presentation in the Temple. The altar-wall is adorned with the Coronation of the Virgin above and below with the Crucifixion.

Everyone who has studied the question is of opinion that the artist who worked in the S. Felice chapel was also active here, but no one agrees which part of the decoration should be ascribed to him and which to the collaborating master (¹).

The question is difficult and complicated for in comparing these frescoes, knowing at the same time that they are by two different artists, we must admit that one is the *alter ego* of the other. Yet, it is beyond doubt that two painters took part in this mural decoration, the resemblance of part of which to the best frescoes in the S. Felice chapel determines the presence of one, who is certainly Altichiero, while the signature of the other — Avanzo — has been read below one of the frescoes in this

---

(¹) *Vasari*, who speaks of a fresco of the Last Supper in this chapel, simply says that the upper part was by Avanzo and the lower frescoes by Altichiero. For other opinions, v. *Venturi*, op. cit., V, p. 986; *Schubring*, op. cit., p. 66. *Selvatico*, in a Guide to Padua of 1848, professes to have read under the fresco of the baptism of King Sevio an inscription which would point to the completion of an undertaking and from which *Schubring*, op.cit., p. 52, infers that from that moment we can admit the presence of a third artist. Later *Schubring*, in Thieme-Becker, Künstler Lexikon, II, p. 270, attributes, part of the frescoes to this unknown painter. For the attribution of some of the paintings, v. also *J. Schlosser*, Oberitalienische Trecentisten, Leipzig (1921).

Fig. 65. Altichiero, the Coronation of the Virgin. St. George's Chapel, Padua.
Photo Anderson.

sanctuary. There are however some faint differences to be discovered which lead me to ascribe to Altichiero the Coronation of the Virgin (fig. 65) in which the Virgin and the Saviour are seated on a throne resembling a Gothic church and are surrounded by large groups of angelic musicians, the two scenes from the life of St. George in the upper row, as well as the fresco in which the founder and his family adore the Virgin, and three of the paintings below. In the first fresco, we see St. George killing the dragon just outside the gate of a city over the crenellated walls of which the king and his suite look on; the rather ungainly figure of the princess is half hidden behind the saint's horse (fig. 66). The baptism of King Sevio forms the subject of the following fresco; it takes place in a spot surrounded by magnificent buildings, among which a great many people are depicted. The next scene illustrates St. George drinking a cup of poison without receiving any harm thereby; a miracle that resulted in the conversion of the magician who had prepared the potion. The incident occurs in the courtyard of an imposing palace, from the windows of which many persons look down at the saint and the surrounding mob. Altichiero's manner is here less evident, as also in the third scene of this row, in which the statues of pagan gods fall and break in the temple — a building always in the same style — to which the saint had been brought by force to adore them. The picture which separates these last two frescoes and which represents St. George martyred on the wheel is decidedly by the other artist who worked here, and one wonders if the scene at either side might not also be from this hand, especially as Altichiero's manner is again very evident in the last fresco. This one represents the decapitation of St. George who is seen kneeling in front of a row of soldiers; a town is depicted on the left of the landscape which forms the background to the scene.

On the opposite wall, Avanzo's signature was discovered below the last scene from the legend of St. Lucy. However, as the purport of the inscription is unknown, we cannot be sure that it was only this fresco that the artist signed; on the contrary it seems to me highly probable that the inscription bore reference to the artist's entire activity in the chapel.

The representations from the life of St. Catherine, above, seem

Fig. 66. Altichiero, St. George killing the dragon. St. George's Chapel, Padua.

Photo Anderson.

to be again from the hand of Altichiero but I am inclined to admit here also, not the collaboration, but rather the assistance of Avanzo.

The first scene, representing St. Catherine's refusal to sacrifice to the heathen idols, is full of movement, for the Christians do not perceive the princess's disdain until they, themselves, out of fear have bent to adore. The painting is badly damaged as is

140 THE PAINTERS OF PADUA, VERONA AND TREVISO.

also the following one in which three moments — the saint conversing with the philosophers, their preparation for martyrdom and their death by fire — were united. In both frescoes,

Fig. 67. Altichiero, the Decapitation of St. Catherine. St. George's Chapel, Padua.
Photo Anderson.

however, fragments of important pieces of achitecture are still visible. The next scene is in a less ruined condition and shows us how the wheel on which the saint was about to be tortured breaks and falls on her oppressors. Many people looking from the windows of a curious-shaped building are seen drawing back in fright. The hand of Altichiero is again very obvious in the scene of the saint's decapitation (fig. 67) which takes place outside the gate of a city and before a group of soldiers; against the rocky landscape on the right we see two angels carrying away the saint's soul and higher up another two apparently close her coffin.

The fresco of the Crucifixion (fig. 68) above the altar is almost

Fig. 68. Altichiero, a detail of the Crucifixion. St. George's Chapel, Padua.
Photo Anderson.

certainly also by Altichiero. The two criminals are represented at the sides of Christ; one of the angels flying around carries away the soul of the one who repented. Below the Cross many soldiers on foot and on horseback intermingle with the faithful, among whom the fainting Virgin has almost fallen to the ground. Some of the figures seem to have been copied from the composition of this subject in the S. Felice chapel.

The five scenes on the entrance wall are of simple composition and comprise but few figures. In the Annunciation we see the Virgin in her room, towards which the angel flies. The Adoration of the Shepherds (fig. 69) takes place in a rocky landscape; the Virgin with the Child lying on her knee sits on the threshold of a little wooden hut built against the rocks; St. Joseph stands outside leaning his elbow on the side of the cabin, while the shepherds approach from the left; they are depicted a second

Fig 69. Altichiero, the Adoration of the Shepherds. St. George's Chapel, Padua.

Photo Anderson.

time, in the distance receiving the angel's message. This fresco is very characteristic of Altichiero's manner.

The Adoration of the Magi occurs on the same spot, seen however at another angle. Angels are now depicted by the Virgin's side; before the Infant Christ kneels one of the kings while the others stand behind; their servants in exotic costumes are looking after the animals.

The Flight into Egypt is somewhat damaged, but one can still distinguish Joseph leading the ass in a somewhat deserted landscape while the servant has stopped behind to quench his thirst at a spring. A town is represented high up in the mountains.

The Presentation in the Temple (fig. 70) is placed in the interior of a very elaborate Gothic cathedral. The parents with a companion approach from the left towards the priest who receives the Infant from His Mother's arms; on the other side the

Fig. 70. Altichiero, the Presentation in the Temple. St. George's Chapel, Padua.

Photo Anderson.

prophetess Anna is seen indicating the principal group to three women.

Avanzo probably helped Altichiero in the execution of several of these frescoes. It is likely that we also owe to Avanzo the decorative part, such as the figures in the vault, in the frieze and around the windows, as well as the four scenes from the life of St. Lucy, and, as I said before, the martyrdom of St. George on the opposite wall (fig. 71).

This scene is shown in front of a Gothic palace; two angels

descend and destroy with their swords the wheel to which the saint was about to be attached; the torturers are terror-stricken while the people who had gathered to witness the event draw back in fear. Within the building we see, on the left, the baptism of the magician who had prepared the poisoned drink and on the right the saint appearing for the second time before King Dacian, the moment after the martyrdom.

Fig. 71. Avanzo, the Martyrdom of St. George. St. George's Chapel, Padua.
Photo Anderson.

The series from the life of St. Lucy begins with the martyr led by soldiers before her judge (fig. 72).

The saint is conducted into the small court-yard of a Gothic building in the loggia of which are seated the judge and members of his staff. The second scene shows us St. Lucy standing immobile despite the fact that six oxen, dragging with all their force and with much persuasion from the herdsmen, are unable to move her (fig. 73 and plate II). The miracle takes place in a crowded street of which the Gothic houses on one side form the background. Then follows the martyrdom of St. Lucy in which we see her

DETAIL OF A MIRACLE OF St. LUCY
By Avanzo, Oratory of S. Giorgio, Padua.

THE PAINTERS OF PADUA, VERONA AND TREVISO. 145

tortured by fire, in boiling oil and stabbed with daggers, in three different parts of one building (fig. 74). The central division of this fresco shows us an interesting study of the nude. The last

Fig. 72. Avanzo, St. Lucy before her Judge. St George's Chapel, Padua.
Photo Anderson.

fresco depicts the saint's funeral; in the portico of a beautiful Gothic church she is represented lying on her bier surrounded by priests and faithful friends; to the left, through a window of the church, we see St. Lucy receiving the Last Sacrament (fig. 75). It was underneath this fresco that the famous signature of

Fig. 73. Avanzo, a Miracle of St. Lucy's. St. George's Chapel, Padua.
Photo Anderson.

Avanzo was inscribed. We have to place our trust in those who, in former days, were able to decipher the inscription, for all that remains now is some vague trace of lettering, which can be interpreted in almost any manner.

The first to read the signature was Foerster who made it out to be: "*Avantus Ve* . . . . ." and thinking the first name might

Fig. 74. Avanzo, the Martyrdom of St. Lucy. St. George's Chapel, Padua.

Photo Anderson.

perhaps have been *Avantiis* he completed the inscription as: "*Jocobus de Avantiis Veronensis*".

After that, Marquis Selvatico in the 1842 and 1846 editions of his guide to Padua relates that he discovered the name *Jacobus* but in 1869 he denies this, saying that the signature

Fig. 75. Avanzo, the Funeral of St. Lucy. St. George's Chapel, Padua.
Photo Anderson.

found there was: "*Avancius Ve . . . . .*" In 1852 Gonzati (¹) discovered the following two-lined inscription:

Avancius . . . . ix (?)
hoc ps pinxit ms nov . . . . ma me (²).

(¹) *Gonzati*, op. cit, I, p.282, affirms that the name was written in red, overlaid in black.

(²) *Schubring*, op. cit., p.67, completes this last line as: "*hoc opus pinxit mense Novembris anima mea*" which seems to me rather incoherent.

From all this we can come to the conclusion that the name inscribed was a Latin form of Avanzo, and Schubring's statement that there was no room in the inscription for other words excludes Foerster's hypothesis regarding the prenomen Jacobus; with this also falls through the interpretation of *Avantiis* for the second word, since this form necessitates the existence of a prenomen. It seems to me that the only reason Vasari, the "Anonimo Morelliano", Foerster and Selvatico had for wishing to place the name *Jacobus* before that of *Avanzo* and for changing, on account of this, the second name of *d'Avanzo* or *Davanzo*, was only caused by their conviction that the signature was that of the Bolognese painter, Avanzi, who really had this prenomen. All the old writers who give the name of Jacobus to the painter who was active in Padua are, for the greater part, also those who call him Bolognese. We have consequently no reason to believe that our artist's forename was Jacobus.

Whether the *Ve*... that was seen after the name of the painter, can be interpreted as *Veronensis* or not is a question which has given rise to a certain amount of unfruitful controversy between Bernasconi and Lauderchi, who, at the same time, tried to throw some light on the problem which of the two painters was the master and which the assistant ([1]).

Although we cannot be certain about it, the documents concerning the S. Felice chapel, nevertheless, lead us to suppose that Altichiero was the principal artist employed here and the author of the best frescoes; a comparison forces us to ascribe to him a considerable number of the paintings in the S. Giorgio chapel, and just those which are superior to that part of the decoration near which Avanzo's signature was found.

I think, however, that all the frescoes of the latter chapel belong to the art of Altichiero who must have directed the whole enterprise but who found in Avanzo a faithful and skilled helper who yielded to his guidance and inspiration, much in the same way as Lippo Memmi did to Simone Martini, and whose only shortcoming, probably, was his lack of originality.

The variety of opinion about which of the different frescoes

([1]) *C. Bernasconi*, Studi sopra la storia della pittura italiana dei secoli XIV e XV e della scuola pittorica veronese, Verona, 1864, pp. 35, 165 and 179.

should be attributed to the one and which to the other suffices in itself to demonstrate to what extent the manners of the two artists resemble one another; however comparing Altichiero's painting, as we know it from the frescoes in the S. Felice chapel, with that which, in the oratory of S. Giorgio, we believe to be from the other hand, I should say that the fundamental difference lies in a soberness and concentration found in the former's works and not in the latter's, not only in the compositions but also in the figures and the faces. Especially in the portrayal of the features, Altichiero obtains a beauty and refinement wanting in the art of Avanzo whose faces are less expressive and less fine, whose proportions are less perfect and whose drawing is a little heavier. The types however are the same in both cases and in their general tendencies the two artists offer no variety of manner.

There are only two other works, both frescoes, one in Padua, the other in Verona, that I think should be attributed to Altichiero. The former is the fresco above Dotto's tomb in the chapel to the right of the choir in the Eremitani church; the principal part represents the Coronation of the Virgin who with the Saviour is depicted sitting on a large monumental throne. A kneeling knight presented by a saint and two other figures are seen to either side while eight medallions with saints' busts line the arch, above which is represented the Annunciation; in one spandrel we see the Virgin sitting in a loggia while in the other is the kneeling figure of the angel. Four somewhat effaced figures of saints are depicted around the sepulchre. I am of opinion — and I think few can doubt it — that this fresco is by the same artist as the Coronation in the S. Giorgio chapel.

The fresco which in Verona adorns the chapel of the Cavalli family in St. Anastasia is more important (fig. 76) ([1]). The scene is placed in a Gothic hall at one end of which the Virgin is seated on a canopied throne surrounded by angels. The Child Jesus, bending forward on His Mother's knee, stretches out His hands to the first of the three Cavalli who, one behind the other, each accompanied by his holy protector, kneel before Him. The attitude of the Child, the knights and saints in costumes of the period,

---

([1]) C. *Cipolla*, Ricerche storiche intorno alla chiesa di S. Anastasia, L'Arte, 1914, p. 413.

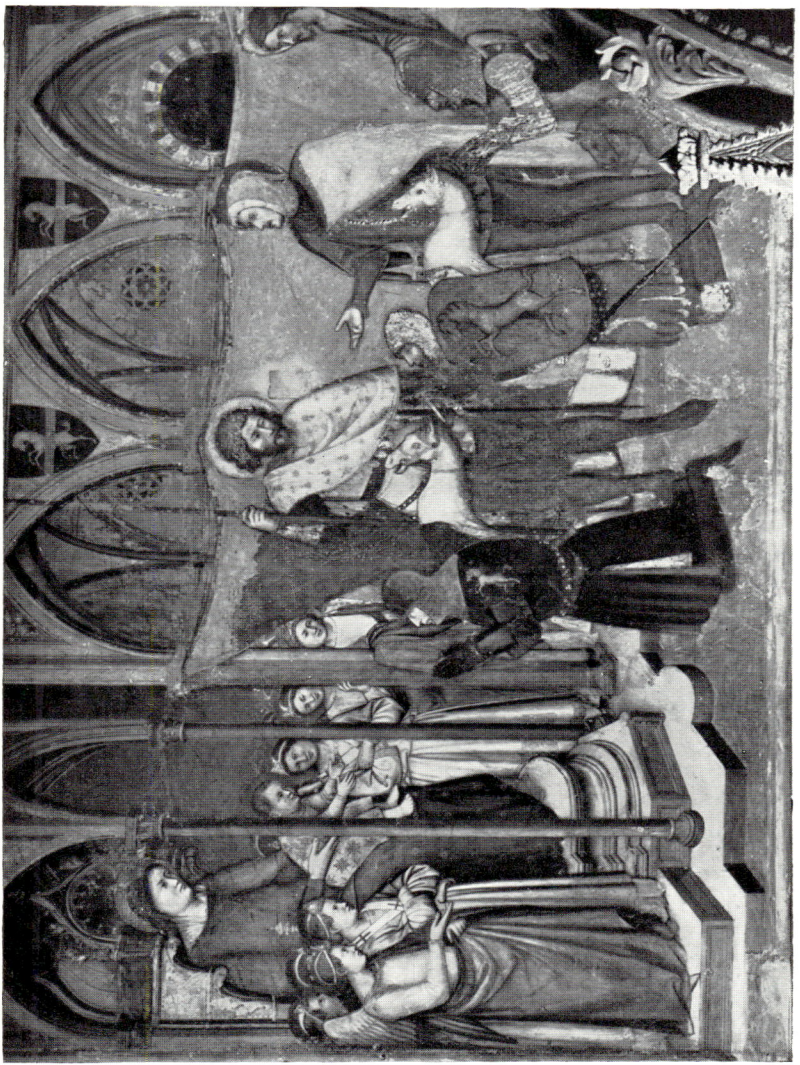

Fig. 76. Altichiero, Madonna and adorers. Cavalli Chapel, St. Anastasia, Verona. Photo Alinari.

the eloquent gestures of the latter, as well as the pose of the angel who has raised the curtain dividing the site of the event from the rest of the hall, all give to this fresco the intimacy of a "scène de genre".

Some of the figures in this picture are among the most beautiful that Altichiero ever depicted. Federigo Cavalli, who is buried here, died in 1390, and in all probability the fresco was executed shortly after his death.

One of the figures mentioned by the "Anonimo" in the Giant's Hall of the Palazzo del Capitano del Popolo, Padua, still remains visible. It is a very damaged and considerably restored image of Petrarch at his desk and is found in a room which nowadays forms part of the University Library. It seems quite probable that this is a work from the hand of Altichiero which, besides, would confirm the information furnished by Savonarola that the artist decorated the Carrara palace in Padua (¹).

Altichiero dominated the school of painting of the end of the 14th century in Padua as well as in Verona. In the former city Altichiero had some individual adherents of slightly later date, such as Giusto di Menabuoi and Jacopo da Verona, but besides their productions, there are a number of anonymous paintings in which his direct influence is manifest.

The artist whom I think we should associate most closely with the master, is the one who decorated the tomb of Federigo Lavellongo who died in 1373 and was buried in the church of S. Antonio. Here the Virgin is represented seated on a globe, surrounded by six angels some of whom indicate the knight, completely mailed, who is stretched on the ground while others present to the Virgin a knight — apparently the same but depicted a second time — kneeling in adoration.

Altichiero's influence seems to have been less direct on the painter who executed some isolated figures of saints and the Madonna and Child between two saints in a chapel — the one to the right of St. Antony's — in the basilica of S. Antonio.

In the cloister, the Bolfaro tomb, constructed between 1382 and 1390, is, apart from the beautiful sculptures, adorned with a fresco of the Coronation of the Virgin, which, although somewhat repainted, shows some of the characteristics of Altichiero's art.

In the corridor leading from the church to the cloister, the sepulchre of Bolzanello and Niccolo da Vigonza of about 1380

(¹) Signor Moschetti's attribution to Guariento seems to me incorrect, v. *A. Moschetti*, Padova, Bergamo, 1912, p. 62.

Fig. 77 School of Altichiero, the Coronation of the Virgin. Museum. Padua.

Photo Ist. Art. Graf.

is also decorated with a painting of the Coronation of the Virgin; here she is depicted sitting on an architectural throne amidst many saints and surrounded by a series of medallions. The work has obviously been inspired by Altichiero.

Other works belonging to Altichiero's school are found in the Eremitani church. In the chapel to the left of the choir there are some fragments of isolated figures of saints as well as a Madonna with a devotee on a tomb of 1381; all are considerably damaged but nevertheless the style, in which Altichiero's influence is evident, can still be recognized (1). Besides the decoration of Dotto's tomb, there still exist in the chapel to the right some remnants of mural decoration.

A very damaged detached fresco representing the Coronation of the Virgin amidst angels making music and offering flowers, and surrounded by a border of medallions, is preserved in the town gallery (fig. 77). It is the work of a very good pupil of Altichiero's. In the same gallery we find a fragment of another fresco representing the head of a saint; it belongs to the same school but is of little importance.

Of the paintings in Verona, the one that most closely approximates to Altichiero's manner is a detached fresco of the Crucifixion now in the town gallery (no. 513, fig. 78), but originally in the cloister of the Trinita church. The attribution to the master himself that we find in the catalogue, is not entirely without foundation, especially if we consider the present restored and repainted condition of the work. However, I think it more prudent to classify it as a school production but by a pupil whose style shows a strong resemblance to the master's. Fifteen angels fly around the Crucified, while below, large groups of people, some on horseback, are massed around the Cross; among them are to be noted the Magdalene clinging to the foot of the Cross and the Virgin fainting in the arms of her companions.

Some other fragments of fresco painting from the church of Sta. Felicita, now in the same museum (nos. 519—38, fig. 79) are also attributed to Altichiero in the catalogue. Again his inspiration is very clear but the author of these was manifestly not so

---

(1) *Schubring*, op. cit., p. 86, is of opinion that the isolated figures have a pronounced Florentine character.

THE PAINTERS OF PADUA, VERONA AND TREVISO. 155

closely connected with the master as the foregoing. The greater part of these remnants are heads of isolated saints, but there is also a Madonna with some half-length figures which no doubt once formed part of a scene.

Above two of the entrances to the church of S. Fermo, we find a representation of the Crucifixion; the one in the lunette over

Fig. 78 School of Altichiero, the Crucifixion. Museum, Verona.
Photo Lotze.

the lateral door has been rightly ascribed to Turone with whom we shall deal later on; the other belongs to the school that we have at present under discussion. This work is considerably repainted. To the right of the Cross are depicted four saints and to the left five, one of whom seems to be the holy protector of the donor, a knight clad in a coat of mail who kneels at this side (fig. 80).

Another work belonging to Altichiero's school is a fresco of 1397 on the left wall of the church of S. Zeno; it was executed for Pietro Paolo dei Capelli whom we see kneeling with other

156 THE PAINTERS OF PADUA, VERONA AND TREVISO.

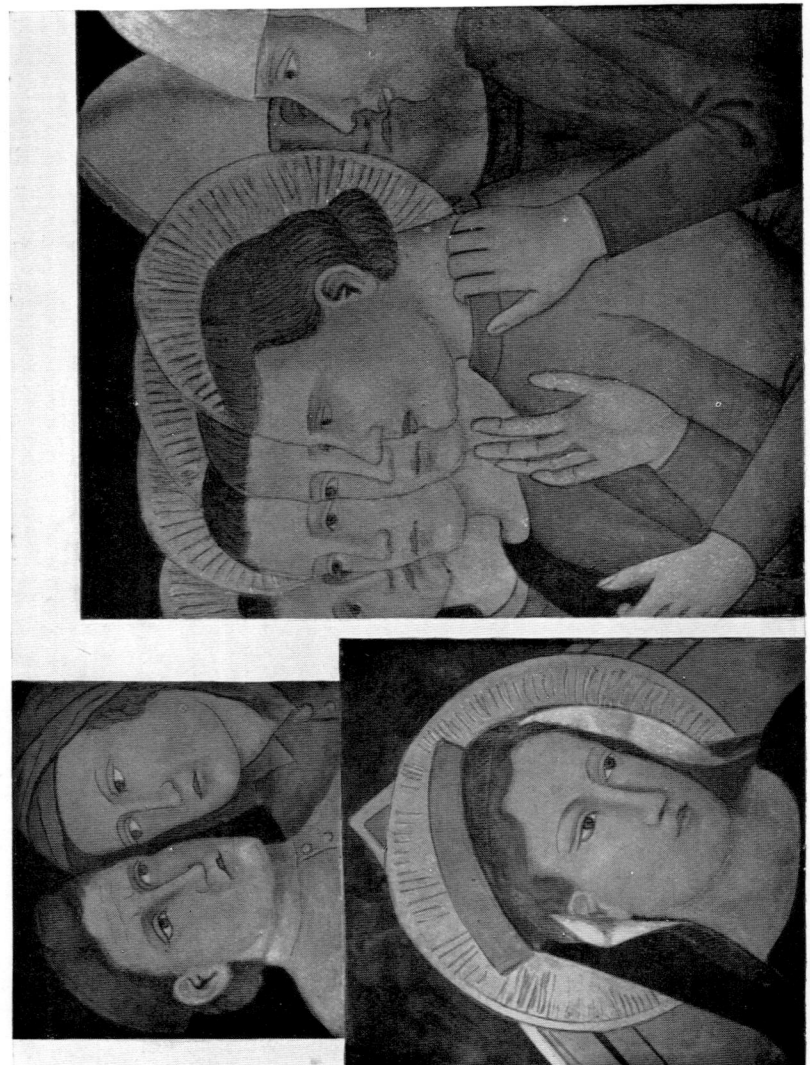

Fig. 79. School of Altichiero, fresco fragments. Museum, Verona.
Photo Lotze.

monks before the Virgin enthroned and escorted by saints. More closely analogous to Altichiero's own works is a fresco of the Madonna with two saints and a child kneeling in adoration, in the church of S. Stefano.

THE PAINTERS OF PADUA, VERONA AND TREVISO. 157

Fig. 80. School of Altichiero, the Crucifixion. S. Fermo, Verona.

Photo Brogi.

The lunette over the tomb of the Bevilaqua family in the Pellegrini chapel of St. Anastasia is adorned with an important fresco, but it is of slightly later date and might have been executed even after 1400. It shows us the Virgin on a monumental throne around which fly four angels; she is escorted by five saints while to either side of the steps of the throne kneels a knight; the one on the right is accompanied by his little son towards whom the Child Jesus, leaning over His Mother's arm, eagerly stretches out His hand (fig. 81). It is a beautiful painting and, although more evolved, can still be ranked as a production of Altichiero's school [1].

In the Cavalli chapel of the same church, we find, besides the fine fresco by Altichiero himself, another by a faithful adherent, representing St. Eligio working in his smithy [2].

We cannot really classify Altichiero and Avanzo as true Giottesque artists, even though their art was in all probability based on Giotto's, whose Paduan series of frescoes was always under their eye and whose reported visit to Verona also deserves a certain amount of consideration.

Altichiero, like Giotto, produced a popular narrative art, and his ample majestic figures show much resemblance to those of the great Florentine. The differences however are many and of great importance. His frescoes, besides showing a slight dissimilarity of iconography, do not portray, before everything else, the psychological side of the event, but rather tend to form beautiful pictures of extensive and elaborate composition, generally comprising numerous figures, and reproducing the impression of a moment rather than dramatic action. The latter are less expressive of tragic action than in Giotto's art, but there is a greater diversity of type which gives a very individual character to his works. As Schubring remarks, it is the beginning of portrait painting.

Some of his frescoes show us the genuine "scènes de genre"

---

[1] *C. Cipolla*, op. cit. 1914, p. 402. *Crowe and Cavalcaselle*, op. cit., III, p. 238, mention a fresco of Altichiero's school in a palace in the Piazza dei Signori of which I can find no trace.

[2] *Medin*, La leggenda profana di S. Eligio e la sua iconografica Atti del R. Istit. Venet. di Scien. Lett. e Arte, LXX, 1910—11, p. 799.

THE PAINTERS OF PADUA, VERONA AND TREVISO. 159

Fig. 81. Evolved follower of Altichiero, Madonna, saints and adorers. St. Anastasia, Verona. Photo Lotze.

peculiar to more northern countries (¹); they are characterized by the abundance of detail, the natural attitudes of those taking part, the faithful reproduction of contemporary costumes, arms and other instruments, the depiction of dogs in spaces not other-

(¹) Although it must be admitted that the examples we find in Germanic countries are of slightly later date.

wise occupied, and, above all, by the richness of architecture. The last mentioned is an element that entirely separates the artist from the Giottesque tradition.

Altichiero and Avanzo show us compositions full of figures, and if the moment represented did not provide sufficient material, then the artists united several incidents on one picture. Giotto rarely did this, but it is more commonly met with in Sienese painting. Moreover, the sense of beauty and the minute treatment, especially of the features, but of other details as well, are factors whose origin must be looked for in Siena, where more attention was also paid to architectural backgrounds.

The architecture itself is very different to that which we find in Sienese painting; it fulfils quite another function in the compositions in which it is but little less important than the figures with which it unites to form a complete image.

The artist's taste for architecture is abundantly displayed in the great diversity of buildings he depicts in his works; there are even instances where, according to the text, the architecture should not vary — as in the different events in the Countess Lupa's castle in the S. Felice chapel — that the painter shows us buildings dissimilar one from the other. Venetian architecture was imitated in Verona, but the probability is that many of Altichiero's beautiful motifs were freely copied from buildings he had seen in Venice; as for the style and manner in which they are employed, both are quite different from anything we find in the Florentine school. Still, certain details seem to have been borrowed from Giottesque artists; thus in the fresco of King Ranieri taking counsel, in the Presentation in the Temple and the central part of the martyrdom of St. Lucy, there is a loggia with a low wall, very similar to that which the so-called Maso shows us in his frescoes in Sta. Croce, Florence; the balcony from which the judge looks down at the saint's torture in the last of these scenes, or in the miracle of the six oxen seems to be another feature adopted from Florentine art. The painter obtains some remarkable effects of perspective which, however, is not always absolutely exact; this is markedly noticeable in the first lunette of the S. Felice chapel where the angle that the aisles form with the apse is very peculiar.

A comparison of the architectural backgrounds of Altichiero

and Avanzo with those that Semitecolo shows in his four panels is sufficient to convince us that it was here our artists borrowed their ideas, motifs and technique. In their art, as in their precursor's, the marked perspective of the backgrounds gives a greater depth to their pictures and adds to the field of action. The architectural backgrounds in the Presentation in the Temple and the death of St. Lucy are but more finished renderings of what we find in Semitecolo's entombment of St. Sebastian; Altichiero and his companion however place their figures more skilfully in the interior of the buildings and not before them as the earlier artist did.

There has been a great deal of controversy about the origin of Altichiero and Avanzo's art and whether its foundations were laid in Verona or Padua ([1]). From documentary evidence we gather that Altichiero was in all probability Veronese and Avanzo, Paduan. Certainly as a link between Giotto and the Giottesque and Altichiero and Avanzo, Padua possessed the masters Guariento and Semitecolo whose influence on our artists was very great; I would even say that in Altichiero's types and technique, there are certain features strongly reminiscent of Guariento's art. Guariento's Coronation of the Virgin in Venice seems to have inspired Altichiero in his representation of this subject in the S. Giorgio chapel, while the imposing architectural throne he depicts therein is clearly the model adopted by Altichiero and Avanzo.

On the other hand, prior to this, Verona had produced no artists of great skill, anyway not one of sufficient force for us to look upon him as the master of Altichiero and Avanzo, and I wonder what painters Messrs A. Venturi and Testi had in mind when for once they agree in thinking that our artists were inspired by Veronese masters of a previous generation.

I am inclined to admit, therefore, that circumstances in Padua were more favourable to the formation of this art; Giotto, Guariento and Semitecolo are not in themselves however sufficient to explain it, and apart from our artists' extraordinary personal talents, I think that we are forced to admit an acquaintance with

---

([1]) Regarding this question, v. *J. von Schlosser*, Ein Veronesisches Bilderbuch u. die höfische Kunst des XIV Jahrh., Jahrb. der Kunsth. Samml. d. Allerh. Kaiserhauses, XVI.

the Sienese school and a fairly strong influence from the North, where, though the extant instances are of slightly later date, "scènes de genre" had already probably made their appearance in German mural decoration, and where illustrations from the lives of noblemen and other secular representations were very much in vogue. This was especially the case in South Germany and Tyrol where the frescoes in the castles of Runkelstein and Lichtenberg are the best known examples of this branch of art in the 14th century ([1]).

I do not find in our artists' style much connection with the Lombards or with Antonio Veneziano, for the spirit of their art is much more modern and of a much higher aesthetic level. The two nude figures in the S. Giorgio chapel are alone sufficient to demonstrate the new artistic conceptions that these painters introduced.

The frescoes of Altichiero and Avanzo are the finest manifestation of the artistic movement which existed at that moment in Verona, Padua and Treviso and in which we might even include the painted tombs, that I have already mentioned, in the church of Sta. Corona in Vicenza. It is a movement in which elements from Florence, Siena and perhaps also from Germany unite and the genius of Altichiero — the greatest Italian painter of the 14th century outside Tuscany — made of this composite art a new and fairly independent school. The type of Madonna on the imposing architectural throne which they seem to have borrowed from Guariento, spread throughout Northern Italy, Emilia and, by means of Nelli, even into Umbria.

Padua's most capable artists, after Altichiero and Avanzo, was Giusto Menabuoi or "da Padova" ([2]). The great problem — one, however, that I do not think very difficult to solve — in connection with this painter is whether it was he or Antonio and

---

([1]) *H. Janitscheck*, Gesch. d. Deut. Malerei, Berlin, 1890, p. 198. *O. Doering*, Deutschlands Mittelalterl. Kunstdenkmäler als Geschichtsquelle, Leipz., 1910, p. 328. *Woltmann u Woermann*, Die Malerei des Mittelalt. bearbeitet von M. Bernath, Leipz., 1916, p. 208. *J. von Schlosser*, Die Wandgemälde aus Schloss Lichtenberg in Tirol, Vienna, 1916. *F. Bürger*, Die Deutsche Malerei, II, p. 232.

([2]) *J. von Schlosser*, Giusto's Fresken in Padua, Jahrb. der Kunsthist. Samml. d. Allerh. Kaiserh., 1896.

Giovanni da Padova who executed the frescoes in the Baptistery of their native town.

Giusto was the son of Giovanni di Menabuoi of Florence (¹), and his name appears in the roll of painters of this city in 1387. He was made a citizen of Padua during the life of Francesco Carrara (²). We know that a Madonna of 1363 from his hand existed in Milan (³) and there is a signed triptych of 1367 in the National Gallery, London, while from hearsay we learn that he decorated St. Augustine's chapel — to the right in the Eremitani church — which was constructed in 1370 and destroyed in 1610.

Then, if we do not ascribe to him the frescoes in the chapel of the Blessed Luca Belludi on the left of the choir of S. Antonio which was built in 1382, we have no mention of him until 1400, the date inscribed on the tombstone of his two sons.

A statement made by the "Anonimo" has given rise to some confusion with regard to this artist's works, for this writer, generally very accurate, informs us that above the door leading to the cloister of the Baptistery, which contains this painter's most extensive production, the signature: *"Opus Joannis et Antonii di Padua"* was inscribed, and comparing these frescoes with those in the chapel of the Blessed Luca Belludi, he discovers such a striking resemblance that he ascribes them all to the same hand. Although this declaration, and above all the precision with which he asserts it, are of some importance, all the same I do not think that the statement can be exact. Savonarola, who, as Signor Moschetti remarks (⁴), was born before Giusto's death, says in his description of Padua that it was this artist who executed the Baptistery frescoes as well as those of the Blessed Luca's chapel. Campagnola, Rizzo and Vasari are all of the same opinion.

(¹) *Campagnola* affirms that Giusto too was Florentine, but *Rizzo* calls him Paduan; the inscription on his sons' tomb ran: " . . . . *filii quondam Magistri Justi pictoris qui fuit de Florentia"*.

(²) *Bandolesi*, Pitture di Padova, etc., Padua, 1795, p. 281.

(³) *Crowe and Cavalcaselle*, p. 240. The picture belonged to a Dr. Fasi and according to Cavalcaselle bore a strong resemblance to Gaddi's works. The signature was: *"Justus pinxit Hoc opus fecit fieri Dona Soror ixotta, fillia qdam Dni Simonis de Tersago MCCCLXIII mesis Martii"*.

(⁴) *A. Moschetti*, Antonio da Padova, in Thieme-Becker, Künstler Lexikon, II, p. 4.

Moschini has since expounded the hypothesis that Giusto, with whom he associates Altichiero, painted the external decoration of the Baptistery, long since disappeared, while Antonio and Giovanni should be held responsible for that of the interior (¹), but nowadays the contrary is more freely admitted. Moschini himself in later years seems to have changed his mind about this question.

In any case I feel sure that the frescoes in the interior of the Baptistery are by the same hand that executed the triptych in the National Gallery, consequently by Giusto da Padova. In admitting this, Antonio and Giovanni da Padova disappear from our horizon, for there is not one other work that can be assigned to them, and the inscription recorded by the "Anonimo" must have been in connection with some other activity, either the frescoes on the outside or even some architectural work, since, although there is no lack of painters of the name of Antonio in Padua (²), there is nothing to prove that this inscription bears reference to a pictorial decoration.

It is but natural that the triptych in the National Gallery, London (no. 701, fig. 82) (³) has all the appearances of a Florentine work for it probably dates from that period of the artist's career prior to his settling in Padua. It is true that the Coronation of the Virgin was the favourite subject of North Italian painters but it is also a composition well represented in the Florentine school.

Daddi shows it to us in his triptych now in Berlin, and Giusto's painting in London seems to have been inspired, not only in the general arrangement but also in technique and sentiment, by Daddi's art. In the centre we see a group of saints around the throne as in the older artist's work, while in the wings are the Nativity and Crucifixion with a figure of the Annunciation above either scene, as in all the triptychs by Daddi and his followers. In the sweetness of expression and beauty of form, a similar degree of Sienese influence is manifest. The Gothic throne fol-

---

(¹) *G. Moschini*, Della origine etc. della pittura padovana, Padua, 1826, pp. 11 and 21.

(²) *A. Moschetti,* op. cit.

(³) This picture was the property of Prince Ludwig von Oettingen Wallerstein but afterwards passed into the collection of Albert, Prince Consort.

lows a Florentine model, but one, however, which does not appear in the group of works with which we have compared the picture; Giusto on account of his late date cannot have been one of Daddi's own pupils. The date we see at the foot of the picture is: *MCCCLXVII;* the signature: *"Justus pinxit in Archa" (?)* is inscribed on the back.

Fig. 82. Giusto da Padova, Triptych, 1367. National Gallery, London.

A curious iconographical detail in the Nativity is the presence of a mid-wife who receives the Child from His Mother's arms while another waits near the bath. The external surface of the wings is adorned with three rows of scenes illustrating the story of the Virgin; they are: Joachim driven from the Temple, the angel appearing to Joachim, the Meeting at the Golden Gate, the Nativity of the Virgin Mary, her Presentation in the Temple and her Marriage. All the scenes display the qualities of the best works of Daddi's school; in many instances the iconography corresponds to that of Taddeo Gaddi's decoration in the Baroncelli chapel.

A considerable lapse of time must certainly have passed between the execution of this triptych — a work undoubtedly painted in Florence — and that of the frescoes in the Baptistery of Padua. We know nothing concerning the date of Giusto's activity in Padua except that the frescoes in the chapel of the Eremitani church were made shortly after 1370; and when he is mentioned in 1387 as being in Florence, he must have returned for a certain time to the city of his birth. The fact that he is named after Padua and not after Florence makes it very probable that he passed the greater part of his life in the former city. As I shall point out later, Giusto was well acquainted with Paduan art when he painted the Baptistery frescoes, and for this reason we must admit that he lived many years in Padua before making them.

In spite of fairly extensive restorations, the decoration of the Baptistery of Padua remains one of the most important series of frescoes of the Italian Trecento that we possess.

The number of paintings is very great. On the left wall (fig. 83), opposite the apse we see three rows, each of three scenes: the Nativity; the Adoration of the Magi; the Presentation in the Temple; the call of the first two Apostles, SS. Peter and Andrew; the summons to the Apostle Matthew, who is seen sitting at the receipt of customs (a scene very rarely represented); the Marriage at Cana; the Prayer in the Olive Garden; the Betrayal of Judas; and Christ before two of His Judges, one of whom, Caiaphas, is seen rending his robe. On the end wall we find, above, the Presentation of the Virgin in the Temple, the Annunciation and the Visitation, while, on the next row, the fresco between the scenes of the Massacre of the Innocents and the young Saviour teaching in the Temple imitates a framed altarpiece, the principal figures of which, the enthroned Virgin and six saints, are painted in a niche; two of the saints, SS. John the Evangelist and John the Baptist present the kneeling donor, Fina Buzzaccherina. In the upper part of this painting there are many angels and the Holy Ghost in the form of a dove. The frame is adorned with four figures of saints and the pinnacles with half-length figures of the Saviour and four angels. Below

Fig. 83. Giusto da Padova, Scenes from the Life of Christ. Baptistery, Padua.
Photo Alinari.

there is an enormous, rather ugly figure of St. John the Baptist which, without any reason, has sometimes been ascribed to another hand; there are two flying angels at the sides while numerous devotees kneel at his feet. The two other frescoes on this row show the Entry into Jerusalem and the Last Supper.

The other lateral wall is dedicated principally to St. John the

Baptist. On the uppermost tier we see Zacharias in the Temple; the Nativity of St. John, and Zacharias inscribing the name of his new-born son; below follow the meeting of St. John with the Saviour, the Baptism, St. John in prison, and Christ curing several sick people simultaneously, while on the lowest row are the Dance of Salome, the beheading of St. John with the head offered to Salome's mother, and the Resurrection of a dead man on a bier (the young man of Jair).

In the centre of the fourth wall, above the arches leading to the apse we find an important representation of the Crucifixion with the three crosses (fig. 84). A multitude of people is gathered below, many of them on horseback; in the foreground we see the fainting Virgin on one side and on the other the soldiers casting lots for Our Lord's cloak; some angels fly around the central cross above which the sun and the moon are depicted on either side of a pelican in its nest feeding its young. To the left we see above, the Flight into Egypt and lower, the Transfiguration; two scenes which form the continuation to those already found at this level on the first wall. To the right the Descent into Limbo and the Holy Women at the Empty Sepulchre are depicted one above the other. On the wall to the right and left of the apse further events are represented; on the left we find the Bearing of the Cross over which is seen Pilate washing his hands: the painter has connected the two scenes by showing one of Pilate's suite leaning over the separating border and looking down at the procession on the road to Calvary. The wall on the other side is occupied by a painting of the Ascension.

The principal scene of the apse itself is that on the end wall representing the Saviour in majesty within an aureole, holding the Holy Lamb on His knee; at His feet are the symbols of the Evangelists and around him the celestial hierarchies. Numerous small scenes from the Apocolypse adorn the other walls and the window embrasures. Busts of saints are depicted on the intrados of the various arches.

The cupola of the chapel is also very richly decorated (fig. 85). In each of the pendentives is represented an Evangelist seated at his desk between two half-length figures of saints with his symbol in a medallion below. Then a long series of scenes from the Old

THE PAINTERS OF PADUA, VERONA AND TREVISO. 169

Fig. 84. Giusto da Padova, the Crucifixion. Baptistery, Padua.
Photo Alinari.

Testament beginning with the Creation, forms, as it were, a circular frame around the vault, the decoration of which is composed of a central medallion containing the Saviour, in the midst of cherubim, surrounded by hundreds of figures of angels and saints arranged in five regular circles which, at one place, are interrupted by the image of the Virgin Orante, crowned and standing in an aureole which is surrounded by angelic musicians.

Lastly we find in the apse an important altar-piece, the colours of which, however, are rather sombre. The centre is occupied by a figure of the Madonna, to either side of whom are six scenes arranged in two rows, some of them illustrating the story of St. John the Baptist. The terminals show the Baptism of Christ, whole and half-length figures of saints and St. Francis receiving the stigmata; the Pietà and other figures of saints are represented on the predella.

In attempting later on to determine to what artistic current Giusto Menabuoi belongs, we shall have to take into consideration the characteristics of this enormous pictorial monument; all the same I should like to draw attention at the present moment to the fact that this artist's iconography is very different from that which Giotto followed in his frescoes in Florence. It would be useless to point out every occasion on which our artist diverges from this tradition; a comparison of their respective works will convince anyone of the truth of this statement.

The question whether or not Giusto Menabuoi also painted the frescoes in the chapel of Beato Luca Belludi in the church of S. Antonio cannot be answered with certainty. They were so completely repainted in 1786 that a critical study is nowadays impossible. The general aspect and the proportions of the figures, however, do not contradict this attribution.

The chapel was constructed by order of Naimiero and Manfredino dei Conti, and in 1382 consecrated to the Apostles SS. Philips and James; after St. Antony's companion, Beato Luca Belludi, was buried here, the chapel took his name.

In the two lunettes on the left wall are represented St. Philip dominating the demon who, by his noxious effluvium, had killed three of the saint's disciples; their resuscitation; and also the saint preaching in Asia. Below the first lunette St. Philip's crucifixion is depicted: among the figures, several members of the dei Conti family are portrayed. On the same wall we find a representation of St. Antony appearing to Beato Luca and informing him of the deliverance of the town of Padua, a very important view of which is seen in the painting.

The altar wall is adorned with an image of the Madonna to whom saints present some members of the dei Conti family, who are depicted kneeling in adoration. Above this we see the two figures of the Annunciation.

Fig. 85. Giusto da Padova, Vault. Baptistery, Padua.

Photo Alinari.

The frescoes on the right wall illustrate the story of St. James. The lunettes show the Redeemer appearing to him and the saint thrown down by the Pharisees; lower down we see him delivering one of the faithful from a tower in which he was imprisoned, and giving his clothes to a pilgrim. His martyrdom is depicted on the entry wall; he is first stoned and then beaten to death. The altar wall on this side is given up to Beato Luca Belludi: here we see the faithful praying at his tomb and imploring his aid while at the same time the Saviour is shown appearing to him. Numerous half-length figures of saints are also found on the walls of the chapel.

Although now the entire decoration is not very pleasing, it seems probable that the attribution to Giusto — one, moreover made by the almost contemporary Savonarola — is correct.

We discover Giusto's hand in two figures of the Madonna nursing the Child, which are placed in niches near the arch in the Arena chapel (fig. 86) ([1]). Comparing these figures with Giusto's Madonna in the Baptistery, no doubt can exist as to their authenticity, but it is curious that the artist should have painted two identical representations, one as pendant to the other, in this little chapel.

The "Anonimo" records fairly exactly the pictorial contents of the S. Agostino chapel to the right of the nave in the Eremitani church. On one side were depicted the liberal arts with the men who excelled therein; on the other the vices, also with their human representatives. Celebrated students of the religion of St. Augustine as well as the titles of the saint's works also formed part of the decoration. It was, as this author inform us, painted by *"Giusto Padoano"* or as some call him *"Fiorentino"*. Vasari's description is very similar to the "Anonimo's", only he makes no mention of St. Augustine's adherents but adds that the representatives of the vices are seen in the depth of Hell.

An addition made somewhat later to the "Anonimo's" text informs us that the chapel was founded in 1370 by Tebaldo di Cortellieri, a Paduan whose portrait, with an inscription, adorned the wall to the right of the altar.

The frescoes were probably destroyed when alterations were made to the chapel in 1610, but Professor A. Venturi has discovered in a book of drawings in the Print Cabinet in Rome what he believes to be Giusto's own sketches for this work ([2]). However,

---

([1]) *A. Moschetti*, The Scrovegni Chapel, Florence, 1907, p. 52.
([2]) *A. Venturi*, Il libro di Giusto per la cappella degli Eremitani in Padova, *Le Gallerie Nazionali italiane*, IV, 1899. *The Same*, Il libro dei disegni di Giusto, idem, V, 1902.

Fig. 86. Giusto da Padova, Madonna. Arena Chapel, Padua.
Photo Alinari.

these drawings appear to be of later date, probably of the beginning of the 15th century, as Herr von Schlosser remarks([1]).

([1]) *J. von Schlosser*, Zur Kentniss der Kunstlerecher Ueberlieferung im Späteren Mittelalter, Jahrb.der Kunsthist.Samml.des Allerh.Kaiserh.,XXIII, 1903. Professor *A.Venturi's* answer to this appeared in L'Arte, 1903, p. 79.

Nevertheless, this does not diminish the importance of these beautiful designs nor does it make it improbable that they are more or less faithful copies of Giusto's frescoes, but I do not think we can look upon them as the sketches from which Giusto worked, or even very exact copies of this artist's frescoes; the style is later and quite different from Giusto's. There exist some other similar collections of designs ([1]) and Herr von Schlosser has published some drawings that he himself discovered, but these show less connection with Giusto's manner than those from Rome, which, as far as the fragmentary remains allow us to judge, seem to have been directly inspired by the paintings.

The series of frescoes in the Paduan Baptistery is consequently the only work by which we can judge Giusto's art, since the triptych in the National Gallery is a production of the period when the painter still belonged to the Florentine school, and the frescoes in the chapel of Beato Luca Belludi have undergone too much restoration.

Giusto's artistic evolution seems to have been fairly logical and simple; an artist without great originality, he was Florentine in Florence and Paduan in Padua, for the decoration of the Baptistery is obviously the work of a painter who was strongly influenced by Altichiero and Avanzo ([2]). There are too few Christological scenes by the latter artists to enable us to make a detailed iconographical comparison, but one would certainly say that the compositions of the Crucifixion and Presentation in the Temple were inspired by Altichiero's examples.

All the features which constitute the difference between the

([1]) In another chapter we shall deal with the Bolognese miniatures of the second half of the 14th century, preserved at Chantilly, illustrating the same subjects. *L. Dorez*, La canzone delle Virtue delle scienze di Bartolommeo di Bartolo da Bologna, Bergamo, 1904. *F. Filippini*, Bolletino d'Arte del Ministero della Pubbl. Istr., 1911, p. 60. *J. von Schlosser*, Ein Veronesisches Bilderbuch etc., publishes some profane miniatures which, in certain details — especially the costumes — show analogies with Paduan art of the second half of the 14th century but which however seem to belong to a later period and probably date from after the year 1400.

([2]) *Cavalcaselle* speaks of his connection with the Lorenzetti but of this I am unable to find any trace.

types in Giusto's triptych of 1367 and in his work in Padua seem to be due to Altichero's influence. The types of his figures especially, are no longer Giottesque but reproduce — although imperfectly — the delicate sweetness, the graceful forms and the specific drapery of Altichiero and Avanzo; the faces too are frequently modelled on those we find in the frescoes of these two artists, and, as in their works, each scene gives the impression of a moment, rather than a picture full of dramatic action after Giotto's manner. Nevertheless Giusto was not so skilful a draughtsman, nor did he possess such fine aesthetic conceptions as his two predecessors.

The chief characteristic of Paduan painting lies in the importance given to architecture, as well as the manner in which the artist uses it as a setting to his figures. Even Florentine artists of the end of the 14th century, such as Agnolo Gaddi and Spinello Aretino only used architecture as an ornamental background to their pictures, depicting a building of little importance with no depth and often isolated and incongruous as is sometimes the case in Giotto's works. From this standpoint Giusto belongs entirely to the Paduan school; his frescoes of Jesus at the age of twelve teaching in the Temple, the Marriage at Cana, the Last Supper and many other scenes are depicted taking place in spacious halls of an excellent perspective such as we never find in contemporary Florentine painting.

That special style of architecture that Altichiero favoured so much is exemplified in the church which forms the background to Giusto's fresco of the Call of St. Matthew. Our artist displays likewise the same taste for decorative detail, especially mosaic ornaments, and even shows us certain characteristics peculiar to "scènes de genre", as for example the little dog in the Marriage at Cana, which we find earlier in one of Altichiero's paintings. All this leads us to believe that when Giusto went to Padua he followed the school then in favour there, but never became one of its distinguished members. His works, however, possess great decorative merits, his colours are warm and bright and he obtains some clever relief effects by a strong opposition of light and shade, but his drawing is often faulty and on that account his figures lack charm while the general effect of his work is provincial.

The frescoes in the chapel of S. Michele, now dedicated to the Virgin of Lourdes, in Padua, are of very inferior quality; their chief interest lies in an inscription over the door, giving the date 1397, the name of the founder, a certain Bartolommeo de Bobis, and the artist's signature: ..... *"pinxit quem genuit Jacobus Verona figuras"* (¹). Here we have another example of a Veronese artist working in Padua, the first being Altichiero.

Jacopo was born in 1355 and he died after 1442. In 1404, he worked in Verona for the Carrara family; his sons Lamberto (1375—99) and Battista (1385—circa 1464) were both painters in Verona.

The frescoes that he has left in Padua deserve but a short description. They represent the Nativity, the Adoration of the Magi with the journey in the background and other details, such as the movement of the horses and the elaborate landscape, which divert one's attention from the main image; some of the figures may well be portraits of members of the founder's family. Above the arches we see the Annunciation, the Archangel Michael, and the Expulsion from Sodom, and on the other wall the Death of the Virgin (fig. 87) and the Descent of the Holy Ghost; in the entry is found the Ascension as well as some fragments of other scenes, while the sacristy contains a fresco of the Madonna amidst saints, worshipped by the donor.

These frescoes belong to Altichiero's school for the same reasons as did Giusto's; the facial types and proportions of the figures betray the same source of inspiration; some of the frescoes, as for example the Annunciation, display the artist's taste for architectural perspective as it was conceived by Altichiero and Avanzo, while it is especially in this same fresco that we note these intimate details which make of a picture a "scène de genre". The four figures, obviously portraits, seen in the right angle of the Death of the Virgin, are treated in that same realistic

---

(¹) *Schubring*, Altichiero, p. 121. *The Same*, in Thieme-Becker. Künstler Lexikon, II, p. 270. G. *Biadego*, Il pittore Jacopo da Verona, Treviso, 1906. *Crowe and Cavalcaselle*, op. cit., p. 237, believes this artist to be Avanzo who at his time, was still known under the name of Jacopo, and that their inferiority to the frescoes in the S. Giorgio chapel can be explained by the fact that in part they were left to pupils.

Fig. 87. Jacopo da Verona, the Death of the Virgin, 1397. S. Michele, Padua.

Photo Alinari.

manner which constitutes one of the features of Altichiero's art and his companion's.

With these frescoes we come to the end of 14th century painting in Padua, since it is useless to dwell on the two very damaged figures of St. Antony in the choir of his church, a Madonna on a pillar to the left of the Beato Luca's chapel and some other fragments of even less importance. Five figures of saints in grisaille in the chapel of the first cloister of S. Antonio are of more interest than these isolated remnants.

Schubring is of opinion that Padua did not really possess a genuine school of painting; he remarks that the number of outside artists was very great and informs us that of the eighteen painters mentioned by Moschini as active in Padua between 1382 and 1400, only three were natives of the town ([1]).

I do not think that Schubring's first statement is correct. Although Padua did not possess an important school whose influence was wide spread, it produced all the same a group of artists who had their own local peculiarities and who were united one with another.

I hope, indeed, I have succeeded in demonstrating, that a connection exists between Guariento's art and that of Altichiero and Avanzo, and that to Altichiero we can link Giusto and Jacopo da Verona. A feature of great significance for this centre of painting is the architectural perspective; it is an element that seems to have begun with Semitecolo and one which we also find in Treviso, but not in Verona which, apart from being the native city of Altichiero and Jacopo da Verona, had no connection with Padua.

Verona produced a large number of paintings in the 14th century ([2]), but with the exception of those belonging to Altichiero's school, they are of mediocre quality and in no way sufficient to

---

([1]) The "Anonimo" mentions a "Marino pittore" who painted in tempera the altar-piece in the chapel that Tebaldo di Costellieri had constructed in 1370 in the Eremitani church and which Giusto decorated. A "Bertolino del quondam Jacopo di Brescia" was active in Padua in 1382. *Moschini,* Pittura in Padova, p. 9.

([2]) *G. Biadego,* Verona, Bergamo, 1914, p. 74.

THE PAINTERS OF PADUA, VERONA AND TREVISO. 179

explain in Padua the appearance of this great artist who, however, is preceded by several worthy painters.

A certain number of Veronese painters are known to us only by name; they are Poja (1298), Gerardo (1311), Daniel (1354) ([1]), Antonius pictor and Bartholomeus pictor quondam magistri Nicolai (1367) ([2]); others, some of whose works have survived are Maestro Cicogna or Cigogna (1300—1336), Turone (1360), Giacomo da Riva (1379—1423) Martino (1396—after 1409), Boninsegna de Clocego, active from 1407 until 1429, whose signature Maffei found in the Salerna chapel of the church of St. Anastasia ([3]), and Jacopo da Verona with whom we have just been dealing.

Consequently, Maestro Cigogna is the earliest Veronese painter of the 14th century, whose works have come down to us, and these works reveal him as an artist of but little importance ([4]).

The oldest production that we have from his hand is the decoration of the church of S. Martino at Corrubio, near Verona. On the right wall we find some figures of saints and rather a curious allegorical representation, in which the souls of the faithful seem to be sailing in boats. The name of the artist and the date, 1300, are inscribed ([5]). He adorned the façade with a scene of the Crucifixion. In the interior of the church some other paintings includ-

---

([1]) This painter signed an altar-piece that *Maffei* (Verona Illustrata, III, p. 510) saw at the "Padri del Oratorio".

([2]) *Maffei*, op. cit., III, p. 148 and *Bernasconi*, op. cit., p. 14. *Maffei* again speaks of a picture at S. Pier di Castello signed: "*Nicholaus filius magistri Petri pictor pinxit hoc opus Veneciis*". He believed him to be a contemporary of Giotto's. It may be that the Bartholomeus Magistri Nicolai who is mentioned in 1367 was the son of this Venetian.

([3]) A fresco of the early 14th century in this chapel has, without any reason, been ascribed to him and this has led people to believe that an artist of that name also existed in the 14th century. *C. Cipolla*, Il pittore Boninsegna, Archiv. Venet., XLV, 1882, p. 213. *G. Gerola*, Il pittore B. etc. e la famiglia di Martino, Atti del R. Ist. Veneto di Scienze, XIX, 1910. *The Same*, Thieme-Becker, Künstler Lexikon, IV, p. 300. *Cipolla*, op. cit., L'Arte, 1915, p. 162.

([4]) *L. Simeoni,* Maestro Cicogna, Madonna Verona, I, 1907, p. 214. *P. M. Tua*, Per un elenco delle opere pittoriche della scuola veronese prima di Paolo, Madonna Verona, 1912, p. 104. *Biadego*, op. cit., p. 76.

([5]) "*Anno Domini MCCC indicione XIII Xpletum fuit hoc opus per me magistram Cigognam die Martie (?) ultimo Madii ad honorem Dei et Beate Marie......tata*".

ing a Madonna, saints, a Coronation of the Virgin and a figure of St. Martin on horseback, might perhaps also be assigned to this artist.

In the church of S. Felice at Cazzano he painted an allegorical fresco, very similar to the one at Corrubio, a Madonna, St. Martin and other figures; a fragment of the signature: *"Ci.... a pinxit"* and the date, 1322, are still visible. We find his name, for the third time, under a fragmentary fresco, originally in the Palazzo Comunale of Verona, now in the town gallery (1090). The inscription begins: *"MCC.... XV C....pinxit"* etc , which has been completed as *"MCCLXXVI Cigogna pinxit"*; but to me this seems unlikely since the original date might sooner have been either 1315 or 1325. The style of the painting makes it very probable that the C..... really did form part of Cigogna's signature.

In any case Cigogna is not very significant for the development of Veronese painting; his coarse provincial Byzantinism derives sooner from Venice and he had no adherents in the city of Verona.

Some contemporary frescoes in the church of S. Fermo display quite a different artistic movement. Above the arches of the chapels to the sides of the apse are depicted the Adoration of the Magi and the Coronation of the Virgin, while over the chancel arch we see the figures of the prior Daniel Gusmerio and Guglielmo di Castelbarco holding the model of the church. This group of paintings is very different from the rest of the decoration in this part of the church and are all doubtless by the same hand [1]. The compositions of the scenes at the sides show a Giottesque simplicity; the forms too are somewhat archaic and the technique rudimentary. On looking closely at these frescoes we find them to be rather damaged [2], although seen from a distance this is not visible. The two kneeling figures are very fine specimens of early portrait painting. Faces and expressions are both full of individuality and the artist has by no means flattered his subjects. Behind the figure of Guglielmo di Castel-

---

[1] *G. Gerola*, Il ritratto di Guglielmo di Castelbarco in S. Fermo di Verona, Madonna Verona, I, 1907, p. 86. *A. Da Lisca*, Studi etc. sulla chiesa di S. Fermo Maggiore di Verona, Verona, 1909, p. 46.

[2] *Idem.*

barco is depicted his family coat of arms, a lion drawn in a very characteristic manner, while behind the prior is an inscription which has been deciphered as: "*Mille Tecente quatuorda*" which is evidently meant to be 1314. This year coincides with the dates that these two persons had certain works carried out in the church; moreover Guglielmo di Castelbarco died in 1320.

The frescoes in S. Fermo may be said to initiate Veronese painting which — Altichiero and his adherents excepted — can be said to constitute an elementary Giottesque school. Dated works are very rare.

The battle scenes which we find at Castelbarco, near Verona, were in all probability executed shortly after 1319; they belong to a different style of painting, being rather archaic in appearance but expressive all the same. They might be classified in the group of Tyrolese works, for Italian features are entirely absent (¹).

Two other pictures of but slightly later date than the frescoes in S. Fermo offer us further examples of very individual portraits. The first of these is kept in the Rosario chapel in St. Anastasia and represents Martino Scaliger and Taddea da Carrara, whom he married in 1327, in adoration before the Virgin who is escorted by S.S. Dominic and Peter the Martyr. The second picture which is preserved in the church of Sta. Maria Antiqua shows the Madonna again adored by Martino Scaliger, who in this instance, is accompanied by Alberto Scaliger.

Both are important works not only on account of the crude realism of the portraits but also because they furnish us with the earliest examples of these devotional pictures which afterwards became so frequent, and of which Altichiero has left us a specimen.

Of the rather ordinary and traditional painters who were inspired by Giotto's manner and to whom we owe the greater part of the Veronese frescoes of about the middle of the 14th century, the name of one, Turone, has come down to us; from his hand we possess a signed and dated altar-piece (figs. 331 and 332), originally in the Sta. Trinita convent, now in the town gal-

---

(¹) Verhandl. des 7en Internat. Kunsthist. Kongresses in Innsbrück, 1902, p. 77.

lery. The inscription runs: *"Hopue Turoni MCCCLX"*. That Turone was really Veronese is established almost without doubt by the presence of other works from his hand in this city and also by the fact that we find members of this name in the town council in 1405 and in 1435.

The principal panel of this polyptych shows the Trinity: God the Father sitting on a throne holds in front of Him the Cross to

Fig. 88. Turone, Polyptych, 1360. Museum, Verona.

Photo Lotze.

which the Saviour is attached, the dove being placed on the latter's nimbus. Date and signature are inscribed on the pedestal of the throne. Within the arcades formed by the frame, the saints Zeno and John the Baptist on the left, and Peter and Paul on the right, are represented, each holding his emblem. St. Paul is apparently depicted about to draw his sword from its scabbard. Eight medallions in the elaborate framework contain busts of the Evangelists and four angels, all winged; the two lateral terminals are adorned with half-length figures of SS. Catherine and Lucy and the much larger central one with a representation of the Coronation of the Virgin who, contrary to what we generally

Fig. 89. Detail of fig. 88.   Photo Lotze.

find in Venetian painting, is depicted kneeling before the Saviour, while around the throne are placed nine angels.

Besides some rather unusual iconographical details, it will be noted that Turone is not one of the most purely Giottesque of the Veronese painters. In the work of this rather mediocre artist we discover certain traces of suavity, reminiscent of Siena [1].

---

[1] *Cavalcaselle* remarks a connection with Ottaviano Nelli and the followers of Taddeo di Bartolo.

The sturdy, sometimes even heavy proportions, however, are borrowed from Giotto. The drawing, especially of the drapery is hard and rigid; the figures of the Coronation are rather coarsely executed.

Cavalcaselle was the first to attribute to Turone the Crucifixion over the entrance in the church of S. Fermo (fig. 90), an attribution which is now generally admitted ([1]). The composition is crowded. Eight angels, dramatically expressing their grief, fly around the Crucified; groups of horsemen are seen to either side of the Cross while the foreground is occupied by the faithful and the Jews. In this fresco the artist has made a great display of realistic expression which in many instances is exaggerated. Comparing the faces with those in the polyptych, particularly the bearded old men seen full-face in the fresco with the St. Peter of the altar-piece, any doubt as to the accuracy of the attribution disappears, although the fresco is of better quality and does not show the clumsy drawing that we remarked in the panel painting.

I do not think, however, that Cavalcaselle was right in finding the hand of the same artist in some of the frescoes in the Cavalli chapel in St. Anastasia.

In Verona there is a tradition of another panel signed by Turone that represented the Saviour arising from His tomb between the Virgin and St. John; but the work has apparently since migrated to Russia ([2]).

Turone was about the best of the traditional artists who adorned the churches of Verona; he lacked neither spirit nor temperament — his Crucifixion is full of life and expression — but he was not a good draughtsman. His productions possess little artistic value, their great shortcoming being their want of refinement.

As the other painters whose dates are known to us bring us at once to about the end of the 14th century, I think it better to

---

([1]) *Schubring*, op. cit., p. 89, is the only one who contradicts this opinion; he believes that this work is introductory to Altichiero's composition in the S. Felice chapel, Padua, and finds much connection between the two paintings. To me this is quite incomprehensible. *Maffei*, Verona Illustrata, III, p. 146, first thought that it was by Giotto, then by Cimabue!

([2]) *G. Trecca*, Catalogo della Pinacoteca comunale di Verona, Bergamo, 912, p. 22.

Fig. 90. Turone, the Crucifixion. S. Fermo Maggiore, Verona.
Photo Alinari.

mention here the works which seem to be of considerably earlier date; but I must limit myself to a short enumeration, since we are dealing with paintings about which we possess no information

Fig. 91. Veronese School, two Madonnas and saints, 14th century.
S. Zeno, Verona. Photo Lotze.

whatsoever. Votive pictures seem to have been very much in vogue in Verona just then, because this group is uniquely comprised of such works, all isolated frescoes adorning the walls of the different churches. On the whole they manifest a strong adherence to the Giottesque tradition, thus giving a resemblance of

THE PAINTERS OF PADUA, VERONA AND TREVISO. 191

account of the fact that they are evidently profane paintings, apparently representing a festive procession.

The frescoes in the church of St. Anastasia ([1]) are on the whole of better quality. The pillars are adorned with what were once beautiful figures but are now greatly ruined. Two good

Fig. 96. Veronese School, St George slaying the dragon, 14th century. S. Zeno, Verona — Photo Lotze.

Giottesque frescoes are found in the Cavalli chapel; one shows the Madonna "della Misericordia", covering the kneeling adorers with her cloak, between a holy bishop and a saint (fig. 98); the other and more feeble represents, on the entrance wall, the Madonna sitting on a simple throne attended by four full-length figures of saints (fig. 99). We find besides in this church the important composition of the Virgin enthroned between saints

---

([1]) *C. Cipolla*, op. cit.

Fig. 97. Veronese School, Scenes from the legend of St. Nicholas, 14th century. S. Zeno, Verona.

Photo Lotze.

THE PAINTERS OF PADUA, VERONA AND TREVISO. 193

and worshipped by a knight that I mentioned as being frequently attributed to Boninsegna ([1]); isolated figures of saints of good execution; an Evangelist with a devotee; the Saviour arising from His tomb between four saints; and a Baptism of Christ painted in a somewhat different style and repainted. Other less important paintings of the same period are scattered on the walls of the church.

Also in S. Fermo, we find some frescoes of the 14th century

Fig. 98. Veronese School, Madonna della Misericordia, 14th century. St. Anastasia, Verona.   Photo Lotze.

made under a Giottesque influence. On the entrance wall there are some legendary illustrations, among which the most important is a representation of the martyrdom of the Franciscan monks at Ceuta, a fresco of 1327 showing five monks put to death before the sultan. In the transept there was a long cycle of scenes from the life of St. Francis; we can still recognize the saint giving his cloak to the poor nobleman, the Bishop of Assisi covering him with his mantle, the confirmation of the rules of the order and the vision of St. Francis borne to heaven in a chariot;

([1]) *Biadego*, Verona, p. 101.

the other paintings have been effaced. In the opposite transept there remains but one scene, which represents the foundation of a religious order: naked figures are seen kneeling before a pope who, escorted by ecclesiastical dignitaries, hands them monastic habits.

The arch which separates the transept from the nave is adorned with medallions containing human figures. In the vault of the apse we find the symbols of the Evangelists, and lower down a figure of the Saviour between the Virgin and St. John.

Among the large number of frescoes which have been detached and brought to the Pinacoteca, there are also some which might be styled Giottesque, but they are of but little importance.

Belonging to this early period of Veronese painting, Maffei [1] further mentions some other works which have since disappeared. In a niche in the church of St. Agnese he found some repainted frescoes with the date 1329. The church of S. Pietro Martire, which was formerly dedicated to St. George, contained several representations of the latter saint, in one instance worshipped by some knights, one of whom died in 1355, an indication that this fresco must have been of earlier date.

In comparison with the large number of frescoes that we find in this group, there are relatively few panel paintings executed in this style. The picture showing most connection with Giottesque art is an altar-piece, considerably repainted, in the Gallery (no. 356), originating from the church of Sta. Caterina. It represents, in the centre, the marriage of St. Catherine (fig. 100). The Child standing on His Mother's knee bends forward towards St. Catherine who kneels to the right of the Madonna's throne; two angels hover in mid-air, each holding a crown above the saint's head. To the sides against an ornamental gold background, we see SS. Rusticus, Martin and Lucy to the left, and SS. Zeno and Fermo to the right. The picture is executed with care and possesses a certain amount of merit; form and type have obviously been inspired by Giotto's art. The throne is halfway between the older simpler model and those of a more complicated pattern that we shall find in later works.

---

[1] *Maffei*, op. cit., p. 147.

THE PAINTERS OF PADUA, VERONA AND TREVISO. 195

A very interesting picture and one in which reminiscences of Giottesque art are clearly evident, is that in which thirty small scenes relate the story of the Bible from the Creation to the Last Judgment, as well as some scenes illustrative of the life of the Virgin. This panel also comes from the convent of Sta. Caterina,

Fig. 99. Veronese School, Madonna and saints, 14th century.
St. Anastasia, Verona. Photo Lotze.

but is now preserved in the Gallery (no. 362). It has been attributed to both Taddeo di Bartolo and Altichiero, but to me it seems a provincial manifestation of Giotto's art and in all probability Veronese [1].

---

[1] As such it has been published by *H. Semper*, Ein Bildtafel vom Anfang der XIV Jahrh. in Museo Civico zu Verona, Madonna Verona, I, 1907, p. 124. That this is a picture of the beginning of the 14th century is highly improbable, I think its actual date must be somewhere near 1350.

Fig. 100. Veronese School, the Marriage of St. Catherine and saints. Museum, Verona.

In the Pinacoteca we find still a little triptych (no. 256) showing the Crucifixion between SS. Peter and Paul and the figures of the Annunciation. The form and composition of the panel are again Florentine but it is doubtless a Veronese production; in it we discover some traces of Gothicism which in later years constitute the great characteristic of such masters as Stefano da Zevio.

In the North, Guariento and his adherents had helped to spread the model of the Giottesque crucifix and in Verona several examples are to be found. We have already mentioned the one in S. Zeno; two others, but of slightly later date, are preserved in the Pinacoteca, the one (no. 257) is insignificant, the other (no. 857) which comes from the church of S. Silvestro is of more artistic value and reveals to a greater degree its connection with the Giottesque tradition. There is still another specimen in the sacristy of SS. Nazaro e Celso but it is repainted and unimportant.

Only two of the numerous artists to whom we owe paintings of the end of the 14th century have been identified: they are Giacomo da Riva and Martino.

The former ([1]) is mentioned on several occasions; his name is found in documents of 1374, 1375, 1386, 1392, 1400, 1409, 1413 and 1416, while we know that he died in, or before 1418.

Part of a fresco representing the Madonna seated on a simple throne nursing the Child is preserved in the church of S. Stefano. The artist has left his name and the date, 1388, in the following inscription: *"Mille Trecento otanta otto fu impenta per Messer Giacomo da Riva."* Beauty and refinement are wanting in this painting, which is executed in a manner that forces us to rank its author among the feebler artists of the city. This fresco however allows us to ascribe to the painter another picture of the Madonna in the same church, although with some hesitation. Here the damaged painting shows us the Virgin surrounded by a mandorla, the Child bending towards an adorer who is accompanied by SS. John the Baptist and James. On account of its resemblance to the authentic work, we can with more certainty attribute to Giacomo another fresco of the Madonna, nursing the Child, on the wall to the right of the entrance of the church of S. Zeno.

Martino, on the other hand, reveals himself as an artist a good step ahead of the traditionalistic painters of the previous generation. Cavalcaselle makes a mistake in calling him Altichiero's contemporary. Not only does the one painting we have from his hand date very probably from 1396, since it adorns the pulpit executed that same year by Antonio da Mestre, but there are divers later records of his existence. In the tax register of 1409 he is spoken of as *"magister Martinus pictor quondam Antonii"*, while during that same year we find him receiving a certain

---

([1]) *P. Sgulmero*, Giacomo da Riva, pittore in Verona nel secolo XIV, Archiv. Stor. per Triest, l'Istria e il Trentino, IV, 1889, p. 159. *G. Biadego*, Un ignoto pittore Trecentista a Verona, Bolletino del Ministero della Pubbl. Istr., 1911, p. 173.

payment; we are informed that in 1410 he lived in the "Contrada di Pontepietro". He died in 1413, and in 1418 his son, also a painter, is mentioned as "*Zeno pictor quondam magistri Martini*" ([1]).

The fresco, close to which we find the signature: "*opus Martini*", adorns the right wall of the church of S. Fermo (fig. 101). Above, it shows the Crucifixion and two incidents from the history of Elijah and below the four Doctors of the Church, each sitting on an elaborate throne before a desk surrounded by other very ornate pieces of furniture and fragments of architecture. The centre of the fresco has been destroyed by the addition of a pillar, while of the frame, only the part on the right hand side has been preserved. It comprises a long series of medallions containing busts of prophets with two heads seen in profile between each.

Martino must have been a fairly capable painter; the execution of the faces and other details is finely treated, the variety of expression and type very remarkable; but I do not agree with Herr Schubring in finding a very definite connection with Altichiero. I share his opinion, however, in believing that Martino's art formed, to a certain degree, the introduction to that of Stefano da Zevio ([2]). His types betray a knowledge of Tommaso da Modena's frescoes in Treviso.

The number of frescoes which date from this later stage in the development of Veronese painting and which show those Gothic elements that dominated the art of Stefano da Zevio, is very considerable. The imposing architectural throne, whose introduction into Veronese painting can be accounted for by Altichiero's influence, is frequently seen in these productions; in the numerous representations of the Madonna the throne is still more complicated and not always in the best of taste.

The church of St. Anastasia is full of these frescoes. On the left wall we see, besides the less important figures of saints, three figures of the Madonna (fig. 102) and in the last chapel to the left

---

([1]) *Bernasconi*, op. cit., p. 214. *R. von Eitelberg*, Ueber einige neu entdeckte Wandgemälde in Verona, Mittheil. der K.K. Central Comiss. zur Erforshung der Baudenkmäler, II, 1857, p. 201. *G. Gerola*, Il pittore Boninsegna, p. 414.

([2]) *G. Biadego*, Verona, p. 98, noticed the connection between the two masters. *Schubring*, Altichiero, p. 125, ascribes to Martino a picture of the Madonna with SS. Zeno, James and Apollonia in the Gallery of Verona.

Fig 101. Martino da Verona, St. Hieronymus and other figures.
S. Fermo, Verona.

Photo Lotze.

of the choir three others, some of them accompanied by saints and adorers. In the same chapel, we also find a representation of the Saviour between two saints and other large figures of saints at the back of a tomb. In the Cavalli chapel the Madonna, before whom kneels the recently deceased knight, is depicted on a low seat surrounded by numerous angels. The type of the latter, as well as the attitude of the Virgin, shows a decided resemblance to what we shall find in Stefano da Zevio's painting. In the adjacent Pellegrini chapel, besides the Madonna and saint that I classed as a production of Altichiero's school, there is another fresco of the end of the 14th century showing the enthroned Virgin. A fresco on the exterior of the church, over the entrance, represents SS. Dominic and Zeno recommending some monks and other persons to the Holy Trinity.

The church of S. Zeno conserves in the choir a fragment of a late 14th century fresco of an enormous bishop — doubtless the titular saint — sitting on an elaborate throne with his hand raised in blessing.

Two fragmentary frescoes of the Madonna are found in the church of Sta. Maria della Scala; both show thrones that are almost edifices. The one in which St. Antony Abbot is depicted seems to be by the same artist as the Madonna surrounded by angels in the Cavalli chapel (¹).

As panel painting in this manner may be cited that representing St. Mamaso in the Pinacoteca (no. 124) of Verona.

In all the foregoing works we can discover traces of Gothicism which, in the 15th century, reached its summit.

The insufficiency of artistic personalities has forced me to limit my description of Veronese pictorial works of the 14th

---

(¹) The following 14th century paintings in Verona might also be mentioned: a Madonna and other figures in a lunette over the entry to S. Fermo; half-length figures of saints on the principal beams of the same church; in the Baptistery, a votive Madonna and some other paintings, the most important of which is the repainted fresco in the right apse showing the Saviour in majesty above and the Virgin lower down; in St. Eufemia, over the entry, an almost effaced fresco of an enthroned bishop; several fragments from this church are now in the Pinacoteca (Nos. 565, 567—570). Some unimportant remnants are found in S. Giovanni in Valle and in the crypt of the same church. A fresco of the Saviour in benediction in the lunette over the entry of SS. Siro e Libera is not without merit and already shows some resemblance to the works of Stefano da Zevio. Still another fresco in the Pinacoteca of Verona (No. 545) is interesting only on account of the subject: the enthroned Virgin, some saints and a person crucified, probably St. Wilgefortis (*E. Fea*, Madonna Verona, V, 1911, p. 36). In the vicinity of Verona there are also some 14th century paintings at S. Felice, at Cazzano, where, besides those by Cicogna, we find among them a fine Giottesque fresco of the Lord on the Cross between the Virgin and St. John (*Simeoni*, op. cit.) and in the Pieve of Tregnagno (*C. Cipolla*, Madonna Verona, V, 1911, p. 186).

THE PAINTERS OF PADUA, VERONA AND TREVISO.

Fig. 102. Veronese School, Madonna and saints, about 1400.
St. Anastasia, Verona.   Photo Lotzé

century to a mere enumeration. Apart from Altichiero and his pupils there were none but very mediocre artists.

What I have said, however, is enough to show the existence of two consecutive styles which are easily differentiated; the first very simple, dominated by somewhat rudimentary reminiscences of Giotto's art; the second more elaborate and approximating the flowery Gothic that flourished in Verona during the first half of the 15th century. Although the architectural thrones of the latter group seem to have been borrowed from Altichiero's works, I do not think that this artist, outside the little group of his genuine adherents, exercised any influence in Verona.

The frescoes of Collalto near Conigliano have sometimes been classed among the works of the Veronese school, but, as will be demonstrated later on, they belong to the school of Rimini. In the frescoes detached from the church of Sta. Margarita of Treviso and now in the Gallery of that town, the influence of Altichiero prevails over the Giottesque. Signor L. Bailo (¹), to whom we owe the conservation of these important paintings, and Herr von Schlosser both think it possible that they are works by Tommaso da Modena — who, in 1352, painted in the church of S. Niccolo of the same town — but at the same time they attach much importance to their similarity to the art of Altichiero and Avanzo (²). Personally, I do not find sufficient resemblance between Tommaso's art and this cycle of frescoes to attribute this decoration to the Modenese artist. His influence, however, is apparent in the design of the faces.

The series commences with (1) the representation of St. Ursula between four companions and with two devotees kneeling at her feet. It is a fresco in which the figures are lacking in grace and the faces rather ugly. (2) The first incident taken from the saint's legend shows the pagan king of the Anglo-Saxons sending two ambassadors to request St. Ursula's hand in marriage for his son. (3) We then see him delivering a letter to the saint's father (fig. 103); (4) followed by her travelling companions she bids farewell

---

(¹) *L. Bailo*, Relazione degli affreschi salvati nella demolita chiesa di Sta. Margarita, Treviso, 1883. *The Same*, in Bolletino del Museo Trivigiano, Sept., 1886.

(²) *J. von Schlosser*, Tommaso da Modena u. die ältere Malerei in Treviso, Jahrbuch der Kunsthist. Samml. d. Allerh. Kaiserh., XIX, Wien, 1898, p. 240 and also in his small book recently published, Oberitalische Trecentisten, Leipzig, 1921, p. 7. *Cavalcaselle* accepts this attribution to Tommaso, so also do *Testi* and *Venturi* who discovers in them an influence of the Bohemian school. I do not know any earlier Bohemian paintings which show even a distant connection with these frescoes. *Schubring*, Altichiero, p. 97, is of opinion that they are later in date, executed probably after 1400.

THE PAINTERS OF PADUA, VERONA AND TREVISO. 203

to her father and on the same fresco we find represented how she obtained her future husband's consent to be baptised. Then follow (5) the baptism (fig. 104); (6) her voyage on the Rhine in which she and her companions are seen sailing towards the city of Cologne; (7) St. Ursula in Rome visiting the Pope; (8) the

Fig. 103. Scene from the legend of St. Ursula, 1370—'80. Museum, Treviso.
Photo Garatti.

Pope dreaming that he is martyred together with the saint; (9) in a consistory he divests himself of his pontifical insignia (fig. 105) in spite of the cardinals' protests and (10) with the saint and her suite leaves Rome; (11) back in Cologne they prepare themselves for their martyrdom and (12) they are all killed by the Huns.

As to the actual artistic value of these frescoes the painter in

204 THE PAINTERS OF PADUA, VERONA AND TREVISO.

no way equals Altichiero, nor do his figures possess that serene beauty of expression, feature and proportion, of the forms in the decoration of the two Paduan chapels. The Treviso master was a narrator of true Giottesque tendency; he emphasizes the details

Fig. 104. Scene from the legend of St. Ursula, 1370—'80. Museum, Treviso.
Photo Garatti.

of his recital, his figures are very intent and the action dominates the composition and artistic attributes of the picture. However, the great care with which every detail is depicted is a charming trait of this artist's. In the two scenes showing the ambassadors and in the one in which the saint prepares for her departure, there is a remarkable subtlety of attitude and expression. The rendering of the cardinals' disapproval of the Pope's action is a chef d'oeuvre of psychology. The scene of the massacre is an agitated conflict, perfectly presented.

The artist was also inspired by profane painting, with the

Fig. 105. Scene from the legend of St. Ursula, 1370 – '80. Museum, Treviso.
Photo Garatti.

result that his frescoes have the aspect of "scènes de genre". The details of the costumes, the courtiers whose figures fill up the corners of the pictures, and the intimate, yet worldly and irreligious appearance of these frescoes, lead us to classify them with this group of works.

The perspective of some of the buildings is reminiscent of Altichiero; the church that gives depth to the scene of the baptism, for example, is very similar to the buildings in the frescoes of the St. George chapel or rather to the Giottesque manner in which Semitecolo presents his edifices as a background rather than encompassing his figures. Some of the other backgrounds are also depicted sooner after Giotto's manner; for instance the loggia before which St. Ursula's father receives the letter, or again the room seen in section showing at the same time part of the façade, in the fresco representing the saint's farewell. The way in which the painter, in the first illustration of the saint's legend, shows us the king's throne, isolated and without the addition of any accessories or architecture, is also very Giottesque, while certain figures such as the saint and her four companions in the first fresco, the saint and the figure to the right — her mother? — in the scene of the father reading the letter, and several figures in St. Ursula's farewell are of broad robust proportions, obviously inspired by Giotto [1].

The result of the above comparison is that although the spirit of his art and the technique of his perspective betray a certain connection between the master of Treviso and Altichiero's school, we cannot, without considerable reservation, place him in this group, since we find in his works just as important features borrowed from the Giottesque tradition. This cycle of frescoes from the life of St. Ursula dates from about 1370—1380, that is to say almost contemporary with Altichiero's activity, but the work of the master of Treviso is less perfect and slightly more archaic than this great painter's art.

If we cast a glance at the art of miniature painting and of design in Padua and Verona during the 14th century, we discover that it was again in the former of these two cities that the artistic development was the greater.

Schubring [1] speaks of a codex with illustrations from the Old Testament that he found in the Library of Rovigo; it is written in Venetian dialect and he is of opinion that the work is Paduan of about 1350. He finds that the artist's compositions and his pronounced taste for architecture — though slightly different in type — are reminiscent of Altichiero's art, while the

---

[1] *Schubring*, op. cit., p. 94.

Fig. 106. The Adoration of the Magi, Veronese Miniature, 2nd half of the 14th century. Biblioteca Capitolare, Verona.   Photo Lotze.

intimacy and care of detail are characteristic of "scènes de genre". If the date and school to which Schubring assigns these miniatures be correct, then we would have in them a sort of introduction to that art which shortly afterwards developed under the guidance of Altichiero and Avanzo; however they seem of later date and have been more justly ascribed to the last years of the 14th century [1].

[1] *H. J. Hermann*, Jahrb. der Kunsthist. Samml des Allerh. Kaiserhauses, XXI, p. 123.

The fancy for profane paintings, in which we observe a decided fondness for chivalry, resulted in several collections of drawings which in all probability were inspired by existing paintings. The *Liber de principibus Carrariensibus et gestis eorum* of Pietro Paolo Vergerio in the Museum of Padua [1] contains portraits of the princes of the house of Carrara, which were probably painted from those that Guariento made in their palace and which are mentioned by the "Anonimo Morelliano".

Anyhow we can be certain that the portrait we find of Petrarch in a codex in the Darmstadt Library, dating from the last years of the 14th century [2], is copied from the fresco representing the great poet which was originally in the Giants' Hall. As both works are extant, there can be little doubt about their quasi-identity; though naturally we must not forget the present ruined condition of the fresco.

To the same group of drawings copied from paintings, I think also belong those in the National Gallery, Rome, that Signor Venturi thought might have been sketches for Giusto da Padova's frescoes in the Erimetani church. This, if true, would explain the later date of the drawings, which, I think, belong to the beginning of the 15th century [3].

We find no trace of this worldly and rather unusual art in Verona where the Giottesque tradition also dominated this form of painting. Some antiphonaries in the Chapter Library show illuminations which prove that the art of miniature-making was well represented in this town (fig. 106) but these examples do not possess many points in common with the Veronese school of painting.

---

[1] *Lazzarini*, Libri di Francesco Novello da Carrara, Atti e Mem. della R. Acc. di Scienze, Lett. ed Arti in Padova, XVIII, p. 1.

[2] As I have said before, *von Schlosser* believes these illustrations to be of later date and influenced by Pisanello.

[3] In the article previously cited in Jahrb. der Kunsthist. Samml., XXIII, *von Schlosser* attributes to the Veronese school of miniature painting some illuminations in a little book in the Hofmuseum, Vienna, that he believed had been made for the Cerrati family of Verona. *Venturi* (L'Arte, 1904, p. 79) assigns them to a German artist. *P. Toesca*, Pittura e miniatura nella Lombardia, p. 338, is of opinion that they are productions of the Milanese school of the end of the 14th century and I think this is the correct attribution.

CHAPTER III.

PAINTING IN LOMBARDY AND PIEDMONT.

Among the numerous paintings of the 14th century that we find in Lombardy (¹), there is a certain number that can be grouped together on account of the predominating influence of Giovanni da Milano; apart from these works we discover a fairly prolonged persistence of 13th century art, a little group of Giottesque paintings — this influence spread from Verona towards the end of the 14th century — and many productions of a local art which does not seem to belong to any of these categories. In all districts a little distant from one of the important artistic centres, we find evidence of the existence of a similar provincial art.

Further, about the year 1400, we note in Lombardy the budding of Gothic painting whose great development was an international movement, being represented in Verona in the person of Stefano da Zevio. Although this movement started some years before the 15th century in Lombardy, Giovanni de Grassi being mentioned as early as 1389, its florescence took place in the 15th century and I shall treat it in its entirety when I reach that period.

The persistence of the Byzantine tradition after Giottesque art had penetrated into Lombardy, is rather curious and proves the existence side by side of two different tendencies. After the infiltration of elements of Giotto's art into other districts, the

---

(¹) Almost all the material that is in any way useful for our knowledge of 14th century art in Lombardy has been treated by Signor *P. Toesca* in his excellent book: La pittura e la miniatura nella Lombardia, Milan, 1912. This book was rather superficially criticized by *Betty Kurth* in Kunstgesch. Anzeigen, to which Signor *Toesca* replied in L'Arte, 1913, p. 136. *V. Constantini*, La pittura lombarda, Milan, 1922, p. 75 et seq., makes a brief mention of 14th century works without giving any data or new ideas.

archaic forms were fairly soon replaced, but in Lombardy we find, even up to about the middle of the 14th century, works still executed in the style of the 13th.

The most important series of frescoes painted in the manner of the previous century is the one that decorates the castle of Angera, on the south shore of the Lago Maggiore (¹). Besides some purely ornamental frescoes which adorn other parts of the building, we find, in the large hall, extensive mural paintings, the principal representations of which are the battles between the archbishop, Otto Visconti, after whom the hall is named, and Napoleon della Torre and his adherents.

The original plan of the decoration included a rich ornamentation of the vault and lower parts of the walls. As an arch divides the side walls into two different parts, there are consequently six separate surfaces; the lunettes above contain representations of the planets, while below in each space there are two scenes illustrating the war-like bishop's campaigns; each of the six compartments is enclosed in a frieze in which are depicted here and there other astronomical images. The decoration is considerably damaged, and in some places, especially on the east wall, the frescoes have entirely disappeared.

The subjects and spirit of this work lend themselves to a comparison with the frescoes of Castelbarco, but in making this comparison we discover that we are here dealing with the manifestation of quite another artistic tendency. Just these details which, at Castelbarco seemed to be of German origin, are at Angera thoroughly Italian. The style of drawing is still strongly reminiscent of the Byzantine tradition but the colours and sense of realism that we notice throughout these representations, are already characteristic of a newer art.

As for the date of this cycle of paintings, Signor Toesca has pointed out that it must be after 1314, the year that the castle was definitely taken by the Visconti, but it is probable that the ornamentation was started forthwith because it certainly dates from the first quarter of the 14th century (²). Executed very much

---

(¹) L. *Beltrami*, Angera e la sua rocca etc., Milan, 1904. *Toesca*, op. cit., p. 157.

(²) And not between 1342 and 1354 by order of the archbishop, Giovanni II Visconti as *Beltrami*, op. cit., p. 15, says.

in the same style are the almost contemporary frescoes in the vaults of the church of S. Bassiano at Lodi Vecchio (¹). The decoration of the vaults was ordered by the association of oxen-drivers (²); the frescoes were probably executed in 1323 since this is the date we find in the inscription of a statue in relief in the interior of the church, representing a man on horseback leading two oxen: "*MCCCXXIII Paraticum Boateriorum fecit fieri hoc celum*" (sic) (³). Moreover it was probably the donors' occupation that led the painter to depict on one of the four vaults, heavily laden waggons drawn by two oxen and each driven by a man. The other vaults show the four symbols of the Evangelists (fig. 107), and four medallions containing the Doctors of the Church, while the fourth one is only adorned with a painted design without any figures. This decoration is of a certain importance since it furnishes us with a second example of painting of the first quarter of the 14th century, in which, at least the drawing is dominated by the archaic Byzantine tradition.

Other paintings of this period in which the same Byzantine characteristics are equally evident are to be found at Lodi. On a pillar in the church of S. Francesco, there is a rigid representation of the Baptism of Christ before Whom the water rises in a very primitive manner (⁴). Near the tomb of Antonio Fissiraga who died in 1327 there are two other paintings. One of them, which is but little superior in quality to the frescoes in S. Bassiano, shows the nobleman stretched on his deathbed, two choristers swinging censers and numerous clerics standing behind (⁵). The archaism of the design is evident in the mannerism of the details, as for example the shape of the dead man's beard. The stiffness of the composition, with the row of stereotyped monks, is surprising at such a late date. The figures of SS. Clement and

---

(¹) D. *Sant' Ambrogio*, Lodi Vecchio San Bassiano, Milan, 1895. *Toesca*, op. cit., p. 155.

(²) Really those who undertake any transport with their oxen.

(³) *Sant' Ambrogio*, op. cit., p. 28 pl. XX. This date coincides perfectly with the decision which was taken in 1321 to carry out some restoration to the church, op. cit., p. 31.

(⁴) *Toesca*, op. cit., p. 173.

(⁵) *Idem*, p. 182.

Helen in the same church might be paintings from the hand of the same artist (¹).

The second fresco which we find over the tomb of Fissiraga, is by a much more skilful artist and one who is not any later (²).

Under an architectural canopy the crowned Virgin is depicted holding the Child Who bends towards an old man who is kneeling before Him holding a model of the church; behind him are seen a holy bishop and St. Francis. The somewhat remarkable artist who painted this fresco belongs to a transition stage between the Byzantine style and Giottesque art. From the former he borrowed his facial types and his schematic execution, but the robust proportions of the figures and the triangles on the baldachin — one adorned with a relief of St. George killing the dragon — are essentially Giottesque elements. I would even say that the marked perspective of the above mentioned baldachin is superior to what we generally find in Giotto's own works.

Signor Toesca has justly ascribed to the same master another painting of the Virgin and Child in this church (³); it is even more Giottesque than the foregoing work. In the Baptistery of Varese, a fragment of a composition, similar to the one on the Fissiraga tomb, shows the Madonna under an almost identical canopy with St. John the Baptist who, as before, is of rather Byzantine appearance (⁴). I think from this artist's hand are also a Madonna "della Misericordia", a fragment of which alone remains close to the previous fresco, and a Virgin and Child with two adorers, all half-length figures, in the lunette over the entry (⁵).

Some other frescoes of this period, which are less Byzantine in technique but more primitive in execution, have been transported from the convent of Sta. Margherita in Como to the Broletto of the same town (⁶). The scenes depicted are taken from the legend of SS. Liberata and Faustina.

(¹) *Toesca*, p. 185.
(²) *Idem*, op. cit., p. 183, pl. VIII.
(³) *Idem*, p. 184.
(⁴) *Idem*, op. cit., p. 185.
(⁵) *Idem*, p. 186.
(⁶) *Carotti*, L'Arte, XI, 1908, p. 143. *Toesca*, op. cit., p. 175.

Fig 107. The Symbols of the Evangelists, 1323. S. Bassano, Lodi Vecchio.

The artist has retained the childish compositions, the stiff forms and fragmentary architecture of 13th century art, but feeling and expression belong to the 14th century and, together with some of the physical proportions, seem to be the result of a knowledge of Giottesque works.

In Milan itself we find several examples of the persistence of the 13th century manner. The most important of them is the mural decoration of an annex to the "Monastero Maggiore", behind S. Maurizio (¹). On account of certain technical details an earlier date than the middle of the 14th century cannot be assigned to these paintings. They show a long series of figures of saints, each one enclosed in an arch; the row is broken by a representation of the Saviour on the Cross between the Virgin and St. John. It is a work of little artistic importance and of a crude execution; the archaism is very pronounced.

The tower of S. Marco preserves some fragments of fresco painting from which we are able to gather that the original decoration comprised an image of the Madonna and two rows of saints, one above the other (²).

Some of the better conserved figures have beautiful heads but they are designed in the conventional Byzantine manner with prominent and rather hard features.

A crucifix in the church of S. Eusturgo is probably still a late 13th century production; the body of Christ shows, to a certain extent, the curve we find in crucifixes of this period. The fulllength figures of the Virgin and St. John depicted at the ends of the cross-bar, and the angel enclosed in a medallion at the summit again exemplify the continuity of the older style of painting (³).

The oratory of Sta. Maria, near Voghera at Pontasso, contains some frescoes of the beginning of the 14th century (⁴), which, as in all the works mentioned until now, prove the persistence of the Byzantine tradition in Lombardy in the early 14th century, by the side of and sometimes even intermingling with the new tendencies about to develop.

A fresh impetus appears in Lombard painting shortly after 1330. According to Vasari, Giotto was called to Milan by Azzo

---

(¹) *U. Nebbia,* Note intorno alla chiesa di S. Maurizio al Monastero Maggiore, Rassegna d'Arte, XI, 1911, p. 13.

(²) *Toesca,* op. cit., p. 175.

(³) v. Vol. I, p. 318.

(⁴) *V. Cerioli,* L'oratorio di S. Maria del Pontasso, Riv. di Scien. Stor., 1908.

Visconti after his consent, in 1334, to become architect of the Cathedral of Florence; we have no absolute proof of the truth of this statement, and still less that the artist ever went to Milan. What makes the story highly improbable is that the construction of Azzo Visconti's palace was begun after 1339, consequently after Giotto's death. It is interesting to note that this prince had certain frescoes executed there, illustrating episodes from the

Fig. 108. The Adoration of the Magi, fresco, circa 1350. S. Abondio, Como.

Punic war and a series of heroes, beginning with Hercules, a subject very frequently repeated in later centuries, and he included in it portraits of himself and of Cangrande della Scala. It is one of the oldest examples that we know of humanistic representations ([1]).

The first Lombard paintings, in which the dominating element is the Giottesque, are of an earlier date than the master's hypothetical sojourn in Milan. Moreover we have already observed

---

([1]) *v. Schlosser*, op. cit., p. 178.

a certain Giottesque influence in the work of the anonymous painter who decorated the tomb of Fissiraga who died in 1327.

The most extensive cycle of Giottesque paintings is somewhat later and is almost entirely free of Byzantine elements. It adorns the apse of the church of S. Abondio at Como (¹). The conch contains the somewhat repainted figures of the Saviour, St. Peter, the Virgin, the Baptist and St. Paul. Then follow, in six rows intersected by the windows, twenty scenes illustrating the Life of Christ from the Annunciation until the Entombment (figs. 108 and 109). The frieze below and at the sides shows half-length figures of prophets and saints; the different scenes are separated by a border adorned with medallions containing heads and chimera.

These paintings, which seem to be from more than one hand, are not of good quality; they are evidently the production of some provincial local artists who had only a limited knowledge of Giotto's art, and did not even follow his iconography. Nevertheless the simplicity of composition, together with the forceful depiction of dramatic action, the facial types and expressions, and the construction of the forms point to a Florentine inspiration. A similar manifestation of the Giottesque influence is found in a fresco in the Broletto of Como; it represents a young man wearing a crown of flowers receiving an inscription from a skeleton. A painting of a saint, also in the Broletto whence it was transported from Sta. Margherita, belongs to the same tendency (²).

The other traces of Giottesque art in this region are of but little importance.

In the archiepiscopal palace in Milan, however, there are some fragments of what once must have been very fine paintings of the Giottesque school; they probably formed part of a scene of the Massacre of the Innocents and doubtless belonged to the decoration that we owe to Bishop Giovanni Visconti (1342— 1354) whose coat of arms is represented close by (³). Reminiscences exist of a painting showing him in adoration before the

---

(¹) *Toesca*, op. cit., p. 190.
(²) *Toesca*, op. cit , p. 196.
(³) *Toesca*, op. cit., p. 208.

Virgin, whilst, the "Anonimo" speaks of frescoes, still resplendent in his day by very old masters (¹).

Besides the older paintings in the tower of S. Marco, there are some figures of saints of about the middle of the 14th century. The Giottesque inspiration is evident but the work is very mediocre (²).

Fig. 109. The Presentation in the Temple, fresco, circa 1350. S. Abondio, Como.

More genuinely Giottesque and slightly earlier in date is a large fresco in the church of S. Michele at Monza, that Signor Toesca is of opinion represents the saints praying for the faithful on All Saints' Day, as the Golden Legend describes in connection

---

(¹) *Anonimo Morelliano*, p. 54, "In la corte archiepiscopale le pitture a fresco che risplendono fin hoggidi come spechii furono di man de maestri vecchissimi".

(²) *Toesca*, op. cit., p. 210.

with this feast(¹). The fresco shows St. Peter enthroned as Pope and before him about twenty saints are depicted. The figures are well proportioned, majestic and imposing, and the faces are beautiful. It is one of the finest Lombard paintings belonging to the Giottesque school.

Not any inferior is the fragmentary fresco representing the tree of St. Bonaventura in the church of Sta. Maria Maggiore, Bergamo (fig. 110). At the foot of the tree, we see the Virgin, St. Francis and St. Clare to the left, St. John and two Franciscan monks to the right and St. Bonaventura kneeling in the centre; near him is placed the kneeling figure of the donor who, according to the later inscription, which is no doubt a true copy of the original, was a certain Guido di Suardi, while the date of execution is given as 1347. The scenes in medallions between the lower branches that have not been destroyed, illustrate the beginning of the story of Christ. This master was an excellent Giottesque artist but his design is a little harder and his figures slightly longer than Giotto's Florentine followers show us in their works (²).

Close by, in the monastery of S. Francesco at Vimercate (³), we find some paintings of minor importance, belonging, however, to the same artistic movement and dated 1354.

The persistence of the Giottesque tradition in the second half of the 14th century is manifest in a fine fresco of a half-length figure of the Virgin with the Child standing on her knee, in the church of S. Agostino, Cremona (⁴).

(¹) *Toesca*, p. 212. D. Sant' Ambrogio, who dates it from about 1400, has interpreted it as a representation of a votive mass: Il grandioso dipinto di una messa votiva nella chiesa di S. Michele di Monza, Rassegna d'Arte, 1907, p. 62.

(²) The most important painter in Bergamo between 1363 and 1403 was Pierino de Nova (*Tassi*, Vite dei pittori Bergam., I, 1776 p.2, read the name as Paxino or Pecino). I do not know for what reason some fragments of frescoes in the campanile of Sta. Maria Maggiore have been attributed to him. There also existed a Michele di Ronco di Milano, v. *Crowe and Cavalcaselle*, op. cit., p. 253.

(³) *Toesca*, op. cit., p. 213.

(⁴) *Idem*, p. 266. A Cremonese painter called Polidoro Casella was active in 1354. *Crowe and Cavalcaselle*, op. cit., p. 255. These authors mention a large Madonna with the donor dated 1370 in the Cremona Cathedral that they believe is a possible work of this artist.

PAINTING IN LOMBARDY AND PIEDMONT. 219

Fig. 110. The Tree of St. Bonaventura, 1347. Sta. Maria Maggiore, Bergamo.

Photo Ist. Art. Graf.

In the left aisle of the church of S. Francesco of Lodi we find a fairly long cycle of scenes from the life of a holy bishop (¹), evidently a work of the second half of the 14th century; the general appearance of the figures, as well as the animated action and simplicity of composition, may be looked upon as derived from Giotto's art of which, however, it is but a provincial manifestation.

The group of painters, in which Giovanni da Milano was the most prominent figure, cannot be explained by a simple evolution of Giottesque elements, the earliest trace of which we find in Lombardy in the first quarter of the 14th century. Giovanni da Milano, who constitutes such an obvious link between Lombardy, his native country, and Florence, where we find him active; who had fellow artists of the same origin so closely connected with him that their works have been attributed to him; yet who, on the other hand, seems to be in his proper place among the Florentine painters, is only a factor in the artistic movement that may be called the Lombardo-Florentine. Consequently the painters who worked in Viboldone, Mocchirolo and Lentate in the second half of the 14th century were not late Giottesque artists, but may be considered to a certain extent as forming a colony of the contemporary school of Florentine painting.

In what way this close connection between Lombard and Florentine painters was brought about is not very clear, for Giovanni da Milano's migration to Florence, where he is mentioned in 1350, and where he took up his residence, does not explain how a marked Florentine influence dominated a group of Lombard artists, more especially as this influence is to be observed prior to the above mentioned date. I think we must assign Giovanni's choice of home to the renown that Florence had attained in his native country.

Even the Bergamo fresco of 1347 shows such a Florentine form of the evolution of Giottesque art that we may suppose its maker to have been familiar with works of Giotto's immediate followers. A series of frescoes in the church of Castel S. Pietro, near Balerna in the region of Como, is excuted in the same style (²). The church

---

(¹) *Toesca*, op. cit., p. 266, note 1.
(²) *Toesca*, op. cit., p. 188.

was built in 1343 and in all probability was decorated immediately after. Besides some half-length figures of saints in medallions on the walls, we see in the apse an image of the Saviour in benediction enclosed in an aureole and surrounded by the symbols of the Evangelists; lower down are depicted the summons to SS. Peter and Andrew, the capture of St. Peter (?), his crucifixion; then follow the Annunciation, a figure of the Madonna, and over the door the Navicella.

This master was not one of the good artists of the group with which we are at present dealing. His drawing is somewhat clumsy and his colours without any charm, but nevertheless he is not entirely devoid of interest, since his work can be called Florentine, and offers us an example of that stage in this school after the death of its great founder and before Giovanni da Milano went to Florence. On account of certain Lombard features that Giovanni brought with him to Tuscany, it may be inferred that he was active in his native country while resident there.

For the artist, Giovanni da Milano[1], we have records that allow us to follow his activities from 1350 until 1369 [2]. It is more than probable that we can identify Giovanni da Milano with Johannus Jacobi da Como whose name is found in the first of these years in the list of foreign artists then working in Florence, all the more so as when Giovanni da Milano matriculated in 1363 in the "arte dei medici e speciale" he is mentioned as being the son of Jacopo di Guido. From the tax register it appears that at the end of the same year he lived in the quarter of S. Pier Maggiore, and that he possessed some property in the region of Ripoli, while in 1365, he signed the picture now in the Accademia of Florence but originally in the church of S. Gerolamo, representing the dead Christ surrounded by the Virgin, St John and the Magdalene. The same year he contracted for the extant frescoes in the Rinuccini chapel of Sta. Croce, and in this document he is called "Johannes pictor de Kaverzaio" which certainly may be taken to mean Caversago,

---

[1] *C. F. von Rumohr*, Italienische Forschungen (new ed.), Frankfort, 1920, p. 279. *W. Suida*, Florentinischen Maler um die Mitte des XIV Jahrhunderts, Strasbourg, 1905, p. 28. *O. Sirén*, Giottino, p. 53. *P. Toesca*, op. cit., p. 217. *W. Suida* in Thieme-Becker, Künstler-Lexikon, XIV, p. 127.

[2] *Vasari-Milanesi*, I, p. 584, note 2; p. 572, note 2; p. 584, note 1.

a small village near Como. In 1366 he obtained for himself and his offspring the citizenship of Florence (¹), and the last time we find him is among the artists whom Urban V employed to adorn the Vatican (²).

His name is still found on a polyptych in the Gallery of Prato which, however, is undated.

Vasari furnishes us with the usual unreliable information concerning this artist; he relates that he worked with Taddeo Gaddi and was so friendly with him that at his death, Taddeo appointed Giovanni and Jacopo del Casentino the guardians of his sons, Agnolo and Giovanni, especially charging the former with their artistic instruction.

This little anecdote is far from the truth, because not only at his father's death was Agnolo Gaddi of an age at which a guardian was no longer required, but also nothing in Giovanni's art leads us to believe that he ever worked with Taddeo. Consequently we need not dwell on Vasari's record of the works that our artist made in collaboration with his supposed master. He mentions, however, the altar-piece of the Ognissanti church that von Rumohr saw there in the Gondi-Dini chapel, but that has since been transported to the Uffizi, and attributes to him a panel on the Gherardo da Villamagna altar which must have borne the date 1364 (³), and a crucifix, a Madonna and St. Clare and scenes from the history of the Virgin in Assisi (⁴).

Vasari who, in a sentimental way likes the subjects of his writings to end their lives in the city of their origin, informs us

---

(¹) Giornale Storico degli Archivi Toscani, II, 1858, p. 65.

(²) An attempt, without any foundation, to identify Giovanni da Milano with Giovanni de' Grassi, was made by *G. B. Calvi*, Notizie sulla vita e sulle opere di principali architetti, scultori e pittori che fiorivano in Milano etc., I, Milano, 1859, p. 85.

(³) *Vasari*, who says Taddeo Gaddi died in 1350, tells us that Giovanni executed this panel fourteen years after his master's death.

(⁴) *Vasari* does not even state in which church these paintings were to be found. Could it possibly be that the first part bore reference to the three panels of the end of the 13th century in Sta. Chiara (v. Vol. I, p. 339). *Von Rumohr* was entirely mistaken in believing that the scenes from the Childhood of Christ were the frescoes in the transept of the Lower Church and in his acceptance of this attribution to Giovanni.

Fig. 111. Giovanni da Milano, Joachim driven from the Temple, fresco, 1365. Sta. Croce, Florence.

Photo Alinari.

that Giovanni returned to Milan where he executed many works before expiring.

The oldest and most important work that we have by Giovanni da Milano, and the one which is best documented, is the partly repainted (¹) cycle of frescoes in the Rinuccini chapel or choir of the sacristy of Sta. Croce, Florence (²); the entire decoration, however, is not from the master's own hand. In May of the same year — 1365 — that the artist made the contract for the execution of these paintings, we find him asking the Capitano of the Compagnia of Or San Michele, who had ordered them, for more time in which to finish them, which request is granted.

Giovanni's iconography differs in many points from Giotto's. This is at once evident in the first fresco, Joachim driven from the Temple (fig. 111). The main action, although placed in the centre of the picture, is dominated by the imposing architecture; the perspective is well shown and the building full of devout persons. The angel's message to Joachim and the Meeting at the Golden Gate are illustrated in the next fresco. The former is very similar to Taddeo Gaddi's representation of this event in the Baroncelli chapel of the same church, where, if it will be remembered, it also formed half of a fresco. Joachim is seen lying on the mountain looking up at the angelic apparition, while below is depicted one of the shepherds with his flock of sheep.

The scene on the right half, shows a good deal of correspondence to the examples by Giotto and Gaddi, particularly resembling those of the latter in its general disposition, as well as in the absence of that charming tenderness that Giotto expresses in his Paduan cycle. Giovanni, like his two predecessors, represents the servant, with pointed bonnet and satchel slung on a stick, following his master. Anna is accompanied by several women, while the city behind its walls is another feature that Giovanni depicts in common with the other artist active in Sta. Croce.

The Nativity of the Virgin is a charming, homely scene and

(¹) *Crowe and Cavalcaselle*, op. cit., II, p. 187, note 1.

(²) These paintings which *Vasari* assigned to Taddeo Gaddi, were ascribed to Giovanni da Milano by *Crowe and Cavalcaselle*, before any documents were found concerning them.

one in which Giovanni's characteristic drawing is very evident (fig. 112). Anna, sitting up in bed is seen washing her hands; three women at the bed side amuse the new-born Child Who has just been bathed, while a fourth accepts a gift from a neighbour who stands in the door-way.

It is generally acknowledged that the two lowest frescoes on this wall — the Presentation of the Virgin in the Temple and

Fig. 112. Giovanni da Milano, the Nativity of the Virgin, fresco, 1365. Sta. Croce, Florence.

Photo Brogi.

her Betrothal — are not by Giovanni da Milano (¹). In the former the artist has followed Taddeo's composition, even to such an extent that we might even call it a free copy. There are only a few features reminiscent of Giovanni's art; he probably did not even provide the rough sketch but referred the artist to Taddeo's example in the Baroncelli chapel. This is not the case for the Betrothal in which the moment represented is when Joseph, guided by the high-priest, places the ring on the Virgin's finger,

---

(¹) I find no reason to believe, as Signor *Toesca* does, that the assistant artist was Giovanni del Biondo.

while the rejected suitors break their rods; the event is witnessed by many persons.

The story of Mary Magdalene is depicted on the opposite wall. In the lunette we see the saint washing Christ's feet in the house of the Pharisee. In the building, which is shown in section, Our Lord is represented seated at table with three other persons; three domestics serve the food while Mary Magdalene kneels below and the seven devils are seen fleeing away. On the second row we see, in the house of the two sisters, the Magdalene sitting at the Saviour's feet, intent on what He says and Martha reproaching her with her idleness while several people look on; here too is depicted the Resurrection of Lazarus in quite an unknown composition: Lazarus, supported by some friends climbs out of a large flat marble sarcophagus behind which are the Saviour and the two imploring sisters; other figures are seen to either side, those on the left apparently standing in the gateway of the city, outside whose walls the incident occurs. The variation on the usual composition is not a happy one for the picture is clumsy and awkward; with the exception of Lazarus, Martha and Mary Magdalene, the figures are not at all characteristic of the master's work and we may conjecture that the greater part of this fresco was probably left to an assistant. Nor are the two last scenes by Giovanni's own hand. The first representing the Holy Women at the Empty Sepulchre shows the Maries in conversation with the three guardian angels and combined with it is the Noli me tangere. The iconographical peculiarities here consist in the number of angels at the grave and the wall enclosing the garden in which both events are depicted. The other scene shows the miracle that we found in Mary Magdalene's chapel in the Lower Church of Assisi; the merchant returning by sea to Marseilles finding his wife alive on the island where he had left her dead on the outward-bound journey. The finest part of this decoration is the painting of the vault where the imposing and grandiose figures of Our Lord and four prophets are represented in medallions, while the busts of the Twelve Apostles in the entrance arch are scarcely less beautiful.

Giovanni's request that he might be allowed to finish these frescoes at a later date than he had first stipulated, the fact that important parts were left to assistants whose artistic capabilities,

Fig. 113. Giovanni da Milano, Pietà, 1365. Accademia, Florence.
Photo Brogi.

Giovanni must have known were not of a very high standard, and, notwithstanding the great technical qualities of the work to which we shall return later, the inferiority of even the best parts of this decoration to the contemporary Pietà in the Accademia, all prove that for one reason or another, the enterprise was undertaken with but little enthusiasm on the part of the master.

Had the only two dated works not been executed in the same period of Giovanni's career, we should have been able to form a better idea of his artistic evolution. The panel of the dead Saviour with the Virgin, the Magdalene and St. John (fig. 113), bears the inscription: *"Io Govani da Melano depinsi questa tavola i(n) MCCCLXV"* (¹).

Even without the documents of the one and the signature of the other we should certainly have considered these two works as productions of one artist executed in the same manner and spirit, but the technical qualities of this picture are so much finer that it may be classed with the best Florentine panel paintings of the Trecento. His individual style which was evident in the frescoes of the Rinuccini chapel, is here very marked and gives much more character to the work.

The polyptych in the Gallery of Prato (fig. 114) shows, below the central panel, the signature: *"Ego Johanes de Mediolano pinxi hoc opus"*. This important altar-piece represents above, the enthroned Virgin in the centre with SS. Bernard and Catherine to the left and SS. Bartholomew and Barnabas to the right, each on a separate panel, the apex of which is adorned with a medallion containing a bust. Below each of the lateral saints a scene illustrates an event from his or her life; with the exception of the one from the legend of St. Bernard (to whom we see the Virgin appearing) the incidents represented are those of the saints' martyrdoms. Under the broader central panel are the two figures

---

(¹) *G. B. Calvi*, op. cit., p. 90, doubtless refers to this work in speaking of a panel which he saw in the old convent of Sta. Caterina, signed: *"Gio da Milano"* and dated 1365, representing the dead Christ seated on the ground, supported by two angels. This is all the more probable since *von Rumohr* saw the picture now in the Accademia in this convent which was then a store-room of the Accademia. Herr *Suida*, Florentinische Maler, p. 28, infers from *Calvi's* statement that there must have been a second panel bearing the same date.

of the Annunciation each framed in a separate arcade. On the predella we find six events from the Life of Christ: the Nativity, the Adoration of the Magi, the Presentation in the Temple, the

Fig. 114. Giovanni da Milano, polyptych. Gallery, Prato.
Photo Brogi.

Prayer in the Garden of Gethsemane, the Betrayal of Judas and the Calvary

The very refined execution and the artist's taste for ornamental detail, which is very striking, for example, in the mosaic decoration of the various thrones, serve to reveal the inferiority of the fresco cycle in the Rinuccini chapel where we certainly do not see Giovanni at his best. The exquisite calligraphic design of the figures, the minuteness of detail and the brilliant colouring make of this picture a work very superior to the artist's mural paintings.

In comparing the two dated works of about 1363 and of 1365 with the signed altar-piece, we discover in the former productions an increased strength of design, especially in the form of the body and of the features, so that we may safely assume the picture in Prato to be of earlier date. Herr Suida has propounded the theory that as the picture bears another inscription telling us that Frate Francesco was the donor, and that as it was originally in the church of the hospital of which Frate Francesco was rector in 1354, it may be taken for granted that the painting was executed about that time. An interval of about ten years between this work and those mentioned above seems rather too much; it may be possible, however, that rectors were appointed for more than one year and that it is of somewhat later date.

There are two other paintings that we can compare with Giovanni's dated works and that seem of contemporary or even later execution.

The more important of them is a large part of a polyptych which was transferred from the Ognissanti church to the Uffizi Gallery (fig. 115). We have now only five parts of the polyptych which must originally have comprised seven on account of the representation of the days of the creation in the spandrels of the lateral panels. The central one no doubt showed an image of the Madonna. On each of the five principal parts that still exist are represented two figures of saints; they are SS. Catherine and Lucy, Stephen and Lawrence, John the Baptist and Mark, Peter and Benedict, James and Gregory. Below each pair a small panel shows a group of about twelve figures of saints. Comparing these figures with those in the foregoing works, we discover a broader and freer treatment than we found in either the mural decoration or the Prato polyptych, a lack of that severe individual style which was so admirable in the Pietà of 1365, and a decided increase of Gothicism in the drapery, most evident perhaps in the small figures but also to be observed in some of the others, in particular that of St. John the Baptist. The artist's excellence in the drawing of the features has in no way diminished.

Fig. 115. Giovanni da Milano, part of the Ognissanti polyptych.
Uffizi, Florence. Photo Anderson.

The Gothic element is still more marked in three panels — once doubtless having formed part of an important altar-piece — in the National Gallery; they represent the seated figure of the Almighty, holding the globe and a key, the Virgin, and St John pointing to the Madonna and holding a scroll with an inscription bearing reference to her; half-length figures of angels are seen in the medallions of the terminals (fig. 116). In none of Giovanni

Fig. 116. Giovanni da Milano, God the Father, the Virgin and the Baptist. National Gallery, London.

da Milano's other works do we find such beautiful drapery and such refinement in the drawing of the features. I am inclined to look upon these panels as one of his late works, more especially as the smooth regular features are less vigorously designed than in his other productions.

We shall now deal with those paintings which I think can be placed in that period of the artist's career that preceeded the one in which he executed the two dated works. In doing so I think that it is best to work backwards so that we shall begin with those that most closely approximate the year 1365.

Fig. 117. Giovanni da Milano, Madonna. Gallery, Strasbourg.

Of about the same period as the frescoes in the Rinuccini chapel, consequently later than the Prato altar-piece, is, I believe, a picture which I venture, for the first time, to ascribe to Giovanni da Milano, although it is not one of his most characteristic works. It is a half-length figure of the Virgin standing, holding the Child on her left arm, in the Gallery of Strasbourg. A half-length figure of the Saviour in a trefoil above bestows a blessing with one hand and holds an open book in the other (fig. 117).

A somewhat damaged fresco in the Carmine church, Florence (fig. 118), shows much connection with the foregoing panel and the Prato altar-piece, and although the quality of painting is less good, I think we might perhaps include it with Giovanni's late works (¹).

On a Gothic throne adorned with Cosmati mosaics, the Virgin sits holding the Child Who bends towards a knight, kneeling in adoration to the left of the throne; a nun in similar attitude forms his pendant on the right. Two saints stand to either side, those nearest the donors, SS. James and John the Evangelist(?) presenting them to the Virgin with a protecting gesture. The other two saints are SS. Antony Abbot and Barbara. On the whole it is not a very characteristic work of the master's and the question of its attribution must remain problematic.

The same may be said of a polyptych in the sacristy of the same church, representing the enthroned Virgin with two angels in the centre, and two saints to either side, each on a separate panel (fig. 119). This painting, which is very often ascribed to Andrea da Firenze, shows much more connection with Giovanni's manner; the long-necked silhouette of the young deacon, Leonard, to the left and the figure of St. John the Baptist are even very peculiar to the master's art, and the fine quality of the painting excludes the possibility of its being only a school work.

A charming picture of a decidedly earlier date is the small triptych in the Accademia, Florence (fig. 120). It shows in the centre the Madonna seated on a cushion which, although placed at the height of a chair, does not seem to be supported by anything; two miniature donors kneel in the left lower corner. On the left wing are four saints — SS. Catherine, John the Baptist, Dorothy and Antony Abbot — and the angel Gabriel above; on

(¹) Signor *Toesca* does not agree with this attribution.

the right the figure of the Virgin Mary completes the representation of the Annunciation while below is depicted the Crucifixion with the Madonna, St. John and Mary Magdalene at the foot of the Cross and four little angels hovering around the Crucified. In the dispersed de Marquard collection, Florence, I remember

Fig. 118. Giovanni da Milano (?), Madonna and saints. Cloister, Carmine Church, Florence. Photo Anderson.

seeing, a small picture of the Madonna, similar in shape to the central panel of the triptych in the Accademia and showing a strong resemblance in execution. I think it may be attributed to the same period in Giovanni's career. (¹)

Two other works by Giovanni da Milano do not display the fine technical qualities that we have noticed until now in all his

---

(¹) A short time ago, I saw it again, for sale first in Florence and then in Rome, and a further examination only helped to confirm my first impression.

Fig. 119. Giovanni da Milano, polyptych. Carmine Church, Florence.
Photo Reali.

PAINTING IN LOMBARDY AND PIEDMONT. 237

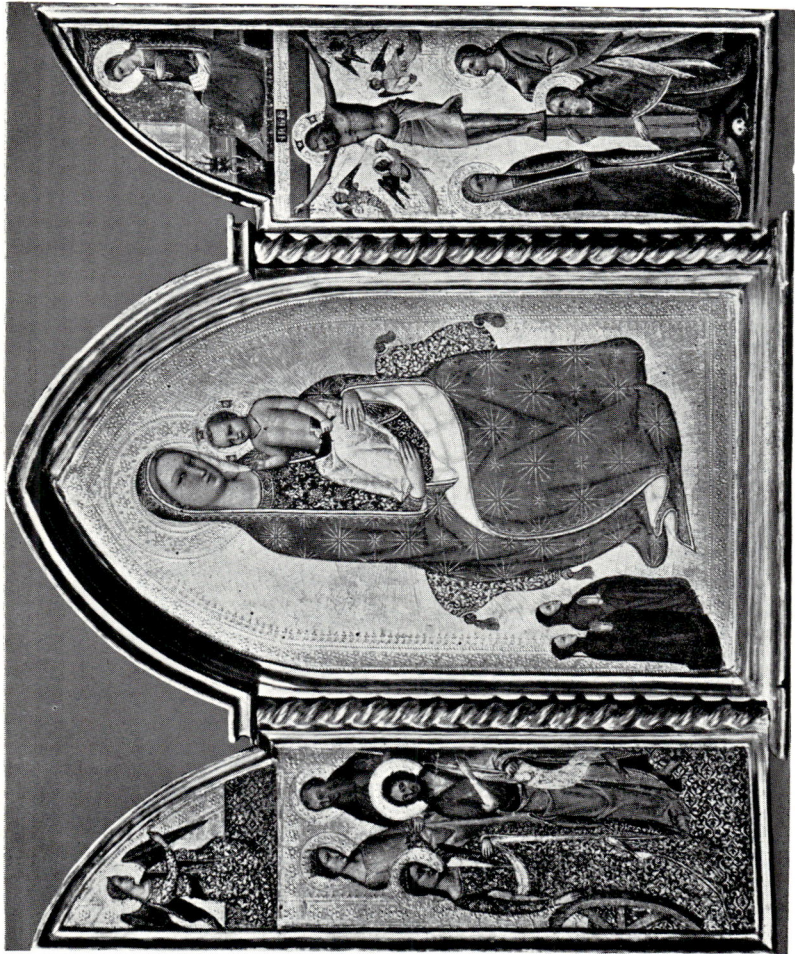

Fig. 120. Giovanni da Milano, triptych. Accademia, Florence.
Photo Brogi.

productions; they are, however, so characteristic of the master that we can have little doubt as to their authenticity.

One of them which I think is going to be transferred from the Roman National Gallery to the new museum in the Palazzo Venezia, is composed of eight small panels (fig. 121).

In the centre the Virgin, sitting on a throne inlaid in marble, holds the Child standing on her knee; two angels are placed at either side. Above on the left the Annunciation is seen taking place in a room; a lectern separates the angel and the Virgin who has just risen from her seat; both pieces of furniture are again adorned with marble mosaics. The adjacent panel on the right shows the Nativity which takes place under an open shelter against a rocky background; the Madonna, sitting on the ground under the shelter, gazes at the Child Whom she holds in her arms; the animals look over the top of the manger while Joseph sits pensively nearby. On each of the panels at the sides of the central one, two saints are represented; to the left they are SS. Nicholas and Lawrence(?) and to the right SS. Julian Hospitator and James.

The three panels on the lowest row show the Crucifixion with the Virgin, St. John and two small angels; the mourning over the Lord's body under the Cross; and SS. Margaret and Catherine.

The figures do not display the forceful drawing and mannered form of Giovanni's later works but they are very graceful although somewhat flat.

The second of these two works which we can be sure are from Giovanni's hand, is an Annunciation on two panels in the Pisa Gallery. It is even earlier than the previous picture and in all probability one of Giovanni's youthful productions. The kneeling angel is represented on one panel and on the other the Virgin seated, holding a book in one hand and pressing the other to her bosom in a gesture of timidity. The drawing is rather clumsy but the folds of the drapery are well depicted. The Virgin's head is very characteristic of Giovanni da Milano and justifies our attribution to this master.

Mr. Sirén has ascribed to this artist a drawing in the Print Cabinet in Berlin representing the Crucifixion ([1]); the appearance of the drawing which in manner is reminiscent of the Pietà of 1365, upholds the attribution ([2]).

([1]) O. *Sirén*, Florentiner Trecento Zeichnungen, Jahrb. der K. Preus. Kunstsamml., 1906, p. 209.

([2]) I think the following works can be considered as the master's own: *Amsterdam,* Lanz coll , Crucifixion with four figures under the Cross; *Florence,* Acton coll., small panel of the Madonna between two saints (?); *London,* Roger Fry coll., the wing of an altar-piece showing many saints,

Fig. 121. Giovanni da Milano, the Virgin, saints and scenes from the Life of Christ. Palazzo Venezia, Rome.

Photo Anderson.

There are many elements in Giovanni da Milano's painting that make us qualify him as a member of the Florentine school, but at the same time he retains many characteristics of the art of his native country which, however, as I have already said, was very much dominated by Florence.

In the Florentine school, Giovanni should be classed with the group of Orcagnesque artists; his works nevertheless are strongly reminiscent of Daddi's art and even of Giotto's. From the former he borrowed certain Sienese peculiarities that mislead some writers into believing that Giovanni himself was influenced by the Sienese school. I do not find any reason to believe this, while his connection with Daddi is very manifest in the figures of the triptych in the Accademia, Florence,

an attribution made by Mr. Sirén. *Modena*, belonging to the advocate Bergolli, a Virgin and Child in an attitude of affection, one third life size (Crowe and Cavalcaselle, op. cit.). *Paris*, Martin Le Roy coll., Pietà, the Virgin holding the dead body of Christ on her knee. *Philadelphia*, Johnson coll., the angel delivering St. Peter from prison (O. Sirén, The Burlington Magazine, XIV, 1908—9, p. 192 and accepted by Mr. Berenson in his catalogue of the collection p. 5). Whether an enthroned Madonna, originally in the Artaud de Montor collection and known from the reproduction in the catalogue, was really by Giovanni himself, is difficult to say. A considerable resemblance to the master's manner certainly existed (Suida, Florentinische Maler, pl. 27 attributes it to Giovanni). Many of the other attributions have already been rightly protested against by Signor Toesca. I do not think that any of the following works, although they all show his influence, are by Giovanni da Milano: *Arezzo*, Gallery (13), standing Madonna dated 1367 (Rassegna d'Arte, 1915, p 84; Salmi, Catal. della Pinac. comun. d'Arezzo, Citta di Castello, 1921, p. 19: influenced by Giov. da Milano). *Berlin*, Gallery, mourning over the Lord's body under the Cross; the form of the tomb, however, is identical with that in the fresco of the Resurrection of Lazarus in the Rinuccini chapel. *Cracow*, Czatoryski Museum, Madonna between SS. Lawrence and Dorothy; Giovanni's influence is manifest but the work is too inferior to be from the master's own hand (M. Logan Berenson, Dipinti italiani a Cracovia, Rassegna d'Arte, 1915, p. 1). *Florence*, Uffizi, Store-room (4696), two female saints (Salmi, L'Arte, 1913, p. 210, note 5: Orcanesque, influenced by Giov. da Milano); Horne Museum, St. Paul and the Baptist (75, 76), (attrib. by Horne to Giov. da Milano but sooner the outcome of the combined influences of this artist and of Andrea da Firenze). *New York*, Metropolitan Museum, a lunette with the half-length figure of the Madonna and two adorers, apparently a school work (Sirén, Giottino und seine Stellung in der Gleichzeitigen Florentinischen Malerei, Leipzig, 1908, p. 91); Historical Society, Crucifixion, previously in the Artaud de Montor collec-

especially in those of the Crucifixion on the right wing. On the other hand the plastic and other qualities of the Prato polyptych and the one from the Ognissanti church, now in the Uffizi, are those of a genuine follower of Orcagna.

Whether Giovanni da Milano became familiar with the Giottesque style of painting in Lombardy or whether he studied it in Florence cannot be ascertained, but the fact remains that he owes certain features of his art to this tradition. The compositions are similar as well as the obvious desire to relate the narrative in the most concise manner. It is true that in Lombard painting the artist generally surrounds the principal actors with a fairly large number of persons, who, however, take no part in the proceedings, which are depicted with Giottesque simplicity. The com-

---

tion (Suida, Florentinische Maler, pl. 25, ascribes it to Giovanni da Milano, P. Toesca, op. cit., p. 283, to the miniaturist Giovanni di Benedetto. In the catalogue of the Artaud de Montor collection and in that of the Historical Society this picture is ascribed to Botticelli!). *Parma*, Gallery, nos. 427 and 433, two panels each showing four figures of saints; a school work. *Philadelphia*, Johnson coll., (120), triptych, Nativity, Crucifixion, saints and Annunciation (Berenson in his Catal. of the collection calls it school of Allegretto Nuzi). *Prato*, S. Domenico, lunette over the door on which is represented the Virgin between SS. Nicholas and Dominic (Crowe and Cavalcaselle, op. cit., have attributed it to Giovanni and this has been generally accepted as correct but I think it is a school work). *Rome*, National Gallery, Coronation of the Virgin, considerably repainted (Sirén, Monatsheft für Kunstwissensch., 1908, p. 1122; Suida, op. cit., pl. 18 and Sirén, Giottino, p. 91). I do not agree with this attribution and find the picture shows more connection with Nardo di Cione (v. Vol. III, p. 490[1]); Vatican Gallery, no. 62 a triptych with the Crucifixion and scenes from the Passion; nos. 93—95, the meal in the house of the Pharisee, the Crucifixion and Noli me tangere; no. 79, the Ascension (Sirén, Giottino, p. 92; later the same writer, Alcuni note aggiuntive a quadri primitivi nella Galleria Vaticana, L'Arte, 1921, p. 59, retracts the attribution to Giovanni of the former pictures but maintains that of the Ascension (Toesca, op. cit., p. 226 notes 2—3, makes a mistake in stating that Sirén attributes the first two to Giottino). In my opinion all these pictures are somewhat later productions of the Florentine school; there are, however, in the Vatican Gallery two other pictures which show a much closer connection with Giovanni's art: no. 67 Nativity of the Madonna and no. 66 Crucifixion with two angels, the Virgin, St John and an adoring Dominican monk (Sirén, L'Arte, loc. cit., attributes the first of these panels to Maso-Giottino, the second to Andrea da Firenze, v. Vol. III, pp. 421[1] and 441).

positions are very different in the frescoes in Sta. Croce that Giovanni left to an assistant.

The way in which Giovanni surrounds his figures and the manner in which he uses the site of the action as the background (compare for example Giovanni's fresco of Joachim driven from the Temple with Giotto's representation of the Lord driving the merchants from the Temple) are typical Giottesque features. Then again both artists represent an interior in an almost symbolic manner, the unreality of which is very incongruous with the naturalness of the action.

In the scene of the meal in the house of the Pharisee, Giovanni shows both the exterior and interior of the room at the same time by the simple means of suppressing one wall, and this is thoroughly Giottesque. Giovanni has that directness of depicting an event that Giotto himself possessed. His expressions and attitudes, in fact the entire action of his pictures, are very real without any mystical idealism, while those scenes, in which the presence of some august personage ought to give a certain solemnity, are rendered in an even simpler manner than by Giotto himself.

The characteristic in Giovanni's art that betrays his adhesion to the Lombard school sooner than to the Florentine, is his peculiar chiaroscuro technique, so different from the plastic effects we see in the works of the good Florentine artists. The elongated proportions of rather fantastic elegance, resulting in somewhat feebly constructed forms, is another detail which links him with the Lombard painters and differentiates him from the Florentines; as too his warm brilliant colouring, reminiscent of Sienese painting, and his curious and often ugly faces, with their exaggeratedly individual features. In his frescoes in the Rinuccini chapel and in the paintings at Viboldone, Mocchirolo and Lentate, we find grimacing faces alongside those of a charming regular beauty, a contrast never seen in Florentine productions.

Moreover, as I have already remarked, the chief actors in Giovanni's scenes are not grouped in a more complicated manner than in Giottesque art, but he, as other Lombard artists, adds a large number of accessory figures, which, as it were, constitute the audience. Lastly, the intimacy, the introduction of contemporary costumes, the numerous homely details which give his pictures the appearance of "scènes de genre" (v. the Nativity of the Virgin) and the effects of perspective that add considerably to the depth of his representations are all elements that belong to North Italian painting — we have already found them in Padua and Verona (¹) — and not to the Florentine school. Further, as I have previously had occasion to mention, Giovanni's iconography is not Florentine; the manner, for instance in which Lazarus is depicted coming out of his tomb is not at all traditional.

In short, Giovanni da Milano who was active in Florence and native of Lombardy where the art of this Tuscan city was so widely disseminated, nevertheless shows in his works a good number of characteristics which are not of Florentine origin but which he possesses in common with his fellow countrymen. On the other hand Giovanni introduced the chiaroscuro technique into Florence where it was accepted and developed until it reached its acme in Masaccio's paintings.

Almost contemporary with Giovanni da Milano's appearance in Florence is the execution of some frescoes in his native country, those in the church of Viboldone, near Milan, which the inscription dates from 1349 (²). The paintings in question are found in the choir; those on the walls, although belonging to the same school, are of later date. The principal fresco represents the Virgin sitting on an imposing throne to the left of which are placed the archangel Gabriel, near whom kneels the donor, and St. John the Baptist and to the right SS. Nicholas and Bernard.

The date is seen below the central part. Above the arch there is an important fragment of a Last Judgment. The Saviour is represented in a mandorla surrounded by eight angels; below are the Saved with three little naked figures emerging from their tombs and the Damned in Hell tortured by Satan and devils. At either side the Apostles form a row headed by the Virgin and St. John. The painting is of excellent quality and very fine technique, showing graceful figures such as are to be found in Florentine works executed under a Sienese influence. Types,

---

(¹) I agree with Signor *Toesca*, however, that there does not exist a very close connection between Giovanni and Altichiero.

(²) *W. Suida*, Le opere di Giovanni da Milano in Lombardia, Rassegna d'Arte, 1906, p. 11. *The Same*, Studien zur Trecento Malerei, Repert. f. Kunstwis., XXXI, p. 212.

proportions and the chiaroscuro technique all bear a very strong resemblance to what we find in Giovanni da Milano's art without, however, there being any question of indentifying the artist who was active here with this master (¹).

These frescoes are the only works belonging to this group that we can date from the middle of the 14th century; all the others are later. At the end of the nave of the same church we find some examples of such paintings which may be assigned to about the year 1370 (²). The arch that separates the nave from the choir, is adorned with a representation of the Crucifixion in which four angels hover around the Redeemer, and groups of agitated people are placed at the sides of the Cross. Above the arch-way we find on one hand the Last Supper, the Prayer in the Olive Garden, the Betrayal of Judas, with the Flagellation and the Calvary lower down and opposite, the Descent from the Cross, the Ascension, the doubting Thomas and Pentecost, while in the four divisions of the vault are depicted the Annunciation, the Adoration of the Magi, the Presentation in the Temple and the Baptism of Christ. These last frescoes are of a quality very inferior to the others and it is only in a vague similarity of form that we are able to find any analogy with Giovanni's art. The other scenes, however, are full of dramatic force, and besides a resemblance of technical details, this artist shows us the same types, the same elongated proportions and the same exaggerated realism, not only in the attitudes and actions but also in the facial expressions, as we found in Giovanni da Milano's painting. His iconography too differs in several points from Giotto's.

Another painter whose works we find in this church was a feeble unrefined artist; nevertheless he seems to have followed Giovanni da Milano's models. We possess from his hand a representation of the Wise and Foolish Virgins, a figure of the Saviour and some prophets (³). The chief interest of these paintings is that they provide us with a proof of the existence of a connection between Giovanni's manner and that of provincial

---

(¹) As *Suida*, op. cit., does.

(²) *G. Cagnola*, Gli affreschi di Viboldone e di Solaro, Rassegna d'Arte, 1907, p. 37. *Toesca*, op. cit., p. 240.

(³) *D. Sant' Ambrogio*, Le vergini sagge e le folli del Vangelo negli affreschi di Viboldone, Rassegna d'Arte, 1905, p. 190. *Toesca*, op. cit., p. 246.

Fig. 122. The Crucifixion, fresco, circa 1365. Oratory, Mocchirolo.

Photo Ist. Art. Graf.

Lombard artists of little importance, a connection which we can doubtless ascribe to the existence of a prototype. The frescoes in the right nave seem to be slightly earlier than those at the end of the central nave in the church of Viboldone; a comparison might be made between them and those in the little oratory of Solaro in the region of Saronna (1). This church was built in 1366 and the decoration was probably undertaken immediately after, so that the paintings must be about contemporary with those in the central nave of the Viboldone church which I ascribed to about 1370.

The principal scene here is again the Crucifixion in which, besides the Saviour, we see some angels and a fairly large number of other figures. To one side the history of the Virgin and her parents is illustrated on three rows of scenes including Joachim and Anna performing charitable acts, Joachim driven from the Temple, the Meeting at the Golden Gate, the Nativity of the Virgin Mary, her Presentation in the Temple, the Virgin's visit to the sanctuary (?) and her Marriage; while the scenes, which comprised the lowest row, are very damaged. On the other side we find the Annunciation, the Visitation, the Nativity with the adoring shepherds and the Flight into Egypt; the entire lower division is occupied by a fresco of the Adoration of the Magi. Further to either side is seen a figure of a saint with a half-length figure of a prophet above; another is visible above the window.

From his tragic sense, force of expression and simplicity of composition one would say that this artist was particularly inspired by Giotto; all the same his types, the elongated form of his heads and figures, and the effects of chiaroscuro which are very pronounced in his art, are all, as we have seen, typical Lombard qualities. Nor is his iconography Florentine; the scene of Joachim and Anna giving charity is, as Signor Toesca remarks, but rarely depicted, nevertheless we find it in other Lombard works of the 14th century.

In Brianza, there exist two series of frescoes in the oratories

---

(1) *D. Sant' Ambrogio.* L'oratorio di Solaro, Arch. Stor. Lomb., XX, p. 842. *Cagnola*, op. cit. *Toesca*, op. cit., p. 233.

Fig. 123. St. Ambrosius chastising the heretics and the mystical marriage of St. Catherine, fresco, circa 1365. Oratory, Mocchirolo.

Photo Ist. Art. Graf.

at Mocchirolo and at Lentate (¹), and although they are of very different artistic merit, I think it best to discuss them together, as they were executed for members of the same family and one more or less after the model of the other. As the paintings, which, in concurrence with Signor Toesca, I believe to be of later date, are found in a church that was built in 1368, we can date the mural decoration from about 1370; the second series must consequently have been executed a few years earlier.

At Mocchirolo the Crucifixion again occupies the principal place, the composition is simpler and the figures larger in proportion with the space the artist had at his disposal (fig. 122). Four angels fly around the Crucified; the fainting Virgin is supported by two companions on the left, St. John stands alone on the right while Mary Magdalene kneels at the foot of the Cross. The vault is adorned with an image of the Redeemer bestowing a blessing in an aureole, and the angles with the four symbols of the Evangelists. To one side we see a representation of the mystical marriage of St. Catherine, who, kneeling beside the Virgin's throne, stretches out her hand for the Child Jesus to place the ring on her finger; close by St. Ambrosius, seated at a desk, flagellates the heretics (fig. 123).

Opposite, the members of the Porro family, who had the church constructed, are portrayed kneeling in adoration before the enthroned Madonna. The father offers a model of the church to the Infant Christ; behind him kneel his wife and four children behind whom again are depicted a second woman with four other children (fig. 124). Many angels are represented above, some carrying models of churches others playing on musical instruments. The different frescoes are surrounded by beautiful borders of an ornamental pattern in which some busts of saints or prophets are seen.

There is no reason to believe that these frescoes are from different hands. I think we owe them all to one painter who was one of the best Lombard masters of the 14th century. Like all gifted artists, he is not at all monotonous; the tragic event of the Crucifixion has inspired him to represent it in vigorous lines and

---

(¹) *G. Carotti*, Pitture giottesche nell' oratorio di Mocchirolo, Arch. Stor. Lomb., 1887, p. 765. *Suida*, op. cit., *Toesca*, op. cit., p. 248.

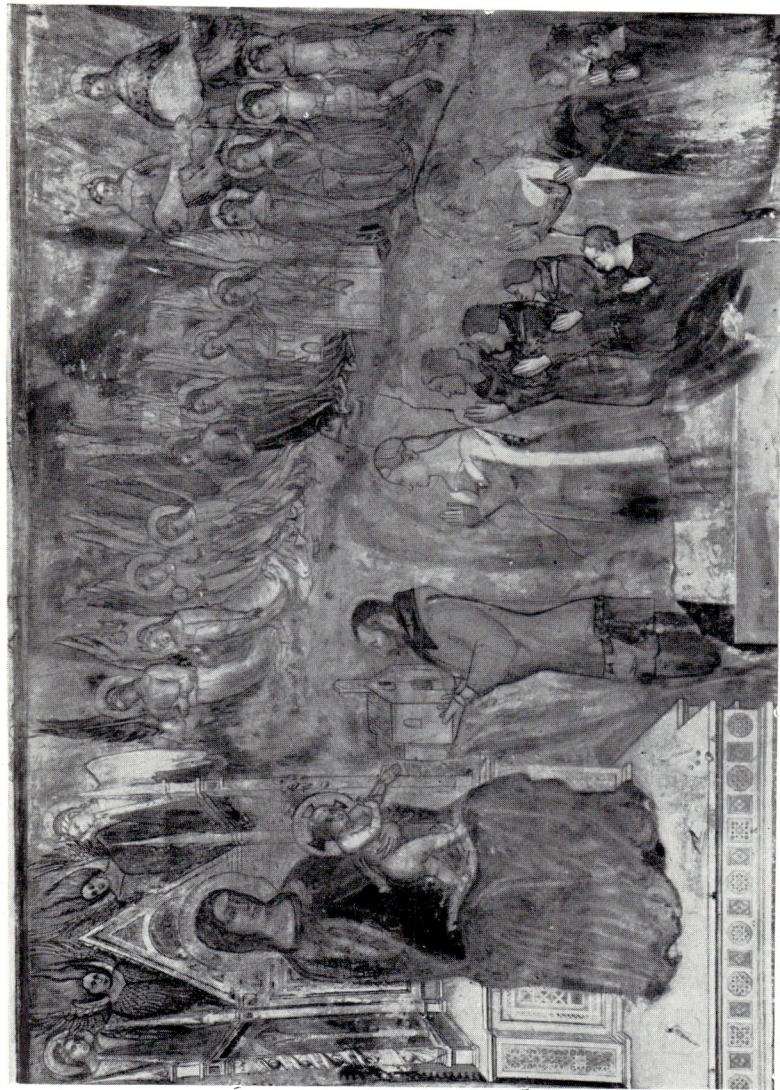

Fig. 124. The Porro family adoring the Virgin, fresco, circa 1365. Oratory, Mocchirolo. Photo Ist. Art. Graf.

with marked realism, while he has conceived his images of saints in a more idealistic manner and displays more refinement in their execution. The noble profile of St. Catherine in particular, is exquisitely subtle and possesses a finesse and sweetness of expression that almost equals the Sienese masters, of whose works the figures of St. Ambrosius and of the Saviour in the vault also remind us. The portraits of the Porro family, on the other hand, are markedly individual and not in every case very flattering. The two Madonnas and the angels are among the least pleasing figures. Their forms, somewhat too robust, as is the case with most of this artist's figures, are reminiscent of the Florentine school and not of the Sienese. The warm and sometimes even brilliant colouring, however, is an element common to the latter of these two schools rather than to the former.

We find reminiscences of Giovanni da Milano's art in the types, especially of the figures of the Crucifixion and the chiaroscuro technique.

The church of Lentate, near Mocchirolo, that Stefano Porro, Galeaggo Visconti's counsellor, founded in 1368, is adorned with a long series of frescoes (¹). Here it is easy to distinguish the work of two different artists, one very superior to the other. The latter, however, so closely followed the style of his more talented contemporary, that the combination was evidently that of master and pupil. The better of these two artists executed the fresco in the choir that corresponds to the principal painting at Mocchirolo. Here the donor, carrying a model of the church, his wife, three sons and three daughters kneel before St. Stephen, the patron saint of the head of the family (fig. 125). From the same hand are the representations on the chancel arch of the Resurrection of the Dead, with a curious series of naked people rising from their tombs, and of the Last Judgment, with a large number of saints and an image of the Madonna. This painter is not, as has been sometimes imagined, the same as the one who worked at Mocchirolo, although he obviously imitates his style of painting. Although not without merit, these paintings are of an inferior quality of technique, as well as of colouring and individuality. Comparing the two series of portraits we find those at Lentate, especially of the younger members of the family, lacking personality; all the children have the same straight little mouth with firmly closed lips.

(¹) *Suida*, Studien etc., p. 212. *Carotti*, op. cit., *Toesca*, op. cit., p. 256.

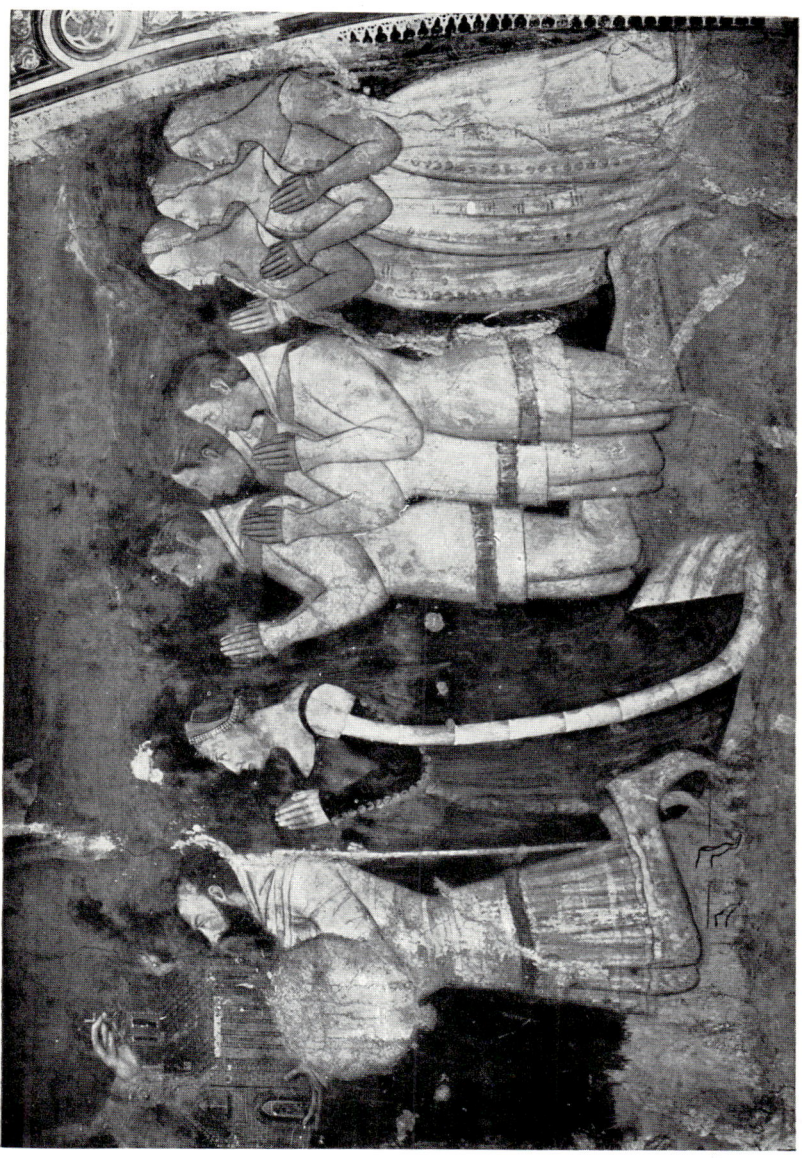

Fig 125. Stefano Porro, his wife and family adoring St. Stephen, fresco, circa. 1370. Oratory, Lentate.

Photo Ist. Art. Graf.

In the rest of the decoration which includes an important Crucifixion in the usual place (fig. 126), the marriage of St. Catherine, St. George slaying the dragon and the story of St. Stephen and his relics narrated in a great many small scenes (fig. 127), we but rarely find the master's hand. The assistant's work can be recognized not only by the curious shape of the mouths he depicts, sometimes even grimacing, but also by the form of his hands with

Fig. 126. A Detail of the Crucifixion, circa 1370. Oratory, Lentate.
Photo Ist. Art. Graf

thin tapering figures, those of the master being sooner fat and rounded. I think, however, that at least the scenes illustrating the end of the saint's life and those concerning the priest Lucian are for the greater part from the hand of the principal artist. The compositions of this cycle of scenes are very simple, sometimes even poor; their great quality is the forceful display of dramatic feeling which however, on account of an exaggerated effort to produce realism, has often resulted in vulgarity.

A fragment of a fresco in the tower of the church of Trezzo, also in Brianza, should, on account of the subject as well as the

Fig. 127. Scenes from the legend of St. Stephen, circa 1370. Oratory, Lentate.
Photo Ist. Art. Graf.

style of the painting, be associated with the works with which we have just dealt at Mocchirolo and Lentate.

Here again a bearded man in contemporary costume kneels in adoration (¹). Close to him is the figure of a standing saint (Mary Magdalene?) but this was no doubt one of the figures at the side of the Madonna who, with the rest of the fresco, has disappeared.

Returning to Milan we find in the church of the abbey of Chiaravalle some mural paintings in which Signor Toesca (²) recognizes two different hands; to the better of the two he ascribes the saints above the tribune, while he thinks the other executed the scenes from the Virgin's life under the cupola. Both artists, especially the latter, were inspired by the Florentine school; and it is curious to note that in their hardness of outline and lack of charm, these frescoes reveal the masters' close connection with that movement which, just at this time — 1370-1380 — manifests itself in the Florentine school.

The same phenomenon will be observed at Vertemate, near Como, in the decoration in and around the apse of the old church of the monastery (³).

The chief representation here is the Coronation of the Virgin in the midst of saints and groups of angels; we see also the dead Saviour, towards Whom angels are flying, and below this fresco, two scenes from the life of St. Benedict. Of the two medallions one is empty, the other shows Abraham, his hand arrested at the moment he is about to strike his son. These paintings are very superior to those we found at Chiaravalle; they can even be compared to the good Florentine productions of the end of the 14th century, and more than one writer has remarked their resemblance to the works of Angolo Gaddi. We find the same facility of drawing and a certain similarity of proportions and types, but also the same superficiality and want of inspiration. A Lombard feature, however, is the manner in which the relief of the faces is depicted by strongly marked light and shade.

Some very fine figures, executed in quite another manner, will be found in the decoration of S. Biagio at Bellinzona (³).

(¹) *U. Nebbia*, La Brianza, Bergamo, 1912, p. 23.

(²) *Toesca*, op. cit., p. 242.

(³) *D.S.*, La Badia di Vertemate, Arch. Stor. Lomb., 1905, III, p. 214. *Toesca*, op. cit., p. 242.

Around a rather crude image of St. Christopher, doubtless the work of a local little master, is a frieze adorned with six busts, each in a diamond-shaped frame, very finely executed and of great charm, reminding one strongly of the productions of the best followers of the school of Simone Martini. It is remarkable that the Infant Christ on St. Christopher's shoulder is apparently of the same technique as the busts in the lozenge-shaped ornaments and greatly superior in quality to the image of the giant saint; it is, however, probable that the actual appearance of this last figure is due to restoration. Some scattered fragments reveal that the entire façade was once decorated, but with the exception of the painting just described, there remains only the fresco in the lunette, representing the half-length figure of the Virgin between those of SS. Peter and Blaise. It is a work without doubt by the same artist who executed the busts in the frame around St. Christopher, for it displays the same sweetness of feeling and finesse of technique. It cannot be said that this master was solely dependent on the Sienese school; his elongated forms and strong contrasts of light and shade betray his Lombard origin; his source of inspiration was in all probability the same as Giovanni da Milano's.

It is possible that the Lombard artists got their model for the frescoes representing the donor and his family kneeling in adoration before the Virgin, from Verona, where similar compositions were more frequent, and where we find the magnificent example by Altichiero in the Cavalli chapel.

An important and earlier Lombard fresco somewhat of the same type is the one already described of 1327 on the Fissiraga tomb at Lodi, but the chief characteristics — the adorers seen in profile, dressed in contemporary costume and depicted about the same size as the Virgin — are here absent.

Besides those at Mocchirolo and Lentate, there exist three other devotional frescoes, now detached and preserved, two in the Bergamo Gallery and one in the Brera, Milan. Those in the former gallery are undoubtedly by the same artist and show respectively two knights kneeling before the Virgin to whom SS. Catherine and Francis seem to recommend them, and a knight with his page adoring the Madonna to whom he is presented by SS. Barbara (?) and Bartholomew (fig. 128).

Fig. 128. A Knight and his page adoring the Virgin, circa 1380. Gallery, Bergamo. Photo Ist. Art. Graf.

The former fresco bears the inscription: "*MCCCLXXXII die XVIIII Augusti*" (¹). These paintings are not of very fine technique; certain Giottesque elements in the figures are reminiscent of the contemporary Veronese school sooner than that

---

(¹) *Crowe and Cavalcaselle*, op. cit., p. 254. *Toesca*, op. cit., p. 273. *G. Frizzoni*, Le Gallerie dell' Accademia Carrara in Bergamo, Bergamo, 1907, p. 15, seems to have been unaware of the existence of this inscription and dates the first fresco from the beginning of the 15th century. *C. Ricci*, Rassegna d'Arte, 1922, p. 140, is apparently also ignorant of the fact that one of the frescoes bears a date and assigns them both to about 1400.

Fig. 129. Simone da Corbetta, Madonna, saints and adorer, fresco, circa 1382. Brera, Milan. Photo Alinari.

of Lombardy, but the strong light effects used on the faces is a very characteristic Lombard feature.

The fresco in the Brera (no. 138, fig. 129), is of greatly inferior quality and is probably the work of a provincial artist who reproduced a traditional composition in a very rustic manner. Here, besides the enthroned Madonna and the knight kneeling in adoration, we see St. Catherine of Alexandria, a female saint holding an arrow and St. George. The principal interest of this fresco which is entirely lacking in artistic merits and which formerly adorned the tomb of Theodoric de Chur in the Servi Monastery in Milan, is the inscription giving the name of the artist which it originally bore and which has been handed down to us by older writers; it ran: *"Hoc opus fecerunt fieri Enricus et Reinardus p aīa (anima) Teodorici de Coira qui obiit sub anno MCCCLXXXII Septebris. Symon de Corbeta fecit"* (¹). Cavalcaselle attributed to the same Simone da Corbetta some fresco fragments in the Brera store-room, representing the Virgin and Child with some other figures and an image of St. Christopher, while Signor Toesca remarks a resemblance to Simone da Corbetta's manner in an even more inferior painting of the Madonna and two saints in the church of S. Giorgio at Bellano.

Another mediocre Lombard artist whose name has come down to us is Bassanolo de Magneris; he has left us an enthroned Madonna amidst saints with a representation of the Crucifixion below (²), in the church of S. Cristoforo on the Naviglio, near Milan. In neither the manner of Simone da Corbetta nor of Bassanolo do we discover any characteristics peculiar to Lombard painting.

Before passing to Lombard works of later date, I should like to discuss the panel paintings of this more primitive period. With the exception of those that Giovanni da Milano executed in Florence, they are extremely rare. A panel of the Madonna to whom a saint presents the kneeling donor, rather similar in composition to the above mentioned frescoes, is preserved in the Museum of Worcester, U. S. A (³). There exists a series of panel paintings, however, that is almost entirely unknown and that may be classed with the best productions of the 14th century (⁴).

(¹) *Crowe and Cavalcaselle*, op. cit., p. 249. *Toesca*, op. cit., p. 391.

(²) *Toesca*, op. cit., p. 392.

(³) Worcester Art Museum, Catalogue of paintings and drawings, Worcester, 1922, p. 5 and Art News, 9th June 1923, ascribe it to the French school of the early 15th century.

(⁴) As far as I know Mr. *Langton Douglas* is the only writer who mentions them (*Crowe and Cavalcaselle*, op. cit., p. 126 note 1) but he attributes them to Bartolo di Fredi and his pupils, an attribution which I cannot accept. The catalogue describes them as Sienese school of the second half of the 14th century.

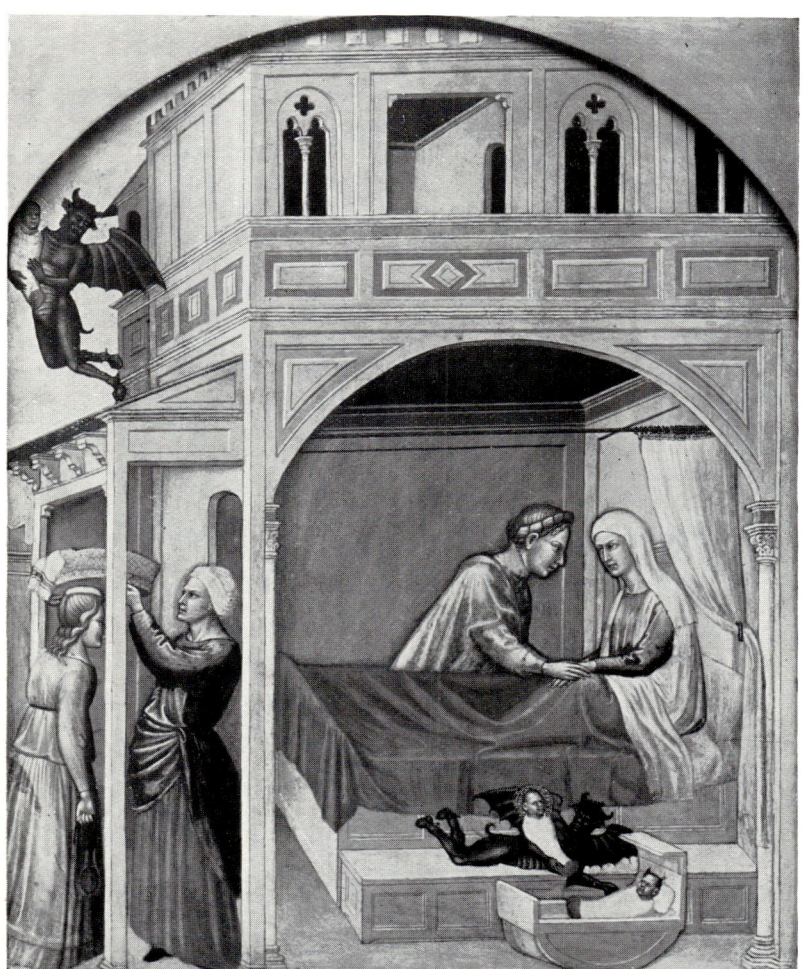

Fig. 130. Lombard School(?), Scene from the legend of St. Stephen, 2nd half of the 14th century. Städelsche Kunstinstitut, Frankfort.

These pictures which are a fair size (74 × 59 and 69 × 59 c.m.) are seven in number and are found in the gallery of the Städeliche Kunstinstitut in Frankfort on the Main (3 A—G).

The scenes illustrate the life of St. Stephen and represent ([1])

([1]) The first four scenes are but rarely illustrated; the interpretation of the entire series is given in the catalogue. *H. Weizsäcker,* Catalog des Gemälde-Gallerie des Städelschen Kunstinstituts in Frankfurt a.M., Frankfort, 1900, p. 319.

Fig. 131. Lombard School (?), Scene from the legend of St. Stephen, 2nd half of the 14th century. Städelsche Kunstinstitut, Frankfort.

(1) the devil carrying away the newborn Stephen and placing in his cradle a diabolic child (fig. 130); (2) the infant who was nourished by a white deer found by the bishop; (3) on a sign from the saint the statues of heathen gods over the gate of a town falling in fragments (fig. 131) (4); the saint's return to his parent's house where he finds the child that the Devil had substituted still in his cradle and combined with this, the saint causing the demoniacal child to be destroyed by fire (fig. 132); (5) St. Stephen consecrated deacon by a bishop (St. Peter?) (fig. 133); (6) the

Fig. 132. Lombard School (?), Scene from the legend of St. Stephen, 2nd ha of the 14th century. Städelsche Kunstinstitut, Frankfort.

saint disputing with members of the libertine sect in Jerusalem, and (7) the stoning of St. Stephen.

I think it highly probable that these panels belong to the Lombard school but cannot be absolutely certain about it. The feeling for refined beauty that emanates from them reminds us of the works by Giovanni da Milano and the artist of Mocchirolo, but they surpass the work of those artists in their high artistic merits, harmony of form and richness of colouring.

The types, however, belong to the Lombard school; in the first scene, the figure of the woman in bed with her head veiled is very much after Giovanni's manner. We also note throughout the series the strong lights on the faces and the very subtle chiaroscuro effects which are peculiar to Lombard painting. I think, however, that the master, to whom we owe these panels, was familiar with Altichiero's art, and it is from this source that he acquired his taste for harmonious forms, regularity of feature, the narrative but not tragic spirit of his recital, as well as his extensive architectural backgrounds and perspective. It is true that the style of his buildings is not the same as Altichiero's, but it is evident that he possessed the same interest in architecture, which, far from being merely an accessory as in Giottesque art, fills up his compositions and draws our attention just as much as the figures themselves. Then again in interior scenes his figures are well surrounded and not only set against a background of the site of the event, while the perspective, especially of the fourth picture, gives a very real impression of depth.

This artist too, like the great masters of Padua and Verona, pays particular attention to detail which he treats in as meticulous a manner as the Sienese. The contemporary costumes, the familiar gestures and the intimacy that prevail in these pictures occasionally give them that appearance of "scènes de genre", so frequent in North Italian art (¹). These remarks, consequently, lead us to attribute the above very fine pictures, which must have been executed about 1370—1380, to a Lombard master who was influenced by the art of Altichiero and Avanzo.

A later Lombard work but of mediocre quality is a Nativity of the Virgin, with the women preparing the bath and others behind the bed, in the Museum of Strasbourg.

The Lombard school apparently spread beyond the frontiers of the region because in the church of St. Catherine at Tiers, in Tyrol, we find frescoes of 1384 illustrating the legend of the titular saint, which show much in common with the style of painting then current in Lombardy (²).

(¹) The coiffure of the woman standing behind the bed in the first scene is also, I think, North Italian.
(²) Bürger, Die Deutsche Malerei, II, p. 237.

Fig. 133. Lombard School, Scene from the legend of St. Stephen, 2nd half of the 14th century. Städelsche Kunstinstitut, Frankfort.

Towards the year 1400, Lombard art, like Veronese painting acquired certain cosmopolitan Gothic elements which resulted in a very mannered style of drawing. This form of art flourished in Lombardy, however, before it attained its full development in Verona and we find there a certain number of examples even of the 14th century; but this movement only reached its culmination in the 15th century and for that reason, as I have said before, its entire production will be treated in another volume.

There are all the same a few Lombard works that belong to the transitional stage between 14th century painting and the later form of art dominated by the Gothic style, and these, I think, should be discussed now.

The earliest evidence of the appearance of the new form of art will be found in a series of scenes originally in the chapel, but now on the left wall of the church of Sta Maria de' Ghirli at Campione([1]). The paintings are twelve in number; six of them represent the angel telling Joseph of the approaching miracle, the Visitation, the Nativity and, at a lower level, the Beheading of St. John the Baptist, Salome bringing the saint's head to her mother and the two women in the prison near the dead body. The other six frescoes are considerably damaged and for that not easily interpreted; one of them might be the Presentation in the Temple and another the Entombment.

The Giottesque school and the influence of Lippo Memmi have been mentioned in connection with these frescoes, but I find no trace of either. They are before all, Lombard works and the facial types and drawing bear a certain resemblance to those of Giovanni da Milano and the masters of Mocchirolo and Lentate, but none the less, there is a considerable difference to be noted. The iconography is very curious and shows no similarity to Giotto's; the compositions are of an extreme simplicity reduced to the essential figures as in the frescoes at Lentate; the buildings are all open loggias, not the rooms cut in section as in Florentine art, but generally constructions consisting of a roof supported on pillars, and represented sometimes from an angle.

The Gothicism is evident in the forms, the proportions and particularly in the drapery which in some of the pictures, is as exaggeratedly Gothic as in the works of de Veris and de' Grassi, that belong to the following stage in the development of this form of art. The frescoes of Sta. Maria de' Ghirli probably date from about 1380.

([1]) *E. Gerspach*, Gli affreschi di Campione, L'Arte, V, 1902, p. 161. *F. Malaguzzi Valeri*, Campione, Rassegna d'Arte, 1908, p. 172. *Toesca*, op. cit., p 263. The fresco of the Last Judgment, which also adorns this church, is a late Gothic work.

Perhaps even an older example of this style of painting is found in Mantua in the church of S. Francesco, where a long series of frescoes on different zones originally illustrated the legend of a Franciscan saint but now only the scene representing his death has been well preserved (¹). This interesting fresco shows us the saint stretched on his bier surrounded by several figures. It is doubtless the realistic individuality of the features that has led Signor Toesca to associate this work with the name of Tommaso da Modena. I think the painter is of later date than the Modenese artist. The Gothicism which, besides in the draperies, is also slightly manifest in the shape of the heads and the delineation of the features, is here in an even more embryonic stage than at Campione.

The vaults of the lateral apsides of the Cremona Cathedral are adorned with frescoes executed in this manner (²). The Old Testament scenes in the triangular divisions not only show a Gothic design that forces us to classify them with the cosmopolitan Gothic productions, but also a taste for intimate details and a realism of narration that confirm our hypothesis. The religious representations here have acquired the aspect of "scènes de genre". This decoration is of slightly later date than the foregoing works.

Some traces of profane Gothic painting is preserved at Brianzale, near Lecco, in an old castle — now a farm — that originally belonged to the Porro family, whose coat of arms is still visible. The decoration includes animals and hunting scenes with figures in elegant costumes of the time, and is the work of a predecessor of Pisanello (³).

A little panel of the Crucifixion with three angels, the Virgin and St. John and Mary Magdalene at the foot of the Cross in the

---

(¹) *A. Patricolo*, La chiesa di S. Francesco a Mantova, Rassegna d'Arte, 1911, p. 35. *Toesca*, op. cit., p. 271.

(²) *L. Lucchini*, Il Duomo di Cremona, Mantua, 1894. *Toesca*, op. cit., p. 397. *B. Vidoni*, La pittura cremonese, Milan, 1824, p. 18. *Rosini*, Storia della pittura italiana, II, p. 147 and other writers of later date attribute these frescoes to Polidoro Casella, a Cremonese painter who is mentioned in 1345, but this decoration is without any doubt, of much later date.

(³) *A. Magni*, Riv. Archeol. della Prov. e Dioc. di Como, 1906, p. 51. *Toesca*, op. cit., p. 396.

church of S. Giorgio in Palazzo in Milan, also reveals a certain tendency towards Gothic forms ([1]).

Of somewhat later date but belonging to the same style are the paintings in the Albizzate Oratory, near Varese ([2]) where Signor Toesca discovers the work of two different artists; one who executed the Saviour in benediction in a mandorla, surrounded by the symbols of the Evangelists and the other and better master who painted the figures of the Apostles in the apsides and, with some assistance, the frescoes on the walls representing incidents from the lives of St. John the Baptist and a holy bishop, in numerous little scenes of very simple composition. The figures are not very beautiful and the forms somewhat feeble but the fine outlines are characteristic of Lombard painting while certain Gothic elements are evident in the drawing of the draperies.

In Milan itself a beautiful Gothic fresco is that, which adorns the tomb of the Robiani family in S. Lorenzo ([3]). It represents the Madonna seated on a complicated throne modelled on those we find in Veronese works, while SS. Lawrence and Ambrosius each present an adorer. Here again Gothic elements in the forms and the draperies intermingle with Lombard peculiarities such as the types of the figures and the chiaroscuro effects.

Besides the works that we have just dealt with, there is a fairly large number of other paintings, but they are mostly by local little masters and only serve to demonstrate the richness of pictorial production in Lombardy at this period ([4]).

([1]) *Toesca*, op. cit., p. 329, attributes it to the miniaturist Anovelo da Imbonate without, in my opinion, sufficient foundation.

([2]) *Toesca*, op. cit., p. 269.

([3]) *Toesca*, op. cit., p. 294.

([4]) The following works might still be mentioned: *Bergamo*, Pinacoteca, frescoes from the old convent of Sta. Marta some of which are finely executed and one dated 1388 (L. Angelini, Affreschi trecenteschi scoperti in Bergamo, Rassegna d'Arte, 1916, p. 9). Crowe and Cavalcaselle, p. 254, mention some other frescoes in the town but they have since disappeared; *Bormio*, in an arch to one side of the parish church and priest's house, a fresco of 1393, the Saviour in a mandorla in benediction and a series of half-length figures of the Virgin, prophets and Apostles, archaic in appearance (Rassegna d'Arte, 1906, p. 137); *Domodossola*, S. Quirico, Madonna and saints by a local artist but influenced by the Giottesque tradition (C. Errera L'Ossola, Bergamo, 1908, p. 45); *Galliano*, some of the figures of saints in

PAINTING IN LOMBARDY AND PIEDMONT. 267

In our survey of Lombard painting of the 14th century we have arrived at the following conclusions.

Firstly, the influence of the archaic art of the 13th century persisted for a long time in this region, traces of it being found even as late as 1330. Secondly we note a strong Florentine influence which resulted in the formation of an isolated local branch of the Florentine school of painting; while towards the end of the 14th century we observe the appearance of a tendency towards Gothicism in Lombard works, at a slightly earlier date than we find it in Verona, and which as we shall shortly see, owed its development to the art of miniature painting. Lastly we find in this district a fairly large number of pictorial productions

---

the crypt of the basilica of S. Vincenzo, most of them, however, are 13th century works (U. Nebbia, La Brianza, p. 136); *Incino*, St. Eufemia, Madonna with two saints and adorers, crudely executed (Idem, p. 102); *Lodi*, S. Francesco, divers isolated votive frescoes of the Madonna with saints, and an Annunciation at Dovera near Lodi, all works in the Gothic style of the end of the 14th century (Toesca, op. cit., p. 401 et seq.); *Lodi Vecchio*, S. Bassiano, Madonna, Annunciation, a holy bishop, St. George killing the dragon, a series of saints and the decapitation of a martyr, fairly archaic productions of local artists (D. Sant' Ambrogio, Lodi Vecchio, pls. IX, XIV and XV); *Mantua*, Palazzo Ducale, some figures of saints (Venturi, Stor. dell' arte ital.,VII,1,p.210, attributes them without any reason to Tommaso da Modena; Toesca, op. cit., p. 272 note 1); Museum, some detached frescoes. Crowe and Cavalcaselle, op. cit., p. 256, cite some other paintings in and around the town that I think have since disappeared: *Milan*, S. Pietro Celestino, fragmentary frescoes including the symbols of the Evangelists, figures of saints, the head of a saint and a figure of the Saviour perhaps from a representation of the Last Judgment; these paintings betray a Tuscan influence (D. Carotti, L'Arte, XI, 1908, p. 142); S. Siro, apse, the Lord in a mandorla between the symbols of the Evangelists (Rassegna d'Arte, 1910, p. 50). Lanzi and Rosini mention some Giottesque frescoes in the sacristy of Sta. Maria delle Grazie; in the museum of the Castello Sforza there are very few works which seem to date from the 14th century; a very mediocre painting of a saint (Helen?, no. 34) may, however, be noted. *Sirmioni*, S. Pietro in Movino a poor fresco of the end of the 14th century (G. Soletro, Lago di Gardo, Bergamo, 1912, p. 32); *Varese*, Baptistery, fresco of the Madonna and of a saint protecting a palace (Toesca, op. cit., p. 151). Rosini, op. cit., vol. II, p. 206, reproduces a little picture — two adorers — that he says is a Milanese work of the 14th century and is signed by a certain Maestro Giuseppe. Judging from the illustration I should say it was of later date and signed: "*M. Georgi*".

by local minor artists, that play no part whatsoever in the artistic evolution.

It has been stated as a certain fact that the explanation of the influence of the Florentine school on Lombard painting is found in Giovanni da Milano's art, but as I have already had occasion to point out, this is by no means sure, and I would even go so far as to say that the hypothesis is highly improbable.

The penetration of Giotto's art into Lombardy might be explained by the presence in Milan of the master himself, and if he did not go in person, in all probability the sumptuous Milanese princes had his most brilliant representatives sent from Florence.

In the first half of the 14th century Florence and Siena were the only two really important artistic centres, and it is evident from the appearance of Lombard painting that it was the former that dominated Lombardy. Moreover, if we believe Vasari, Stefano, whom the Aretin biographer confounds with other Florentine artists, but who really was one of Giotto's pupils, went to Milan, where he undertook a considerable number of works for Matteo Visconti, but on account of illness was forced to return to Florence ([1]).

That the artistic intercourse between Florence and Lombardy was constant and entirely independent of Giovanni da Milano's migration to the Tuscan capital in 1350, is proved by the existence of a more or less developed form of Florentine art in Lombardy prior to this date. Further, what we still know of Giovanni da Milano justifies us in believing that he definitely settled in Florence where he arrived in 1350, acquired the rights of citizenship in 1366 and was still resident there in 1369 when he and other artists were invited by the pope to decorate the papal palace. Consequently far from having introduced Florentine art into Lombardy, Giovanni da Milano executed paintings in Florence that show decided Lombard characteristics. These will be recognized in the proportions of his figures, his types, his chiaroscuro technique and his liking for giving religious pictures the appearance of "scènes de genre", while even his iconography does not belong to the Giottesque traditions.

These peculiarities which differentiate Giovanni from genuine

---

([1]) *Vasari-Milanesi*, I, p. 450.

Florentine artists, are, I think, decidedly Northern. The types in the North of Italy are different from those in Central Italy, but I believe Giovanni's elongated and slightly conventional proportions owe something to Gothic sculpture of more Northern countries. Certainly the aesthetic canon of Giovanni's art and of his compatriots was different from that of the Florentines, the latter being more natural and at the same time more classical.

The more profound study of chiaroscuro effects has always been a characteristic of works executed in Northern regions where climatic conditions produced light effects very different from those we find in more Southern localities.

Lastly the "tableau de genre" is more in keeping with the Northern mentality than with one purely Italian; the sense of dramatic realism in the latter is antagonistic to the intimate worldly details of the former. In the works of Altichiero and Avanzo and in the frescoes of the master of Treviso, however, we find the peculiarities of "scènes de genre".

It is to the same spirit that we owe the taste for profane pictures, examples of which are found in the battle scenes in the castle of Angera (similar to those of Castelbarco near Verona), the frescoes in the vaults at Lodi Vecchio and the hunting scenes at Brianzola, while according to a document of 1380, further hunting scenes were asked for by Giangaleazzo Visconti who commissioned Lodovico Gonzaga of Mantua to order several panels with which he wished to adorn his castle ([1]).

To what extent this art found approval in these regions is demonstrated in miniatures, drawings and extant Lombard paintings of slighty later date, as well as in the profane aspect given to religious representations, such for example as the frescoes in the vault of the Cremona cathedral. Traces of this are manifest in almost all the religious paintings made in Lombardy at this time. All the works are less austere in appearance, generally without much dramatic feeling, but full of little intimate details taken from every day life. The spirit of this art is, consequently, very different from Giotto's.

The evolution of the painting that belonged to, or showed

([1]) *Calvi*, Notizie sulle vite etc. dei principali architetti, scultori, pittori etc. in Milano etc., II, Milan, 1859, p. 92.

connection with the cosmopolitan Gothic manner seems to have been based on the influence that the art of miniature exercised on it; this branch of painting provided another means by which Northern elements penetrated into Lombardy. One of the merits of Signor Toesca's excellent book to which I have frequently referred, is that besides the painting, he deals with all the material of miniature art in Lombardy that has come down to us ([1]) which greatly facilitates the following brief survey of Lombard miniatures.

The school of miniature in Lombardy probably originated from Giottesque paintings, but the earliest examples that we know bear a strong resemblance to the Bolognese school.

It cannot be ascertained where these manuscripts were executed. A codex of St. George in the Ambrosiana Library was doubtless transported from one of the churches in Milan. The illuminations show a decided connection in style with those in a "Pantheon" of Goffredo da Viterbo in the National Library. In both we find those large heavy shades characteristic of the Bolognese school of miniatures, but their technique is much finer.

In a missal of the middle of the 14th century that was executed for Roberto Visconti, Bishop of Milan, and that is preserved in the Ambrosiana Library, the influence of the Gothic style is clearly evident. It was probably the result of the artist's knowledge of French miniatures and is even more marked in some drawings illustrating the Life of Christ in a codex of slightly later date in the same library.

Gothic factors, but united with a Sienese manner of painting, are seen in a missal of 1347 from the church of S. Maurilio, Milan, now in the Vatican Library, and in a somewhat similar manuscript in the Capitular Library, Milan. There is no trace of a Bolognese influence in the miniatures of either of these manuscripts. One of the most important Lombard manuscripts of the 14th century is a Book of Hours made between 1352 and 1378 for Branco Sforza, the wife of Galeazzo Visconti, and now preserved in the Munich Library ([2]). It contains a series of thirty-

---

([1]) *Toesca*, op. cit., pp. 200—276.

([2]) G. *Leidinger*, Meisterwerke der Buchmalerei aus Handschriften der Bayerischen Staatsbibliothek, Munich, 1920. p. 15, pl. XXV.

Fig. 134. Giovanni di Benedetto, the Nativity of the Virgin, miniature, 1352—78. Library, Munich.

Photo Riehn and Tietze.

six miniatures enclosed in ornamental borders (fig. 134). In their simplicity of design and composition they remind us of the frescoes at Mocchirolo and Lentate while some of the figures show analogies to certain of Giovanni de Milano's forms. Side by side with the simple forms of the Lombard manner, we note peculiarities borrowed from French Gothic miniatures. Not all the illuminations are of the same fine quality. The artist — Giovanni di Benedetto — has signed his work (¹).

In the Paris National Library there is a Book of Hours (MS. Cat. 757) that bears such a striking resemblance to the one in Munich that Signor Toesca does not hesitate to ascribe both to the same work-shop. This one is of slightly later date and the influence of French Gothicism is still more evident, but in the contemporary costumes and excellent drawing of animals, it has here acquired the aspect of a cosmopolitan art.

A beautiful miniature representing a pope, in the midst of his cardinals, receiving a book from a kneeling figure, is shown in the Museum of the Castello Sforza. It dates from the beginning of the 14th century, but I am ignorant of its place of origin.

With the appearance of Giovanni de' Grassi about 1390 begins Lombard art of the 15th century. Consequently some very important series of Lombard miniatures and drawings of about this date or shortly after, will be treated in an other volume when I am dealing with the productions of this more evolved stage of Gothic art to which they really belong.

The few remarks that have been made concerning miniature painting, suffice, however, to prove that the Gothicism which appears in other pictorial productions towards the year 1370, is probably due to an influence exercised by the art of miniature in which this tendency is manifest as early as about the middle of the century, its source of origin being, in all likelihood, France.

Piedmontese painting of the 14th century (²) may be considered as a sub-division of the Lombard school or at least as dependent on it. Documents go to prove that at this time there was no lack of artists nor of paintings, but we do not possess a single work

---

(¹) In the list of Giovanni da Milano's school works I have already mentioned a Crucifixion in the collection of the Historical Society, New York, that Signor *Toesca* attributes to this artist.

(²) *Gamba*, L'Arte antica in Piemonte, Turin, 1880, p. 527. *Rondalino*, La pittura torinese del Medio-Evo, Atti dello Soc. d'Arch. e BelleArte di Torino etc., VII, 1901, p. 206. *L. M. Giaccio*, Gli affreschi di S. Maria di Vezzolano e la pittura piemontese del Trecento, L'Arte, 1910, p. 349.

authenticated by the name of the painter, while of the anonymous pictures, only a few have been preserved.

In Turin we find a painter of the name of Turineto decorating the Town Hall in 1300, a certain Guido was active in 1312 while Giacomo Arconerio executed a portrait of a bishop who died in 1330, in the church of S. Domenico. There was a family of painters of the name of Jaquerio the first of whom, Pietro, worked in 1340 and died before 1366. His son, Giovanni, signed a work: "*Joannes pictor*" in 1347 that Lanzi still saw in S. Francesco di Chieri, while another Giovanni, who must have belonged to the succeeding generation, is mentioned between 1369 and 1403. Lastly Lanzi speaks of a Pietro, son of Pietro di Novarra, who in 1370 executed some frescoes in the Sylva Castle at Crevola d'Ossola [1].

As in Lombardy, profane paintings must have been abundant and doubtless the mural decorations of the various castles belonged to this category of art. Besides the frescoes in the castle of Turin, we know that the one at Rivoli was adorned in 1310 with paintings representing the cortège of Henry VII and about the same time the castles of Susa and Avigliana were also decorated.

The oldest Piedmontese paintings of the 14th century do not belong, however, to the Lombard school. They are the frescoes on the tomb of the abbot Tommaso Gallo in the church of S. Andrea at Vercelli and show the abbot at his cathedra teaching his pupils, and above him the Coronation of the Virgin and four angelic musicians. I think Signor Toesca is justified in assigning this monument to about the middle of the 14th century and in recognizing a French influence in the Gothic style of the work, which, is further evident in the sculptural part of the tomb [2].

The three works that allow us to speak of a Piedmontese group of paintings — they show too much dependence on the Lombard manner for us to use the term school — are the frescoes at Vezzolano, those in the church of S. Domenico in Turin and

---

[1] For other names v. *Rondalino*, op. cit. *A. Caffara*, Pittori e altri artisti medioevale in Pinerolo, Bollet. Stor. Bibliogr. subalpino, I, Turin, 1896, nos. II and III.

[2] *Toesca*, op. cit., p. 197. *E. Mella e R. Pasté*, S. Andrea di Vercelli, Vercelli, 1907, p. 485, date this tomb to the 13th century.

those at Piobese Torinese (¹). The series of frescoes at Vezzolano is by far the most important (²). Besides the paintings of the 13th century, we find in one of the arcades of the cloister a Madonna with two angels swinging censers of a crude technique but excuted under a strong Gothic influence. The vault was decorated by a more talented artist, but of the four Doctors of the Church that comprised this ornamentation, only St. Gregory seated at a desk remains visible. In the arches that divide the vault from the lateral parts a series of medallions contain heads of saints seen full face and portraits — or at least very individual faces — seen in profile, while the wall is adorned with a fresco divided into four rows (fig. 135), the uppermost of which shows an image of the Lord in majesty surrounded by the symbols of the Evangelists. Then follows a representation of the Adoration of the Magi in which the donor kneeling in adoration is depicted opposite the Wise Men. Below we see three young knights on horseback terrified at the sight of three dead men arising from their graves, a subject that forms the composition of an older fresco in the same church, while the last compartment is occupied by the image of a nobleman stretched on a couch. An inscription which was still legible in 1873 (³), but has since entirely disappeared, recorded that the work was executed in 1354 and adorned the tomb of the seigneurs of Castelnuovo. As others before me have remarked, those paintings show some connection with Lombard art, especially with the types and elongated proportions of Giovanni da Milano's works; this is particularly evident in the figure of the Virgin in the Adoration of the Magi. Further, we find here those clearly cut profiles seen in the devotional pictures at Mocchirolo and Lentate as well as the strong reliefs and chiaroscuro, characteristic of the Lombard school. Typical of this latter is the image of St. Gregory seen full face.

In the church of S. Domenico in Turin some important fragments of a 14th century decoration are still visible in a chapel in

---

(¹) *L. Motta Ciaccio*, op. cit.
(²) *Renier*, Una leggenda carolingia ed un affresco mortuario in Piemonte, Emporium, 1900, p. 377.
(³) *A. Bosio*, Storia dell' antica abbazia e del santuario di N.S. di Vezzolano, Turin, 1873.

Fig. 135. The Lord in Majesty, the Adoration and the Meeting of the Living and the Dead, fresco, circa 1354. Abbey, Vezzolano.

Photo Alinari.

the left lateral nave ([1]). Of a representation of the Annunciation the angel's head alone remains. We see a remnant of a series of

---

([1]) *F. Rondolino e R. Brayda*, La chiesa di S. Domenico a Torino, Turin, 1909. *E. Ferrettini.* La Risurrezione d'una chiesa del Trecento, Rassegna d'Arte, 1909, p. 6. *P. Toesca*, La chiesa S. Domenico a Torino, L'Arte, 1909, p. 461. *L. Motta Ciaccio*, op. cit., p. 349.

adorers kneeling one behind the other with a saint standing near by, the figures doubtless formed part of a composition similar to those we found in Lombardy and Verona. Some of the figures of Apostles are fairly well preserved. Although inferior in quality these frescoes belong to the same school as the paintings of Vezzolano. The figures in profile are certainly Lombard and I think the decoration may be considered a provincial production of this school ([1]); a certain Gothic movement will be noted in the draperies. As to the date of execution, it is in all probability slightly later than that of the Vezzolano frescoes but can hardly be after 1370.

A long inscription dates the fresco at Piobese-Torinese from 1359. The donor and his wife, whose names are given, are depicted in the frame that surrounds the half-length figure of the Virgin nursing the Child between two angelic musicians; beyond the frame we see to the left St. John the Baptist and to the right St. Christopher with the Child on his shoulder. The painting is of little importance as a work of art but is of some interest on account of the date and the really elegant elongated forms reminiscent of Giovanni da Milano's art, but showing a stronger Gothic influence.

Fairly pronounced Gothic elements are evident in the frescoes in the chapel of S. Antonio at Sandigliano in the region of Biella; they represent the Saviour enthroned in a mandorla and a series of Apostle figures but they are of no importance artistically ([2]). Signor Toesca remarks that certain frescoes in the sacristy of the church of S. Francesco in the Susa valley, that leads directly into France, appear to belong to the art of the other side of the Alps. The frescoes in the sacristy and in one of the chapels of the church of S. Antonio at Ranverso, are, besides a painting of the Virgin and Child in a lunette in the Cathedral of Alessandria, the only 14th century Piedmontese works that Cavalcaselle cites ([3]).

([1]) There is no reason to ascribe these paintings to the Umbrian school as has sometimes been done.

([2]) *A. Roccavilla*, L'Arte nel Biellese, Biella, 1905, p. 116. This author is, I think, right in stating that, in spite of the date, 1399, that we find inscribed, these paintings belong to a later period.

([3]) *Crowe and Cavalcaselle*, op. cit., III, p. 255. *Gamba*, L'Abbadia di S. Antonio di Ranverso, Atti della soc. di Arch. e di Belli Arte di Torino, I, 1875.

The frescoes at Ranverso show in the sacristy, the Annunciation, the Prayer on the Mount of Olives, the Calvary, SS. Peter and Paul; in the vault the Evangelists and the Virgin with the Child and two saints on the façade, while in the chapel we see a representation of the Crucifixion with saints and the kneeling donor. Cavalcaselle justly says that we owe these paintings to a clumsy and vulgar artist with a poor colour-sense. The figures of SS. Peter and Paul, that he believes to be from another hand, remind him of the art of the schools of Gubbio and Fabriano.

The paintings at Vezzolano, Turin and Piobese-Torinese can, without any doubt, be considered the most characteristic productions of Piedmontese painting in the 14th century. Moreover they are the only series that show certain features in common.

The dominating influence in these works is certainly Lombard, and one might even classify them with the paintings of this school, except that the Gothic element is here very much more marked than in true Lombard works. In Piedmont this pronounced Gothicism is present even in local productions of no artistic importance such for example as those at Sandigliano or in the Susa valley and is evident also in the Vercelli fresco which shows no connection with Lombard art. It is undoubtedly from France that this Gothic style penetrated into Piedmont and it is possibly to the same source that we owe the symbolic subject of the Vezzolano fresco, the meeting of the quick and the dead.

Although there was sufficient connection between France and Lombardy to explain the direct artistic influence of the former on the latter[1], it does not seem to me quite out of the question that many of the Gothic elements reached Lombardy by means of Piedmont, where Gothicism was much more widely spread and, as far as we can gather, manifest at an earlier date than in Lombardy.

Nevertheless the real florescence of Gothic art — seems to have had its roots in the Sienese school, and it was after passing by Avignon, that this art was disseminated throughout Central Europe as the cosmopolitan Gothic form.

---

[1] Numerous French artists were active in Milan: *E. Muntz,* Les arts à la cour des papes, I, p. 634. *The Same,* L'Ami des Monuments, II, 1888, p. 247.

An interesting fact which increases our knowledge of the technique of painting is recorded in a document which proves that as early as the first quarter of the 14th century, Piedmontese painters prepared their colours with oil [1].

---

[1] *F. Gabolto*, La pittura ad olio in Piemonte nella prima meta del secolo XIV, Boll. Stor. Bibliogr. subalpino, VIII, 1904, p. 179.

CHAPTER IV.

THE PAINTERS OF RIMINI (¹).

At Rimini we find an artistic centre in which the 13th century tradition persisted for a considerable time, and from which the painting in other centres of Emilia depend.

The 14th century pictorial productions of Rimini can be divided into two groups, the one beginning about the year 1300 and flourishing during the first quarter of the century, the other starting with Giuliano da Rimini, who was active as early as 1307, and following immediately on the former.

The Riminese painters of the early 14th century were inspired by the art of Pietro Cavallini. A few years ago I made a special study of this little school and then I grouped together eight works which form a more or less homogenous nucleus. Since then I have added four other works, the nos. II, IX, X and XII of the following list. Consequently twelve paintings belong to this Cavallinesque Riminese school and there are, in all probability, some others whose existence has not yet come to my knowledge. They are: —

I. Rome, Museum in the Palazzo Venezia (originally in the Corsini Gallery), a panel composed of six scenes in three rows, representing: the Nativity, with the Child receiving His first bath; the Crucifixion, the Entombment, the Descent into Limbo, the Resurrection and the Last Judgment (fig. 136).

II. Faenza, Picture Gallery, a small panel showing, above, a

(¹) O. *Sirén*, Giuliano, Pietro and Giovanni da Rimini, The Burlington Magazine, 1916, p. 272. R. *van Marle*, La scuola di Pietro Cavallini a Rimini, Boll. d'Arte del Minist. della Pubbl. Istr., Dec. 1921. In the attributions I make, and in my ideas of the origin of this group of painters, I so frequently hold the contrary opinion to Mr. Sirén that it seems useless to indicate each point of difference. According to him the entire current derives from Giotto's art and Pietro da Rimini is the principal artist.

Fig. 136. Cavallinesque Riminese School, six scenes from the Life of Christ. Palazzo Venezia, Rome.

THE PAINTERS OF RIMINI.

Fig. 137. Cavallinesque Riminese School, Madonna and five saints. Gallery, Faenza.

half-length figure of the Virgin tenderly embracing the Child while at either side is a little angel supporting the drapery which forms the background. The five standing figures on the lower part of the panel are those of St. Francis, an archangel, a holy bishop, St Catherine and St. Clare (fig. 137) (¹). The attitude of

---

(¹) E. Tea, Una tavoletta della Pinacoteca di Faenza, L'Arte, 1922, p. 34, attributes this picture to Cavallini's school. In the gallery it bore the name of Bettino da Faenza, a painter who was active at a much later date than the time this picture was executed.

Fig. 138. Cavallinesque Riminese School, six scenes from the Life of Christ. Palazzo Venezia, Rome. Photo Anderson.

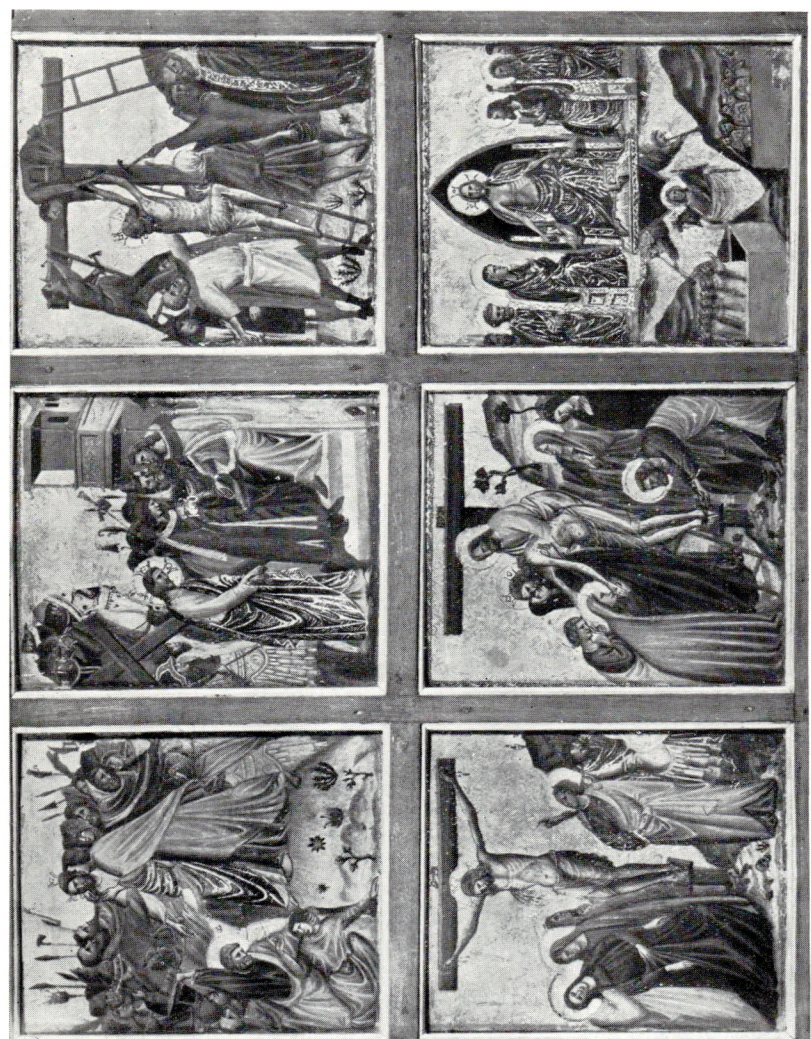

Fig. 139. Cavallinesque Riminese School, six scenes from the Life of Christ. Gallery, Venice. Photo Anderson.

the Virgin and her expression of tenderness, and the elongated forms of the saints lead us to suppose that this is a work from the same hand as the foregoing panel.

III. Rome, Museum in the Palazzo Venezia (from the Corsini Gallery and originally in the Herz collection), an oblong panel comprising six scenes, arranged in two rows, illustrating incidents from the Life of Christ. In order to follow the events chronologically, we must start with the scene in the left upper corner and take them on alternate upper and lower rows. In this manner we find the Descent from the Cross, the Entombment, Pentecost, the Resurrection, the Ascension and the Descent into Limbo (fig. 138) ([1]).

IV. Venice, Accademia, no. 26, a panel of the same form as the previous picture and also composed of six scenes, but the order of events is here followed from left to right, beginning with those of the upper row. The scenes illustrate the Betrayal of Judas, Christ before Pontius Pilate, Christ mounting the Cross, the Crucifixion, the Descent from the Cross and the Last Judgment (fig. 139) ([2]).

V. Munich, Ältere Pinakothek, nos. 979—980, a diptych of which one half represents, in three rows, the Crucifixion, the Flagellation with the Calvary, St. Francis receiving the Stigmata and four saints (fig. 140) and the other half the enthroned Virgin with two saints, Christ washing the feet of the disciples and the Last Judgment (fig. 141) ([3]).

VI. Urbino, the Picture Gallery, one half of a diptych showing the Crucifixion with the Madonna of the Annunciation above (fig. 142). The other half of this diptych was formerly the property of Monsieur Alphonse Kahn, Paris and is now for sale in London; it represents above the angel of the Annunciation and in the two lower parts the Nativity and the Adoration of the Virgin.

VII. Perugia, Pinacoteca, no. 68, a small panel on which we see St. Mary Magdalene borne to heaven by four angels, and the

---

([1]) This picture belonged to the Stroganoff collection (v. L'Arte, 1914, p. 264) and was shown at the exhibition of Sienese art in London where it was described as a work from the hand of a Sienese pupil of Giotto's.

([2]) Signor *A. Venturi* has ascribed this picture to the same master as the previous. Signor *Testi* has rightly protested against this attribution which I, too, think has been made without sufficient grounds.

([3]) In the old catalogue it was attributed to Cavallini but is now ascribed to the Roman school. Signor *A. Venturi* believes it to be a work of Cavallini's old age. Mr. *Berenson* was formerly of the opinion that it was a youthful work of Giotto's. O. *Sirén*, L'Arte, IX, 1906, p. 327, gives it to a Romagnole follower of Giotto's.

Fig. 140. Cavallinesque Riminese School, one half of a diptych. Ältere Pinakothek, Munich. Photo Hanfstaengl.

Fig. 141. Cavallinesque Riminese School, one half of a diptych. Ältere Pinakothek, Munich.   Photo Hanfstaengl.

Fig. 142. Cavallinesque Riminese School, one half of a diptych. Gallery, Urbino. Photo Minist. del. Pubbl. Istr.

figures of SS. Bartholomew, John the Baptist, Lucy, Francis, Dominic, a holy bishop and St. Christopher (fig. 143). According to a paper pasted on the back, this panel came originally from Bologna.

VIII. Gloucester (England), the collection of Sir Hubert Parry, the Adoration of the Magi and the first bath of the Infant Christ (fig. 144) ([1]).

IX. Rome, private collection (previously in the Sterbini collection), the Baptism of Christ in the presence of two angels with a figure of the Almighty appearing above (fig. 145)([2]).

X. Rome, Vatican Gallery, store-room, no. 132, a panel showing a subject that I am unable to interpret: an angel apparently speaks to a child dressed in heavy skins, and points to a child of similar appearance who is seen praying in the background. The painting seems to be from the same hand as the foregoing panel.

XI. New-York, Lehman collection, a panel showing in the triangular upper part the Last Judgment and below, arranged in two rows, the Virgin enthroned between a holy bishop and St. Peter the Martyr, the Crucifixion, St. Thomas Aquinas in glory and the Nativity of Christ (fig. 146).

XII. Bologna, the Picture Gallery, no. 231, the Crucifixion with a great many people and St. Francis kneeling below; at the sides we see one above the other SS. Francis and Catherine (?), and SS. Bartholomew and Clare. The Entombment and the Descent into Hell are depicted at the foot of the panel. The work has been too much repainted for us to be certain about the date of its execution but it seems to belong to the present rather than to the subsequent group.

Some of the characteristics that enable us to group these pictures together are as follows: the subject matter which almost invariably illustrates the Saviour's life; the usually small size of the panel on which several scenes are united as in Byzantine icons; the design of leaves and flowers which adorns the gold background; the technique suitable for miniature painting, the

---

([1]) *R. Fry*, Burlington Magazine, II, 1903, p. 118, attributes this picture to Cavallini's school but later in The Atheneum, 4th June 1914, classifies it as a production of the Giottesque Roman school.

([2]) *A. Venturi*, La Galleria Sterbini in Roma, Rome, 1906, p. 48, attributes this picture to Jacopo di Paolo of Bologna.

THE PAINTERS OF RIMINI.

Fig. 143. Cavallinesque Riminese School, the Ascension of Mary Magdalene and seven saints. Gallery, Perugia.   Photo Anderson.

Fig. 144. Cavallinesque Riminese School, the Adoration of the Magi and the Bathing of the Child Christ. Parry Collection, Gloucester. Photo Mansell.

Fig. 145. Cavallinesque Riminese School, the Baptism of Christ. Pasini Collection, Rome.

gilt woven textures and a predilection for the representation of the Last Judgment though it is a subject more suited to works of larger dimensions (¹). Several of the Crucifixions show the Cross made from the trunk of a tree.

In the above quoted article I have already expounded at length

(¹) The only panel paintings that I know of this early period representing the Last Judgment are the one belonging to the Sienese school at Grossetto (Vol. I, p. 373) and the one which together with five other scenes of the Florentine school, is preserved in the Berlin Museum. Both are 13th century productions and somewhat different from what we find in the school of Rimini.

the reasons that led me to look upon this group of works as a link between Cavallini's school and that of Baronzio and the other Riminese artists of the period. The arguments are found in the technique of the painting, as well as in the iconography to which subject we shall return later.

That a connection exists between these works and Cavallini's art is demonstrated by the fact that many of them have been attributed to the master himself or to his pupils: the types of the greater part of the figures, the manner by which relief is obtained in the drapery as well as in the faces, the majestic proportions in spite of the limited size of the pictures and the details borrowed from classical plastic art, all point to a connection with Cavallini's school and not with Giotto's, of whose influence there is no trace in any of these works.

On the other hand many peculiarities force us to associate this group of paintings with the works of Giuliano, Baronzio and other similar Riminese artists, and the combination of these two predominating elements supports the hypothesis that we are here dealing with the productions of a transitional art between Cavallini's and the school of Rimini. The resemblance to the latter is particularly evident in the facial types. This is very marked in the second picture in the Palazzo Venezia, in which the almost cone-shaped figures with sharp features, pointed noses and narrowly slit eyes are, as it were, introductory to Baronzio's art. Moreover we discover in Baronzio's school a correspondence in the iconographical details, in the partiality for the Last Judgment and in the model of the pictures with numerous small scenes.

The Riminese school of painting to which the works I have mentioned above are but preliminary, is one of the most important of the local groups, not only on account of the quality of its work, which, especially at the beginning, was of a very high standard, but also because of its abundant production. Although the town of Rimini was apparently the principal centre, this art, at the beginning of the 14th century, was spread throughout Romagna. Among the works belonging to the early group, we find one at Faenza and one at Bologna whence the picture at Perugia also originated. In admiring this last painting, the most beautiful of these little panels, we should not forget that Oderisi da Gubbio

Fig. 146. Cavallinesque Riminese School, the Last Judgment and four other scenes. Lehman Collection, New York.

and Franco Bolognese, two miniaturists extolled by Dante (¹),

(¹) Purgatory, XI, 79 et seq. "Oh, said I to him, art thou not Oderisi, the honour of Gubbio and the honour of that art which in Paris is called illuminating? Brother, said he, more pleasing are the leaves which Franco Bolognese paints; the honour now is all his and mine in part".

whose praise of artists was restricted to a chosen few, were active in this town. There is certainly nothing that justifies us in believing this panel in the Gallery of Perugia to be the work of one or other of those artists, but it is not unlikely that it belongs to their school.

From the end of the 13th century onward, we find a considerable number of artists in Rimini. Besides Giuliano, Baronzio, Pietro and Francesco da Rimini examples of whose work have come down to us, we find mention of the following: Frater Fusculus (1292—1306), Zagnonus (1295), Magister Johannes (1300), Nerio the Miniaturist (1306), Zangolo (circa 1336), Paolino Ciciolo (1345—1346), Gregorio (1348), Miginio (1370—1398), Giovanni di Alinerio (1377—1397), Antonio Giacomelli da Imola (1379—1384), and Giangolino (1381—1387) ([1]). Ravenna also possessed many artists, a few of whose names may be cited: Maso and Bindino da Faenza (1314), Rastello da Forli (1352—1368), Nanne da Ravenna (1368—1396), Tommaso da Faenza (1373), Marco da Lencisa (1392) Paolo Pittore (1403) ([2]).

The generation of artists that followed those whom I believe to have been directly inspired by Cavallini and who left us the twelve paintings which have just been discussed, may be divided into two groups. One, in which Giuliano, Baronzio and Pietro da Rimini may be included, created a more or less individual art, while the other produced works which belong to the same style and show but little change from the painting of the early group of the Riminese school.

Of the six pictures that comprise the latter group, five are preserved in the Vatican Gallery and some of them are extraordinarily beautiful. No. 54, for example, showing above the Crucifixion with Mary Magdalene and St. Francis kneeling at the foot of the Cross and below the figures of St. Paul, St. Peter in papal vestments, and St. Louis of Toulouse (pl. III) is without any doubt one of the most beautiful panel paintings of the Trecento ([3]). Hardly inferior to this work is a picture of the Descent

---

([1]) *L. Tonini*, Rimini nella signoria de' Malatesti, IV, Rimini, 1880. *A. Brach*, Giotto's Schule in der Romagna, Strasbourg, 1902, p. 74.

([2]) *S. Bernicoli*, Arte e artisti in Ravenna, Felix Ravenna, Jan. 1912.

([3]) Formerly Mr. *Berenson* believed this to be one of Giotto's youthful works. It is catalogued as a production of Giotto's school. *L. Venturi,*

CRUCIFIXION AND SAINTS
School of Rimini of the first half of the XIV century, Vatican Gallery.
Photo Anderson.

THE PAINTERS OF RIMINI. 295

from the Cross (no. 56, fig. 147) which is catalogued as a production of Giotto's school. The extraordinary depth of feeling which the artist has been able to express and the beauty of the

Fig. 147. Riminese School, Descent from the Cross. Vatican Gallery.
Photo Anderson.

drawing are quite exceptional. A pointed panel representing the Crucifixion (no. 52, fig. 148), also catalogued as belonging to

L'Arte, 1915, p. 9 and *O. Sirén*, L'Arte, 1921, p. 25, both attribute this panel to Baronzio. Although I found the basis on which this attribution was made rather weak, I thought at first it might be possible, but since I have changed my mind, and now think that it is a work of much finer quality than anything Baronzio has ever produced.

the great Florentine's school, no doubt possessed the same qualities, but it has suffered somewhat through restoration. We note here the Cross made with the branches of a tree. Less beautiful, but all the same belonging to this group and showing

Fig. 148. Riminese School, the Crucifixion. Vatican Gallery.
Photo Anderson.

particular connection with the last mentioned picture, is a little oblong panel (no. 44) which, in the gallery, is said to be painted after the manner of Lorenzetti; it represents St. Francis, St. John the Baptist, St. Louis of Toulouse with a miniature adorer and St. Julian of Cilicia (fig. 149).

Very inferior in execution to all these works is a panel (no. 42) on which we see, above, the Crucifixion with but a limited

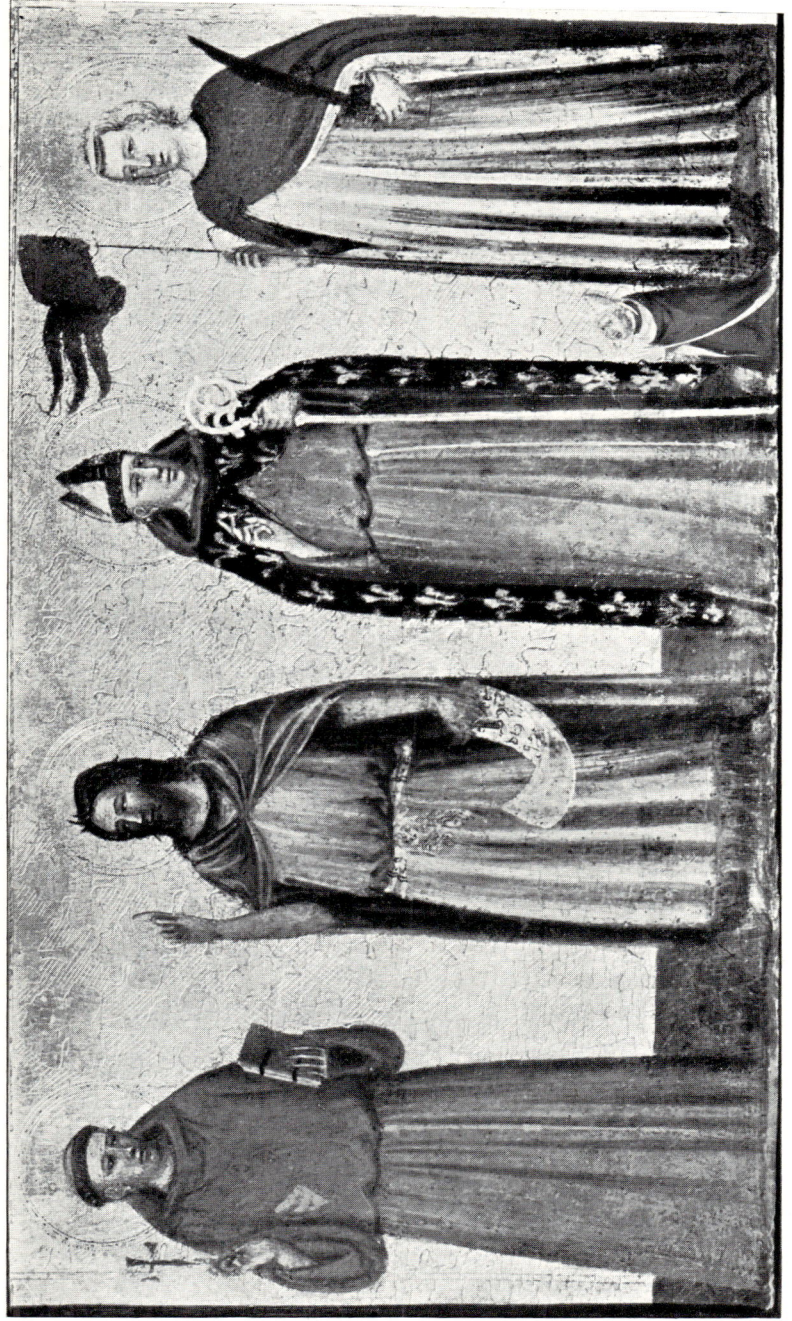

Fig. 149. Riminese School, four saints. Vatican Gallery.
Photo Anderson.

number of people, including St. Mary Magdalene at the foot of the Cross, and SS. Peter and Paul at the sides, each standing in front of a piece of architecture; below we find the Holy Women at the Empty Sepulchre together with the Noli me tangere, (fig. 150), a combination which is reminiscent of one of the foregoing pictures on which the Saviour, rising from His tomb, was depicted in the presence of the holy Maries (¹).

A little panel, perhaps a piece of a predella, in the Lehman collection, New York, may be classified with this group of works. It shows the beheading of the Baptist, the dance of Salome with the saint's head, and the king and his guests seated at table.

A feature that all these pictures have in common with those of the previous group is the ornamental design of leaves and flowers in the gold background.

A triptych in the Jarves collection, Yale University, seems to be the work of a provincial follower of the Riminese school of painting (fig. 151) (²). Incidents in the Life of Christ, from the Annunciation to the Descent from the Cross, are represented without the least sequence. The beheading of St. John and the executioner bringing the saint's head to the king are also depicted, but the execution is very crude and the drawing even infantile. In the Presentation in the Temple, which is seen at the foot of the left wing, and in the Flagellation, which we find on the third row of the right wing, Italo-Byzantine architecture, borrowed from Tuscan art of the 13th century, is to be noted.

Open loggias, as shown in the second scene concerning the Baptist — second row of the right wing — are met with in Giotto's works at Assisi (³) and in the paintings that Cavallini's pupils executed in Naples (⁴).

The other artistic movement in Rimini started during the period that the Cavalinesque painters were still flourishing. The

---

(¹) *O. Sirén*, op. cit., attributes this panel to Giuliano da Rimini or to the Bolognese school before 1330.

(²) *O. Sirén*, A descriptive catalogue of the pictures in the Jarves Collection etc., Newhaven, London, Oxford, 1916, p. 29, ascribes it to a Romagnole follower of Giotto.

(³) Scene of the death of the knight of Celano.

(⁴) In the Apparition to the pilgrims on the road to Emmaus.

Fig. 150. Riminese School, the Crucifixion and Noli me tangere. Vatican Gallery.

Photo Anderson.

first artist, and probably also the founder of this current, was Giuliano da Rimini (¹).

We find Giuliano's signature on an important panel representing the Virgin seated on a throne behind the back of which two angels are seen, while eight figures of isolated saints form two rows of two, one above the other at either side; they are St. Francis receiving the stigmata, the Baptist, St. Clare and St. Catherine on the one side and St. John the Evangelist, St. Mary Magdalene kneeling before an angel, St. Agnes and St. Lucy on the other (fig. 152). Above we read: "*Anno Dni Millo CCC Septimo Julianus Pictor De Arimino fecit hoc opus tempore Dni Clementis PP. Quinti.*" This picture, originally at Urbania in the neighbourhood of Urbino, was bought by Mrs. Gardner and now forms part of her collection in Boston.

The painting is not wanting in characteristics. The bodies are heavily built, the necks often long and the hands beautiful; the faces are of a long oval shape with high foreheads, the eyes, nose and mouth, which are very small and finely drawn, offer a strange contrast with the largely constructed figures.

We do not know anything about this artist except that he died before 1346. From the document that mentions him at this date, it may be gathered that he owned some property (²).

The painting that we can most closely approximate to the authentic work, and which, besides, is generally attributed to the same artist, is a Coronation of the Virgin in the Urbino Gallery (fig. 153). The Virgin, who wears a robe threaded with gold, bows her head towards the Saviour; a holy female martyr is depicted in each of the lateral panels, while of the pinnacles only the two containing half-length figures of SS. Clare and Francis have been conserved.

A more important work by the same artist is the decoration of the refectory of the abbey at Pomposa, situated between Ferrara and Ravenna; the church and Chapter room of the monastery have been adorned by other painters. Although the frescoes are very superior to the two panel paintings, they are

---

(¹) *A. Brach*, op. cit., p. 63 and passim. *O. Sirèn*, Burlington Magazine, XXIX, 1916, p. 272. *Thieme-Becker,* Künstler-Lexikon, XIV, p. 213.

(²) *L. Tonini*, op. cit., IV, p. 390. A painter of Urbino of the same name is mentioned in 1366 and 1367.

THE PAINTERS OF RIMINI. 301

Fig. 151. Outcome of the Riminese School, Triptych. Jarves Collection. Yale University.

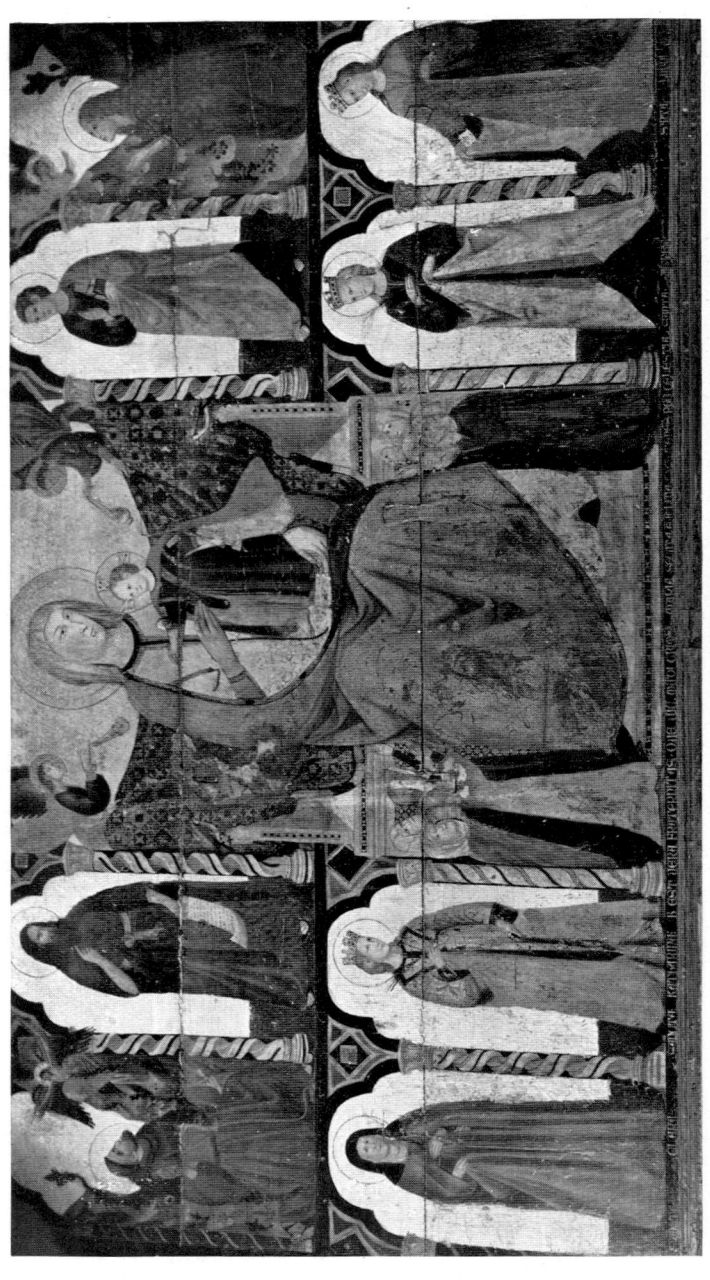

Fig. 152. Giuliano da Rimini, Madonna and saints, 1307. Gardner Collection, Boston.

obviously by the same hand. Only part of the mural decoration now remains.

The wall in which the present entrance has been made, was adorned with a representation of the Prayer on the Mount of

Fig. 153. Giuliano da Rimini, the Coronation of the Virgin and saints. Gallery, Urbino.

Olives but only parts of the figures of the three sleeping disciples and of the angel speaking with Christ are visible. Opposite we see a fragment of a fresco showing a saint seated at a lectern (¹). On the other wall three of the frescoes have been fairly well conserved; they are the Last Supper, the Saviour in majesty in the midst of four saints and a miracle performed by the abbot,

(¹) *Brach*, op. cit., does not mention this figure.

Guido da Pomposa. The first (fig. 154) of these paintings shows the Lord and His disciples seated at a round table — this form belongs to the old iconographical tradition no longer followed by Giotto (¹) — bread and dishes are placed on the table and a large plate in the centre contains a fish, a piece of which the Saviour is about to take in His hand. St John with closed eyes rests his head on Christ's shoulder. Only twelve Apostles are depicted.

In the second fresco we see the Saviour seated on a throne holding an open book and bestowing a blessing; He is escorted by the Virgin Orante and St. John the Baptist, while to the extreme right and left are Benedict and Guido, the holy priors of the abbey (fig. 155).

In the illustration of the miracle, the holy abbot, Guido, is represented sitting at a table which is all prepared for a meal; standing near him is the disguised Bishop Gebehardus of Ravenna who has come to inspect the monks' mode of living which report has said to be too luxurious; the followers of the bishop and of the prior are placed at either end of the table (fig. 156). The miracle consists in the changing of the water into wine in the prior's cup which the bishop holds in his hand.

As I said before, Giuliano's frescoes are very superior to his panels, and it is only the beauty of the former that can in any way be compared with that of the works of the Cavallinesque group of artists. The faces, particularly in the last fresco, are very beautiful, the forms finely proportioned and the design very subtle. Further we note a great variety of expression and gesture, the contrast between the bishop's surprise and the saintly tranquility of the abbot in the third fresco, being very remarkable. The types of the figures in the Last Supper are sooner those we find in the panels. They show no connection with those of Giotto's, to whom the fresco was formerly attributed and to whose school it is still always ascribed. Nor is the iconography Giottesque, while the soft clear colours and chiaroscuro effects remind us of Cavallini's art (²).

(¹) Cavallini's pupils at Naples represent a semi-circular table.

(²) *Brach*, op. cit., who believes that the painters of Rimini were directly inspired by Giotto, is struck by the resemblance between these frescoes and the paintings in the Upper Church, Assisi, which I attribute to Cavallini and his helpers.

THE PAINTERS OF RIMINI.

Fig. 154. Giuliano da Rimini, the Last Supper. Refectory, Pomposa.
Photo Minist. del. Pubbl. Istr.

As for the date of these frescoes, Federici, the historian of Pomposa, has recorded an inscription, once visible in the refectory, informing us that the building was constructed in the year 1304 at the time of Pope John XXII and of the abbot, Mark (¹). But these dates do not coincide, since the potificate of John XXII was from 1316 until 1334, and in 1304 there was no prior of the name of Mark. The name of the Pope seems to me the most likely indication to go upon — especially as there are no other popes of the same name who approach him chronologically — and although some have tried to demonstrate by intricate calculations that the monastery was founded between the years 1317 and 1320, I think it wiser to consider the more protracted period of 1316—1334 as that during which these paintings were executed (²).

Consequently they are of later date than the panel at Urbania which to all appearances is contemporaneous with the Coronation of the Virgin at Urbino. The two panels are then in all probability, productions of a youthful stage in the artist's career while the Pomposa frescoes, which are greatly superior, were no doubt executed at a more mature period.

Giuliano's hand can, I think, be discerned in the frescoes that were revealed by the earthquake of 1916, in the church of S. Agostino in Rimini (³). These paintings, only fragments of which have survived, adorn the apse and right lateral chapel of the church.

The principal representation in the apse is a large Madonna enthroned and holding the Child. The robes and background are richly ornamented. The Madonna is more grandiose in appearance than in the panel of 1307, but the type, as, too, that of the Child, is the same. An aureole of angels is depicted over head.

(¹) *Federici P. Placidi*, Rerum Pomposionarum Historia, Rome, 1781. For the rest of the literature on this abbey, v. *Brach*, op. cit., p. 11 note 1.

(²) *Federici*, op. cit., p. 279, tells us that a painter of the name of *Magister Cheyus pictor Florentinus* is mentioned in a Pomposa record of 1317.

(³) *Fr. Filippini*, Gli affreschi nell' abside della chiesa di S. Agostino in Rimini e un ritratto di Dante, Boll. d'Arte del Minist. della Pubbl. Istr., 1921, p. 3. It is quite incomprehensible to me how this writer can attribute these beautiful frescoes, which show all the characteristics of the Riminese school of painting of the first half of the 14th century, to the mediocre artist, Bittino da Faenza who is mentioned in 1398 and who died in 1427. He even places them about the year 1420, almost a century after the period from which I think they actually date.

THE PAINTERS OF RIMINI. 307

Fig. 155. Giuliano da Rimini, the Lord amidst the Virgin and saints.
Refectory, Pomposa.

Photo Minist. del. Pubbl. Istr.

Above this fresco there is a large image of the Almighty between the two SS. John, while below we see a picture of the Noli me tangere. On the walls, the story of St. John the Evangelist ([1]), to whom the church was originally dedicated, is illustrated.

On the left are depicted the story of how he caused the statues of the heathen gods at Ephesus to fall and break, and his martyrdom in boiling oil; while on the right we find St. John writing on the Island of Patmos, together with his return to Ephesus in a bark, and the resurrection of Drusiana.

Among the scattered fragments on the lower part of the wall, we can distinguish a scene of a dispute which might perhaps be that between St. John and the pagan priest, Aristodelas. Opposite, we see the ascension of St. John whom angels carry to heaven where he is received by Christ. The chancel arch was adorned with a fresco of the Last Judgment, but the painting here is badly damaged. The composition is quite traditional: the Christ as Judge was seated in the centre with angels flying above and the Virgin and Apostles in a row below with two angelic figures in the centre. Nothing remains of the dead arising from their tombs.

In the chapel to the right where the paintings have also suffered through restoration we can still distinguish a Nativity, probably of the Virgin, her Death and the Assumption in a very elaborate composition.

In all these frescoes the artist has depicted a great many people who take no part in the action. Worthy of note is a group in the resurrection of Drusiana, one of the figures crowned with a wreath of laurel indicates with his thumb the incident to another person (fig. 157). Some writers are of opinion that the latter figure is a portrait of Dante and the former that of Petrarch ([2]), but although there is a vague resemblance between the traditional effigie of the divine poet and the personage depicted here, a comparison, especially with the figure to the left in the fresco of the miracle of the abbot of Pomposa, will clearly demonstrate that the type, the drawing of the features and the penetrating gaze are characteristic, not of the figure, but of the artist who has repeated the same model more than once.

([1]) *Filippini*, op. cit., has interpreted the signification of these paintings.
([2]) *Filippini*, op. cit.

Fig. 156. Giuliano da Rimini the Miracle of Abbot Guido. Refectory, Pomposa. Photo Minist. del. Pubbl. Istr.

A comparison with the frescoes at Pomposa will justify our attributing those in the church of S. Agostino to Giuliano da Rimini. We find the same types, the same proportions and a similar treatment of the draperies, hands and relief. The spirit of recital is also the same and some of the expressions and gestures identical. These works seem to point to a more advanced stage in the artist's development than the frescoes in the refectory of the Abbey.

Fig. 157. Giuliano da Rimini, Detail of the Resurrection of Drusiana. S. Agostino, Rimini.
Photo Bezzi.

The paintings in the Pieve of Bagnacavallo(¹) have also been attributed to Giuliano da Rimini. Here we find in the apse an image of the Saviour in majesty — not unlike the corresponding figure at Pomposa — with two angels and the four Evangelists and their symbols at the sides. Lower down we see the Saviour on the Cross, which is made from the branches of a tree, between the Virgin and St. John, while the Twelve Apostles form two

---

(¹) *Brach*, op. cit., p. 75, v. also *A. Messeri*, Di un insegna e poco nota basilica cristiana dei primi secoli, Boll. d'Arte del Minist. della Pubbl. Istr., 1910, p. 345.

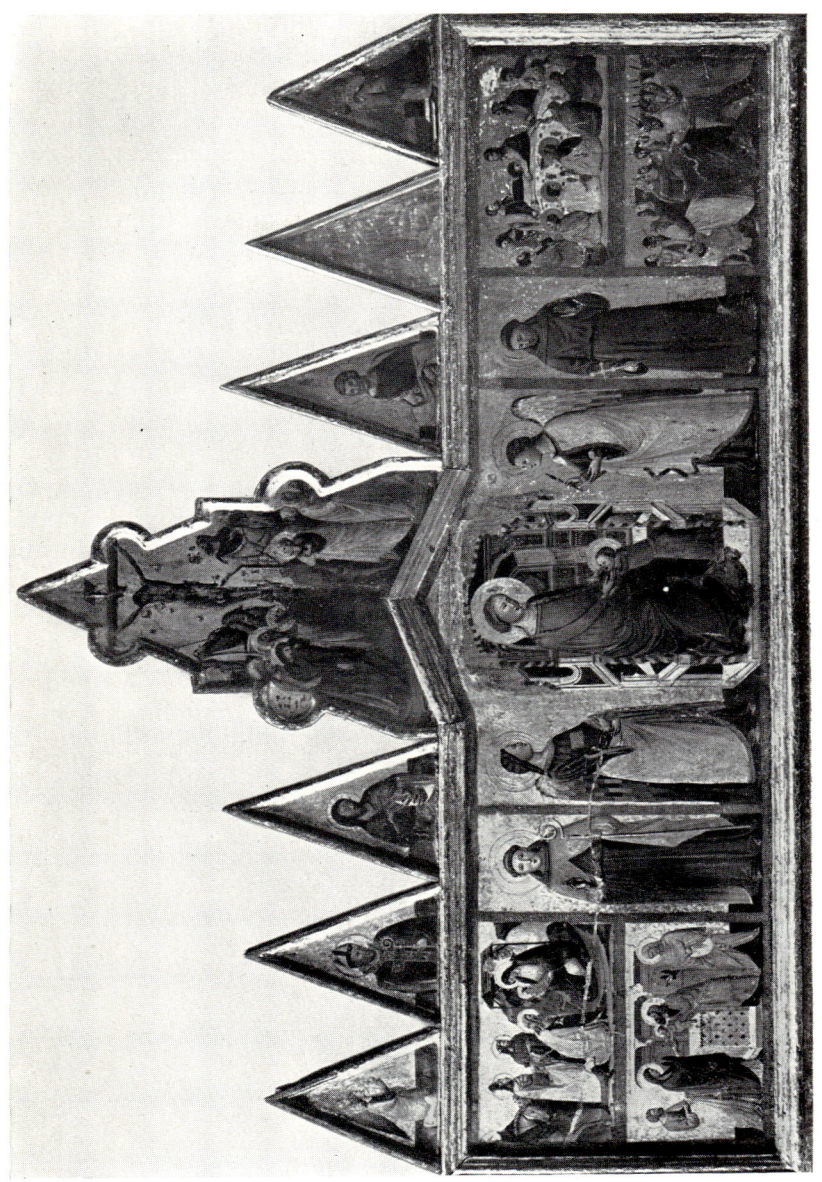

Fig. 158. Baronzio, Atar-piece, 1345. Pinacoteca, Urbino.
Photo Minist. del. Pubbl. Istr.

rows laterally. Although this decoration was entirely repainted when it was discovered in 1792, none the less we note such striking analogies between it and that of the refectory of Pomposa that we can ascribe both cycles to one and the same artist. Further, an inscription, most of which is still visible, on that part of the wall which separates the frescoes tells us that the painter was from Rimini but unfortunately his first name has been effaced. The inscription runs: ".... *De Arimino pro Animabus Simonis et Aliorum Suorum mortuorum tempore Domini Guidonis De Comitibus De Cunis rectoris domini istius Plebis Benvenut. frater ejus fecit fieri hoc opus*". The names mentioned in the inscription furnish us with the approximate date of the painting, since the Guido, who is spoken of, was rector of the Pieve in 1323 but was replaced in 1332, while Benvenutus was prebendary in 1313 but in 1320 went to Rimini as ambassador ([1]), and it may be that he brought back the artist whose work we find here. Consequently these frescoes were executed between 1313 and 1332, and in all probability after 1320, although the manner that the artist has followed here shows much connection with that of the panel of 1307 ([2]).

Giuliano then was the apparent founder and certainly by far the greatest artist of the Riminese school of painting after the Cavallinesque influence had waned. No other painter of this group succeeded in producing the harmonious beauty of form and design that we find in the frescoes of Pomposa and Rimini. The regularity of the features of some of his faces and their animation and intensity of expression rank Giuliano da Rimini among the great masters of the beginning of the 14th century.

I should like to lay particular stress on the fact that his painting — as too that of the entire school of Rimini — does not originate

---

([1]) These documents have been published by *Balduzzi*, Dei dipinti murali nella Pieve di Bagnocavallo, Atti e momorie delle R.R. Deputazione di Stor. Patr. per l'Emilia, Nuov. Ser., II, 1877 (*Brach*, op. cit., p. 77).

([2]) *Brach*, op. cit., p. 79, attributes still to Giuliano a marriage of St. Catherine and saints in the Verona Gallery (no 356) that I have already mentioned with other Veronese paintings. *Sirén*, op. cit., gives to this artist the panel of the Virgin and saints, dated 1308, at Cesi in Umbria which I have classified (Vol. I, p. 544) as a provincial work of Cavallini's school. He further believes it possible that Giuliano collaborated in the execution of the frescoes in Sta. Maria in Porto fuori, Ravenna, but this I do not think.

Fig. 159. Detail of fig. 158.

from Giotto's art but descends directly from Cavallini's, though interpreted in a more modern spirit.

The supposition that all the Riminese painters of the following generation are dependent on Giuliano is, in all probability, correct, while Giovanni Baronzio ([1]) can be considered his pupil.

([1]) *Brach*, op. cit., p. 69. *E. Calzini*, in Thieme-Becker, Künstler Lexikon, II, p. 520.

Concerning Baronzio, we possess only two dates, 1344 and 1345, that we find on his signed works ([1]). The earlier of these is a cross in the church of S. Francesco at Mercatello which was brought to our knowledge only a short time ago ([2]). It is a crucifix after Giotto's model, with a decorated background; the Virgin, St. John and the Almighty are depicted in the terminals; the signature runs: "*Johes Pictor fect hoc opus, Fr. Tobaldi M..... MCCCXLIIII.*"

It is a very fine work though inferior in quality to the beautiful pictures of the Cavallinesque artists of Rimini.

The altar-piece of 1345 was transported many years ago from the Franciscan monastery of Macerata to the Gallery of Urbino (figs. 158 and 159) ([3]). In the lower part of the frame an inscription which is now almost illegible ran: "*Anno Dni Millo CCCXL G(uin)to Tpe Din Clementis P.P. oc opus fecit Jo(a)nnes Barontius de Arimino*" ([4]). The central group is composed of the Virgin seated on an elaborate throne and fondling the Child Who stands at her knee, an angel seen in profile at either side and beyond them a holy abbot carrying a crook, and St. Francis. The two scenes one above the other at either side are, to the left, the Adoration of the Magi and the Presentation in the Temple and to the right the Last Supper — which takes place at a round table — and the Betrayal of Judas. One of the seven pinnacles is missing. The central one which is larger and of a very unusual form shows the Crucifixion with numerous figures; those to the extreme right and left contain the angel and Virgin of the Annunciation, both kneeling, while in the other three are the half-length figures of SS. Louis of Toulouse wearing a beard, John the Baptist and Peter.

This work reveals Baronzio as an artist inferior to his predecessor from whom, however, he borrowed the characteristic

---

([1]) *Tonini*, op. cit., reproduces the following epitaph that he found in the church of S. Francesco, Rimini: "*Johis Barontii et Denta comandi Barontii et Comandi filii quondam magistri Johannis Barontie pictoris di cont. S. Agnetis*".

([2]) *L. Venturi*, A traverso Le Marche, L'Arte, 1915, p. 4.

([3]) *E. Calzini*, La Galleria annessa all' Istituto di Belle Arte di Urbino, L'Arte, IV, 1901, p. 361.

([4]) The inscription has been handed down to us by *Tonini*, op. cit. (*Crowe and Cavalcaselle*, op. cit., II, p. 155 note 2).

Fig. 160. Baronzio, vault of the choir. Sta. Maria in Porto fuori, near Ravenna.
Photo Alinari.

proportions, long necks, sharp features and small mouths, but his exaggeration of these peculiarities makes his figures much less pleasing than Giuliano's. Baronzio also depicts action with much animation, and employs the same soft clear colours which have nothing in common with Florentine art, but remind us sooner of the Roman artists of the end of the 13th century. In his manner of rendering plastic effects, he does not obtain the same subtle gradation as Giuliano, but shows rather strong contrasts of light and shade. He continues the old tradition of ornamenting the gold background with a pattern of flowers and leaves.

The attribution of at least part of the frescoes in the church of Sta. Maria in Porto fuori, near Ravenna, to Baronzio is generally accepted (¹). In my opinion the entire work is by this master who, as was usually the case for enterprises of this size, was assisted by his pupils. Herr Brach has discovered the hand of not less than five different artists; Signor L. Venturi ascribes the decoration to Pietro da Rimini, while Mr. Sirén believes that some of the frescoes might be by Giuliano da Rimini; but, not only do we find nothing in the paintings to substantiate this last hypothesis but I think they are of a posterior date, for Giuliano's activity, which started in 1307, was apparently limited to the first quarter of the 14th century, while the frescoes of Sta. Maria in Porto fuori were executed after 1332, the year that the old church, which, for centuries had been a celebrated place of pilgrimage, was rebuilt (²).

Serafino Pasolini who, in 1676, published a history of a Byzantine relief of the Madonna which is still preserved in this church, informs us that the pictorial decoration was executed between 1337 and 1367 at the time of Abbot Ranuccio da Galliata. The latter in a *Memoria* concerning the history of the Abbey, would himself have furnished these dates. Pasolini, however, was mistaken because Ranuccio was abbot only from 1364 until 1367, but the date concerning the frescoes is very possibly correct (³). In this case the paintings were, in all probability, made shortly after 1337, and I suggest this date on account of the style of the work as much as for the reason that the church was likely to have been decorated after the reconstruction, which, as we saw, took place in 1332.

Above the chancel arch we see a representation of the Last

(¹) *Brach*, op. cit., p. 1. C. W. *Goetz*, Ravenna, Leipz. Berlin, 1901, p. 110. C. *Ricci,* Guida di Ravenna, 5th ed., Bologna, 1914, p. 148, attributes them to the Romagnole school.

(²) *Brach*, op. cit., p. 53. *Cavalcaselle* and *C. Ricci* are of opinion that the church was destroyed by the earthquake of 1348 but, as Herr *Brach* has pointed out, there is no reason to believe this.

(³) *Brach*, op. cit., p. 54.

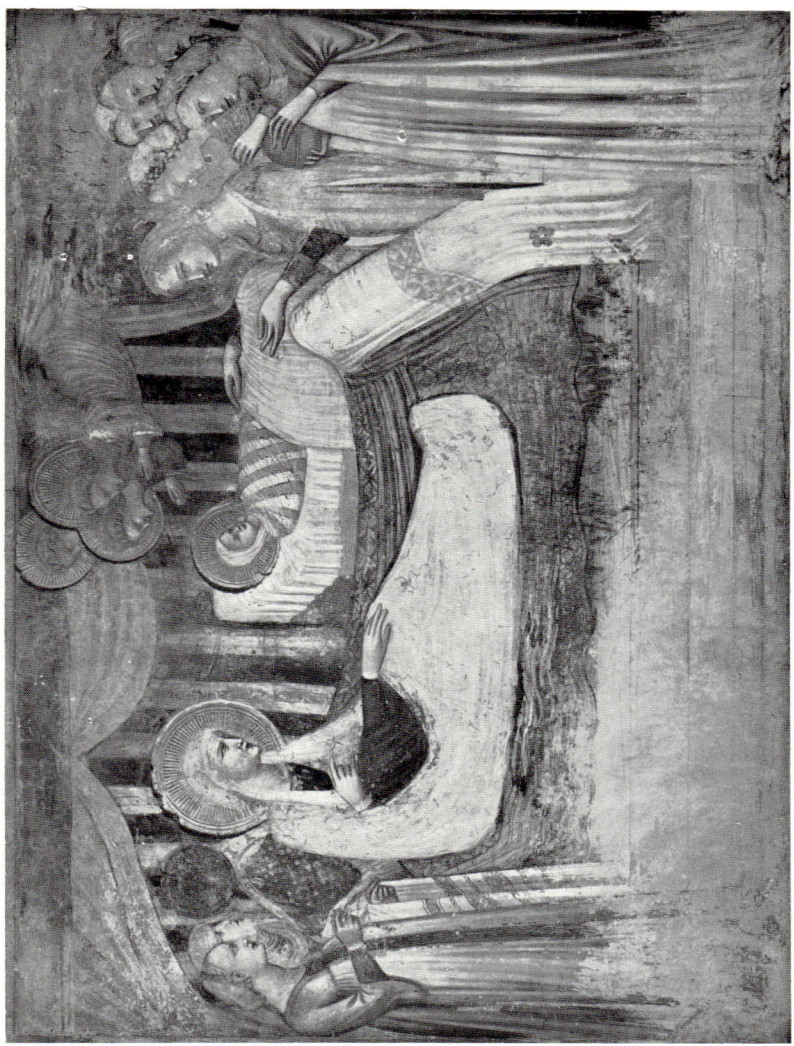

Fig. 161. Baronzio, the Nativity of the Virgin. Sta. Maria in Porto fuori, near Ravenna.   Photo Alinari.

Judgment. The Saviour in a mandorla is depicted with his right hand open palm outwards, his left pronated. Below are shown the Saved dressed in white arising from their tombs and, opposite, devils chasing the Damned into hell which is represented by the open jaws of a monster. The important frescoes at the sides of

Christ portraying the end of the Antichrist's reign are very curious; on one side he orders and assists at the beheading of two old saints, and on the other we see him attacked by four angels with swords and lances while he apparently expounds his false doctrines.

In the chapel each of the four triangles of the vault is adorned with a figure of a Church Father to whom an Evangelist dictates (fig. 160). The latter are seated at lecterns, the former at little desks listening intently or busy with their pens. The symbols of the Evangelists are depicted in the corner above each pair and also serve as the motifs of ornamentation of the pieces of furniture before which the Gospel-writers and Church Doctors are sitting. Their expressions and gestures are fairly animated. The intrados of the two lateral arches are decorated each with six medallions containing the busts of the Apostles while lower down are the figures of SS. Paul, Louis of Toulouse, John the Evangelist and another saint who is unrecognizable on account of the ruined state of the painting, and in the choir the images of SS. Apollinaris and Antony Abbot.

On the left wall we find illustrated the story of the Virgin and her parents.

In the lunette above, we see Joachim driven from the Temple, represented in an agitated scene in which the background is formed by an isolated piece of architecture in rather an archaic manner, but one which Giotto usually employed. Lower down, besides a landscape of the 18th century, are found the Nativity of the Virgin (fig. 161) and her Presentation in the Temple (fig. 162). The former shows us St. Anna sitting up in bed under a baldachin and near her, lying swathed in a cradle, the newborn child over whose head hover three angels. Two women stand at the head of the bed with what appear to be fans in their hands, while six others, one carrying an offering, approach from the opposite side. The mistaken perspective in this scene is very evident. In the Presentation in the Temple we see St. Anna guiding the little Virgin Mary, who carries a candle, towards the priest who, with outstretched hands, inclines slightly to receive her. Many of the figures behind the mother are partly effaced, the three foremost are depicted with gifts in their hands.

Three men in conversation are seen behind the priest; it has

Fig. 162. Baronzio, the Presentation of the Virgin in the Temple. Sta. Maria in Porto fuori, near Ravenna.   Photo Alinari.

been suggested that two of them are supposed to represent Dante and Guido da Polenta or Rainaldo Concoreggio ([1]).

([1]) *C. Ricci*, L'ultimo refugio di Dante, Milano, 1891, p. 287. *The Same*, Ravenna, Bergamo, 1909, p. 40. *The Same*, Guida di Ravenna, p. 151. *Goetz*, op. cit., p. 115. *P. D. Pasolini*, Ravenna e le sue grandi memorie, Roma, 1912, p. 117.

In the background the altar and apse are isolated in the same manner as the building in the foregoing fresco.

On the opposite wall two other scenes from the story of the Virgin are represented; they are the Coronation (in the lunette) and her Death. The former shows in the midst of four angels the Saviour placing the crown on the Virgin's head; in the latter, which is partly destroyed, we see the Virgin stretched on her couch and above, the Lord, surrounded by angelic musicians and prophets, receiving her soul in the form of a small child while the disciples, expressing their sorrow, are grouped around the bier.

The Massacre of the Innocents is also depicted. In the midst of an agitated crowd of women and a large number of children, three soldiers carry out their horrible task; a fourth stands before Herod who assists at the execution of his order. On the same wall a niche which doubtless contained the Sacraments is adorned with an image of the Saviour giving the Eucharist to four Apostles represented in half-figure. Above to the left a young woman and a nun who, it has been suggested, are Chiara and Francesca da Polenta, look from a window (fig. 163).

The apse is almost entirely covered with frescoes of later date. Only two fragments of 14th century painting have been conserved; one shows three holy woman kneeling, the other, which is of more importance, consists of the half of a representation of the Doubting Thomas (fig. 164).

The part in which the disbeliever was depicted has been destroyed by the addition of a pillar, but we see the Saviour, and five Apostles bending towards Him with their eyes fixed on the wound in His side.

In the left lateral chapel, the decoration is considerably damaged. The six half-length figures of saints are still visible in the arch but the painting of the vault has disappeared. Near the entrance there remains an image of a holy martyr. On the right wall we see above, the decapitation of a young saint ([1]) and two scenes illustrating incidents from the life of Pope John I ([2]): firstly, the Pope, followed by two priests, relating to Theodoric how his mission to convert Justinian had failed, and secondly,

---

([1]) Herr *Brach* does not mention this scene.
([2]) *Pasolini*, op. cit., p. 63.

the Pope and his followers, behind the bars of their prison which is guarded by a soldier. A niche between the two frescoes is decorated with an image of the Saviour. Only the figure of a holy pilgrim has been preserved in the apse.

The decoration in the chapel to the right has suffered much

Fig. 163. Baronzio, Chiara and Francesca di Polenta (?) Sta. Maria in Porto fuori, near Ravenna.
Photo Alinari.

less. Over the entrance we see the Saviour in benediction between two prophets, lower on the left is a bearded saint and in the arch six busts of saints. The vault is divided into two parts, the second of which is adorned with four medallions containing angels. On the left wall we find in the lunette above, the call of St. Matthew who is depicted seated at a table while the Saviour, accompanied by a disciple, seems in the act of leaving him after having told him to follow.

Fig. 164. Baronzio, the Incredulity of St. Thomas. Sta Maria in Porto fuori, near Ravenna.   Photo Alinari.

THE PAINTERS OF RIMINI. 323

Fig. 165. Baronzio, the Sermon of Pietro Peccatore. Sta. Maria in Porto fuori, near Ravenna.

Photo Alinari.

On the next row we see the young saint, Pietro Peccatore, with two other persons speaking to cripples who kneel in what seems to be the gateway of a town (fig. 165). Then follows St. John the Evangelist preaching, which, in composition, is very similar to that of the foregoing fresco. On the same wall we find a dragon and an almost effaced figure of a saint which at Brach's time was still clearly visible.

The ascension of St. John the Evangelist is represented high up on the opposite wall; he is depicted in half-length figure carried to heaven by two angels. Of two other frescoes which originally adorned this wall, one has entirely disappeared and only a few fragments that cannot be interpreted remain of the other. The painting of St. John baptising a king in the presence of a saint and the queen is in much better condition. Traces of two figures of saints are seen in the apse.

The walls of the nave may originally also have been covered with frescoes, for high on the right wall we find a representation of the Virgin with four saints and two angels holding the drapery behind the throne. Lower down in another division a figure is depicted in adoration before a young saint, while closeby we see a herd of pigs in a field. The frescoes in the chapel are all framed by rich borders of Cosmati mosaic pattern in which medallions containing heads are scattered.

All the frescoes are not of the same quality, and as I said before, we must admit the presence of some helpers to whom I attribute for example the Presentation in the Temple and the sermon of St. John the Evangelist; but there can be no doubt that it was one master who dominated and directed the whole enterprise, for the decoration in its ensemble is extremely harmonious.

There are still some other paintings by Baronzio. In the church of Sta. Chiara, Ravenna, now the chapel of the Poor-house [1], the vault is adorned with figures of the Evangelists and the Church Fathers, medallions with the Twelve Apostles and ornamental borders imitating Cosmati mosaics; the entire decoration, although less elaborate, being a free copy of the frescoes in Sta. Maria in Porto fuori. The principal painting which is nowadays clearly visible is the Crucifixion; it is depicted around

---

[1] *Crowe and Cavalcaselle*, op. cit., II, p. 156, note 1. *Brach*, op. cit., p. 80. Boll. d'Arte del Minist. della Pubbl. Istr., 1922, p. 338. *L. Venturi*, op. cit., p. 8, with the exception of the Crucifixion which he ascribes to Baronzio, believes all these paintings to be the work of Pietro da Rimini.

the embrasure of a window and shows four angels flying around the Crucified, the Virgin fainting in the arms of two of her companions and St. Mary Magdalene to one side and to the

Fig. 166 Baronzio, the Baptism of Christ. Sta Chiara, Ravenna.
Photo Bezzi.

other St. John, the Centurion and some soldiers. The work is of a strong dramatic effect. Lower down on the left we see traces of the Baptism (fig. 166) and the Prayer on the Mount of Olives.

On the lateral walls there remain on one side, the figure of the Saviour from a scene of the Doubting Thomas, markedly resembling the central figure of the composition in Sta. Maria in

Porto fuori, and on the other, the Annunciation and the figures of SS. Francis, Clare, Antony Abbot, and Louis. On the entrance wall we see against a rocky landscape one man standing and behind him a second holding a horse, a group which originally must have formed part of a representation of the Adoration of the Magi. No doubt can exist that these paintings are the work

Fig. 167. Baronzio, a Detail of the Crucifixion. S. Francesco, Ravenna.
Photo Bezzi.

of the artist whom we have just found active in the church on the outskirts of the town.

Among the frescoes in Ravenna which can be attributed to Baronzio, I think we should include the very damaged Crucifixion in the left aisle of the church of S. Francesco in which the fainting Virgin (fig. 167) and a figure, which some have suggested to be Dante's portrait (fig. 168), are still clearly visible ([1]).

Elsewhere I have had occasion to ascribe to Baronzio a Des-

([1]) *G. Gerola*, Ancora sugli affreschi danteschi scoperti in S. Francesco, Ravenna, 1920. *Santi Muratori*, La chiesa dei funerali di Dante, San Francesco di Ravenna, Rassegna d'Arte, 1921, p. 298. Bolletino d'Arte del Minist. della Pubbl. Instr., 1922, p. 337.

Fig. 168. Baronzio, a supposed portrait of Dante. S. Francesco, Ravenna.
Photo Bezzi.

cent from the Cross on a gold background with a design of leaves, which I saw in the Palazzo Gentile at Viterbo (fig. 169) ([1]). This

---

([1]) R. *van Marle*, op. cit.

picture is very superior in execution as well as in feeling to the one at Urbino and can be classed with the Mercatello crucifix as the finest of this artist's productions. In the very marked finesse of the execution of these two panels Baronzio closely approaches Giuliano da Rimini and the artists influenced by Cavallini.

That Baronzio was a pupil of Giuliano da Rimini's seems to me almost certain. The very peculiar facial types, the characteristics of which I have already mentioned, the elongated proportions, especially striking in the necks, the regular and somewhat hard folds of the drapery, the technique of relief and plasticity, the profound feeling and intensity of action, as well as the clear colours of the Roman school of painting are all found in Baronzio's works but treated in a cruder manner and with a less developed sense of the beautiful. Baronzio pushes the peculiarities that he borrows from Giuliano so far as almost to produce caricature. The expression of the faces of the Apostles to whom the Saviour distributes the Sacraments in the church of Sta. Maria in Porto fuori are regular grimaces. The crucifix of 1344 and the altar-piece of 1345 prove, however, that the artist's productions of almost simultaneous execution are very variable in quality, and his feebler works lead us to believe that the school of Rimini, which shortly before had such a brilliant commencement, had already entered into a stage of decadence with Baronzio, and after a short decline completely died out. There are, of course, still a good many works that belong to this school but none of them comes up to the standard of the productions of its earlier masters.

Baronzio himself seems to have had a fair number of followers. To one of his faithful pupils we owe a polyptych in the church of S. Francesco at Mercatello in which, beside the enthroned Virgin with the Child, we see eight figures of saints each in a separate panel (¹).

An immediate disciple, very much under the master's influence, was the artist who, not without help however, executed the most extensive pictorial monument belonging to the school of Rimini viz., the decoration of the chapel of St. Nicholas at

---

(¹) *L. Venturi*, op. cit., believes this polyptych to be a work of Baronzio's.

Fig. 169. Baronzio, the Descent from the Cross. Formerly in the Palazzo Gentile, Viterbo.   Photo Brogi.

Tolentino. It is easy to understand how this series of frescoes, so imbued with Baronzio's art, has been attributed to the master himself(¹).

The chief decoration of the vault consists once more of pairs

---

(¹) *F. Hermanin*, Gli affreschi di G. Baronzio e dei suoi seguaci in Tolentino, Bolletino della Soc. di Filol. romana, 1905, VII, p. 65. *Vitzthum*, Ueber Giotto's Schule in der Romagna, Sitzungsbericht der Berliner Kunsthistor-

of Evangelists and Church Fathers, each seated before a little table and, as we found in Sta. Maria in Porto fuori, a symbol of an Evangelist in each of the upper angles. Here too all the available space has been filled up with books and little pieces of furniture (fig. 170). The facial types and the attitudes also resemble those of the other decoration. Each of the triangles is enclosed in a border showing numerous medallions containing busts of saints and in each of the four pendentives we find personifications of the seven virtues and of one vice, they are: Justice with Injustice, Temperance with Faith, Courage with Charity and Hope with Prudence.

The walls are entirely covered with frescoes arranged in three rows. On the entrance wall we see, in the lunette, the Presentation in the Temple taking place in a somewhat fantastic building in which the old priest holds the Child, Who turns towards His Mother, while on one side, Joseph, behind whom are depicted two little devotees, bears an offering, and on the other Anna the Prophetess carries a scroll with an inscription. Lower are represented the Holy Ghost descending on the Apostles who are grouped in a semicircle (fig. 171) and the Massacre of the Innocents, which shows many points in common with the composition in Sta. Maria in Porto fuori. An ornamental border with medallions of saints' heads separates this row from the lower one where we find four scenes illustrating the life of the titular saint: firstly St. Nicholas curing a blind man who kneels before him; then follow the saint delivering an innocent person from prison, rescuing ship-wrecked sailors, and praying for the salvation,

---

Gesellsch., 1905, III. p. 18. *Crowe and Cavalcaselle*, op. cit., III, p. 181, apparently include them with the productions of the school of Fabriano. So also does *A. Venturi*, op cit., V, p. 854, who describes the artist as a precursor of Allegretto Nuzi's. I fail to see the connection between the paintings of Fabriano and this work which is so essentially Riminese. Among the numerous differences which divide these two schools the most striking is, that the painters of Fabriano produced an art in which the principal interest lies in the contours while in that of Rimini, as too in the whole of Emilian painting, the artists have given a preponderating place to plastic effects. A comparison of the types will but emphasize the error of this attribution and provide us sooner with an argument in favour of Signor Hermanin's. *A. Colasanti*, Gentile da Fabriano, Bergamo, 1909, p 27, sees but quite a superficial connection between Baronzio and the painter of Tolentino.

Fig. 170. School of Baronzio, Vault. St. Nicholas Chapel, Tolentino.

Photo Minist. del. Pubbl. Istr.

Fig. 171. School of Baronzio, the Descent of the Holy Ghost. St. Nicholas Chapel, Tolentino.
Photo Minist. del. Pubbl. Istr.

— which salvation is granted — of a person who has been hanged (fig. 172).

On the left or altar wall the lunette above is occupied by an

Fig. 172. School of Baronzio, Detail of the kneeling figure of St. Nicholas of Tolentino. St. Nicholas Chapel, Tolentino.
Photo Minist. del. Pubbl. Istr.

important representation of the Virgin's Death, which again shows much correspondence with the composition of this subject in Sta. Maria in Porto fuori; only here we see a fairly large and finely executed group of figures — probably the donors — kneeling in adoration in the centre, while nearby kneels a holy monk, very likely St. Nicholas.

The tier below shows the Saviour at the age of twelve teaching in the Temple while His parents approach from the left — the profusion of architecture is rather remarkable —, the Return from Jerusalem and a scene which can only be the Wedding at Cana (fig. 173). The last mentioned is of curious composition; it is divided into four distinct parts: to the extreme right we see the Saviour, giving orders, seated at a table with a nimbused figure which is somewhat effaced, but probably represents the Virgin; adjacent are the steward and other servants with the jars of water; then follow two people seated at table, without doubt the bride and bridegroom, while on the extreme left two Apostles with three other persons are depicted eating at a round table. Three pairs of miniature adorers are represented on the right of this row. Below we find St. Nicholas curing demoniacs and sick people, whose faces are of an unpleasing realism (fig. 174), the Saviour on the Cross between the Virgin, St. John, another saint and St. Nicholas, with St. Mary Magdalene kneeling at the foot of the Cross clasping Christ's feet (fig. 175), and two scenes from the childhood of St. Nicholas; the one illustrating how St. Nicholas of Bari appeared to the parents, over whose head hovers an angel, and predicted the extraordinary life of their child; the other showing the little St. Nicholas of Tolentino with other childern receiving instruction from their school master (fig. 176).

On the wall opposite the entrance we see in the lunette the Annunciation with two little figures of adorers, the Entry into Jerusalem in which the size of the figures does not harmonize with that of the rest of the decoration, and the Prayer on the Mount of Olives depicted in two episodes: firstly Christ speaking to His disciples and asking them to remain awake, and secondly the disciples asleep while the angel appears to Christ. The lowest row is again adorned with scenes from the life of the titular saint who is first represented eagerly listening to a sermon by an Augustinian monk, then, united with this scene, his reception into the order, and lastly, an angel descending towards the saint and placing a crown on his head. Finally on the last wall we see in the lunette a combination of the Visitation, the Nativity, the angelic Message to the Shepherds and the Journey of the Wise Men. Below are represented the Saviour followed by

Fig. 173. School of Baronzio, Detail of the Marriage at Cana. St. Nicholas Chapel, Tolentino.
Photo Minist. del. Pubbl. Istr.

Fig. 174. School of Baronzio, Detail of St. Nicholas curing the Possessed and the Sick. St. Nicholas Chapel, Tolentino.

Photo Minist. del. Pubbl. Istr.

two angels, descending into Limbo, the entrance to which resembles the gateway of a town, and the three Holy Women visiting the Empty Sepulchre on which the angel is seated and around which the soldiers lie sleeping. These two frescoes are not in a good state of preservation. On the lowest row we find the death of St. Nicholas who is represented lying on a couch surrounded by monks while the Saviour, accompanied by the Virgin, St. Nicholas of Bari and four angels has come to fetch the soul of the dead saint; the other scene on this row shows, how

Fig. 175. School of Baronzio, the Crucified and saints. St. Nicholas Chapel, Tolentino.

Photo Minist. del. Pubbl. Istr.

through St. Nicholas' intervention, a dead woman is resuscitated while being transported to church.

This imposing series of frescoes is executed in rather sombre colours, and for that reason seems, at first sight, to differ more considerably from the other works of this school than is really the case. Another feature which is rather unusual in the painting of the Riminese school is the abundance of architecture. In some scenes, e.g. the Presentation in the Temple, we find very elaborate architecture and in others the artist has depicted buildings even when their presence was in no way required. This leads us to suppose that we have in this decoration a work of a more advanced period of this school and the date of 1350 to 1360 proposed by Signor Hermanin seems quite feasible, although I am inclined to place it slightly earlier.

It is once more the curious facial types, the sharp features, the piercing look, the somewhat hard drapery, the lively gestures and the vivacious spirit of the work that demonstrate the close connection that must have existed between the artist who directed this enterprise and Baronzio. Had not adjacent figures contradicted the hypothesis, we might have ascribed some of the figures in the vault and in the scenes of the Massacre of the Innocents, the Crucifixion, the Entry into Jerusalem and the resurrection of the dead woman to Baronzio himself.

The figure of the school-master shows a striking resemblance to the supposed portrait of Dante in S. Francesco, Ravenna, and to Herod in the Massacre of the Innocents in Sta. Maria in Porto fuori, or again the extremely realistic profiles of the disciples receiving the Holy Communion in the last-mentioned church to the profiles of the sick before the saint at Tolentino. A large part of the rest of the frescoes seems to have been left to another artist who was less familiar with Baronzio's art and no doubt a pupil of the better master. The large number of donors that we find depicted in these frescoes would lead us to suppose that the decoration was ordered by an association of persons.

There are a few crucifixes which show some connection with Baronzio's art. One, in the chapel of the Confraternity of S. Giovanni Decollato at Urbania, bears the signature: "*Petrus de Arimino fecit h* ......" It is a finely executed work in which the morphological types peculiar to Giuliano and Baronzio are manifest. The terminals are occupied by the figures of the Almighty, the Virgin Mary and St. John (¹).

(¹) *Passavant*, in his book on Raphael, describes this cross in the third chapter of the appendix but erroneously attaches to it the signature of Giuliano's panel that is preserved in this town. *Brach*, op. cit., p..67, believes

Fig. 176. School of Baronzio, St. Nicholas at school. St. Nicholas Chapel, Tolentino.   Photo Minist. del. Pubbl. Istr.

it to be probably the work of the artist who was active in the right chapel in Sta. Maria in Porto fuori and says it bears a strong resemblance to a crucifix in the Badia, Arezzo, which is a work of the Sienese artist, Segna di Bonaventura, v. Vol. II, p. 129.

Three other crucifixes are preserved in the Gallery of Urbino; one of them is ascribed to Pietro da Rimini, author of the foregoing work, and may very well be a work of this artist who seems to have belonged to a slightly later generation than Baronzio.

A second crucifix in the same gallery is attributed to Baronzio himself and it really does show a decided resemblance to this master's style. The Virgin's figure is expressive of great agitation; the pelican at the top of the cross is a Giottesque element; four angels are grouped around the feet of the Crucified.

A work executed very much after Baronzio's manner is a crucifix in the church of Talamello in which half-length figures of the Saviour, the Virgin and St. John are seen in the extremities. Formerly some writers have thought it to be a production of Giotto's. The painting is of excellent quality but I think should be placed slightly posterior to Baronzio's activities.

The third cross in the Urbino Gallery (fig. 177) is very large. The master's connection with Baronzio is manifest in the types of his figures but the round shape of his heads differentiates him from the other members of this group (¹). I think the same hand can be recognized in the terminal of a polyptych in the Gallery of Strasbourg representing the Crucifixion (fig. 178). Certain iconographical features of the early productions of the school of Rimini are found in this picture, thus for example the Cross made from the branches of a tree. The curious form of the panel is identical with that of the central terminal of Baronzio's signed altar-piece. Two angels are depicted catching the blood that drips from the Saviour's hands; on the left the Virgin faints in the arms of two of her companions, while on the right we see St. John and the smaller figure of St. Francis kneeling at the foot of the Cross.

Quite after Baronzio's manner is a panel of the Nativity of Our Lord which once belonged to the Kaufmann collection in Berlin (²).

(¹) In the Urbino Gallery this crucifix is attributed to Lorenzetti; it is probably the same as the one that *Crowe and Cavalcaselle*, op. cit., II, p. 156, mention as being in S. Paolo a Montefiori. They cite, loc. cit., another similar cross with the Magdalene but do not say where it is to be found.

(²) *W. Hausenstein,* Die Malerei der Frühen Italiener (Das Bild III—IV), Munich, 1922, pl. 40, considers it to be in the circle of Pietro Lorenzetti.

THE PAINTERS OF RIMINI.

Two panels which on account of their form and miniature-like technique belong to the group of Riminese paintings influenced by Cavallini reveal at the same time, in their types and figures, the master's knowledge of Baronzio's art. One of them, which is found in the Lichtenstein collection, Vienna, shows in three divisions, one below the other, the Adoration of the Magi, the Crucifix-

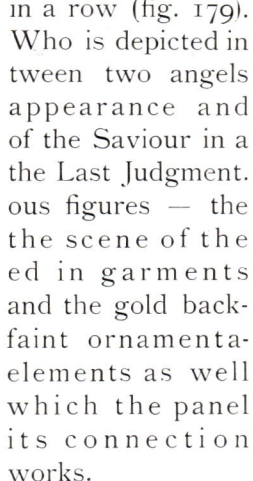

Fig. 177. School of Baronzio, Crucifix. Gallery, Urbino.
Photo Minist. del. Pubbl. Istr.

ion and seven saints in a row (fig. 179). The figure of Christ Who is depicted in the pinnacle between two angels has been given the appearance and attitude of an image of the Saviour in a representation of the Last Judgment.
One of the numerous figures — the Centurion's — in the scene of the Crucifixion is clothed in garments woven with gold and the gold background shows a faint ornamentation. These two elements as well as the manner in which the panel is divided, betray its connection with the older works.
With the exception of the design in the background we find these features in another panel, this one in the Metropolitan Museum, New York, where it is, I believe, ascribed to Baronzio himself (fig. 186).
It is composed of eight scenes arranged in four rows. The uppermost two represent the Coronation of the Virgin and four

angels; then follow the Descent from the Cross with the Entombment, the Descent into Limbo with the Ascension and the Descent of the Holy Ghost with the Last Judgment, which scene shows a certain resemblance to the one we found in the panel of the same form in the Palazzo Venezia. A detail until now unknown in the Riminese school of painting is the quite Giottesque manner in which the figures are placed in the interior of a building in the scene of the Descent of the Holy Ghost, and which is identical with the way in which Giotto depicts this subject in his cycle of frescoes at Padua. Thus we have proof that this work also is the production of a more advanced stage, and does not belong to the group of Cavallinesque painting. Judging from the photograph I should imagine that the panel is in parts considerably repainted.

Among the works belonging to this school in which Baronzio's influence does not predominate, the most important is found rather distant from this region. It consisted in the series of frescoes in the chapel of the castle of Collalto, near Conegliano and Treviso, but the locality was badly bombarded during the war and I think the paintings were very much damaged, if not completely destroyed.

Von Schlosser has rightly ascribed this decoration to two different artists, one of whom executed the representations of Jesus at the age of twelve teaching in the Temple, the Transfiguration, the Death and the Resurrection of the Virgin; and the other St. Prosdocimus, the first bishop of Padua, baptising the Count of Treviso; St. George killing the dragon before the princess who kneels in prayer; St. Ursula and her companions and an image of the Virgin nursing the Child Christ. The former of these two painters is the more traditional and is certainly the older. I do not agree with Herr von Schlosser when he mentions the second group of frescoes in connection with a youthful work of Tommaso da Modena's with whom the painter of Treviso should be identified ([1]).

In the past the castle frequently changed hands; von Schlosser is of opinion that the paintings were executed about 1340 which

---

([1]) *von Schlosser*, Tommaso da Modena. *Brach.* op. cit., p. 88, has already placed them in the school of Rimini.

Fig. 178. School of Baronzio, the Crucifixion. Gallery, Strasbourg.

would coincide with the residence of the Scaliger family and it is quite possible that the decoration was carried out while they were the proprietors.

The artist who executed the first group of frescoes, worked very much after the manner of Giuliano da Rimini. The facial types of some of the old men, the appearance of the beautiful angels in the Resurrection and the folds of the draperies are not, however, always entirely free from Byzantine elements.

The drawing of the second artist is more evolved and he possessed a greater sense of beauty. Even although his morphological types more closely resemble Giuliano's, we also note that abundance of detail, almost entirely limited to the costumes, that characterizes the "scènes de genre", peculiar to Padua and Treviso.

Both artists depict action with a keen sense of reality; expressions, gestures and attitudes are more violent than in the works of the Riminese painters and give to the paintings a certain vulgarity and a lack of tragic and religious feeling, which is another factor they have again in common with "scènes de genre". Architecture is not very frequent in these frescoes, nevertheless, in the baptism of the Count of Treviso, the background is formed by a fine building of Gothico-Venetian style; it does not, however, show the perspective characteristic of Paduan painting but is merely a background to the event which is supposed to take place in its interior.

These two artists, consequently, seem to have united elements of the local art and those of the school of Rimini; their style however is based on the latter and it is highly probable that we are herein dealing with two painters who originally belonged to the Riminese group but whose manner underwent a change on account of the infiltration of Paduan factors.

Another important series of paintings is the later decoration in the Abbey of Pomposa which, on this occasion, adorns the Chapter room (¹). On the end wall we see a somewhat damaged fresco of the Crucifixion in which we can however distinguish the fainting Madonna, the Magdalene at the foot of the Cross, the angels flying around the Crucified and a good many of the other figures. At the sides and ends of the lateral wall we see four isolated figures of saints enclosed in frames resembling portals while twelve other figures, no doubt the Apostles, form three pairs on either of the side walls, each pair depicted in the

---

(¹) *Brach,* op. cit., p. 40, believes them to be of earlier date than the frescoes in the refectory and the church, but I hold the contrary opinion. The description given by Herr *Brach* leads me to believe that in his day the paintings were for the greater part covered.

Fig. 179. School of Baronzio, the Crucifixion and other scenes. Lichtenstein Collection, Vienna.

opening of a mullioned window (fig. 181). The colours of these paintings have entirely disappeared and if some traces of paint had not survived on the other frescoes it might have been thought that these figures were executed in grisaille.

The excellent drawing, especially of the drapery, reveals the artist's adherence to the school of Rimini. The work probably dates from the beginning of the second half of the 14th century.

Some frescoes which were of considerable significance for our knowledge of the Riminese school of painting existed in the cloister of S. Francesco, Bologna, but in 1882 the wall was demolished ([1]).

There were three rows of scenes with the Crucifixion and the Resurrection one above the other, in the centre; the others all illustrated the life of St. Francis and showed the stigmatization, with the saint's apparition to the Pope, the death of the knight of Celano, the ordeal by fire before the Sultan, the healing of the man wounded in the chest and, above, three other scenes which are impossible to decipher from the only photographs of them that exist ([2]), but of which one might very probably have represented St. Francis' apparition at Arles.

The iconography of the scenes of the Franciscan legend has some points in common with that of the cycle that Giotto and his pupils have left at Assisi, but also a good many differences, and there is no reason to believe that the artist who worked at Bologna followed the Assisan frescoes. For as far as the reproduction allows us to judge the technique of the painting is not Bolognese but sooner shows a connection with that of the school of Rimini; moreover formerly the decoration seems to have borne the signature: *"hop Francisci Ariminensis"* ([3]). The name of Francesco da Rimini whom Malvasia, in his book on Bolognese painting, wishes to include with the artists of this town, appears in a Riminese document of 1348, when he is mentioned as deceased. A tomb of a painter of this name existed in 1362 in the church of S. Francesco, Rimini ([4]).

([1]) *Brach*, op. cit., p. 84.

([2]) Reprod. in *Brach*, op. cit., pl. 10.

([3]) *A. Rubbiani*, La chiesa di S. Francesco in Bologna, Bologna, 1886, p. 148. *Brach*, op. cit., p. 87.

([4]) *L. Tonini*, op. cit., p. 391.

Fig. 180. School of Baronzio, the Coronation of the Virgin and other scenes. Metropolitan Museum, New York.

In and around Rimini we still find a certain number of works belonging to this school. The most important is a fresco in a room to the left of S. Francesco which originally formed part of the church of S. Antonio. Here Galeotto Malatesta, out of gratitude for the Virgin's protection during the plague of 1348, had himself represented in adoration before the Madonna whom we see escorted by SS. George and Antony ([1]). Of the donor, only the head covered with a helmet remains visible, but it is highly probable that the fresco was one of those devotional paintings that we frequently met with in Verona and Padua; and if this be so, it is one of the early examples of this type of picture.

A fragment of an extremely small fresco that Brach reports having seen in the Hotel of the Aquila d'Oro, represented the angel of the Annunciation, St. Ursula and her companions, and some other saints, but it has since disappeared, as has also a figure of the Saviour that Cavalcaselle saw on the wall of the garden of the Casa Romagnoli and that according to Brach dated from the 13th century.

As examples of crucifixes similar to those we found at Urbino, may be cited one in the sacristy of S. Agostino (the earliest, but a considerably damaged specimen) and that in the Isotta chapel in the Tempio Malatesta (almost entirely repainted and of little interest) while Cavalcaselle mentions others at Verucchio and Villa in the vicinity of Rimini ([2]).

In Ravenna, apart from the frescoes with which we have already dealt in the church of S. Francesco, we find on the left wall a second Crucifixion, on the one opposite, a Presentation in the Temple, and in the Polenta chapel a fragment of yet another Crucifixion and a representation of Abraham offering hospitality to the angels ([3]) while some heads and other débris of frescoes are scattered throughout the church. In the vault of S. Giovanni Evangelista we find once more depicted in the four triangles the Evangelists and the Church Fathers with the symbols of the Gospel-writers over head. The figures, which are here somewhat differently placed, are entirely repainted but

---

([1]) Atti e Mem. della R. Dep. di Stor. Patr. p. la Romagna, VII, 1868. L. *Tonini*, op. cit., IV, p. 131. *Brach*, op. cit., p. 83.

([2]) *Crowe and Cavalcaselle*, op. cit., II, p. 156.

([3]) *Santi Muratori*, op. cit.

CHAPTER V.

THE PAINTERS OF MODENA [1].

In Modena, we find a good deal of evidence that leads us to suppose that the artistic activity during the 14th century was fairly great. Besides such artists as Tommaso, Barnaba, Serafino Serafini, his son Paolo, and Fra Paolo da Modena, whose works have survived, there are records of the following painters: Ugolino, Bonane and Paolo in 1306, Barisino dei Barisini, the father of Tommaso, in 1317, Niccolo di Pietro Patecchi in 1353, Raniero da Porte and Giovanni Diddo in 1357, Niccolo da Reggio in 1359 and 1363, Bartolommeo Diddo together with the afore-cited Giovanni in 1387 [2] and Bonifacio, the son of Tommaso in 1391.

Painting in Modena seems to have made a considerable advance at the beginning of the second half of the 14th century when Tommaso, Barnaba, and Serafino Serafini, all three natives of the city, were contemporaneously active there; but they apparently did not find constant employment in the city of their birth, for they migrated elsewhere for more or less protracted sojourns, as did also, at a later period, Paolo, the son of Serafino.

Thanks to the documents that Signori Bertoni and Vicini have published, we are well informed as to the lives of these three principal Modenese painters. We now know for certain that Tommaso was born, not at Treviso of a Modenese father [3] and still less in Bohemia as has been thought, but in Modena. His father was the painter, Barisino dei Barisini who, as I have already said, is mentioned in a deed of 1317. As we have a record

---

[1] *von Schlosser*, Tommaso da Modena etc.

[2] *G. Bertoni e E. P. Vicini*, Tommaso da Modena, pittore modenese del secolo XIV, Memorie della R. Deput. di Stor. Patr. per la Prov. di Modena, ser. V, vol. III, p. 141. A painter of the name of Ugolino is mentioned in a Modenese document of 1279; it is perhaps the same as the one whose name is recorded in 1306.

[3] A theory expounded by *Federici*, Memorie trevigiane sulle opere di disegno, Venezia, 1803, I, p. 65.

telling us that Tommaso was not yet fourteen years old in 1339, and another of the following year that he had already passed this age, the year of his birth must have been either 1325 or 1326. He is mentioned in documents of 1342, 1344 and 1346 but from 1346 until 1359 he seems to have been absent from Modena except for what must have been a short visit in 1349, for that same year he is found in Treviso ([1]). In 1352 he signed some frescoes in Treviso; he was still there in 1358 but the following year he returned to Modena where further mention is made of him in 1366, 1367 and 1368. There is no other record of him until his death which occurred in 1379, far from Modena where his children certified his decease.

It seems to me highly probable that Tommaso went to Bohemia as we find evidence of his activity there in the castle of Karlstein but he was very likely an unknown artist when he first went. The theory held by Signori Bertoni and Vicini that this was after 1368 and that the Emperor Charles IV, when passing through Modena on his way to Rome in 1368, must has asked him to come ([2]), has been opposed by Signor Venturi on the grounds that Karlstein was founded in 1348 and the prebendaries of the chapels appointed in 1357, before which date the decoration must have been executed. Further he remarks that foreign elements in Tommaso's frescoes in Treviso lead one to suppose that the artist was familiar with Northern art before he executed them ([3]).

This seems hardly possible, especially as a document informs us that in 1367 Theodoric of Prague, who painted part of the decoration of the chapels of Karlstein, was rewarded for his services and further, that at least one of the chapels — that dedicated

---

([1]) *G. Bertoni e E. P. Vicini*, Tommaso da Modena a Treviso, L'Arte, 1916, p. 349.

([2]) *J. Neuwirth*, Mittelalt. Wandgem. u. Tafelbilder der Burg Karlstein in Böhmen, Forschungen zur Kunstgeschicht Böhmens, I, Prague, 1896 and *The Same*, Prague. Leipzig-Berlin, 1901, thought that Tommaso went to Bohemia between 1352 and 1357 and that the Emperor must have become aware of his existence during a voyage he made in 1354; but it has been pointed out that on this occasion Charles IV did not visit Treviso. *H. Lambert*, in the Oester.-Ungar. Revue, XXIV, shared this opinion.

([3]) *L. Testi*, La pittura veneziana, I, p. 261, also believes that the panels of Karlstein were executed before 1352.

THE PAINTERS OF MODENA.

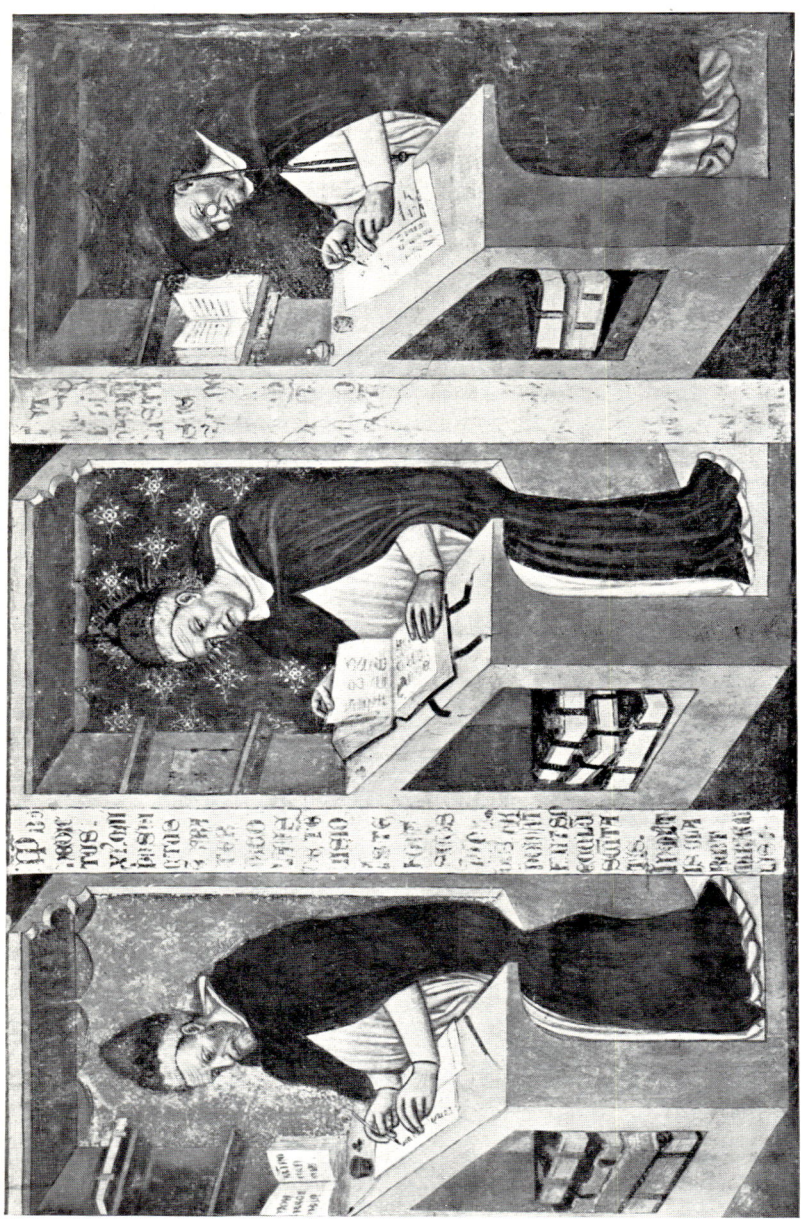

Fig. 182. Tommaso da Modena, the Blessed Leo V and Benedict XI and the venerable Hugues de St. Cher, 1352. Chapter Room, S. Niccolo, Treviso.

Photo Alinari.

to the Holy Cross — was consecrated in 1365 (¹). Another fact that contradicts Signor Venturi's hypothesis is that Tommaso was twenty-four years of age when he went to Treviso and twenty-six when he finished the forty figures that comprise his work there; for the paintings at Karlstein he also required a certain length of time so that, according to Signor Venturi, he would have been requested to work for the King of Bohemia when he was scarcely more than twenty years old. This can hardly be admitted.

Finally the difference in style that Signor Venturi justly notes between the frescoes of 1352 and the works at Karlstein, also leads us to suppose that a considerable lapse of time separates them, the former having been executed in the master's first manner, because it is hardly likely that at this early stage in Tommaso's career, his style had already undergone a change; while the pictures that we find in Bohemia bear more resemblance to the works of his compatriot, Barnaba, from which we can infer a certain influence of the latter artist; and as he appears for the first time only in 1361, he belongs, consequently, to a slightly later generation than Tommaso. Here, it seems to me we have proof that the paintings in Karlstein really are productions of a late stage in Tommaso's career.

I think therefore that the oldest work by Tommaso that we know is the decoration of the Chapter House of S. Niccolo in Treviso (²) which he signed near the door: "*Anno Domini MCCCLII Prior Tarvisinus ordinis praedic depengi fecit istud capitulum et Thomas pictor de Mutina pinxit istud.*"

The decoration consists of forty holy, blessed or venerable figures of monks from the Dominican order. The three principal figures with which the series begins are represented in a different manner from the others. They are the founder of the order, St. Peter the Martyr and St. Thomas Aquinas who are depicted full-face, each showing to the spectator a text from an open book. All the other figures are seen in full or partial profile sitting at little desks with an open book before them and others at their feet.

(¹) H. *Janitschek*, Geschichte der Deutsche Malerei, Berlin, 1890, p. 202. *Neuwirth*, op. cit. No mention is found of Nicolas Wurmser, who collaborated in the ornamentation of these chapels, until the year 1357.

(²) G. *Milanese*, La chiesa monumentale di San Niccolo in Treviso, Treviso, 1904. J. J. *Berthier*, Le chapitre de S. Niccolo de Trévise, Rome, 1912.

Fig. 183. Tommaso da Modena, Albertus Magnus, 1352. Chapter Room, S. Niccolo, Treviso. Photo Alinari.

The inscriptions which separate the figures from one another mention the chief merits of each of the brothers (figs. 182—184).

These frescoes are really a glorification of the studious life of Dominican friars; each figure is represented either reading or writing; two of them — Cardinal Malafranca and the Blessed Bernard da Traversa — display their texts, while others interrupt their reading to consult commentaries, and some study scrolls of parchment. The venerable Cardinal Hugues de St. Cher is seen wearing eye-glasses as he writes; Nicholas of Rouen uses a magnifying glass, while some are busy trimming their quill-pens. The painter's greatest merit is the variety with which he has depicted these forty figures which, on account of the similarity of the subject, might otherwise have resulted in rather a monotonous cycle. Not only the types, which are of a realism by no means flattering, are of a marked individuality and very different one from another, but also the attitudes and above all the impressions that the subject of their texts produces on the Dominicans, are rendered with a diversity full of verve and fantasy.

On the other hand Tommaso's technique is not above criticism. The perspective in general and of the desks in particular is invariably false; while the artist has made no attempt to give any depth to his images. The drawing is hard, the habits fall in heavy folds and the hands are clumsy; all the contours are indicated by thick black lines.

Among the frescoes on the pillars of the church of S. Niccolo, we can ascribe to Tommaso only those on the fifth pillar on the north side, representing the Baptist carrying a scroll and a globe, St. Agnes holding a lamb, St. Romuald sitting on a monumental throne with two devotees kneeling before him, St. Jerome sitting in a cell surrounded with books and with one open on his knee (fig. 185). These figures are executed with more care than the portraits of the Dominicans in the Chapter House; the technique is more refined, the drapery hangs in softer folds, while the features and expressions are not depicted with the crude realism of the other images but rather produce the impression of a calm and profoundly religious spirit. As we know that Tommaso was still in Treviso in 1358, it is highly probable that these works are of later date than the paintings of 1352.

All the other frescoes in this church were executed by Tommaso's disciples, or artists who were inspired by his manner, and certain Venetian elements in the decoration lead us to believe that it was left to local painters.

The third pillar on the left is adorned with a figure of the

Fig. 184. Tommaso da Modena, the Blessed Giovanni da Vicenza, 1352. Chapter Room, S. Niccolo, Treviso. Photo Alinari.

Virgin reading a book that St. Thomas holds before her, and a representation of St. Francis receiving the stigmata. On the fourth and sixth pillars we see the Virgin with the Child and a saint, and again the stigmatization of St. Francis.

The pillars on the other side show, on the first, St. Michael crushing the devil; on the second, the Virgin reading from a book that St. Thomas presents to her and a holy bishop blessing a knight; on the third St. Christopher carrying the Child Jesus and St. Nicholas of Bari; on the fourth, St. Catherine in the midst of four angels with two donors at her feet (¹); and on the sixth the figure of St. Martin. In the chapel to the right of the choir we find some frescoes which do not betray such a close connection with Tommaso's art. They represent the Virgin and saints and the Adoration of the Magi with saints and a donor. The paintings are less good in quality, nevertheless the forms, the colour and the sweetness of expression betray an influence of Tommaso's second manner (²).

Among the other works in Treviso that belong to Tommaso's school we might cite a Madonna in a side chapel of Sta. Maria Maggiore (³), a Crucifixion in a lunette in the Cathedral, another fresco in this church, while a third in the crypt, although still belonging to this group, shows much less connection with Tommaso's style of painting. Cavalcaselle ascribes to the master's own hand a fresco of the Virgin nursing the Child, escorted by four saints, and another of St. Marius in the Rinaldi chapel of S. Francesco. The former of these two frescoes bears an inscription with the date 1353. The church is now used by the military authorities; personally I do not know these paintings but von Schlosser disputes this attribution.

I have already pointed out that Tommaso da Modena's activity at Karlstein dates from the later part of his career. As one of the artists, Theodoric of Prague, who was active there, is mentioned as painter to the Emperor in 1359 and again in 1367 as being rewarded for his services, and as Tommaso is found still in Modena in 1368, he cannot have directed the entire decoration of the castle, unless, instead of being called by the Emperor in 1368, he went to Bohemia during the time that elapsed between 1359 and 1366.

In any case Tommaso's activity there cannot have been limited to the production of only a few panels which could just as well have been painted in his native city. It has already been remarked, however, that the quality of the wood — beech — makes it

---

(¹) *von Schlosser* believes that this fresco is also by Tommaso.

(²) *Cavalcaselle* quoting *Fedirici*, op. cit, I, p. 195, is of opinion that these paintings might date from 1366.

(³) *von Schlosser* also ascribes this fresco to the master.

Fig. 185. Tommaso da Modena, St. Jerome. S. Niccolo, Treviso.
Photo Alinari.

very probable that they were executed in Bohemia. Further than that, the appearance of the figures, the ornamental background and the manner in which the figures stand out against it, provide us with the almost certain proof that these panels belonged to the decoration of one of the chapels — the one dedicated to the Holy Cross. The pictures show us the half-length figures of the Virgin holding the naked Child Who plays with a little dog, between St. Wenceslaus of Bohemia and St. Dalmasius (fig. 186). At the foot of the image of the Virgin we read: *"Quis opus hoc finxit Thomas de Mutina pinxit. Quale vides lector. Barisini filius auctor"* (¹). This altar-piece which, in 1780, was transported from Karlstein to the Vienna Gallery, has, since 1901, been restored to its original site.

Karlstein also possesses two panels in magnificent frames, which probably belonged formerly to a polyptych. They represent the half-length figure of the Virgin with the Child Who fondles His Mother's face, and the dead Christ erect in His tomb with two archangels above. These pictures are considerably damaged, the face of Christ being quite effaced; at the foot of this image we find the signature: *"Thomas de Mutina"*.

The other paintings at Karlstein reveal the great influence that our artist exercised on local painters.

The names of Nicolas Wurmser of Strasbourg and Theodoric of Prague from among the artists who worked there have survived.

An authentic work by the latter shows the Saviour on the Cross between the Virgin and St. John (²); this panel manifests the artist's great inferiority to Tommaso and I see no reason for ascribing to him the half-length figures of SS. Ambrosius and Augustine (³), as is generally done, which bear much more resemblance to Tommaso's own manner, not only in the appearance of the figures and the realistic faces, which can easily be compared with those of the Dominican monks at Treviso, but also in the form and decorative part of the panels, which correspond with what we found in Tommaso's signed panel representing the Virgin between two saints.

(¹) Previously there was some doubt as to whether it read Barisini or Rarisini but since the discovery of the document concerning Tommaso's father, this has been cleared up.

(²) *F. Burger*, Die Deutsche Malerei, I, p. 161. This picture was also removed from Karlstein but later returned.

(³) *F. Burger*, op. cit., p. 163. These panels also were taken to Venice but have since been restored to Karlstein.

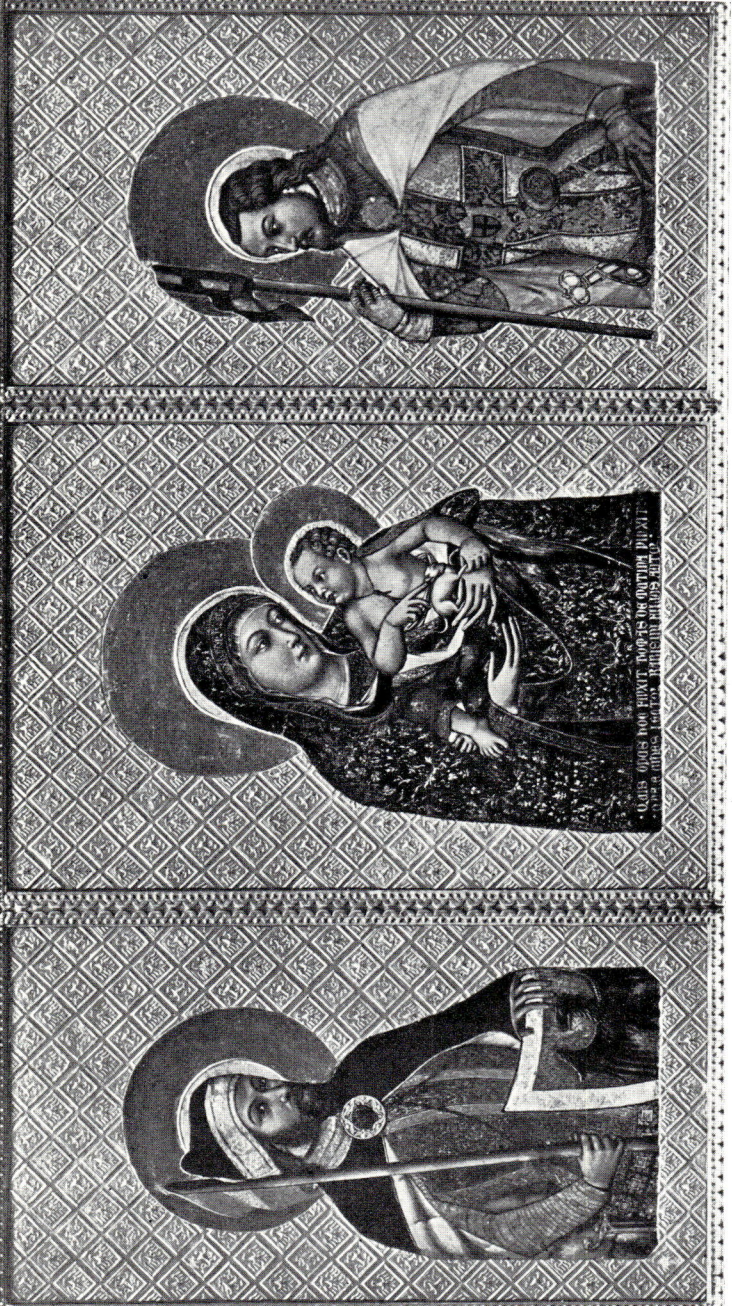

Fig. 186. Tommaso da Modena, the Madonna with SS. Wenceslaus and Dalmasius. Karlstein, Bohemia.
Photo Hanfstaengl.

Further, in the chapel of the Holy Cross — one of the three chapels that the castle possesses — we find 133 panels showing half-length figures of saints, which seem to be directly inspired by Tommaso, and it is even probable that the best of them were executed by the master himself. In the two other chapels which are dedicated to the Virgin Mary and St. Clare, Tommaso's influence is not so evident and although Cavalcaselle attributes the paintings here to Tommaso also and to his helpers, I think they are for the greater part the work of German artists, assisted perhaps by some Italians who were not dependent on the Modenese painter. This was no doubt the decoration that was completed before 1367. The other frescoes in the castle, as for example the illustration of the legend of St. Wenceslaus on the walls of the stairs, are also of German workmanship, influenced however by Italian art.

It has been supposed that Tommaso collaborated with Theodoric of Prague in the execution of the scenes relating the legend of St. Wenceslaus in a chapel of the Prague Cathedral, but too little of this decoration has survived to enable us to form an opinion.

Tommaso's influence on the Bohemian school of painting has been considerably exaggerated. We certainly note some Italian elements in the productions of this centre; they are not, however, due to a knowledge of Modenese art but rather to that general dissemination of the Italian influence which originated in Sienese painting of the 14th century and which we meet with in different artistic centres of that period throughout Europe, especially in French miniatures and the paintings of Cologne.

The gallery of Tommaso's native town possesses a work signed by him: "*Thomas fecit 1385*" ([1]). Even before the discovery of the document which informs us that the artist died in 1379, it was noticed that part of the inscription was not original. The 8 is very curious and is written horizontally. Signori Bertoni and Vicini believed that the date must have read 1365 but in all probability the work was executed at a still earlier period which would approximate it to the frescoes of Treviso, and 1355 seems to me a more likely date. The picture is divided into an upper

---

([1]) *A. Venturi*, La Galleria Estense in Modena, Modena, 1882, p. 424.

and a lower division; above, we see the Virgin and Child in the centre with St. Jerome extracting the thorn from the lion's paw and St. Bruno at the sides, and below, the Descent into Limbo with SS. Catherine and John the Baptist laterally. Below the image of the Madonna the following is inscribed: *"Pulcros Aurora mater Pia Ugo decora p̄. nobis ora et in mortis nos suscipe ora. Thomas fecit 13 ∞ 5"*. It has often been doubted (Cavalcaselle, von Schlosser) if this is the same artist but it seems probable, although this is certainly not one of the master's more characteristic works; and the condition of the picture moreover adds to the difficulty of solving this question.

I do not think that any of Tommaso's other works have survived, for I have already remarked that I do not concur with the attribution to him of the frescoes from the story of St. Ursula in the church of Sta. Marguerita in Treviso and those at Colalto [1].

Summing up the artistic career of Tommaso da Modena, we find that he had two different manners; during the first he executed the frescoes of Treviso, and to the second the panels at Karlstein belong.

The somewhat crude technique and exaggerated realism which verges on vulgarity and to a certain extent detracts from the aesthetic value of his works, rank Tommaso, in his first manner, with his contemporaries of Bologna. His paintings are nevertheless, markedly individual and full of vigour and fantasy,

---

[1] *P. P. Weiner*, L'Arte, 1909, p. 222, ascribes to him a Madonna seated on a cushion suckling the Child with angels in the background which belongs to his own collection and which was shown at the exhibition of old art held in Petrograd, but it is a painting that I would sooner classify as a production of Daddi's school. More in the manner of Tommaso, although I do not think from his own hand, are a panel of the Lord's Supper, three representations of the Madonna and four saints in the Gallery of Bologna, which are attributed to Tommaso by *A. Venturi*, L'Arte, 1924, p. 14. Nor am I of opinion that Tommaso can be accredited with a diptych representing the Virgin suckling the Child, and St. Jerome, in the Johnson collection, Philadelphia, which Mr. *B. Berenson* in his catalogue of the collection (no. 153) ascribes to the master. A figure of St. Catherine in the Accademia of Venice was falsely signed: *"Io Toms pictor de Mutina pin, anno MCCCLI"*; this picture — probably a German work of the 15th century — is no longer exhibited in the Gallery. *A. Venturi*, Storia dell' arte italiana, VII[1], p. 210[1], believes that a fragment of a Crucifixion and some figures of saints in the window embrasures of the old chapel in the castle of Mantua are also by Tommaso da Modena.

and it is the presence of these peculiarities that makes his series of Dominican monks an extremely interesting work of art. At Karlstein, on the other hand, we find that he has acquired a very refined technique and creates beautiful forms with an artistic ideal and a religious spirit reminiscent of the Sienese masters. That this transformation is due to Barna's influence can hardly be disbelieved. It is not only the spirit and artistic direction of Barna's works that are manifest in Tommaso's later productions but certain details, such as the tapering figures of the Byzantine artists, the type of the Child Christ in the two panels — the one which originally must have formed part of a polyptych seems to have been copied from Barna's picture now in Boston — and the chiaroscuro effects which are skilfully blended without any sharp contrasts of light and shade; these are all elements which are absent in the frescoes of Treviso and the panel in the Modena Gallery but which Tommaso obviously borrowed from Barna, in whose art they constitute an all important factor. Further, a certain evidence of this change is already seen in the figures in the church of S. Niccolo, which for this reason I believe to have been executed at a slightly later date than the frescoes in the Chapter Room.

We have perhaps also to admit in Tommaso's art some influence of the painters of Padua and Verona who, moreover, were represented in Treviso itself; it was doubtless they who aroused our artist's interest in homely details, such as the variety of features and attitudes, and in such items as furniture and books which make of each image of the Dominican monks at Treviso a picture from every-day life. To the same artistic direction, Tommaso also owes the elaborate details of the rich costumes of the two saints to the side of the Virgin at Karlstein, and the dog — a characteristic peculiar to "scènes de gènre" — in the hands of the Infant Jesus, where this animal seems so out of place. A strange legend exists that Tommaso da Modena made oil-paintings.

Tommaso's compatriot, Barnaba da Modena flourished at a slightly later date [1].

---

[1] S. *Varni*, Appunti artistici sopra Levanto, Genoa, 1870, pp. 48 and 140. G. *Bertoni e E. P. Vicini*, Barnaba d. M., Rasegna d'Arte, 1903, p. 117, give all the documents concerning Barnaba and his family. A. *Venturi*, Barnaba d. M., in Thieme-Becker, Künstler Lexikon, II, p. 507.

Fig. 187. Barnaba da Modena, Madonna, 1369. Kaiser Friedrich Museum, Berlin. Photo Hanfstaengl.

His family was of Milanese origin but his great-grandfather, Ottonello, took up residence in Modena where we find mention of his grandfather, Barnaba, in 1324, and his father, Ottonello, in 1332 and 1367 when he made his will in which his son, Barnaba, is already referred to as "Magister".

The family name is recorded in deeds of 1380 and 1383 as "Agoclari". The painter's mother was called Francesca Cartari.

Barnaba da Modena is mentioned for the first time in 1364 when we find him decorating the Palazzo Ducale of Genoa (¹), an enterprise sufficiently important for us to suppose that he was no longer very young at that date. In 1367 he signed the Madonna now in the Gallery of Frankfort. The one in Berlin dates from 1369, and the one in Turin from 1370, in which year we know from a document that he restored an altar-piece for the "Loggia dei Banchi" in Genoa. We have other works of 1374 and 1377, whilst in 1380 he was called from Genoa to Pisa to finish the frescoes illustrating the life of St. Ranieri in the Campo Santo (²). On his way to Pisa we are informed that he passed by Modena where he sold a house; but he did not execute the solicited task and in November 1383 is back once more in Genoa; after which date no further mention is made of him.

Consequently we have five dated works by Barnaba da Modena and they extend over a period of ten years, but the difference between the first and the last of these paintings is so slight that it hardly shows any evolution. Moreover most of these pictures strongly resemble one another; they represent the half-length figure of the Virgin, draped in material threaded with gold, holding the Child in her arm, both facing the spectator. The chief difference that we note is in the appearance of the Child, so alive in the first works and of a very conventional aspect in the others.

Further, in the works which I think can be placed at the beginning of Barnaba's career, we note very marked contrasts of light and shade in the portrayal of the features and this, as time wore on, gradually disappeared.

Of the period prior to the year 1370, we possess only two dated works, the Madonna in the Stadelsche Kunstinstitut of Frankfort

(¹) C. *Aru*, Bollet. d'Arte del Minist. della Pubbl. Istr , 1921, p. 272 note 15. This date has erroneously been given as 1361 and 1367.

(²) *Bonaini*, Memorie inedite intorno a etc. Francesco Traini, Pisa, 1846, p. 99.

Fig. 188. Barnaba da Modena, Madonna. Fine Arts Museum, Boston.

(no. 1), originating, according to the catalogue, from Bologna ([1]), and the one in the Kaiser Friedrich Museum, Berlin (no. 1171, fig. 187). The inscription at the foot of the former runs: "*Barnabas de Mutina pinxit M. Anna (ianuario?) MCCCLXVII*". The panel in Berlin shows the same signature, only the date,"*MCCCLXVIIII*" follows directly on the word "pinxit". The difference between the one and the other of these two pictures, apart from the fact that in the former the Child is engaged in scratching His foot, while in the latter He feeds a little bird and wears a coral mascot, lies in the more refined forms and more vigorous drawing of the Frankfort panel while in the Berlin picture the shadows are more sharply marked.

The fine forms and about the same degree of plasticity are to be noted in another painting, which, except that the figures are turned towards the opposite side, is very similar. It belonged to the collection of Mr. Langton Douglas but in 1915 was acquired by the Fine Arts Museum of Boston (no. 2, fig. 188) ([2]). A good deal of difference is noticeable here in the threads of gold which are less brilliant and do not join to form broader strips. The Child is again seen wearing a coral mascot; His type which characterizes this stage of the master's career, is very pronounced in this picture.

A Madonna in the church of S. Matteo at Tortona, near Alessandria, that Signor Toesca discovered (fig. 189) ([3]), shows a certain resemblance to the Berlin panel, displaying the same sharp contrasts of light and shade.

Reminiscent of the Tortona Madonna is a rather damaged work in the Schiff collection, Pisa; it is of a slightly more archaic aspect. The Child is depicted scratching His feet. This picture is signed: "*Barnabas Demutina pinzit*" ([4]).

It is very probable that some of these panels were executed before the year 1367 although we have not been able to ascer-

---

([1]) Arch. Stor. dell' Arte, II, 1888, p. 90.

([2]) *F. Mason Perkins*, Un dipinto ignorato di Barnaba da Modena, L'Arte, 1915, p. 222.

([3]) *P. Toesca*, Dipinti di Barnaba da Modena, Bolletino d'Arte del Minist. della Pubbl. Istr., 1923, p. 291.

([4]) *F. M. Perkins*, Una tavola di Barnaba da Modena, Rassegna d'Arte, 1916, p. 203.

Fig, 189. Barnaba da Modena, Madonna. S. Matteo, Tortona.
Photo Minist. del. Pubbl. Istr.

tain when Barnaba's career started. Considering that his father is mentioned in 1332, Barnaba must almost certainly have been active a considerable time before 1367.

To the second half of Barnaba's career but apparently not to the latter end of it, belongs an important signed polyptych — another discovery of Signor Toesca's ([1]) — in the church of Lavagnola, near Savona (Liguria); it represents the half-length figure of the Virgin, nursing the Child, and four full-length figures of saints, while in the pinnacles we see four busts of saints and the Lord on the Cross between the Virgin and St. John who are seated on the ground. The appearance of the Child, and particularly the chiaroscuro effects in this figure, as well as in the lateral ones, are very similar to what we found in the Tortona panel, but the proportions of the Virgin are larger and the saints at the sides are a little wooden.

The same characteristics, above all a certain rigidity of form, are noticiable in a panel representing the Baptism of Our Lord in the presence of two angels who carry His gold-woven garments (fig. 190). This panel, which is enclosed in a frame which must have served as a reliquary, belongs to a private collection. In the hands and feet, which are of a very elongated form, we observe an archaism which is absent in the artist's other works.

The change especially in the aspect of the Child, Who is now conceived in rather a rigid manner, is evident in the painting of the Madonna in the Gallery of Turin (no. 21) which, from a technical standpoint, is the finest of Barnaba's productions (Pl. IV)([2]). The panel was taken from the church of S. Domenico in Rivoli near Turin; it is signed: *"Barnaba de Mutina pinxit MCCCLXX"*. The Child Jesus, Who holds an unrolled scroll with an inscription and again wears the coral mascot, is the least pleasing part of this picture, but the charm of the Virgin's face and the fineness of the forms and the modelling make this a very attractive work.

That Barnaba's figures became heavier after this date is demonstrated in a picture of 1374 which, after having belonged to the collection of Lord Wensleydale who exhibited it in Manchester in 1857, and then to that of the Earl of Carlisle, was

---

([1]) *P. Toesca*, op. cit., places this work towards the end of the artist's life.
([2]) *E. Jacobsen*, La R. Pinac. di Torino, Arch. Stor. dell' Arte, 1897, p. 122.

acquired in 1913 by the National Gallery (no. 2927, fig. 191) (¹). It is a fairly large panel and is composed of four scenes: the Coronation of the Virgin in the midst of a large group of angelic musicians; the Trinity with the four symbols of the Evangelists and the Virgin and St. John sitting grieving on the ground as in representations of the Crucifixion; the Virgin and Child, to

(¹) *D'Agincourt*, op. cit., IV, p. 408, Pittura, pl. 133, mentions and reproduces this picture whose fate was unknown to him.

Fig. 190. Barnaba da Modena, the Baptism of the Lord.
Private Collection.

Fig. 191. Barnaba da Modena, the Coronation of the Virgin and other scenes, 1374. National Gallery, London.

whom an angel presents two donors, and the Crucifixion with a great many figures. The criminals are depicted, one on either side, the Virgin who has fainted, lies on the ground, tended by

Fig. 192. Barnaba da Modena, Madonna and Crucifixion. Gallery, Modena.
Photo Alinari.

her companions, while opposite a group of soldiers gamble for the clothes of Christ. A row of busts of the Twelve Apostles is found at the foot of the panel. The signature: "*Barnabas de Mutina pinxit 1374*", is inscribed on the pedestal of the Virgin's throne. In spite of the charm that emanates from this finely executed work, it is clear that a certain change has taken place in the master's manner; this is most noticeable in the faces which are rounder and in the figures which are sturdier.

The same forms are to be noted in another picture, on which Barnaba has left his name but no date; this one, which was formerly in the Puccini collection, Pistoia, is now preserved in the Modena Gallery (fig. 192) (¹). It is divided into two parts, on the lower of which we see the Virgin and Child between the Baptist and St. Catherine and the two figures of the Annunciation in the spandrels. In the pointed upper part the Lord is depicted crucified between the Virgin and St. John, while Mary Magdalene embraces the foot of the Cross. In the left corner of this part the signature: "*Barnabas de Mutina pinxit*" is inscribed.

The forms resemble those in the picture of 1374; they are still graceful and finely executed but are nevertheless heavier than those we found in the earlier works.

The figures are still broader in two little panels which must have belonged to a picture resembling the one of 1374. One of them represents the Descent of the Holy Ghost and also belongs to the collection in the National Gallery (no. 1437, fig. 193). In a room of which the ceiling and part of the back wall are alone visible, the Virgin and the Twelve Apostles, on whose heads fiery flames descend, are seated together in a circle. Some of the heads of the old white-bearded disciples are very fine, but those seen in profile are markedly inferior, and I think we may consider this to be Barnaba's least beautiful production.

The other little panel which represents the Ascension and was formerly in the Sterbini collection but now belongs to Signor Pasini, Rome, shows a better technique (fig. 194) (²). In a rather barren landscape, we see the Saviour in a mandorla in mid-air between two angels, while a third, kneeling on the ground, seems

---

(¹) *A. Venturi*, La Galleria Estense etc.

(²) *A. Venturi*, La Galleria Sterbini in Roma, Rome, 1905, p. 53, and L'Arte, 1905, p. 429.

to explain the event to the Twelve Apostles, the Virgin and a holy companion all of whom kneel at a slightly lower level. Although the execution is less fine, the round heads and proportions of the figures are reminiscent of those in the panel of 1374 and that in the Gallery of Modena.

A picture of the Virgin, now in the church of S. Giovanni Battista, but formerly in that of S. Francesco at Alba, between Turin

Fig. 193. Barnaba da Modena, the Descent of the Holy Ghost. National Gallery, London.

(Bra) and Alessandria, dates from 1377. A detail, which, until now, Barnaba has not shown in any of his other half-length figures of the Virgin but which we noted in the enthroned Madonna in the altar-piece in the National Gallery, is the presence of the two angels holding the tapestry behind the Virgin, who in this case is represented suckling the Child. The artist's signature is the same, the date alone being changed: "*Barnabas de Mutina pinxit MCCCLXXVII*". The gradually increasing breadth of the figures is again very evident.

A panel bearing a strong similarity to the foregoing is found in the chapel of S. Secondo in the Cathedral of Ventimiglia: the Child carries a long scroll and the two angels holding the drapery are visible in the back ground ([1]). I think we can attribute to the same period the considerably damaged picture of the Virgin nursing the Child, which is preserved in the church of SS. Cosme e Damiano of Genoa ([2]).

The two Madonnas which we now find in the Pisa Gallery were in all probability executed in 1380 when the artist was called to this town. It is recorded that while in Pisa Barnaba painted four pictures, one of which Cavalcaselle saw at Ripoli, a few miles from Pisa, and describes as a full-length Virgin suckling the Child between SS. Andrew, Bartholomew, Peter and a holy bishop while four angels hold up the drapery behind the Virgin's throne ([3]).

In the church of S. Francesco, there were two panels by Barnaba, one of which, representing the Coronation of the Virgin between SS. Francis, Louis of Toulouse, Antony of Padua and the Blessed Gherardo, was described by Da Morrona ([4]), but it also is lost. The other has been transferred to the Gallery of the town. It shows, against a very ornate background, the Virgin nursing the Child; four angels' heads are depicted behind the Madonna's halo, and in medallions in the spandrels the angel and Virgin of the Annunciation (fig. 195). The work is undated but is signed: *"Barnabas de Mutina pinxit"*. Not only on account of the composition but also because of the similarity in the modelling of the figures, this work forms a little group together with the Madonnas of Alba, of Ventimiglia and probably with the Madonna of Genoa also; the execution in this last case, however, is finer and there emanates from the picture a much greater depth of feeling as well as a finer sense of idealism.

Another painting by Barnaba in the Pisa Gallery originated from the monastery of S. Giovanni dei Fieri; from there it was

---

([1]) *P. Toesca*, Opere di Barnaba da Modena in Liguria, L'Arte, IX, 1906, p. 461. *L. Venturi*, L'Arte, 1918, p. 272.

([2]) *P. Toesca*, op. cit.

([3]) *Crowe and Cavalcaselle*, op. cit., III, p. 211. In spite of the name, "*Jacobus Compagnius Pisanus*" that appeared at the foot of the panel, Cavalcaselle assures us that it was undoubtedly a work from Barnaba's hand.

([4]) *Da Morrona*, Pisa illustrata etc., 2nd ed., III, Livorno, 1812, p. 90.

Fig. 194. Barnaba da Modena, the Ascension. Pasini Collection, Rome.

transported to the principal chapel of the Campo Santo but has since been taken to the Gallery. It is the largest work of Barnaba's that has survived. The life-sized Virgin is enthroned holding the Child erect on her knee; He again wears a coral mascot and holds in both His hands a long inscription; eight angels surround the central figures, the two who kneel below also carry unrolled scrolls (fig. 196). At the foot of the picture we read the artist's signature: *"Barnabas de Mutina pinxit"* and on the frame a part of another inscription: ".... *cives et mercatores Pisani pro salute a ....*"

It is rather a commonplace work, showing but little inspiration. The artist's tendency to create broader forms has deprived this picture of all the charm of his earlier productions. The Virgin's expression is sweet but her face is not very pleasing; the two angels below show the same shape of head and the same relief as the figures in the picture of 1374 and in that at Modena, but they are less graceful; while the others are but very mediocre figures and we cannot be mistaken in assigning this panel to Barnaba's decadence [1].

The œuvre of Barnaba da Modena extends over a sufficiently long period for us to form a fairly good idea of his art which is perhaps more unexpected and surprising than complicated. Barnaba was a painter of the second half of the 14th century who still retained some Byzantine elements, such as the garments of material threaded with gold and the shape of the hands.

At the beginning of his career, Barnaba, judging from his art, was an aesthetic eclectic who paid but little attention to the change that had taken place in Italian painting since the 13th century. I do not think we should reproach him with his primitive style, for he probably painted in this manner from choice. The depth of feeling that emanates from his earlier works in particular, as well as the refined technique classifies him as an artist of great merit. His types lead us to suppose that he was inspired

---

[1] Other works attributed to Barnaba are: a Madonna which formerly belonged to Signor Pedulli, Florence (*Perkins*, op. cit.), one in the Gallery of Cologne and another in that of Savona (idem). I have included the second with the productions of Lorenzetti's school; as for the last which Signor Toesca also ascribed to Barnaba, we know now that it is by Niccolo da Voltri, a painter with whom I deal in Vol. V and who was inspired by Barnaba and Taddeo di Bartolo (*L. Venturi*, L'Arte, 1918, p. 269). I. B. *Supino*, Un dipinto di Barnaba d. M., Rivista d'Arte, 1905, p. 13, assigns to him a Crucifixion in the Campo Santo, which is by the "Master of the Triumph over Death" to whom he himself (Campo Santo, p. 68) as well as *Thode* (Repertor. f. Kunstwiss., 1888, p. 21) previously attributed it. *Suida*, L'Arte, 1907, p. 183, gives to this artist a Madonna in the Budapest Museum, which is obviously by Taddeo di Bartolo, v. Vol. II, p. 549.

Fig. 195. Barnaba da Modena, Madonna. Gallery, Pisa.
Photo Brogi.

by the Sienese school and perhaps also by that of Rimini in which garments threaded with gold were favoured until a late date.

Barnaba made an excellent début, producing works of great charm but gradually his pictures deteriorated, losing the graceful forms and spiritual qualities which characterized his early paintings. His influence is very evident in the art of Niccolo da Voltri (a Ligurian painter of the following generation), in the last manner of Tommaso da Modena and perhaps also in Taddeo di Bartolo who worked at Genoa in 1393.

Although it is chiefly in Liguria and Piedmont that we find his pictures, we must not forget that it is only between 1364 and 1383 that the documents refer to his activity in these districts, so that we may suppose that at a previous period he studied and exercised his art in Modena. He did not break all connection with his native town, for record is made of certain business transactions there in 1380 and 1383.

Serafino Serafini was another Modenese painter but of a very different artistic temperament. His merits have been exaggerated by writers of past centuries. Marc Antonio Guarini, in his "Compendio historico" of the churches of Ferrara printed in 1612, relates in verse the facts that in 1373 he decorated the chapel of the Petrati family in the Cathedral of Ferrara by the order of Brother Aldovrandino and at the expense of Donna di Francesca di Lamberto. Vedriani, who studied the artists of Modena fifty years after Guarini, says that the name of Serafino Serafini was glorious up until his day. However he made a mistake in copying the date given by Guarini and speaks of 1376, an error that has given rise to much confusion.

The documents concerning Serafino Serafini have again been brought to light by the study of Signori Bertoni and Vicini [1] who demonstrate that the artist was some years senior to Tommaso and Barnaba.

In 1349, when his father died, Serafino was at least twenty-five years old, because he was appointed his brothers' guardian; on the other hand the fact that his brothers were still so young as to need tutelage — which would have ceased had they reached fourteen — makes us suppose that Serafino himself could not have been much older than twenty-five. Consequently he must have been born between 1320 and 1324. He started life as a

---

[1] *G. Bertoni e E. P. Vicini*, Serafino Serafini pittore modenese del secolo XIV, L'Arte, 1904, p. 287.

Fig. 196. Barnaba da Modena, Madonna. Gallery, Pisa.
Photo Alinari.

dealer in earthenware and his name is recorded in 1350, 1352, 1353 and 1354. His wife was called Bartolommea Ricciardi. In 1361 and 1362 we find him in Ferrara where he possibly settled down for we are informed that he sold all his property in Modena, and as we have already seen, he was active in Ferrara in 1373. In 1384 ([1]) he signed and dated the large altar-piece in the Cathedral of Modena, his only surviving work; in 1387 he is mentioned in a document of that town without, however, any proof that he lived there; in 1393 he is back in Ferrara where his name appears in a deed of sale ([2]).

The unique work that has come down to us represents, in the centre, the Coronation of the Virgin: the Saviour and the Madonna are seated on an elaborate throne surrounded by angels while the donor and his wife kneel at their feet.

The figures in the lateral panels are: to the left, St. Christopher carrying the Child on his shoulder, and St. Nicholas, and to the right St. Gemignanus and St. Antony Abbot. In the central pinnacle we see the Crucifixion with the Virgin, St. John and Mary Magdalene; SS. Onuphrius and Catherine are depicted in the adjacent pinnacles while to the extreme left and right are the angel and Virgin of the Annunciation (fig. 197). The predella shows the Saviour and the Twelve Apostles ([3]). At the feet of the central figures we see, besides an invocation of the donors, the signature: *"Seraphinus de Seraphinis pinxit 1384 die iovis XXIII Marcii"*. The artist was probably more than sixty years old when he executed this work. The style of the painting is very different from Tommaso's and Barnaba's and reminds us sooner of that of the painters, such as Giovanni da Bologna, who

---

([1]) It is not clear whether the date reads 1385 (*Cavalcaselle, Venturi*) or 1384 (*Bertoni e Vicini; Dondi*, Notizie storiche ed artistiche del Duomo di Modena, Modena, 1896, p. 22:).

([2]) *L. N. Cittadella*, Documenti sguardante la storia artistica di Ferrara, Ferrara, 1868, p. 365.

([3]) *P. Cavedoni*, Dell' ancona di Serafino di Serafini nel Duomo di Modena etc., Modena, 1856. *A Dondi*, op. cit., loc. cit., propounds the hypothesis that the donors are Bartolommeo de la Molza and his wife, Betta, for the former in a will made in 1362 decreed that after his death, an altar dedicated to SS. Antony Abbot and Christopher should be founded in the Cathedral. He died in 1388.

formed the link between Venice and Bologna. The complex form of the polyptych is reminiscent of Venice where the Coronation of the Virgin was so favourite a subject and where we also find

Fig. 197. Serafino Serafini, Polyptych, 1384. Cathedral, Modena.
Photo Anderson.

thrones of a similar model to that in Serafino's altar-piece. Such thrones however are even more frequent in the productions of the Paduan and Veronese artists. Although the figures are stumpier, the contours bear a resemblance to those of the Bolognese artists; the Virgin has certain points in common with the images that Lippo Dalmasio and Vitale have left of her, but

Serafino's technique belongs to a different artistic movement, his drawing and his effects of light are very subtle and the exaggeratedly indicated plasticity of the Bolognese painters is absent is his work. On the whole he seems to have been a talented artist possessing a good deal of originality and independence.

Paolo, the son of Serafino Serafini, has left his name on a picture which is found in the South of Italy. It is a half-length figure of the Madonna and, since 1503, has been the object of much veneration in the Metropolitana of Berletta (fig. 198)([1]). Although the drawing is not very fine, as will be noted in the modelling of the hands and the feet, it is a work of considerable charm, approaching in spirit the art of Siena.

This element is even exaggerated in the figure of the Child, Whose appearance for that reason is rather curious, but the grace of the Virgin's figure, her beautiful face and spiritual expression reveal Paolo di Serafino as a very capable artist. I think it is also possible that this painter was influenced by his fellow-citizen, Barnaba, whose works have a different aspect but from whose art Paolo's forms, technique, especially of relief, and spirit might very well descend. The panel, which is rich in decorative detail shows at the foot an inscription, the third line of which runs: *"Paulus filius Magistri Safini de Safini Pitori de Mutina pi"*.

It has only of late been noted that this panel had a pendant, representing a half-length figure of the Redeemer seen in full-face, bestowing a blessing and holding a long, slender rod surmounted with a cross (fig. 199). This picture has the same charm, but also the same mistakes in the drawing, as the previous one.

There is still a third work in the same Cathedral, undoubtedly from the hand of this artist, although the quality of the painting is a good deal inferior (fig. 200). The picture is considerably damaged; the features and expression of Christ lack the charm of Paolo's other works.

There was another Modenese painter of the name of Paolo.

([1]) Arch. Stor. dell' Arte, 1889, p. 491. *Bertoni e Vicini*, L'Arte, 1904, p. 294. A. *Colasanti*, Opere d'arte ignote o poco note, Bolletino d'Arte del Minist. della Pubbl. Istr., 1910, p. 184.

Fig. 198. Paolo Serafini da Modena, Madonna, Cathedral, Barletta.
Photo Minist. del. Pubbl. Istr.

Fig. 199. Paolo Serafini da Modena, the Saviour. Cathedral, Barletta.

In the Gallery of the town we find a painting on canvas representing the Madonna of Humility seated on the ground suckling the Infant Christ; an adoring priest kneels close by while two medallions contain the figures of the Annunciation. At the foot of the picture we read:*"La nostra Donna. D'Umilta MCCCLXX, F. Paulus De Mutina fecit ord. p. Dic. IIII I Die Nat."* (¹). Consequently it must be the work of a Dominican monk of the name of Paolo. If the painting really be-

Fig. 200. Paolo Serafini da Modena, the Saviour, Cathedral, Barletta.
Photo Minist. del. Pubbl. Istr.

(¹) *P.Bortolotti,* Intorno un quadro di Fra Paolo di Modena, Mem. della R. Acc. di Sc. Lett. ed Arti di Modena, serie VI, vol. II, p. 45. *Baldoria,* Un quadro di Fra P. d. M. nella Galleria Estense. *The Same,* Ancora sul quadro di Fra P. d. M., Rassegna Emiliana, 1888.

longs to the period that the date indicates ([1]), it has been greatly changed by restoration; nevertheless we can still distinguish that the artist's style was the outcome of an intermingling of Sienese elements and those borrowed from the school of Fabriano.

Besides such masters as Tommaso, Barnaba, Serafino and his son, Modena possessed some other painters, who worked in a less individual manner, but of whose productions few remains are to be found, and those chiefly in the Cathedral, where but little of the once fairly extensive decoration has survived ([2]). On the left wall, apart from the enormous figure of St. Christopher that I have classified with the works of the 13th century, we see a Virgin with the Child between St. Peter and a holy bishop dating from the beginning of the 14th century; some figures of saints are depicted on this wall, as well as on that adjacent. Beside two figures of saints of the 13th century near the right apse, we find an Annunciation and a curious composition of the Virgin, the Child Christ and an angel kneeling in adoration, but unhappily the object of their veneration has disappeared. Certain details seem to confirm the possibility that this is a 13th century fresco which has been painted over at a later date.

A fresco which has been detached from the Cathedral and is now preserved in the Gallery of Modena shows the Virgin seated on a simple but imposing throne nursing the Child between St. Bartholomew and a bishop ([3]). The type of these frescoes, as well as the form of the throne, reminds us of similar compositions in Verona but the technique shows more resemblance to that of the Bolognese school. They are provincial-looking works of but little importance ([4]).

A fresco of the Madonna with a holy bishop and a female devotee which once showed the date 1334, was also detached

---

([1]) Mr. *Langton Douglas,* in *Crowe and Cavalcaselle*, op. cit., p. 208 note 3, is of opinion that it is a copy of an older picture.

([2]) *Dondi*, op. cit., p. 179.

([3]) *G. Bertoni*, Atlante storico artistico del Duomo di Modena, Modena, 1921, p. 70.

([4]) In the Gallery there are still some 14th century panels by local artists; we might mention a half-length figure of the Madonna with the Child (not numbered) said to be in the manner of Barnaba; no. 13, a triptych showing the Madonna, Pietà and saints, and no. 44, a panel from a predella.

from the walls of the Cathedral and brought to the Gallery [1].

At Carpi, which lies about ten miles to the north of Modena, there exists a fairly important series of frescoes in one of the chapels of the "Sagra". We find the images of the Church Doctors on the walls, the symbols of the Evangelists in the vault, the figures of the Annunciation, St. Christopher and other saints on the entrance arch, and the Adoration of the Magi in the lunette. Signor A. Venturi [2], who places these frescoes among the best productions of Emilia, draws our attention to the details that the artist has borrowed from the Bolognese school; and it is quite true that this decoration bears more resemblance to the works of the painters of Bologna than to anything we have found in Modena.

---

[1] *P. Bortolotti,* Di un murale dipinto nel 1334 etc. del Duomo di Modena, Modena, 1891.
[2] *Venturi,* Storia dell' arte, VII^1, p. 208.

CHAPTER VI.

THE SCHOOL OF BOLOGNA (¹).

The Bolognese school of the 14th century was as productive as it was wide-spread, and it is one of this period of which the greatest number of works has been preserved. It certainly was not the school that produced the most fascinating painters; on the contrary, as we shall see later, the Bolognese masters frequently employed a rather crude technique and are more interesting for the vivacity and vigour with which they depict their figures, than for their esthetic sense.

In the controversy which has arisen as to whether or not Bolognese painting is an outcome of the art of miniature, I am quite of the affirmative opinion, without, however, excluding the fact that other influences collaborated in the formation of this school of painting as we see it at the last quarter of the 14th century, the period of its greatest activity.

Miniaturists are found working in Bologna as early as the middle of the 13th century, and from the first years of the 14th onward we find many series of illuminated manuscripts, at the beginning chiefly registers and rules of different corporations. Towards the year 1350 the celebrated and prolific miniaturist,

---

(¹) *C. C. Malvasia*, Felsina Pittrice, vol. I, Bologna, 1841. *P. Zani*, Enciclopedia metodica critico-ragionata delle belle arte, Parma, 1819–1822. *A. Bolognini Amorini*, Vita dei pittori ed artefici bolognesi, Bologna, 1841—1843. *Brach*, op. cit. *F. Gerevich*, Sull' origine del Rinascimento Pittorico in Bologna, Rassegna d'Arte, 1906, p. 161; 1907, p. 177 *The Same*, Le relazione tra la pittura e la miniatura bolognese nel Trecento, Rassegna d'Arte, 1909, p. 196; 1910, p. 29. *R. Baldani*, La pittura a Bologna nel sec. XIV, Documenti e studi per cura della R. Deput. di Stor. Patr. per la Romagna, III, 1909, p. 375.

Fig. 201. Bolognese Miniature, illustrating a Decretales, 1st half of the 14th century. Library, Siena.   Photo Brogi.

Niccolo di Giacomo makes his appearance (¹). The number of manuscripts he adorned is very great, and in the second half of the 14th century his pupils and other Bolognese miniaturists produced such a quantity of work that nowadays we find hundreds of codices adorned by them dispersed among the libraries of Europe. It was especially the "Decretales", with or without illuminations, that were copied in Bologna.

We are led to believe that painting in Bologna took its origin in the art of miniature not only by the fact that the production of miniatures was so great, but also because as early as the first half of the 14th century we note in certain illuminations that curious realism and lack of refinement which some decades later characterize the works of such painters as Simone dei Crocifissi; and the miniaturist, Niccolo di Giacomo, only developed the tendency manifest in the art of previous generations. Miniatures of the first half of the 14th century often retain some archaic elements of the Duecento to which is added the somewhat heavy and coarse technique so characteristic of Bolognese works (fig. 201), but at this period there is no trace of the vulgar design and ugly forms that are peculiar to Bolognese miniatures when, fifty years later, that art became an industry.

In all probability the Bolognese school of miniature started with Oderisi da Gubbio and Franco da Bologna whom, as I have already remarked, Dante praised in his Purgatory; clearly saying that in this art Franco surpassed Oderisi. Although the latter was Umbrian by birth, the site of his greatest activity was apparently Bologna, and Benvenuto da Imola calls him the greatest miniaturist of this town. He was known under the name of "Oderisio di Guido da Gubbio da Bologna" and is found active

---

(¹) *F. Malaguzzi Valeri*, I codici miniati di Nicolo di Giacomo e della sua scuola in Bologna, Atti e Mem. della R.Deput. di Stor. Patr. per la Romagna, 1892. *The Same*, Le miniature nell' archivio dello stato a Bologna, Arch. Stor. dell' arte, 1894, p. 1. *The Same*, La miniatura in Bologna del XIII al XVIII secolo, Arch. Stor. Ital , 1896, p. 262. *The Same*, Catalogo delle miniature e disegni posseduti dell' arch. di Stato a Bologna, Atti e Mem. della R. Deput. di Stor. Patr. per la Romagna, 1898. *L.Ciaccio*, Appunti intorno alla miniatura bolognese del sec XIV, L'Arte, 1907, p. 105, *Hermanin*, Vita d'arte, I, 1908. *Gerevich*, op. cit. *A. Erbach von Fuerstenau*, La miniature bolognese nel Trecento, L'Arte, 1911, pp. 1 and 107.

in 1268 and 1271 (¹). The Codex of St. George in the archives of the Chapter Room of S. Pietro, Rome, was formerly ascribed, without sufficient grounds, to Oderisi, but since these miniatures have been recognized to belong to the school of Simone Martini there is now no reason to admit, as Vasari affirms, that Oderisi went to Rome (²).

From Dante's reference it may be conjectured that a certain relation existed between Oderisi and Franco da Bologna; the facts that they exercised the same art in the same town makes this very probable but it does not allow us to admit that, through Oderisi, the Bolognese school of miniature originated from that of Umbria since none of the beautiful Umbrian miniatures can be traced back to the time of Oderisi, and there is further no resemblance of style in the two groups. Although on all sides we discover older miniatures than at Bologna, it is in this town that we find the oldest established tradition of this art, which seems to have had a vigorous and uninterrupted existence from about 1260 until the end of the 14th century.

We know no works of either Oderisi or Franco da Bologna. It is true that Rosini reproduces a Madonna signed by the latter artist and dated 1312 (³) from the collection of Prince Ercolani at Bologna but the easy attitude of the Child and the general appearance of the reproduction lead us to believe that it is sooner a painting of the second half of the 14th century. Cavalcaselle has already doubted the authenticity of the inscription. Lanzi saw this picture and also some others attributed to Franco in the Malvezzi Museum of Bologna (⁴); while Malvasia, who, on Vasari's authority, believed that he had been charged to execute miniatures for the Pope's library in Rome, classified Franco as the leading artist of the Bolognese school, with disciples throughout Romagna and Lombardy.

Although Malvasia's theory is little more than mere conjecture, for it was founded on an unreliable argument, I do not think

---

(¹) Giornale di Erudizione artistica (Perugia), II, 1873, p. 1. *Crowe and Cavalcaselle*, ed. *Langton Douglas*, III, p 167.
(²) *Vasari-Milanesi*, I, p. 385.
(³) *Rosini*, op. cit., pl. XI.
(⁴) *Lanzi*, op. cit., III, p. 9, gives the date of the foregoing picture as 1313. *Cavalcaselle* in accordance with *Rosini* corrects it to 1312.

that he is entirely wrong. The Bolognese school of painting followed on that of miniature, which was older and always remained the more important on account of its enormous output; Oderisi and Franco da Bologna were without doubt the greatest figures in this branch of art.

We find few painters in Bologna before the second half of the 14th century. One called "Petrus" is mentioned in a document of 1348 and it was probably he who signed the crucifix, a very tarnished piece of which now hangs in the Pinacoteca of Bologna; we also know that a certain Deodato Giovanello da Imola executed a Madonna for the church of S. Stefano before 1350 (1), but with the exception of Vitale who seems to have been the actual founder of the Bolognese school of painting, there are no other painters of any importance whose works have come down to us.

We are fairly well informed concerning Vitale (2). The earliest mention we have of him is in a document of 1334, in which he is spoken of as "*Vidolino Ryme de Equis pictore*" (3). Bolognini tried to prove that he was related to the noble family of Cavalli. In the foregoing deed, he figures as witness, from which we know that he was then at least twenty-five years of age, so that at the latest he was born in 1309. In 1359 his name still appears in the register of the parish of Sta. Maria Maggiore, and as those who had passed the age of seventy were not inscribed, he could not have been born before 1289 (4). His wife Giovanna di Lorenzo Merciaio died in 1357; they had one son, Francesco. Regarding his dated works, in the Gallery of Bologna there is one signed picture with the date 1320, but no one believes that the inscription, at least that part showing the date, is original. In 1330 he

---

(1) *C. Ricci*, Guida di Bologna, 5th ed., Bologna, p. 92.

(2) *F. Filippini*, Vitale da Bologna, Bolletino d'Arte del Minist. della Pubbl. Istr., VI, 1912, p. 13. L. *Frati*, Un opera ignota di Vitale da Bologna, L'Arte, 1911, p. 442.

(3) *Orioli* in Atti e Mem. della Soc. di Stor. Patr. per la Romagna, Serie III, vol. XXV p. 184.

(4) The document of 1343 mentions that Vitale was "*emancipatus*" (free of his father's guardianship), which state a young man generally attained at the age of 18 or 20; Vitale had doubtless obtained this freedom a considerable time before and I do not think that this word furnishes any direct indication concerning his age as some writers have believed.

Fig. 202. Vitale, Madonna. Pinacoteca, Bologna.

Photo Anderson.

adorned the chapel of Filippo degli Odofredi in the church of S. Francesco, and Oretti, in his treatise on Bolognese painters — the manuscript is preserved in the town library — mentions a work of the same year. Ten years later he decorated the chapel of S. Lorenzo and the "foresteria" (¹).

His name is found in deeds of 1338 and 1347 and an extant picture of the Madonna by him is dated 1345. A document of 1343 is highly interesting as it reveals to us that Vitale was also a sculptor, for in it he undertakes to execute four wooden statues for the Bishop of Ferrara. Another record informs us that in 1353 a picture costing 60 scudi was ordered from him; it is doubtless the one which is nowadays preserved in S. Salvatore for the date is the same, although the number of saints does not correspond to that specified in the contract (²).

It is highly probable that Malvasia named Franco Bolognese Vitale's master only because he did not know the name of another Bolognese painter of the preceding generation; Herr Brach, however, accepts this affirmation since it confirms his hypothesis that, through Oderisi da Gubbio, Bolognese painting was derived from that of Umbria, a theory without any foundation and, as I have already remarked, contradicted by chronological facts.

The panel with the false date of 1320 comes from the church of Sta. Maria del Monte and is now catalogued under the no. 203 in the Gallery of Bologna (fig. 202). Although the work is undoubtedly by Vitale, the signature seems as little genuine as the date; the form of the letters is not even that of the 14th century. It may be that the original signature has been copied but in so doing the transcriber has mistaken the date. We now see: "*Vitalis de bononia fecit anno MCCCXX*", while a little lower, in characters of the same period as the painting, the following is inscribed: "*Hoc opus fecit fieri duā Blaxia paia* (per anima) *magister Johanis de Plaxenxia* (Piacenza)".

The Virgin is represented enthroned, holding with both hands the vivacious Child Who stands on her knee; an angel kneels at either side of the throne, the one to the right presenting a miniature devotee.

As we cannot rely on the authenticity of the date inscribed on

---

(¹) *Gerevich*, Rassegna d'Arte, 1906, p. 165 note I.
(²) *L. Frati,* Un polittico di Vitale da Bologna, Rassegna d'Arte, 1909, p. 171.

Fig. 203. Vitale, Madonna. Vatican Gallery.

Photo Anderson.

this picture, it is difficult to say if it is the oldest work that we possess by this artist. I think, however, it belongs to an earlier period than that between 1345 and 1353 of which years we have two dated paintings.

In this first manner, which is characterized by a fairly marked Sienese influence, Vitale executed two other Madonnas. One of them will be found in the Vatican Gallery (no. 103, fig. 203); it has been considerably restored and a good deal painted over.

The Virgin is represented in half-length figure holding the Child Who bestows a blessing on some members of a flagellant order who kneel in adoration. The signature at the foot of the panel runs: "*Vitalis. de Bononia. F*".

The other painting which I think has been executed at an early stage in Vitale's career is a little triptych in the Bologna Gallery (no. 351). It shows the Virgin and Child in the centre and nine angels in each of the wings, but is less characteristic of the master's manner than the two other works.

I agree with those who believe that Vitale collaborated in the decoration of the church of Pomposa but am of opinion that his part in the enterprise was limited to the ornamentation of the apse not all of which, however, is from his hand, for the large central figure of the Redeemer displays a considerable difference in style to the rest of the decoration.

Signor Baldani makes what appears to me a big mistake in attributing the frescoes of the apse to Jacopo di Paolo; and further I do not agree with him in ascribing the paintings in the nave to the same artist, but I shall return to this subject when dealing with the painters of Ferrara. Baldani argues that his attribution would have the advantage of taking away from Vitale, who, on account of the great number of Madonnas that he has painted, has been surnamed "Vitale delle Madonne", a grandiose composition which forms such a contrast to the subject of his predilection; but to me this argument seems worthless because the painters represented what was ordered from them and their own personal inclination had nothing to do with the subjects chosen.

Nor am I of exactly the same opinion as Herr Brach and Signor Filippini who include in Vitale's activity here, not only the frescoes of the apse but the representation of the Last Judgment on the entry wall, which I consider to be a Ferrarese work betraying an influence of the schools of Bologna and Rimini. At the most I might admit that some figures in the lower part on the right, portraying Hell, might be from this artist's hand.

The decoration of the apse is fairly elaborate ([1]). On the wall we see above at either side a figure of the Annunciation; the conche is surrounded with a border containing a series of half-length figures, most of them carrying inscriptions, in medallions. Lower down on the left a half-length figure of the Virgin with the Child is represented. The apsidal decoration, the right hand part of which is considerably damaged, shows the Saviour in a mandorla surrounded by four groups of angels, giving His blessing and holding an open book; from either side approaches a procession of male and female saints; the one on the left is headed by the Virgin before whom kneels a monk. The four Evangelists writing at desks are depicted on a lower row; they are separated from the Church Doctors, who are represented reading, by two figures of saints. Still lower various scenes illustrate the legend of St. Eustachius; we also see here the three holy priors, Benedict, Maurus and Guido.

I think the frescoes at Pomposa must be of somewhat later date than the above mentioned panels; in general the proportions are larger and the drawing a little harder which makes them approximate to the Madonnas of S. Salvatore and S. Giovanni in Monte, which we shall come to shortly; but the refined technique and the general spirit of the works are still reminiscent of the Sienese school.

I think it very likely that of the two painters who worked at this decoration Vitale was the more important and, as will be pointed out in the following chapter, he exercised an influence on his fellow artist.

The grace and sweetness of Sienese art are not evident in the two Madonnas which I have just mentioned and which, I think, follow chronologically on the frescoes of Pomposa. The one will be found in the 6th chapel to the right in the church of S. Giovanni in Monte; it is often attributed to Lippo Dalmasio; the other which is called the "Madonna della Vittoria" is preserved in the 3rd chapel to the right in S. Salvatore, the church which also possesses the altar-piece of 1353. Cavalcaselle recognized the former as a work of Vitale's. The composition, which is a favourite one with Lippo Dalmasio at a slightly later date,

---

[1] The description that *Brach*, op. cit., gives of this part of the church is not very exact or at least it is not complete.

represents the "Madonna dell' Umilta" seated on the ground holding the Child on her knee.

The "Madonna della Vittoria" has also been ascribed to Lippo Dalmasio, but this mistake has arisen from the fact that an inscription on the back of the panel with this artist's name has wrongly been considered as a signature. Signor Filippini was the first to assign it to its genuine author. The enthroned Madonna holds in her left arm the Child Jesus Who is here of clumsy form and unpleasing appearance.

The picture is rich in decorative detail and the execution very fine but the outlines are a little hard and, as I said before, the Sienese grace has entirely disappeared.

Between these works and the Madonna of 1345, I think we should place a little fresco of the Virgin which adorns a niche to the left of the nave of the church of S. Martino [1]. Here the Madonna is seated low on a cushion suckling the Infant Christ. Four angels hold up a drapery behind her while two others kneel at the sides. Although a certain grace in the figure of the Virgin and a general sweetness of feeling, reminiscent of Sienese art, are more obvious in this panel than in the two previous works, we notice here for the first time in Vitale's productions — and even for the first time in Bolognese painting — that coarseness of execution and crude contrasts of light and shade which become the characteristics of the entire school.

The Madonna, surnamed "dei Denti", of 1345, which formerly hung in the oratory of St. Apollonia, near the church of Mezzaratta, was, for a time lost sight of, but has now been placed in the Davia Bargellini Gallery of Bologna (no. 129, fig. 204). It was the central panel of a polyptych that d'Agincourt reproduced with the four little lateral saints, two on either side one above the other [2]. The Virgin is represented enthroned, sitting on two pointed cushions as in old Byzantine pictures. The Child Who is fairly vivacious grasps His mother's head-dress with His outstretched right hand; a miniature figure of an adorer kneels

---

[1] G. *Cantalamessa*, Di un affresco del secolo XIV, Lettere ed Arti (Bologna), 1889. O. *Maruti*, Archiv. Stor. dell' Arte, 1889, p. 427.

[2] *d'Agincourt*, op. cit , IV^2, p. 397 and Pittura, pl. 127. *Baldinucci*, op. cit., IV, p. 323. *Ricci*, Guida di Bologna, p. 85, gives the date as 1340, as we now see it, the last numerals having been effaced.

Fig. 204. Vitale, Madonna, 1345. Davia Bargellini Gallery, Bologna. Photo Parazzo.

at either side. The pattern on the Virgin's cloak is composed of a repetition of an heraldic chimera. The type of the principal figure has not greatly changed, but the contours are hard and rigid and the refinement of execution, which was so marked in the master's early works, is here little evident. The signature reads: "*Vitala(?)s fecit h. opus. MCCC XL* ...."

Much more attractive is the polyptych of 1353 (fig. 205) in the right transept of the church of S. Salvatore, which, before the documents were brought to light, was attributed to a great diversity of schools and to many different artists. It has been thought a work of the first half of the 13th century ([1]), of the Venetian school of the end of the 14th, from the hand of Simone dei Crocifissi and from that of Cristoforo.

The centre shows the Madonna kneeling before her Son Who places a crown on her head; five angels look over the back of the Saviour's throne. The lateral figures represent St. John the Baptist at whose feet we see a young boy kneeling in prayer, and a holy bishop — probably St. Thomas of Canterbury and not St. Augustine — before whom kneels a monk, doubtless the prior, Riniero Ghislieri who, according to the contract, ordered the picture. To the extreme right and left are two little scenes; those on the left are the Adoration of the Magi and an angel appearing to a holy bishop, and those on the right the martyrdom of St. Catherine and two holy bishops seated together.

The figures are executed with more care than those in the pictures in the Davia Gallery and in S. Martino, and the proportions are larger, but the fine technique of the Madonna in the Vatican Gallery and of the one with the false date of 1320 in the Pinacoteca of Bologna, is absent. In the same manner Vitale has executed a picture on canvas in the Pinacoteca of Bologna (no. 328) representing against a rocky background St. Helen in adoration before the Cross while near by kneels a nun (fig. 206).

We have now come to the end of the list of Vitale's works ([2]),

---

([1]) *Bolognini Amorini*, and *G. G. Roncagli*, in Atti e Mem. della R. Deput. di Stor. Patr. per la Romagna, Serie III vol I, 1883, p 451.

([2]) *Baldani*, op. cit., p. 458, assigns to him a picture of the Death of the Madonna belonging to the art dealer Tavazzi in Rome; and no. 501 of the Pinacoteca, a Madonna which was formerly attributed to Vitale but which has been rightly restored to Lorenzo Monaco (*Toesca*, L'Arte, 1904. p. 171).

Fig. 205. Vitale, Polyptych, 1353. S. Salvatore, Bologna.
Photo Parazzo.

because I do not think that the frescoes of the Nativity, the Ascension and the Virgin with angels, in the church of Mezzaratta that Malvasia, Brach and Filippini attribute to him, are from his hand; they seem to be of slightly later date; besides for as far as we know their names at all, the painters who were active in this church, belong to a later generation.

A certain number of works that old writers attribute to Vitale have disappeared. Oretti, in his manuscript treatise on Bolognese painting that is preserved in the town library, speaks of a panel in the church of the Montalto college showing the figure of St. Antony Abbot and six scenes from his life that was signed: "*Vitalis f.*", and of a fresco on the outside of the church representing the same saint and dated 1330, to which I have already referred. Malvasia mentions two panels in the oratory of St. Apollonia, one representing St. Antony Abbot, St. James and a little angel, the other a holy bishop blessing a pilgrim, and in the church of S. Domenico a painting of the Virgin and St. John adoring the Divine Child in a niche in the choir and a fresco of the Nativity in the cloister. At the end of the passage dealing with Cristoforo, the same author still cites a Madonna in the church of Sta. Maria Maddalena agli Orfanelli; while lastly, Lanzi mentions two holy Benedictines and other figures of saints, which at his time, were to be found in the Malvezzi collection.

Belonging more or less to Vitale's school are: an Annunciation on two panels in the Bologna Gallery (nos. 384 and 385); a large number of scenes from the Life and Passion of Christ, from the Annunciation till the Noli me tangere, in the same Gallery (nos. 257 and 258); and a Virgin and Child surrounded by angels, a fragmentary painting, in the Museum of S. Stefano [1].

How the Sienese elements were introduced into Vitale's art is a question that is impossible for us to answer. The mere fact that from 1301 until 1315, the Sienese, Manno, miniaturist, painter and gold-smith, was active in Bologna does not solve the problem.

---

[1] *Baldani*, op. cit., p. 458, attributes this work to Vitale's own hand. *Filippini*, op. cit., p. 126 note 1, associates with Vitale a figure of a seated bishop in the Pesaro Gallery that I have already included in the Venetian school.

Fig. 206. Vitale, St. Helen adoring the Cross. Pinacoteca, Bologna.
Photo Poppi.

In the Bolognese school of miniature there is no trace of Sienese forms, but it is nevertheless beyond any doubt that the modelling and feeling of Vitale's first works clearly betray the influence of Sienese art.

His treatment and highly developed sense of ornamentation however, force us to seek for the origin of Vitale's technique in the school of miniature, which, in Bologna, was so important and certainly dominated that of painting. To this source we might also trace the change that took place in the second half of Vitale's career, since in this branch we also note many cases in which the diminution of refinement is incontestable, and I think we can safely admit that Vitale was influenced by the miniaturist, Niccolo di Giacomo.

We must not forget that although the number of Bolognese painters was fairly considerable towards the end of the 14th century, we hardly find any contemporary with Vitale, so that our artist, in this town abounding in miniaturists, was probably a rather isolated figure, and it is only natural that his works reflect the changes that miniature art underwent. During the latter half of Vitale's activity Bolognese miniature painting acquired a more fixed aspect on account of Niccolo di Giacomo's enormous production, for his numerous works, as well as the school that he created, exercised a lasting influence on the art of miniature and of painting in his native town ([1]). It was believed by some that this artist's career started in 1320, but this hypothesis is not supported by any facts. His first signed and dated work is a Gradual of 1351 in the Estense Library of Modena, while his last, a register "dei creditori del Monte" in the state archives in Bologna, dates from 1395. He made his will in 1399 and that is the last time we find mention of him. A resemblance in style leads us to believe that the illuminations of certain codices prior to 1351 are from his hand, such for example as those of the "statuti della societa dei drappieri" in the Bologna archives, which date from 1346.

Some important miniatures showing a very marked connection with Niccolo di Giacomo's manner are seen in the "Officium Ma-

---

([1]) For literature on Giacomo v. especially the monographs of *Malaguzzi Valeri, Baldani* and *Ciaccio* cited at the beginning of the chapter.

THE SCHOOL OF BOLOGNA. 411

riae Virginis" of 1349 at Kremsmunster (¹). We should, however, note the existence of a pseudo-Niccolo, a miniaturist who worked side by side with Niccolo di Giacomo and produced

Fig. 207. Niccolo di Giacomo, the Ascension, Miniature. Library, Munich.
Photo Riehn and Tietze.

works strongly resembling his, but whose activities can be traced to a slightly earlier date (²).

(¹) *Neuwirth*, Italienische Bilderhandschriften in Oesterreichisch Klosterbibliotheken, Repert. f. Kunstwiss., 1886, pp. 386—395.
(²) *Ciaccio*, op. cit.

The art of Niccolo di Giacomo (fig. 207) and of those who worked in his manner is composed of elements but rarely found in miniature painting. The forms are strong and sturdy rather than graceful and elegant. The figures are large and well developed, the faces are without any beauty or spirituality; the shape of the heads, as well as of the other parts of the body, is heavy, and the features coarse.

Action is depicted with an exaggerated realism; the gestures are natural but the artist has not attempted to make them pleasing. The drawing is executed in vigorous strokes, and the shadows are large and dark. The types seem to have been borrowed from Vitale, who, however, presents them in a more spiritual manner. With the miniaturists of Niccolo's group began the predominance of the realistic style in Bologna; it very soon replaced the more idealistic current which probably derived from the art of Oderisi and other miniaturists of the earlier generation.

The first Bolognese painter who seems to have been inspired as much by the work of Vitale as the miniatures of Niccolo di Giacomo and his group was Cristoforo, concerning whom we possess a certain amount of information although but two of his works have survived.

Cristoforo's name was known to Vasari who tells us that this artist was active in the church of Mezzaratta but that he is unaware whether he came from Modena or Ferrara [1]. It is much more likely that he was born in Bologna where we find a painter of this name mentioned in documents of 1381, 1391 and 1403.

In 1374 a Cristoforo was paid ten livres for the painting in the Corradini chapel of the church of S. Francesco [2], and in 1389 there existed in Bologna a painter and goldsmith of the name of "Cristoforo quondam Giacomo da Bologna, detto il Biondo" [3].

Malvasia affirms very precisely that a canvas on the altar "de' Torri" in the church of the Celestine monks, representing the Madonna between SS. Antony and Catherine, bore the inscription: *"Cristophorus pinxit Ravagexius de Savigno 1382 fecit fieri"* [4].

---

[1] *Vasari-Milanesi*, II, p. 140.
[2] *Gerevich*, Rassegna d'Arte, 1906, p. 167 note 6.
[3] *Zani*, op. cit., IV, p. 137.
[4] *Malvasia*, op. cit , I, p. 32.

D'Agincourt reproduces two paintings which he believes to have been executed by Cristoforo (¹) but one of them, a fresco in the church of Mezzaratta showing Moses bearing the tables of the law to the people of Israel, is not, as we shall see, from his hand. The other is a panel of the Madonna "della Misericordia" in the same church, one group of men and another of women, no doubt members of confraternities, kneel at the Virgin's feet. It was signed: "*Cristophorus pinxit 1380*", but as this inscription was written according to d'Agincourt on the back of the picture, he was rather doubtful about its authenticity; on the other hand the facsimile that d'Agincourt reproduces of this signature is identical with the one we find on Cristoforo's little picture preserved in the Ferrara Gallery.

In his manuscript, Oretti speaks of a work that Cristoforo executed in 1398.

Senator C. Ricci mentions a picture in S. Cristoforo at Monte Maggiore, signed and dated 1359 (²); while lastly Signor T. Gerevich cites a Madonna with adorers in the collection of Signor Guerina at Novarra, showing the signature: "*Croforus fecit 1387*" (³). As the former of these two works seems to have disappeared (⁴) and the latter is unknown to the public, our judgment of Cristoforo's art must be based on the one signed painting that we have at our disposal viz. the panel in the Ferrara Gallery (fig. 208).

This picture is divided horizontally into two parts, the upper of which shows the Saviour crucified between the Virgin and St. John while Mary Magdalene kneels at the foot of the Cross, and the lower the faithful mourning over their Master's body. Below this scene we read: "*Xpoforus fecit*".

The elements which the artist has borrowed from Vitale's art and from that of contemporary miniatures are evident in the appearance of the figures as much as in the technique, only Cristoforo was not himself a miniaturist as his figures clearly show. He was a true Bolognese artist and his manner particularly resembles that of the painters who come immediately after

---

(¹) *d'Agincourt*, op. cit., VI, p. 420 and Pittura, pls. CLVIII and CLX.
(²) *C. Ricci*, Guida di Bologna, p. 121.
(³) *T.Gerevich*,Cristoforo, in Thieme-Becker,Künstler Lexikon,VIII, p.117.
(⁴) *T. Gerevich*, loc. cit.

him. The dramatic and somewhat crude realism that we note in this picture reaches a climax in Simone dei Crocifissi's works.

Of the numerous attributions made to Cristoforo, I do not think that any of them are reliable(¹). A rather damaged Crucifixion with the Virgin, St. John, the Magdalene at the foot of the Cross and a devotee, in the Schnütgen Museum, Cologne, seems, however, from his hand. Cavalcaselle's attribution to this artist of some frescoes representing the Madonna and Adoration of the Magi, of which but a fragment remains, in the bell-tower of S. Andrea, Ferrara, has a special importance, since, if exact, it provides us with the proof that Cristoforo went to Ferrara to work.

Cristoforo was an artist of some merit and it is chiefly on account of the lack of his works that he takes such a very mediocre place in the Bolognese school. He is, however, of a certain importance because he is the connecting link between the first and second generation of painters and it is to his art that the influence, emanating from the group of miniaturists, owes its continued existence.

Some painters of the Trecento in Bologna are characterized by the foreign elements that they introduced into the local art, changing to a certain extent their manner of painting, so that they can hardly be called true Bolognese artists. They were Jacopo Avanzi, an artist whom I shall call the pseudo-Jacopo Avanzi who was strongly influenced by the painters of Rimini, and Andrea da Bologna who betrays a special familiarity with

---

(¹) *Malvasia* ascribes to Cristoforo several frescoes which have now disappeared; among them a Virgin and St. Antony in the sacristy of S Domenico; a similar painting transported from an old house to the church of S. Andrea dei Padri Penitenziari, and a Madonna between SS. Cosmo and Damian in Sta. Maria Maddalena degli Orfanelli. *Laderchi*, in his catalogue of the Costabili collection, Ferrara (1838) whence the signed picture in the gallery originates, attributes to Cristoforo the panels of the Crucifixion and the Virgin's dream in the Pinacoteca, which I include with the productions of Ferrara, and a panel with the figures of SS. Francis and Dominic from the Corpus Domini monastery in Ferrara which has been lost. *Filippini*, I affreschi della cappella Bolognini, accepts Vasari's and d'Agincourt's attribution of some frescoes in the church of Mezzaratta. *Gerevich* formerly believed that it was Cristoforo who executed Vitale's Coronation of the Virgin in S. Salvatore (Rassegna d'Arte, 1906, p. 167) and even still hesitatingly ascribes to him the frescoes in the Bolognini chapel to which subject we shall shortly return (*Thieme-Becker*, Künstler Lexikon, loc. cit.).

Fig. 208. Cristoforo, the Crucifixion and the Faithful mourning over the Body of Christ. Gallery, Ferrara.

Photo Minist. del Pubbl. Istr.

the art of The Marches where, moreover, he worked for a considerable length of time.

We shall begin with the first of these artists.

The older writers such as Vasari and Malvasia, confounded Jacopo Avanzi of Bologna with Jacopo d'Avanzo of Padua and Jacopo di Paolo of Bologna with whom we shall deal later on. Even at the present time Signor Filippini tends to identify the two former artists ([1]).

Of Jacopo Avanzi we possess but one document and one picture authenticated by the painter's signature ([2]). The document dates from 1384 and records that an enamel — perhaps an enamelled tile — was painted by him for the loggia of the Town Hall; further as Signor Baldani remarks, considering that his son, Bartolommeo di Jacopo Avanzi, is mentioned in 1395 without the father's name being preceded by the word "quondam", it is probable that he was still alive at that date ([3]). We know nothing else concerning Jacopo Avanzi.

His signed work is preserved in the Colonna Gallery in Rome; it represents the Saviour nailed to the Cross, above which a pelican is seen feeding its young, between the Virgin, St. John and the kneeling figure of Mary Magdalene. At the foot of the panel the inscription runs: "*Jacobus de Avanciis de Bononia f.*" (fig. 209).

We must now consider a question of the utmost importance in the study of Bolognese painting of the Trecento, namely the authorship of the frescoes in the church of the "Casa de Mezza" or of Mezzaratta, just outside the city.

From the information that is offered us in a Guide to Bologna of 1792, and by Malvasia, we learn that originally there were not less than three signatures of painters of the name of Jacopo.

([1]) *F. Filippini*, Jacopo Avanzi pittore bolognese del 1300, Atti e Mem. della R. Deput. di Stor. Patr. per la Romagna, 1912, p. 31.

([2]) A picture in the Venice Accademia is signed "*Jacopo Avanzi 1367*" but the signature is false and the picture, which shows the Saviour between the Virgin, St. John the Evangelist and Nicodemus, belongs to the Venetian-Byzantine manner of the 14th century. *Schubring* in Thieme-Becker, Künstler Lexikon, II, p. 270, mentions it as an authentic work of Jacopo Avanzi's.

([3]) *Baldani*, op. cit., p. 44.

Fig. 209. Jacopo Avanzi, the Crucifixion. Colonna Gallery, Rome.
Photo Ist. Art. Graf.

Firstly the series of eight scenes from the life of Joseph on the right wall was signed according to the guide: "*Jacobus fecit*" and according to Malvasia: "*Jacobus Pauli f.*" Then to the left of the entrance there are two rows of frescoes, the upper of which, illustrating the Saviour's youth, the Ascension and the Virgin and Child, bore, Malvasia tells us, the signature: "*Jacobus et Simeon f.*", while on the lower, in which later incidents from the Life of Christ are represented, the same author read: "*Jacbus fecit*" (¹), which inscription has not yet entirely disappeared. Malvasia adds that the frescoes of this church were restored in 1578.

These inscriptions do not always refer to the same Jacopo and I think it probable that the series of frescoes from the story of Joseph is by Jacopo di Paolo, a Bolognese painter of the following generation.

That the Jacopo who, with Simone dei Crocifissi, signed a part of the other frescoes, was Jacopo Avanzi whose authentic panel in the Colonna Gallery we have just considered, can hardly be admitted on account of the difference in style. Simone's share in the decoration of this church is evident in certain of the figures which do not harmonize with the ensemble. Moreover we have not only the combined signature of Jacopo and Simone for some of the frescoes but, according to Malvasia, Simone's signature was found isolated on another part of this wall. I think, then, that for this piece of the decoration we must admit the collaboration of these two artists.

There were other painters of the name of Jacopo, besides Jacopo Avanzo, in Bologna during the 14th century. Firstly there was Jacopo di Paolo but he seems to have been active at too late a date to have collaborated with Simone dei Crocifissi.

As for Jacopino de' Pappazoni or Jacopino de' Bavosi, the former appears in Bologna in 1365 when, with Andrea de' Bartoli, he left for Pavia to work in the castle of Galeazzo Visconti (²),

---

(¹) *Malvasia*, op. cit., p. 28. *Vasari-Milanesi*, II, pp. 141, 142 note 2. *Rosini*, op. cit., II, p. 226. *Crowe and Cavalcaselle*, op. cit., III, p. 199. *Brach*, op. cit., p. 96. *Ricci*, Guida di Bologna, pp. 120 and 240.

(²) *F. Filippini*, Bolletino d'Arte, 1911, p. 57, and Jacobino de' Papazzoni pittore bolognese del' 300, Bolletino d'Arte, 1915, fasc. 6.

while the latter is mentioned in 1368, 1371 and 1383 (¹). It is possible that these two names refer to but one artist. It is a curious fact that in his second will Jacopino de' Bavosi left a candle worth 20 sous to the Confraternity which adjoined the church of Mezzaratta, so that some connection between the artist and the church must have existed, and it is not impossible that he was the author of the frescoes signed Jacobus.

We know that in 1366 Simone made a contract to execute frescoes for this church, but as it was stipulated that the subjects of the paintings were to be taken from the Old Testament and the frescoes were to adorn the east wall, we can be sure that this deed does not refer to the works with which we are at present occupied.

Malvasia gives a fairly detailed description of these frescoes but many of them are almost completely effaced and others have disappeared entirely.

Of the combined work of Jacopo and Simone, the Circumcision of Jesus on the entry wall is in a good state of preservation; the composition comprises a large number of figures but they are for the greater part more characteristic of Simone's manner than of Jacopo's. On the left wall we see, above, some heads from an Adoration of the Magi; a Virgin amidst saints with an adorer kneeling at her feet, but only the last figure remains clearly visible (²); a fragment of the Massacre of the Innocents which seems to be from Simone's hand; the Ascension and the Virgin with the Child. Of the scenes below, the first, of which only a few heads remain, cannot be interpreted; then we find the miracle of the paralysed man who is let down from the roof into the room where the Saviour heals the sick, a painting certainly by Simone; Christ curing other sick people combined with the miracle at the pool of Bethseda (a fairly complete fresco)

(¹) *L. Frati*, Jacopino de' Bavosi, pittore bolognese del secolo XIV, L'Arte, 1911, p. 393.

(²) *Malvasia* does not mention this fresco but instead describes one which seems to have been the Presentation in the Temple, under which appeared the signature of the two artists, Jacopo and Simone. Following on this were the Flight into Egypt, the Massacre of the Innocents and the Wedding at Cana.

and the woman who was taken in adultery brought before the Lord (¹).

The accuracy of the information that Malvasia furnishes regarding the collaboration of the two artists has sometimes been questioned, but not only does the appearance of the painting confirm its authenticity, but that the activity of the two painters was combined is very evident in one of the pictures, which shows the name of only one of the artists. In the fresco of the miracle at the pool of Bethseda which Jacopo alone signed, two different hands are clearly manifest, the one having executed the part on the left, the other the figures to the right, which are not only different in appearance but also are of smaller proportions altogether. The attribution of this part to Simone is indubitable.

As for the figures that the painter Jacopo executed, we find that the proportions, the long shape of the faces, the sharp features and marked light effects resemble those in the works that I consider to be by the pseudo-Jacopo Avanzi; but it must be clear that even if we could attribute these panels and the frescoes at Mezzaratta to the same hand, it would in no way provide any connection with Jacopo Avanzi who signed the Crucifixion in Rome, even although a good many writers include it as a work of the above artist. Signor Filippini has rightly protested against this error.

The artist to whom I attribute the panels I have just alluded to, was dominated by an influence of the Riminese school. His most typical work is a painting in the Vatican Gallery (no. 100) representing the death of St. Francis (fig. 210) (²). The dead saint is stretched on his bier, his bare feet sandalled, his pierced hands folded; above, two angels carry away his soul while behind is grouped a large number of followers. It is a work which clearly reveals that the origin of this master's art should be traced to the school of Rimini. The morphological types so peculiar to this

---

(¹) *Malvasia* describes the fresco with the Miracle at the pool of Bethseda and says it showed Jacopo's signature; then followed, according to him, the Resurrection of Lazarus, signed only by Simone, Lazarus at the rich man's table after which were other scenes, such as the Entry into Jerusalem and the Last Supper.

(²) *F. M. Perkins*, Rassegna d'Arte, 1906, p. 122. *O. Sirén*, L'Arte, 1921, p. 101, calls it a late work.

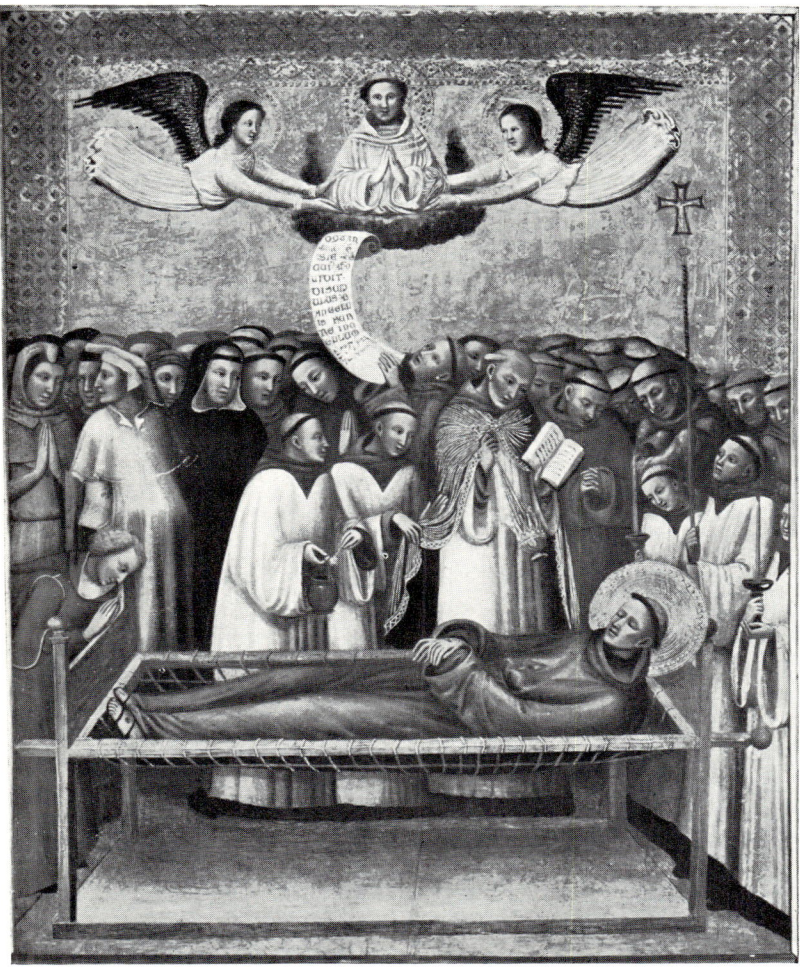

Fig. 210. Pseudo-Jacopo Avanzi, the Death of St. Francis. Vatican Gallery.
Photo Anderson

artistic school, the sharp features and the elongated forms leave us in little doubt as to the truth of this statement.

Five predella panels, formerly in the Gozzadini collection, Bologna, now in that of Mr. Platt, Englewood, are, in this regard, just as characteristic. They represent the Nativity, under an open shelter, combined with the Adoration of the Magi (fig. 211), Mary Magdalene anointing the Saviour's feet, a Resurrection, an angel delivering St. Catherine from her martyrdom on the wheel and the saint's decapitation (¹). An important crucifixion with many figures in the Acton collection, Florence, is executed in the same manner.

The other works by the pseudo-Jacopo Avanzi, in whose manner we detect no change, are preserved in the Pinacoteca of Bologna. A large polyptych (no. 159, fig. 212) shows, below in the centre, the Death of the Virgin and at either side, four small scenes arranged in two rows; they represent St. Gregory and other saints praying on Traiano's tomb, the Annunciation, the Nativity, the Adoration of the Magi, the Flight into Egypt, the Saviour at the age of twelve teaching in the Temple, the Ascension and Pentecost. Higher up, we find centrally, the Presentation in the Temple while the six lateral panels show full-length figures of saints. In the terminals we see, in the larger central one the Virgin supporting the dead body of her Son over His tomb, and in those at the sides, six half-length figures of saints. Another painting of the Death of the Virgin in the same Gallery (no. 170) has many points in common with the principal scene of the above polyptych (²). A rather damaged Coronation of the Virgin with separately framed figures of saints is a work by the same artist.

A certain connection between the art of the pseudo-Jacopo Avanzi and that of the real master of this name who signed the panel in the Colonna collection is evident in an altar-piece showing the Coronation of the Virgin and the Crucifixion (no. 161) and even more marked in a panel of the Crucifixion with several figures, and the pelican above the Cross (no. 160).

I think we should attribute yet another Crucifixion in the Bologna Gallery (no. 380) to the pseudo-Jacopo (³).

(¹) *Perkins*, op. cit., and Rassegna d'Arte, 1911, p. 145. *Baldani*, op. cit., p. 451.

(²) Attributed to Simone dei Crocifissi by Mr. *Langton Douglas* in *Crowe and Cavalcaselle*, op. cit., III, p. 196 note.

(³) The following attributions made by Signor *Baldani*, who does not differentiate between the two artists, are more doubtful: Bologna, Pinacoteca, nos. 363 and 364, two panels with an angel and two saints sometimes wrongly attributed to Simone dei Crocifissi (*Crowe and Cavalcaselle*, ed. *Langton Douglas*, III and *Filippini*, op. cit., p. 96 note); no. 230, a Last Judgment with the Pietà below. I think these are sooner school works. As such Signor *Baldani* rightly cites: no. 167, the martyrdom of St. Cristina; no. 383 St. Gregory writing at his desk. O. *Sirèn*, L'Arte, 1921, p. 25, wrongly attributes to Jacopo Avanzi a polyptych in the Vatican Gallery (no. 6) representing scenes from the Life of Christ. He believes it to be a youthful production.

Fig. 211. Pseudo-Jacopo Avanzi, the Nativity and the Adoration of the Magi. Platt Collection, Englewood, N.J.

All the writers who, in studying Jacopo Avanzi, confound him with the pseudo-Jacopo agree in finding an influence of the Riminese painters in the works that have just been mentioned. This is incontestable. Moreover there are other examples of this influence in Bolognese art. It is particularly to be noted in the miniatures of the "Canzone delle Virtu e delle Scienze" at Chantilly, which were executed before 1349, since Luchino Visconti is mentioned as being still alive (¹). M. L. Dorez who has published this manuscript(²) described the miniatures as Bolognese but executed under a Sienese influence. Signor Baldani on the other hand rightly discovers in them a resemblance to Baronzio's art. The subjects represented correspond to those with which Niccolo di Giacomo illustrated a manuscript of 1354, now in the Ambrosiana Library, Milan, and Signor Baldani concludes that perhaps Baronzio executed a series of frescoes in Bologna in which the virtues and sciences were depicted in a similar manner but which have entirely disappeared. This is obviously only a somewhat daring conjecture, but we have already seen that Riminese artists were active in Bologna, at least it was Francesco da Rimini who adorned some walls of the S. Francesco monastery of this city where other Riminese artists as well are mentioned (³).

Consequently Riminese elements in the work of a Bolognese painter are by no means surprising. Certain iconographical details in the pseudo-Jacopo's works, to which so far I have made no allusion, demonstrate to what an extent the artist was inspired by the examples of this school. Thus, for instance, in one of the panels in the Platt collection, we find the scenes of the Nativity and Adoration of the Magi combined, a peculiarity which, as I have already remarked, the Riminese painters borrowed from the Roman school of the 13th century. In the panel of the death of St. Francis and in the large polyptych in the Bologna Gallery (no. 159) we note the gold texture in the clothing, so characteristic of Riminese painting.

Moreover the picture signed by Jacopo Avanzi shows an iconographical peculiarity taken from the same school, viz. the

---

(¹) *F. Filippini*, Bolletino d'Arte del Minist. della Pubbl. Istr., V, 1911, p. 59.

(²) *L. Dorez*, op. cit. Signor *Filippini* ascribes, without any grounds, these miniatures to Andrea da Bologna.

(³) *Baldani*, op. cit. p. 428.

Cross to which the Saviour is attached is made from the branches of a tree.

Nevertheless I see no serious reason for confounding Jacopo Avanzi and the pseudo-Jacopo Avanzi for they are two artists

Fig. 212. Pseudo-Jacopo Avanzi, Polyptych. Pinacoteca, Bologna.
Photo Alinari.

whose style and temperament are utterly different, and furthermore the pseudo-Jacopo most probably belonged to the generation preceding Avanzi's. The Riminese school flourished, as we saw, at the beginning of the first half of the Trecento and the activity of an artist who was so directly inspired by it cannot be placed later than the beginning of the second half of the 14th century, while we have every reason to believe that Jacopo Avanzi was still alive in 1395. At the most we might admit that the pseudo-Jacopo Avanzi was the master of the genuine artist of this name, but this is only hypothetical and we can in no way be sure about it.

It seems to me possible that the painter who signed the frescoes in the church of Mezzaratta can be identified with the pseudo-Jacopo Avanzi; it is certainly rather curious that he, too, was called Jacopo, but, on the other hand, this coincidence may very well be the only reason for the confusion which these two artistic personalities have suffered.

It is this erroneous identification that has been the cause of the general unjustly severe judgment that has been pronounced on Jacopo Avanzo (¹). Whilst the the pseudo-Jacopo reveals himself — with the exception of the beautiful panels in the Platt and Acton collections — as a rather mediocre adherent of the Riminese school, the real Jacopo Avanzi must, on the strength of the figure of St. John in his signed panel, be considered an artist of exceptional merits, displaying a vigour of draughtsmanship and very advanced plastic effects which force us to qualify him as one of the immediate precursors of the 15th century Florentine artists.

All this, however, does not make me accept Signor Filippini's hypothesis that the Jacopo Avanzi who signed the panel in the Colonna Gallery, was the artist who worked with Altichiero in Padua, but he rightly points out that in order to differentiate these two artists, we should not take into account the pictures in the Bologna Gallery which have been wrongly ascribed to the former.

The art of the true Jacopo Avanzi, just as much as that of the painter whom I have called the pseudo-Jacopo Avanzi, constitutes an alien element in the Bolognese school. In neither one nor the other do we find those forms which at a later date characterize the art of this city, although the strong oppositions of light and shade that are displayed in the works of the pseudo-Jacopo show

---

(¹) Mr. *F. M. Perkins*, on the other hand, is of opinion that Jacopo Avanzi was "not the least gifted of the early painters of Bologna, if not the most talented of them all" (*Crowe and Cavalcaselle*, ed. Hutton, II, p. 159 note 5) but he too identifies the pseudo and the real Jacopo Avanzi.

Fig. 213. Andrea da Bologna, the Decapitation of St. Catherine. S. Francesco, Assisi. Photo Alinari.

a faint connection with the chiaroscuro effects of the Bolognese painters of subsequent generations.

Almost as estranged from the general movement of the Bolognese school as these two painters was yet a third, Andrea da Bologna ([1]).

[1] *F. Filippini*, Andrea da Bologna miniatore e pittore del XIV secolo, Bollet. d'Arte del Minist. della Pubbl. Istr., 1911, p. 50.

Mention is made of him for the first time in 1368 when he was charged with the decoration of the tomb of the Spanish Cardinal Albornoz who, in 1362, had ordered the construction of the chapel opposite the entrance in the Lower Church of S. Francesco, Assisi. The cardinal died in 1367 and was buried in this chapel. It was in all probability at this time that Andrea decorated the entire chapel, for which work he received the sum of 450 florins ([1]). There are two extant works that he signed and dated, the one the polyptych at Fermo of 1369, the other the Madonna of Pausola of 1372, both in The Marches.

No other facts concerning the artist have come to us. An Andrea worked in the church of S. Francesco in Bologna in the first half of the 14th century and a painter called Andrea de' Bartoli went to Pavia in 1365 to decorate the palace of Galeazzo Visconti ([2]), but in neither case do I think the record refers to our artist, the first on account of the date, the second because of the name.

The decoration of the chapel, dedicated to St. Catherine, in the Lower Church of Assisi is fairly important. The intrados of the entrance arch is adorned with six figures, three on either side, five of which are bishops. At the feet of one of them kneels the cardinal founder. The illustrations of the St. Catherine legend

---

([1]) The documents concerning the decoration of this chapel were found in Bologna by Signor *Filippini*. Prior to their discovery the frescoes were sometimes attributed to a certain Pace di Bologna. This is a mistake, even although traces of Pace's activity are found elsewhere in the church of S. Francesco and the inscription on the cardinal's tomb was painted by him. He was employed on the more ornamental part of the decoration, together with Giovanni di Maestro Nicola and Angelino di Corrado di Novarello. *Vasari* who confounds him with Pace da Faenza (ed. *Milanesi*, I, p. 405) informs us that he adorned the chapel of S. Antonio. The sum required for this decoration was bequeathed only in 1360 (*C. Fea*, Descrizione etc. della Basilica, etc. di S. Francesco d'Assisi, Roma, 1820, p. 11) while the painter Pace is mentioned in a register of the accounts of the church in 1354. (*G. Fratini*, Storia della basilica e del convento di S. Francesco in Assisi, Prato, 1882, p. 192). This confirms *Vasari's* statements v. *H Thode*, Franz v. Assisi u. die Anfänge der Kunst der Renaissance in Italien, 2nd ed., Berlin, 1904, p. 301. Regarding Cardinal Albornoz's activities at Assisi, v. also *Filippini*, Rassegna d'Arte Umbra, 1910, p. 55.

([2]) *F. Filippini*, op. cit., p. 57.

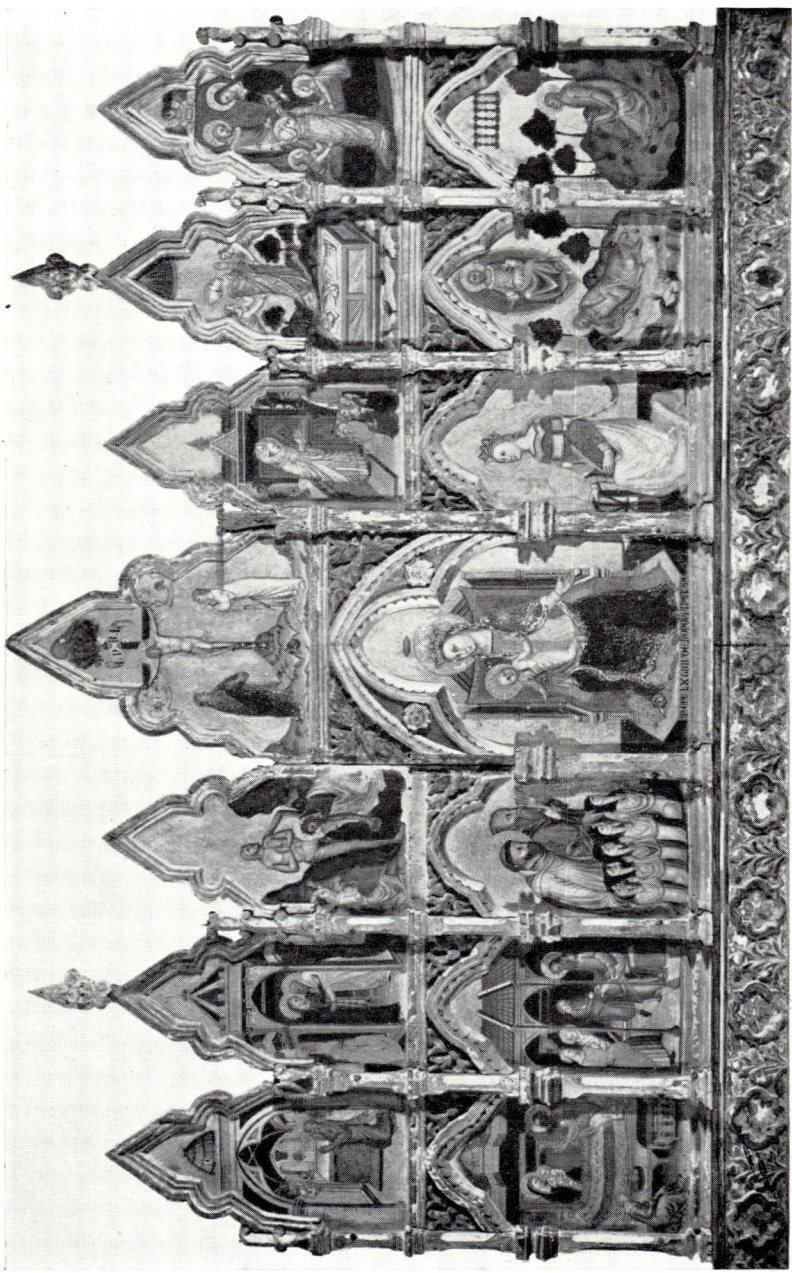

Fig. 214. Andrea da Bologna, Polyptych, 1369. Gallery, Fermo.
Photo Alinari.

begin below on the right, where we see her conversion and her mystical marriage. Above is depicted the saint at the court of Maxencius; on the left she is represented in dispute with the philosophers who, below, are burnt at the stake. Returning to the right wall we find the Empress Faustina visiting her in prison and the beheading of Faustina, while opposite the frescoes show the angels delivering St. Catherine from her martyrdom on the wheel, her decapitation, and angels burying her on Mount Sinai (fig. 213). The groins of the vault, the borders between the frescoes and the window embrasures are adorned with figures of saints and the cardinal's coat of arms. Signor Filippini is of opinion that the same artist also designed the window decoration but there is no sufficient reason for believing this to be true (¹). In a passage, leading to the first chapel to the right of the nave of the same church, which is known as the oratory of S. Lorenzo, there is a representation of the martyrdom of this saint from the hand of the same artist, to whom, moreover, it has been attributed, although some critics find that it only betrays a connection with this painter's art (²).

Andrea da Bologna's second authentic work is a polyptych in the Fermo Gallery (fig. 214). The principal panel is occupied by an image of the enthroned Madonna at whose feet we read: "*MCCCLXVIII de Bononia Nat. Andreas fecit*". On the panels adjoining the central one we see on the right St. Catherine with the wheel and to the left a group of nuns presented by two holy monks. On the extreme left is represented the nativity of St. John (fig. 215), while next to it we find the father writing down the name of his son (fig. 216). The corresponding panels on the right show two visions of St. John the Evangelist on the Island of Patmos. In the left lateral terminals we see an angel appearing

---

(¹) *J. Cristofani*, Le vitrate del' 300 nella Basilica inferiore d'Assisi, Rassegna d'Arte, 1909, p. 153. *E. Giusti*, Le vitrate di S. Francesco in Assisi, Milan (1911), p. 300. *B. Kleinschmidt*, Der Basilika von S. Francesco in Assisi, I, Berlin, 1915, p. 237.

(²) *Filippini*, op. cit., p. 53. *Thode*, loc. cit., associates with the painter who executed the frescoes in the St. Catherine chapel, a painting of the Madonna enthroned between SS. Francis and Antony which we find on the wall to the left of the entrance in the Lower Church. It is a work executed in the manner of Ottaviano Nelli — probably by Ceccolo di Giovanni as we shall see in Vol. V — and bears no resemblance to the frescoes in the chapel.

Fig. 215. The Nativity of St. John the Baptist. Detail of fig. 214.
Photo Alinari.

to Zacharias, the Meeting at the Golden Gate and the Baptism of Christ; the first two scenes are placed in the interior of a house and are rather unskilfully rendered. To the right are three illustrations from the life of a holy bishop, and in the centre the Crucifixion with the Virgin and St. John at the sides, and over the Cross a pelican in its nest. The pedestal of the picture is adorned with twelve medallions containing half-length figures, many of which, however, are badly damaged or have entirely disappeared.

The picture of 1372 is a Madonna of Humility; it is found in the Town Hall of Pausula but belongs to the church of S. Agostino (fig. 217). With a profusion of decorative detail the Virgin is represented sitting on the ground nursing the Child. Below the signature runs: *"De Bononia Natus Andreas ... fatu A. D. MCCCLXXII"*.

Of the various works attributed to Andrea, I can only accept that of the Death of the Virgin in the Ancona Gallery (no. 14, fig. 218) made by Signor L. Venturi, and this not without a certain reserve, since the technique is here more typically Bolognese than in the signed or documented works. The Virgin's bier is surrounded by Apostles while in the background the Saviour in an aureole, accompanied by angels, holds the image of His Mother's soul[1]. A peculiarity of this painting is the dominating cherry-red colour.

On the question as to whether Andrea da Bologna belongs to the Bolognese school or to that of The Marches, opinion is divided. Signor Baldani for instance, denies that the artist belonged to the Bolognese group of painters, and according to him

---

[1] *L. Venturi*, A traverso Le Marche, L'Arte, 1915, p. 13. The other attributions with which I do not agree are a Coronation of the Virgin with six lateral figures made by Signori *Astolfi* and *Colasanti*.(L'Arte, 1902, p. 193 and 1907, p. 413) which I have already included in the Venetian school (v. Vol. IV, p. 88); a polyptych representing the Madonna, Nativity, Adoration of the Magi, Resurrection and Ascension in the Ascoli Piceno Gallery (*A. Venturi*, Storia dell' Arte italiana, VII, p. 184); *L. Venturi*, op. cit., p. 14, rightly ascribes this work to a pupil of Andrea's *O. Sirén*, L'Arte, 1921, p. 101, gives to Andrea a triptych in the Johnson collection, Philadelphia, and somewhat hesitatingly a Nativity in the Vatican Gallery (no. 172). *Filippini*, op. cit., believes, as I have already said, that Andrea executed the miniatures of the codex of the "Canzone delle virtu e delle scienze" at Chantilly.

Fig. 216. Zacharias writing the name of his Son. Detail of fig. 213.

Photo Alinari.

the signatures on the two works in The Marches only state that the master was born in Bologna from which it may be inferred that there was a difference between the city of his birth and the one in which he resided. Senator C. Ricci ([1]) also finds that the connection between the painting of The Marches and Andrea's art is evident while Mr. Perkins ([2]) thinks that he was inspired by Francescuccio Ghissi, one of the artists whose productions are very typical of this school with which we shall deal in the next volume. Signor Venturi, on the other hand, considers Andrea as belonging to the Bolognese school; nevertheless he described the frescoes at Assisi (before the discovery of the document proving them to be by Andrea) as the work of a "Marchegiano" who had borrowed certain elements from Romagnole paintings and whose art was not devoid of a Sienese influence ([3]). Signor Colasanti is of opinion that Andrea's connection with The Marches has been exaggerated ([4]) while Signor Filippini finds that Andrea's art is composed of Giottesque and Sienese factors ([5]).

This difference of opinion regarding an artist who so obviously belongs to a definite school, seems to me incomprehensible. The Madonna of Humility at Pausula is nothing but a free copy of the pictures by Allegretto Nuzi and Ghissi, the two chief artists of the school of The Marches. Not only is the composition identical — even to the moon at the Virgin's feet — but we find the same tendency to emphasize the contours and an almost complete lack of plasticity.

The outline plays the most important part in the art of The Marches and from this standpoint Andrea's Madonna is thoroughly Marchegian.

The same may be said of the figures in the Fermo polyptych, and we may further note here the peculiar proportions which are so characteristic of this school, in which the upper part of the body is often too long. In the frescoes of Assisi, however, we find certain persons whose general appearance and, above all, whose

---

([1]) *C. Ricci*, La pittura antica alla mostra di Macerata, Emporium, March, 1906.
([2]) *F. M. Perkins*, Rassegna d'Arte, 1906, p. 51, coll. 2 note 2.
([3]) *A. Venturi*, op. cit., V, p. 862.
([4]) *Colasanti*, op. cit.
([5]) *Filippini*, op. cit., p. 58.

Fig. 217. Andrea da Bologna, Madonna, 1372. Town Hall, Pausula

Photo Minist. del. Pubbl. Istr.

realistic and not always beautiful facial expression show more connection with the Bolognese manner; this is also manifest in the Ancona panel. Moreover the Pausula Madonna, whose form is more robust than we find in painting of The Marches, clearly reveals the Bolognese origin of the artist. I admit, consequently, that the master was a native of the town after which he is named, but working chiefly in The Marches, he was influenced by the art of this region.

This would also explain the Sienese elements that we have observed in his works, because the school of The Marches was founded by Allegretto Nuzi, in all probability a pupil of Bernardo Daddi who, among the Florentine artists of the period, was the one most inspired by Sienese painting. Andrea's sojourn in The Marches must have been of considerable length since already in the frescoes at Assisi which were executed some years before the two pictures still to be found in The Marches, we note a fairly strong influence of the Marchegian school.

Nevertheless Andrea never entirely lost the characteristics of the art of his native town. It is to Bologna that he owes the dramatic animation and realism of action evident in the frescoes at Assisi, and also a certain coarseness, which we meet within the works of some of his compatriots, such as Simone and Jacopo di Paolo, and from which the painters of The Marches were quite free. He was, however, in constant touch with Bologna which explains how Cardinal Albornoz, who resided there, selected Andrea for the decoration of the chapel which he had ordered to be constructed.

It is in the second half of the 14th century that we find a prodigious pictorial output in Bologna, manifest not only in painting itself but also in miniature art, innumerable specimens of which are scattered throughout the different European libraries ([1]). Simultaneously with this abundance of production we note that the quality deteriorates, and the Bolognese art of the second half of the Trecento is characterized by a negligence and coarseness

---

([1]) One of the artists active at this period was a certain Beltranimo who is mentioned in documents of 1369 and 1370, in the latter of which years he had passed the age of 25. There exists a poem in honour of this artist, L. *Frati*, Beltranimo da Bologna, pittore del Trecento. L'Arte, 1916, p. 161.

Fig. 218. Andrea da Bologna, the Death of the Virgin. Gallery, Ancona.

Photo Minist. del. Pubbl. Istr

of execution which show that the art of painting had developed into a veritable industry. The redeeming qualities of Bolognese works are the animated action, the realism and the dramatic force, even when these effects are obtained with an absolute disregard of the aesthetic.

In miniature, an art in which the fineness of execution is often one of the principal qualities, the coarse clumsy forms are even more evident than in the frescoes and the panels; the best are those in which we find reminiscences of Niccolo di Giacomo's art (fig. 219) ([1]); while the worst are of an almost barbarous appearance (fig. 220).

The most characteristic member of this new group of artists is Simone dei Crocifissi whose signed works we possess in considerable number, for he was a fairly productive artist, and concerning whom we have several documents. Unfortunately there are but few of his works that can be dated with any precision. His name appears for the first time in a record of 1355 in which he is mentioned as "Magister Simon quondam Philippi pictor", being one of the "ventiquinquene hominum capelle S. Domini di quartero porte S. Proculi" ([2]).

He was the son of a shoemaker called Filippo di Benvenuti. In 1359 he married Donella di Gerardino di Giovanni di Conte di Cavalli, a relation of the painter, Vitale, and had two daughters. He is mentioned again in 1363 and in 1365 when his father-in-law, Dalmasio, a painter and the father of Lippo Dalmasio, appointed him his attorney. In 1366 we find him signing a contract with the prior and the "massaro" of the confraternity adjoining the church of Mezzaratta in which he undertakes to execute five frescoes representing scenes from the Old Testament on the east wall of this church, receiving for each one the

---

([1]) *G. Leidinger*, Meisterwerke der Buchmalerei am Handschriften der Bayerischen Staatsbibliothek München, München, 1920, p. 29, attributes the miniature that I reproduce to the Veronese school, but in my opinion it is clearly a Bolognese miniature reminiscent of Niccolo di Giacomo's art.

([2]) *Baldani*, Documenti e Studi pubbl. per cura della R. Deput. di Stor. Patr. per la Romagna, III, p. 460. For other documents, v. *L. Frati*, Dalmasio e Lippo de' Scannabechi e Simone dei Crocifissi, Atti e Mem. della R. Deput. di Stor. Patr. per la Romagna, Serie III, vol. XXVII, 1909, p. 209.

Fig. 219. Bolognese Miniature, 2nd half of the 14th century. Decretum Gratiani, Library, Munich.

Photo. Riehn and Tietze.

sum of 25 lire (¹). In 1380 he was elected magistrate for the months of September and October.

Simone made two wills, one in 1397 and the other in 1399, in both of which the miniaturist, Niccolo di Giacomo, is nominated executor (²). Simone at this time was living in the parish of S. Damiano. His testament leads us to suppose that the proceeds of his great activity were considerable. He expresses therein the wish to be buried near the church of S. Domenico.

We find the artist's name on only one dated work, the crucifix in the church of S. Giacomo Maggiore which bears the date 1370; Malvasia, however, informs us that at the head of the stairway of the "foresteria" in the monastery of S. Francesco there was a Coronation of the Virgin signed and dated 1377, but this work has since disappeared (³). Seeking for other dates concerning the artist, I think we can admit that the picture of Urban V in the Bologna Gallery possesses to such a marked degree the assets of a genuine portrait that we may safely say it was executed during his pontificate, consequently between 1362 and 1370. It is probably the head of the same Pope that we find at the foot of another picture in the Bologna Gallery; while a Pietà in the Davia Bargellini Gallery was executed in accordance with the will of Giovanni di Eithinl who died in 1368 (⁴).

It is very regrettable that we have no more precise indication regarding the evolution of Simone's art which shows a good deal of diversity, and it would have been of the utmost importance had we been able to establish a more exact chronology of his productions.

Nevertheless we can distinguish fairly clearly two manners, one of which betrays a certain dependence on the preceding generation of artists, and especially on Vitale, for which reason we may suppose it to be Simone's first manner; while the other shows many of the characteristics peculiar to the subsequent Bolognese school of painting in which the coarseness of drawing,

---

(¹) I do not know why Signor *Baldani*, op. cit., p. 464, doubts whether it was Simone who executed these frescoes.

(²) *Baldani*, op. cit., makes the mistake of reversing the rôles when he says that Niccolo di Giacomo was the testator and Simone the executor.

(³) *Malvasia*, op. cit., p. 30.

(⁴) *Ricci*, Guida di Bologna, p. 85.

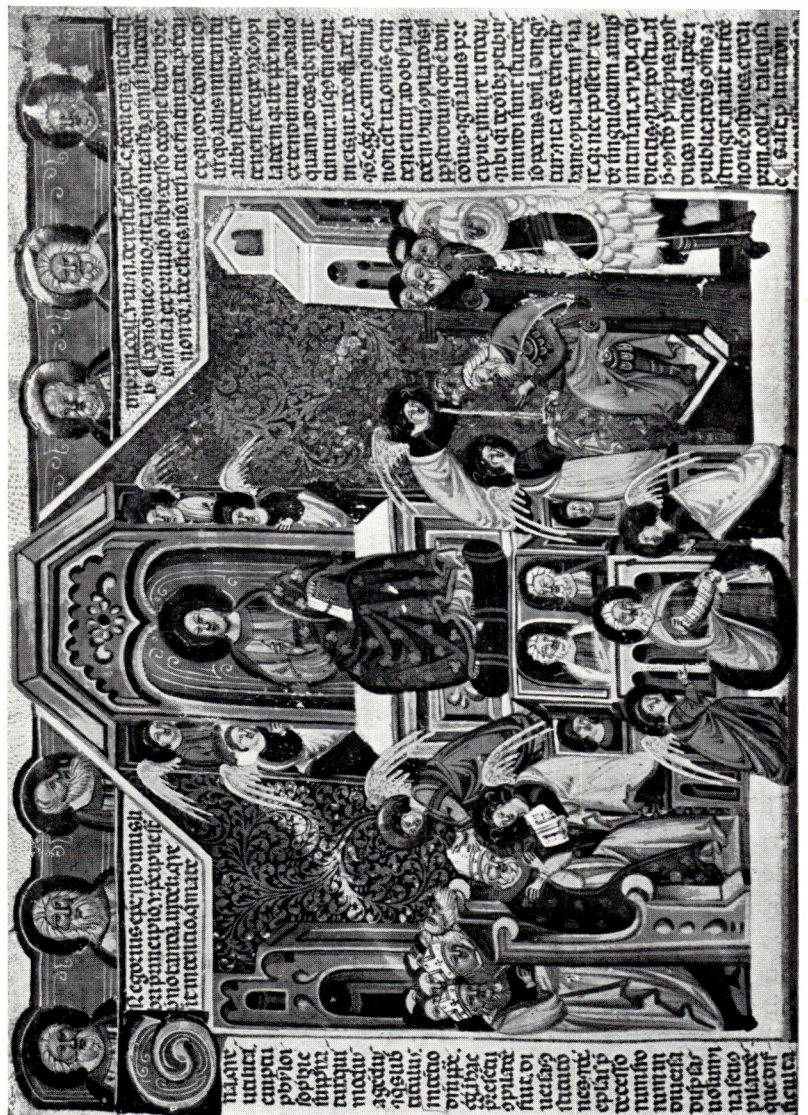

Fig. 220. Bolognese Miniature, 2nd half of the 14th century. Decretales Gregorii IX, Library, Munich.

Photo Riehn and Tietze.

the large shadows and a general lack of beauty are the predominating features.

Examples of the art which was transitional between the painting of the first half of the 14th century and that peculiar to Simone dei Crocifissi, are to be found in a few small panels in the Museum of Nancy (France), representing the Crucifixion and some scenes from the lives of martyrs (fig. 221). These paintings undoubtedly belong to the Bolognese school on account of the drawing of the faces and the helmeted soldiers which we find later in Simone's productions, but the types are too subtle and the drawing too fine for us to ascribe them with certainty to this artist; they might, however, be a work of his youth.

Although the facial types in the large polyptych in the Bologna Gallery (no. 474, fig. 222) have already acquired a certain amount of individuality, Vitale's influence is still manifest. The principal panel shows the Coronation of the Virgin with angels looking over the back of the throne and a tiny figure of the donor kneeling below.

Each of the six lateral panels is occupied by a figure of a saint. Higher, we see in the centre the Crucifixion and at the sides six smaller figures of saints. The terminals show centrally the Resurrection of Christ and a third series of saints, this time still smaller. It is recorded that originally this altar-piece possessed a predella composed of five illustrations from the Life of Christ [1]. This large polyptych does not lack either fineness of execution, grace of form or nicety of feeling. We find that same Sienese element which made Vitale's paintings so attractive and which produces something of the same effect here. At the foot of the central panel we read: "*Symon de Bononia fecit hoc opus*". It is one of the two signatures in which the artist calls himself after his native town; the other was on a work mentioned by Malvasia which has since been lost.

Another Coronation of the Virgin in the same Gallery (no. 164, fig. 223) shows a considerable fineness of execution and feeling but the forms have become less graceful. The Saviour is depicted sitting on the same long seat as the Virgin who clasps

---

[1] Oretti's manuscript furnishes us with this fact, v. *Gerevich*, Rassegna d'Arte, 1906, p. 167.

His left hand as he places the crown on her head with His right. The two figures, behind whom is seen a cross, are enclosed in an elliptical aureole surrounded by angels. Below their feet the words: "S*ymon fecit*" are inscribed.

Fig. 221. Simone dei Crocifissi (?), two holy Martyrs taken to prison. Museum, Nancy.

Photo Bulloz.

The first of the three paintings which can be dated more or less approximately, is the image of Pope Urban V in the Pinacoteca of Bologna (no. 340, fig. 224). The Pontiff is depicted full-face, bestowing a blessing and holding the portraits of SS. Peter and Paul; a little angel is seen behind either shoulder while higher up two other angels place the papal tiara on his head, towards which the Holy Ghost descends. The signature: "*Symon fecit*", and the inscription: "*Beatus Urbanus papa quintus*" are

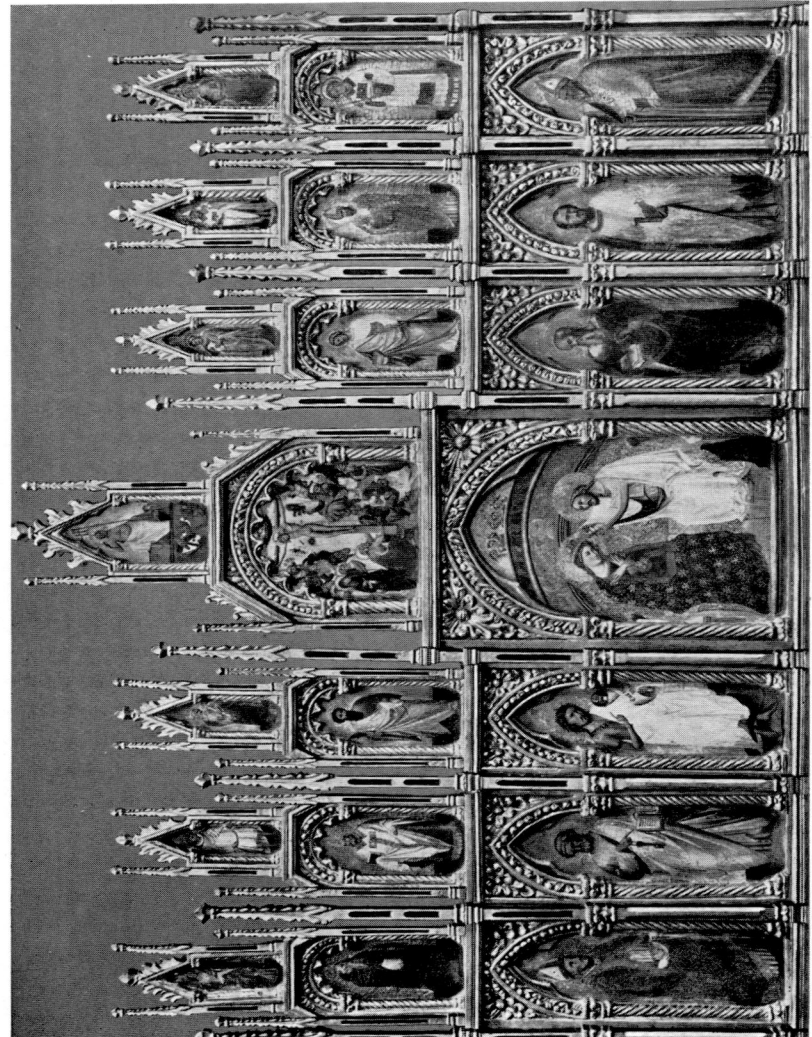

Fig. 222. Simone dei Crocifissi, Polyptych. Pinacoteca, Bologna.
Photo Anderson.

painted at the foot of the panel. A very realistic detail and one which the painter has made very evident is the Pope's squint.

The second picture is the Pietà in the Davia Bargellini Gallery in which Giovanni di Eithinl, who died in 1368, is represented,

Fig. 223. Simone dei Crocifissi, the Coronation of the Virgin. Pinacoteca, Bologna.

Photo Perazzo.

while the third, which can be dated exactly, is a large crucifix of the Giottesque type in the chapel of the Cari family — the third on the right — behind the choir of S. Giacomo Maggiore. We find God the Father represented above, the Virgin and St. John at the sides and two figures at the foot of the Cross where the painter has inscribed his name and the date: "*Symon fecit hoc opus An. MCCCLXX*".

Fig. 224. Simone dei Crocifissi, Pope Urban V. Gallery, Bologna.
Photo Poppi.

There is a very similar crucifix in the Museum of S. Stefano; it is perhaps even a little larger. Of the two figures at the foot of the Cross one is here that of St. Mary Magdalene. The artist has again signed this work but without giving the date. We can, however, admit that these two crosses were executed about the same time, because not only their appearance, but also the technique is identical.

In all the works of this little group the treatment is thorough and the drawing correct but there is no trace of elements due to a Sienese influence; these have been replaced by a vivacity of expression and a somewhat vulgar individuality of facial types. The graceful forms have also undergone a change, being now larger and more robust.

There are some works in which this tendency is not yet very pronounced. The first of these is a little picture of a curious shape in the Bologna Gallery (no. 162, fig. 225) which may also date from the time of Urban V, at least one would say that the bust depicted on the right as pendant to that of St. Theresa is an image of this Pontiff. The Saviour and the Virgin are seated

Fig. 225. Simone dei Crocifissi, the Crucifixion and Christ and the Virgin enthroned amidst saints. Gallery, Bologna. Photo Perazzo.

in the centre in the midst of the kneeling Apostles; two saints present the donors who kneel one on either side. Above we see Our Lord on the Cross between the Virgin, St. John, Mary Magdalene, St. Antony Abbot and St. Augustine, while to the extreme left and right are the figures of the Annunciation. The position of the signature: "*Symon fecit hoc opus*", which we find below the principal figures, proves that this picture is not a fragment as the busts at the sides might have otherwise led us to suppose.

In the collection of the senator, Count Giovanni Gozzadini, which was broken up in 1906, there was an unsigned picture by Simone showing the Coronation of the Virgin and the Crucifixion, with the Saviour and the Apostles in the predella, and above, the Trinity, adored by four angels, and the figures of the Annunciation in the lateral pinnacles (¹). It was a characteristic work of Simone's and bore a strong resemblance to the foregoing picture.

A still rather pleasing work but one in which the forms are a little heavy and the facial types somewhat vulgar is a Coronation of the Virgin in the Museum of Troyes (France) (no. 269, fig. 226) (²). The embroidered curtain which forms a background to the principal figures is held up by four of the nine angels whose heads appear behind the back of the throne. The Twelve Apostles kneel in adoration at the sides.

Comparing another large polyptych in the Gallery of Bologna (no. 163) with the one we have already considered (no. 474) we observe a marked decadence in Simone's art. It is again the Coronation of the Virgin which comprises the principal part of this altar-piece; seven angels look on from above while higher up we see the Crucifixion with the Virgin, St. John and Mary Magdalene. In either row there are six lateral saints, those of the lower one are full-length figures while those in the pinnacles are only half-length. The polyptych came originally from the monastery of S. Michele in Bosco.

Another comparison which should be made is that between the Crucifixion in the first big polyptych (no. 474), which was executed under Vitale's influence, and a panel representing the same subject in the author's collection (fig. 227). Only a slight change will be noted in the composition, but the technique has altered considerably. There is certainly no lack of dramatic force in this picture; the exaggerated facial expressions are in some instances grimaces, while the methods that the artist has employed to obtain certain effects are somewhat crude, the thick

---

(¹) *Baldani*, op. cit., reproduces it, pl. X.

(²) Formerly in the Campana collection, v. *P. Pedrizet et R. Jean*, La galerie Campana et les musées français, Bordeaux, 1907, p. 34, no. 337.

Fig. 226. Simone dei Crocifissi, the Coronation of the Virgin, Museum, Troyes.
Photo Bulloz.

outlines and large shadows being particularly prominent. It is to this manner in the artist's career that belong those frescoes in the church of Mezzaratta with which we have dealt in connection with Jacopo Avanzi. The figures to the right of the scene of the miracle at the pool of Bethseda, for example, show a striking resemblance to those of the above-mentioned panel. To the same group of works belongs a picture of the Madonna della Misericordia, preserved in the villa of Prince Potenziani at Rieti ([1]).

The erect figure of the Virgin, beside whom we see six angels, holds her cloak open above the adorers, who are arranged in two groups, the men to the left, the women to the right. In spite of the coarseness of the drawing, the painting is interesting on account of the marked individuality and animation of the faces. The work is signed: "*Symon pinxit hoc opus*".

In some of Simone's productions we note an even more inferior technique and an absolute lack of desire to create a work of any artistic value; they have all the appearance of mediocre provincial pictures.

The most characteristic production of this stage in Simone's career is a Coronation of the Virgin, painted on canvas, in the Museum of Pesaro (fig. 228) ([2]). The two principal figures and the eight angels looking down on them from above are equally ugly. The signature, "*Symon pinxit*", leaves us, however, in no doubt as to its being an authentic work. A Coronation of the Virgin which I saw recently for sale in Florence is certainly from the hand of Simone, and but little superior to the foregoing work.

To this same manner, which was probably that of Simone's old age, belong two panels in the Museum of Compiègne (France), representing a saint being crowned with a mitre by a Pope (fig. 229) and a saint — perhaps the same — beaten to death at the altar before which he had been saying mass ([3]). The two panels,

---

([1]) U. *Gnoli*, Un dipinto sconosciuto di Simone de' Crocifissi, Rassegna d'Arte, 1912, p. 47.

([2]) G. *Vaccaj*, Pesaro, Bergamo, 1909, p. 108. L. *Serra*, La Pinacoteca e il Museo di Pesaro, 2nd ed., Pesaro, 1920, p. 14.

([3]) Formerly in the Campana collection, v. *Perdrizet et Jean*, op. cit., p. 24, nos. 175—176. These authors are of opinion that the scenes illustrate the life of St. Thomas à Becket but this hardly seems likely as this archbishop was killed by the sword of a soldier.

THE SCHOOL OF BOLOGNA.

which originally seem to have belonged to one altar-piece, are as crude in their technique as the canvas at Pesaro ([1]).

([1]) There is no lack of Simone's works, among which I shall cite the following: *Bologna*, Pinacoteca, Madonna and ten angels signed "*Symon fecit hoc opus*" (unnumbered); Sta. Maria Incoronata, Coronation of the Virgin on the altar (Ricci, Guida etc., p. 113); the dispersed Gozzadini collection, a Coronation of the Virgin signed "*Simon pinxit hoc opus*" which was acquired by Mr. Langton Douglas (v. Baldani, op. cit., p. 465 and Crowe and Cavalcaselle ed. L. Douglas, III, p. 196 note) while another Coronation of the Virgin, showing the same signature, passed from this collection into that of Herr Japs, Berlin (v. Baldani and Crowe and Cavalcaselle, loc. cit.). *Florence*, Uffizi, no. 260 (old number), the Nativity, signed "*Symon pi....*". *Modena*, Pinacoteca, no. 24, Madonna in the midst of ten angels, signed "*Symon fecit hoc opus*". *Paris* (for sale in 1923) triptych with the Virgin in the central panel and a saint in each of the wings.

The following paintings are executed in Simone's manner: *Bologna*, Pinacoteca, no 601, seven scenes from the life of the Madonna; S. Martino, right wall, fragment of a Crucifixion; Museum of S. Stefano, three figures of saints, two panels each with three saints, and the Entombment; Gozzadini collection, SS. Andrew, Antony and the Annunciation (Baldani, op. cit., p. 467). *Faenza*, Pinacoteca, half-length figure of the dead Saviour. *Rome*, (for sale in 1909, Baldani, op. cit., p. 466), triptych, the Crucifixion in the centre with three saints and a figure of the Annunciation in each wing.

Some works inspired by Simone's manner are: *Bologna*, Pinacoteca, no. 166, St. Bernard dei Tolomei, monks and nuns; S. Giovanni in Monte, 6:h chapel to the right, a crucifix; S. Domenico cloister (now an elementary school), a fragment of the Trinity (the word "*Petrus*" is found on this painting. C. Ricci, Guida etc., p. 61, informs us that the signature read "*Petrus Johannis*" and believes in accordance with Crowe and Cavalcaselle that it is the signature of Pietro di Giovanni de Tovaglis who was active between 1410 and 1453. Baldani, op. cit., p. 470, is of the contrary opinion and does not think that the signature has anything to do with this artist); Museum of S. Stefano, crucifix with four saints below, considerably damaged; Gozzadini collection, SS. Francis, John the Baptist and above Petronius and Zamas. *Florence*, (for sale in 1922, the same was for sale in Rome in 1918) an important panel of the Crucifixion with the three crucified, a large number of people and St. Francis at the foot of the central cross.

A certain number of works are known to us only from old records. In *Malvasia* op. cit., p. 30, we find, besides the frescoes at Mezzaratta of which the Resurrection of Lazarus was signed, and the Coronation of the Virgin of 1377 that I have already mentioned, a crucifix in S. Martino (apparently a different work from the Crucifixion that I have just included with Simone's school works); another in S. Pietro signed "*Simon fecit hoc opus*"; a Madonna in S. Petronio; a Coronation of the Virgin in Sta. Margherita and a painting of the titular saint on the altar of the same church; a Madonna pinch-

Glancing back at Simone dei Crocifissi's work it may seem extraordinary that his surname was taken from the subject of the Crucifixion since the number of Coronations of the Virgin that he has depicted is far greater.

The frequency with which this subject appears recalls the Venetian school which had for it a special predilection.

The complex form of his polyptychs may also be accounted for by his knowledge of this school, the works of which were not rare in Bologna. His manner of painting however is in no way Venetian but derives directly from the older Bolognese artists whose style he disfigured with his coarseness of technique. In his vigorous forms and popular dramatic feeling we find elements borrowed from the direct Giottesque tradition to which the type of his crucifixes also belongs.

It is his enormous output that has made us qualify Simone's art as an industry and although he was a fairly gifted painter, his paintings as a whole offer us but little artistic enjoyment.

Lippo Dalmasio de' Scannabecchi([1]), in one of his works, is so manifestly influenced by Simone dei Crocifissi that we may safely say he was his pupil, a fact that is the more likely as he was Simone's nephew. His father, it is true, was also a painter.

---

ing the Child's ear, in the subterranean church of S. Michele in Bosco (the annotator of Malvasia's text states that this picture was in the Pinacoteca but there is no work in the collection corresponding to this description although one of the polyptychs (no. 163) comes from this church); it was signed "*Simon de Bononia fecit hoc opus*" which is the same as the inscription on the other polyptych in the Gallery (no. 474). *Malvasia* further mentions some frescoes in the cloister of S. Domenico, in which two Barons Alemanni were represented receiving fiefs from the people; a Madonna in Sta. Maria Maddalena agli Orfanelli (p. 32). The annotator states that a Madonna in the portico dei Bolognini of S. Stefano, attributed by Malvasia to Lippo Dalmasio (p. 35), was, according to the signature, a work from Simone's hand and only restored by Lippo; the subject however would point to Lippo and not Simone as its author.

Malvasia also speaks of two Coronations of the Virgin and a Madonna in the Vatican but these works have disappeared. *Laderchi*, Descrizione della Quadreria Costabili a Ferrara, Ferrara, 1837, mentions a triptych representing the Virgin and some saints, showing Simone's signature.

([1]) *L. Fratti*, Dalmasio e Lippo de' Scannabecchi.

He was called Dalmasio and was born about 1324 (¹). There are various records of him in Bologna while in 1365, 1380 and 1384 he is mentioned in Pistoia. In 1365 when he left for Pistoia he

Fig. 227. Simone dei Crocifissi, the Crucifixion. Author's Collection.

appointed, as we saw, Simone to direct his affairs in Bologna. Lippo was born about 1352 and he must have accompanied his father to Pistoia since his wife, Antonia di Paolo Sali, was a native of that town.

(¹) *L. Fratti*, op. cit. *Zani*, Enciclopedia, XVII, p. 93. For the origin of the Scannabecchi family, v. *Guidicini*, Cose notabile di Bologna, I, p. 428.

Fig. 228 Simone dei Crocifissi, the Coronation of the Virgin. Museum, Pesaro.

Photo Minist. del. Pubbl. Istr.

He had five children; he made his will in 1410 (¹) and died before 1421.

As for his works, Malvasia (²) mentions a Madonna of 1376 painted with oil colours in Sta. Maria di Borgo Panicale and

Fig. 229. Simone dei Crocifissi, a Saint ordained Bishop. Museum, Compiègne.

Photo Bulloz.

another dated 1391 near the church of S. Andrea. In 1393 he painted, together with Antonio Otonello, a Madonna for the altar of S. Petronio and a St. George with the dragon (³).

(¹) *T. Gerevich*, Rassegna d'Arte, 1906, p. 178 note 1.
(²) *Malvasia*, op. cit., I, p. 35.
(³) *Bolognini Amorini*, op. cit., p. 17, gives the year as 1395; this is repeated by others but corrected by *L. Fratti*, L'Arte, 1910, p. 216.

No doubt the date at the foot of a little panel of the Coronation of the Virgin in the Pinacoteca of Bologna (no. 500) should read 1394, although the 9 not being very clear some writers have misread it as 1324 which is impossible.

The date 1397 is seen on a signed Madonna in the Misericordia church and Malvasia records a painting of 1400 in the Bolognetti Palace, another of 1404 in the church of S. Pietro ([1]) and one of 1405 in the Guidalotti chapel. Two years later Lippo signed a Madonna on a pillar of the church of S. Petronio: *"Lippus Dalmaxii pinsit 1407"*. This fresco was white washed in 1859 ([2]); after its discovery it was detached from the wall and brought to the little museum of the church but the inscription has disappeared. In 1409 he made another contract to execute a crucifix. Malvasia mentions a Madonna of the same date that was preserved in the church of Ceredolo. This writer dwells at considerable length on Lippo and even reproduces his portrait. He informs us that this artist invented oil-painting, that he was extremely pious and always said his prayers before starting to paint and that he became a monk. According to him, Pope Clement VIII granted special indulgence for his Madonna over the door of the church of S. Procolo, while several popes possessed Madonnas from his hand. At least part of this account is false for we know that Lippo never joined a monastic order. Malvasia, however, also speaks of Guido Reni's admiration for Lippo's art and this, naturally, may contain more truth. It seems certain that Lippo was just as productive an artist as his uncle, Simone. Fewer of his works have survived, but Malvasia enumerates more than thirty paintings extant at his time and does not even include in this list some of those which we still possess. Others are mentioned by Bolognini Amorini.

Among Lippo's works that have come down to us there is one, as I said, that reveals him as a faithful follower of Simone dei Crocifissi; it is the Coronation of the Virgin in the Pinacoteca of Bologna (no. 500, fig. 230), consequently not only the style but also the subject reminds us of Simone. The composition too,

---

([1]) *Vasari-Milanesi*, op. cit., II, p. 15, seems to place this painting in the church of S. Francesco.

([2]) *Vasari-Milanesi*, II, p. 15. *Malvasia* gives the name in the signature as: "dal Maxii".

Fig. 230. Lippo Dalmasio, the Coronation of the Virgin. Gallery, Bologna. Photo Perazzo.

is similar to this artist's, for a row of angels' heads appear behind the back of the throne. The apex of the panel is adorned with a half-length figure of God the Father bestowing a blessing and holding an open book.

The inscription at the foot runs: "*1394 di 24 de Avrile Lipo di Dalmase f. per Redolfo di...mbertini*". The panel was probably the centre piece of a triptych. It is the oldest of the three dated works that we possess from Lippo's hand. The style and the coarse execution strongly recall Simone's art.

In another dated work which Lippo painted only three years later there is no trace of Simone's influence and we have every reason to believe that the change in the painter's manner was rather sudden and radical in nature. This work, which bears the date 1397, shows the type of Virgin that Lippo has most frequently represented. It is preserved on the second altar to the right in the church of the Misericordia (fig. 231).

The Virgin, seated on a low cushion in a flowering field, is suckling the Child Jesus; a circle of stars surrounds her head while a luminous glory in the background forms an aureole. The signature: "*Lippus Dalmassi bononiae (?) 1397*", is inscribed on a plain strip in the lower right-hand corner. The appearance of the Virgin is more reminiscent of Vitale than of Simone; the sweetness of the expression too is quite Sienese but the spirit of the work is more modern than Vitale conceived it. The iconographical type is that of the Madonna of Humility which Andrea da Bologna adopted when he worked in The Marches.

A detail never missing in the Madonnas of Allegretto Nuzi and Francescuccio Ghissi, and which Andrea borrowed from them, is the moon at the Virgin's feet. It is seen in Lippo's panel in the National Gallery (no. 742, fig. 232) in which however the Virgin is turned towards the right, while the Child apparently plays with her veil. In each of the upper corners beyond the aureole three little angels are depicted. In Cavalcaselle's time this picture belonged to the Ercolani collection in Bologna. The technique is somewhat harder than that of the foregoing panel.

There is a certain number of similar Madonnas in Bologna. In the Pinacoteca an unnumbered panel shows the almost life-sized Virgin sitting on a cushion among flowers, surrounded

Fig. 231. Lippo Dalmasio, Madonna. Misericordia Church, Bologna.

Photo Poppi.

Fig 232. Lippo Dalmasio, Madonna. National Gallery, London.

by eight angels, it is signed: "*Lippus Dalmaxii fecit*". Another picture in the same collection (no. 752), in which, as in the London panel, three angels are seen above on either side, is also signed by Lippo. In the Spanish College, a considerably damaged fresco representing the Madonna of Humility, again turned towards the right, bears the signature: "*Lipus Dalmaxii pinxit*".

This, however, was not the only type of Madonna that Lippo

Fig. 233. Lippo Dalmasio, Triptych. College of Sta. Croce, Bologna.
Photo Perazzo.

portrayed, for he painted her enthroned in majesty in the fresco of 1407 which was detached from one of the pillars in S. Petronio and is now preserved in the museum of this church. A donor kneels in adoration at her feet; four angelic musicians escort the central figure, while above, God the Father and more angels are depicted.

To this type belongs the triptych in the College of Sta. Croce (fig. 233). Two angels kneel at the sides of the throne on which the Virgin is seated holding the Child standing on her knee. Each of the wings is occupied by two figures of saints, while the terminal above each pair, is adorned with a medallion containing a bust. On the pedestal of the throne we read: *"Lipus Dalmaxii pisit"*.

In the lunette over the entrance of S. Procolo we find a fresco of the Virgin and Child in benediction between St. Benedict and the Pope St. Sixtus. This mural painting is mentioned by Vasari and Malvasia, the latter affirming that it is painted in oil colours. It is certainly among the best of Lippo's works that have survived. Perhaps of even finer quality is the so-called "Madonna del Veluto" which adorns the first chapel to the right in S. Domenico; but this charming picture is very tarnished and seems to have undergone a certain amount of restoration ([1]). A fragmentary fresco in the cloister of S. Domenico shows Mary Magdalene at the Saviour's feet. No trace now remains of the signature of which Senator Ricci still discerned the following letters "...... *maxii f* ......".

([1]) The following works may still be attributed to Lippo: *Bologna* in the chapel outside S. Bartolommeo, a very damaged fresco which was detached from the now demolished church of Sta. Maria di Porta; Sta. Maria della Purificazione, in a little room near the choir, a Madonna; Sta. Maria dell' Orazione, the repainted Madonna on the altar may be a production of Lippo's. A signed panel of the Virgin and Child was for sale in Rome in 1909 (Baldani, op. cit., p. 478). *Rosini*, op. cit., I, opp. p. 20, reproduces a Madonna by Lippo, referring to it in Vol. II, p. 226, without saying where it is to be found.

As school works may be cited: *Bologna*, Pinacoteca, no. 225, an altar-piece from the church of S Marco showing the Coronation of the Virgin, the Crucifixion and saints; no. 232, in which again the Coronation of the Virgin is represented as well as St. Ursula and her virgins and twenty-two other divisions most of which are occupied by saints; the Crocifisso church, which belongs to the S. Stefano group of buildings, a Madonna; S. Stefano Museum, Madonna with the Child, sitting rather low. *Baldani*, op. cit., p. 480, also ascribes to this school two panels, each showing a figure of the Annunciation, in the Gallery of Ravenna.

As Signor A. Venturi points out (¹), it is important to note that a fresco representing the Madonna humbly seated nursing the Child in the midst of four angels, two of whom are playing musical instruments, in the Palazzo Pubblico of Pistoia is a work from the hand of Lippo Dalmasio. It is one of his less fine productions, rather approaching Simone's manner, and as it is probable that Lippo went to Pistoia with his father, that is to say some time prior to the year of his first dated work, we may infer that his more refined manner, showing a connection with Vitale's art, was subsequent to the other and coarser style.

Lippo Dalmasio was one of the artists who largely augmented the already considerable number of Bolognese paintings of the end of the 14th century. His temperament must have been very different from Simone's; he apparently had no sense of dramatic force; his Madonnas are always sweet and unsophisticated and sometimes a little rustic. His technique is generally anything but coarse; but his art is very monotonous.

Vasari further relates that Lippo was a good draughtsman and taught drawing to Galante da Bologna who, however, surpassed his master in this art. Malvasia, on the other hand, finds that the latter was the feebler of the two.

Among the Bolognese artists of the end of the 14th century, Jacopo di Paolo was the most vulgar. According to Signor Frati (²) he probably descended from Orso, a painter active at Reggio in the 13th century who was his great-grandfather; the latter's son, Zanello, was also a painter (1270—74) for in 1357, we find record of a Niccolo di Maestro Paolo pittore di Maestro Zanello di Orso di Reggio, the aforesaid Niccolo being Jacopo's brother; and their genealogy consequently the same. Jacopo di Paolo is mentioned in documents of 1390, 1393, 1394, 1395 and 1400, and again in 1402 when he is charged to make a wooden model of the church of S. Petronio. In 1425 he painted a cupola in the campanile of S. Pietro while in 1426 his name is recorded for the last time together with that of his son, Orazio. The document

---

(¹) *Venturi*, op. cit., V, p. 948.
(²) *Baldani*, op. cit., p. 471. *R. Frati*, Una famiglia di pittori Bolognesi, L'Arte, 1914, p. 263.

of 1393 informs us that he undertook to make sketches of six figures for the Venetian sculptor, Maestro Paolo ([1]).

Of Jacopo's signed works, we possess a Coronation of the Virgin and a Crucifixion in the Pinacoteca of Bologna, an Annunciation in the Museo Civico, part of the altar-piece in a chapel of the choir of S. Giacomo Maggiore, and the frescoes in the church of Mezzaratta, under which, as I have already mentioned, appeared the signature: "*Jacopus fecit* or *Jacobus Pauli f.*" Lastly Crowe and Cavalcaselle profess that a Coronation of the Virgin in the Louvre showed the signature: "*Jacobus Pauli fecit*" but at the present time there is no trace of any such picture.

Jacopo di Paolo's Crucifixion in the Pinacoteca of Bologna (no. 10, fig. 234) marks him as an extremely poor artist. The three crucified figures, as well as those below, are ugly both in form and in feature, the faults in the drawing are numerous, the colours are unattractive and relief and plasticity are entirely missing. The work is signed below: "*Jacobus Pauli f*".

The Coronation of the Virgin in the same Gallery (no. 11, fig. 235) is scarcely more pleasing. The composition resembles that of Simone, with a cluster of angels above the back of the throne, only here the Virgin is depicted kneeling before the Saviour. The signature is identical with the one on the foregoing panel.

The Annunciation in the Museo Civico (no. 221) on the other hand, is of much finer quality. The incident is seen taking place in a Gothic building; the forms are more graceful but the pointed, almost grimacing features are very characteristic of this master. The signature is again the same but the name of the donor: "*Jacobus De Blanchilis*", who is seen kneeling to the left, is also inscribed ([2]).

We find the artist's name: "*Jacobus Pauli-f.*" under the Coron-

---

([1]) *V. A. Gatti*, La fabbrica di S. Petronio, Bologna, 1889, p. 4. I see no reason in this information for attributing to the same artist as Sgr. Filippini does (Bolletino d'Arte del Minist. della Pubbl. Istr., July-August, 1916) the large altar-piece of carved wood in the Bolognini chapel which displays no connection with this master's style.

([2]) This picture was brought from the notarial archives and it is possible that is was painted originally for the oratory of S. Gabriele in the commune of Baregella.

ation of the Virgin of the altar-piece in the Cari chapel of S. Giacomo Maggiore, the greater part of which was executed by Lorenzo Veneziano. In this case the Virgin is seated at the

Fig. 234. Jacopo di Paolo, the Crucifixion. Gallery, Bologna.
Photo Perazzo.

Saviour's side. I see no reason for Signor Baldani to doubt the authenticity of this signature since the painting differs but little in style from the artist's other works, while the types of the figures and the faces are the same. The saints beside the Coronation, the Crucifixion and the figures in the pinnacles are also Jacopo's work.

Lastly, the signature, "*Jacobus f*" that was found under the frescoes illustrating the life of St. Joseph, high up on the right wall in the church of Mezzaratta, is undoubtedly that of Jacopo di Paolo, although the paintings are very badly damaged and it is only here and there that we are able to discover a figure sufficiently well preserved to conform this assertion. I think this decoration is a production of the artist's least pleasing manner.

Among the works which may be ascribed to Jacopo di Paolo, but which are not authenticated by his signature, I shall first mention two panels in the Bologna Pinacoteca (nos. 367 and 368) which no doubt formerly belonged to one large picture. Signor Baldani is of opinion that they formed the wings of a triptych, the centre piece of which was the Crucifixion in the same Gallery (no. 10). Certainly the style corresponds perfectly. Each of the panels shows below two saints, St. James with St. Michael and St. Peter with the Baptist, and above a figure of the Annunciation.

Slightly more pleasing in appearance are the figures of SS. Peter and Paul, Bartholomew and Roch in two other little panels in the same collection (nos. 268 and 269). The only other work in this Gallery that I think we are justified in attributing to Jacopo di Paolo is a picture representing St. Romuald's vision (no. 168) ([1]).

A half-length figure of St. John in the museum of S. Stefano is finely modelled but the facial type is too reminiscent of our artist for us not to attribute it to him. A triptych, showing the Madonna, four saints, the Annunciation and the Pietà, in the same museum, is probably also a work from his hand.

A panel in the Museum of Pesaro, representing the two saints Bartholomew and Constantine may, I think, be assigned to our artist, although the drawing is of better quality and displays certain Gothic effects, absent in his other works ([2]).

([1]) *C. Ricci*, Guida etc., p. 120. *Filippini* calls this picture a school work of Jacopo Avanzi.

([2]) This work has already been attributed to him by *G. Vaccaj*, op. cit., p. 117. *L. Serra*, in his catalogue of the Museum, assignes it to the school of Bologna or that of Siena. *E. Brunelli*, Rassegna marchegiana per le Arti etc., 1923, p. 331, believes this picture to be Bolognese but not by Jacopo di Paolo.

Fig. 235. Jacopo di Paolo, the Coronation of the Virgin. Gallery, Bologna.
Photo Perazzo.

A panel showing a somewhat violent composition of the Crucifixion, formerly in the Chillingworth collection (sold at Lucerne in 1922) bears some resemblance to the painting of this subject in the Pinocoteca of Bologna, in spite of the fact that the execution is less commonplace and here and there shows a certain Gothicism of line (¹).

In attributing to Jacopo the frescoes illustrating the Apocalypse and the Old Testament on the right hand wall of the nave of the church at Pomposa, Herr Brach commits rather a grave mistake(²), and although Signor Baldani in part shares this opinion(³), I think these paintings belong to quite another school and to a different period. Nor do I believe that Jacopo di Paolo's hand can be discerned in any frescoes in the Mezzaratta church other than those representing incidents from the story of St. Joseph, even although Senator Ricci holds him responsible for almost all the frescoes on the right wall (⁴) and Signor Baldani believes that he executed the Nativity over the entrance (⁵). Lastly Signor Filippini ascribes to him a mural painting of the Calvary and the Crucifixion in the Crocifisso church, and the frescoes in the Bolognini chapel of S. Petronio (⁶).

As for Jacopo di Paolo's lost works, we know, through Malvasia, that there once existed a Crucifixion and an Annunciation on the façade of the sacristy — in this writer's day a tower — of SS. Naborre e Felice, which work was signed and dated 1384 (⁷).

There is not one of Jacopo di Paolo's productions but ranks this painter as the weakest and most vulgar of the Bolognese artists of the end of the 14th century. He belongs to a generation slightly later than Simone's and even than Lippo Dalmasio's. By making certain unfounded attributions some writers have at-

---

(¹) As school work may be cited, in the Gallery of Bologna, no. 191, a crucifix; no. 233, a Coronation of the Virgin; no. 270, two saints, one carrying a cross, the other a book; and a panel of a holy bishop in the S. Stefano Museum.

(²) *Brach*, op. cit., p. 109.

(³) *Baldani*, op. cit., p. 472.

(⁴) *C. Ricci*, Guida etc., p. 240.

(⁵) *Baldani*, op. cit., p. 446.

(⁶) *Filippini*. Gli affreschi della cappella Bolognini, Bollet. d'Arte del Minist. della Pubbl. Istr., X, 1916, fasc. 7—8.

(⁷) *Malvasia*, op. cit., I, pp. 30—31.

tempted to raise the standard of this artist's painting, but if we judge him from his authentic works only, he can never be considered anything but a very mediocre artist.

Jacopo di Paolo's art is a clear proof of the fact that the style of the Trecento persisted well into the 15th century. None of his works, with the exception of the Chillingworth Crucifixion, shows any trace of the new manner that made its appearance about the year 1400 or, as in some of the regions in Northern Italy, even earlier.

The works of the two anonymous painters whose productions we find on the walls of the Mezzaratta church, are too important for us merely to enumerate them in the list of Bolognese paintings that will be given at the end of this chapter. To one of them we owe the charming composition of the Nativity with numerous angels surrounding the central group which we find on the wall above the entrance. The type and grace of the figures are reminiscent of Vitale to whom, moreover, Herr Brach ascribes it; Signor Baldani believes it to be by Jacopo di Paolo. It seems however to be a production of the following generation. The marked shadows, as well as the folds of the drapery which are rather hard and a little heavy, remind us of Simone dei Crocifissi's contemporaries.

Formerly there existed in the church of Mezzaratta a series of scenes from the Old Testament. In Cavalcaselle's time a fair number of them still remained although some had already been detached (¹). Nowadays only two frescoes remain plainly visible; they represent Moses receiving the tables of the law and bringing them to the Israelites, and Korah swallowed up by the earth while Moses and Aaron look on. The artist who executed these frescoes (²) was probably Simone's contemporary but his compositions are more concise while his expressions and movements are more moderate and not devoid of a reminiscence of Giottesque simplicity. The artistic value of these paintings is considerable.

In the Bolognini chapel, the fourth to the left, in the church of S. Petronio, we find a series of frescoes in which elements of

---
(¹) *Crowe and Cavalcaselle*, III, p. 199 note 5.
(²) *F. Filippini,* Gli affreschi della cappella Bolognini, repeats *d'Agincourt's* erroneous attribution to Cristoforo da Bologna.

the cosmopolitan Gothic manner are already noticeable but as these features are manifest only in a very rudimentary stage, and because the technique and spirit of the work belong entirely to the 14th century Bolognese school, I think they should be dealt with here, even though the date of their execution is rather in advance of the period to which this volume is devoted.

We are able to determine the exact date of these paintings (¹) for Bartolommeo Bolognini in a will, made in 1408, bequeathed the money for this decoration in case he died before it was finished. As, on the one hand, we see a representation of the election of John XXIII which took place in May 1410, when Bartolommeo Bolognini was still alive, and on the other we know from an annotation that in October 1411 the decoration of the chapel was terminated, we are consequently provided with dates between which the frescoes must have been executed.

They have been attributed to Buffalmacco, Vitale, Giovanni da Modena, who worked in a chapel nearby, to Antonio Alberti da Ferrara, to Francesco Lola and lastly, by Signor Filippini, to Jacopo di Paolo, but I do not think that we have sufficient grounds for any of these attributions not one of which, in my opinion, is correct, not even the last, for the excellent master to whom we owe these frescoes surpasses by far the very mediocre Jacopo di Paolo. Although his figures are full of life and vigour he does not represent, except in the scene of Hell, grimacing faces; his outlines are graceful and slightly Gothic, plastic effects are well marked. These peculiarities as well as the individuality of his types characterize the artist of the Bolognini chapel. Moreover it is not difficult to determine to which group of painters he belongs, but we shall return to this subject later on.

The principal representations in the Bolognini chapel comprise the illustrations of the history of the Eastern Kings, Paradise and Hell. The first of these subjects is depicted in an elaborate and detailed manner. Above we find the preparation for the voyage, the harnessed animals awaiting the travellers; the second picture shows the crossing of a river, one of the horses represented rearing. In the second row we see the Wise Men jour-

---

(¹) *L. Frati*, La cappella Bolognini nella Basilica di S. Petronio a Bologna, L'Arte, 1910, p. 214. *F. Filippini*, Gli affreschi della cappella Bolognini.

Fig. 236. Bolognese School, Detail of the Journey of the Magi, circa 1410. S. Petronio, Bologna.

Photo Minist. del. Pubbl. Istr.

neying through a rocky landscape in which animals are running wild. The mounted travellers, who are escorted by soldiers and servants, are guided by the Star of the East that shines in the sky (fig. 236). On the adjacent fresco is the scene of their meeting with Herod (fig. 237). Lower down, Herod is represented taking counsel in his palace which has the form of an open loggia, in another division of which the three Wise Men sit waiting the result of the consultation. The second fresco here shows, in the midst of much confusion, the departure of the Kings and their suite from Herod's palace, some are depicted mounting while others are seen galloping away. On the fourth row we find the Adoration of the Magi (fig. 238). Melchior, the oldest of the three Kings, having taken off his crown, prostrates himself to kiss the feet of the Child Christ Who sits on His Mother's knee before an open shed; the second looks into a box that a servant holds open for him while the third has just taken from the hands of another servant an object that looks like a reliquary.

Their return by sea forms the subject of the last fresco. One of the two vessels is still attached to the shore, they are busy charging it, a sailor who has climbed on the mast prepares the sails. In the midst of the crowd that fills up the larger boat, we can distinguish the three Magi gravely conversing together.

On the wall opposite we see Heaven and Hell represented as Bartolommeo had indicated in his will. In the upper half the Almighty, over-looking the Virgin who is crowned by the Saviour, is surrounded by the different hierarchies of angels. Lower down rows of saints seated on benches are arranged at either side while the archangel Michael stands in the centre of the foreground with sword and balance.

In the lower half Hell is represented in seven divisions according to the seven capital sins; in each of the compartments, naked figures are seen undergoing the torments of their particular sin (fig. 239). Lucifer seated in the centre devours the damned. As Signor Filippini remarks, the composition of this picture is somewhat different from the other 14th century representations of Purgatory that have survived, and does not seem to be directly inspired by Dante's Inferno.

The election of Pope John XXIII adorns the upper part of the window arch: the Pontiff is seated in the centre in the midst of the cardinals with two bishops kneeling at his feet. Lower down on the arch some scenes from the life of St. Petronius, the titular saint, are represented, while opposite on the entrance wall we find part of a composition of the Last Judgment: the Saviour in the midst of angels. The intrados below is decorated with busts

THE SCHOOL OF BOLOGNA. 473

Fig. 237. Bolognese School, the Meeting of the Magi and Herod, circa 1410.
S. Petronio, Bologna.

Photo Minist. del. Pubbl. Istr.

and full-length figures of the Fathers of the Church, prophets and saints, and the angles of the vault with eight figures of saints.

As other works from the hand of the master of the Bolognini chapel, we might cite two detached frescoes in the sacristy of the Crocifisso church; they belong to the S. Stefano group and represent Christ carrying the Cross and the Crucifixion; both scenes are shown in dramatic and crowded compositions. These frescoes were detached from the walls of the church in 1675 ([1]).

A picture in the Pinacoteca of Bologna (no. 229), on which Paradise is depicted in a composition identical to that in the Bolognini chapel, has also been ascribed to this master ([2]); this is not entirely impossible although the figures of this picture bear more resemblance to Lippo Dalmasio's, than those in the fresco in the Bolognini chapel.

The decoration of the Bolognini chapel really belongs to that branch of painting which we have qualified as "scènes de genre" and which we have met with in Padua and Verona but here the technique of the painting is Bolognese. The characteristics of this art are noted in the rich costumes of the time, the individuality of the faces, the hunting dogs in several scenes in which they are quite out of place, and the irreligious feeling pervading the entire series and making of each scene an image of every-day life. A great many realistic details are also borrowed from daily life; this is very evident in the manner in which the Magi greet Herod. The oldest shakes him by the hand in a friendly way, while the two others salute him with a rustic gesture such as country people still employ when they wish to show their respect ([3]). The movement seems to have disarranged the crown of one of the Kings. Many of the objects are executed in relief, a peculiarity we find especially in Gothic painting of the beginning of the 15th century, as for instance in the works of Gentile da Fabriano.

The marked contrast of light and shade, however, in this decoration is thoroughly Bolognese. Another characteristic of this school is the exaggerated realism, and although we do not find here actual grimaces, as in Jacopo di Paolo's works, the artist, with courageous veracity, represents many very ugly male faces.

([1]) *C. Ricci*, La pittura romanica nell' Emilia, Atti e Mem. dell. R. Dep. di Stor. Patr., serie III, vol. IV, p. 55. *F. Filippini*, Cappella Bolognini. This critic attributes, as I have already said, these frescoes to Jacopo di Paolo. According to old writers this decoration dates from 1115! v. *d'Agincourt*, Pittura, pl. 89.

([2]) *Filippini*, op. cit.

([3]) A very similar gesture is seen on a fresco at Treviso, compare fig. 105.

Fig. 238. Bolognese School, the Adoration of the Magi, circa 1410. S. Petronio, Bologna.   Photo Minist. del. Pubbl. Istr.

Moreover the vigorous drawing and coarse technique, devoid of any finesse, that characterize Bolognese artists, are not absent from these frescoes. It may be conjectured that the master possessed a fantastic imagination, for the landscape in some of the scenes, the view on the stormy sea, and the strange gloomy expression of many of the faces are certainly of his own invention.

The master of the Bolognini chapel introduced in a rudimentary manner the elements of the cosmopolitan Gothic style of the beginning of the 15th century, examples of which we find in this church in the paintings of Giovanni da Modena and Francesco Lola, and although these two artists worked only a few years later — the former in 1420, the later in 1419 — their productions show such a marked evolution of this style that we can hardly consider them as belonging to the Bolognese school of the Trecento. Their right place is with the artistic creations of the following century and for that reason they will be treated elsewhere.

A contemporary of these two artists, however, who painted alongside Francesco Lola, worked entirely in the manner of the 14th century. It was Luca da Perugia who signed a fresco in the Pepoli chapel — the second to the right — in the church of S. Petronio (figs. 240 and 241) (¹). The Virgin is seated on an imposing architectural throne escorted by three saints on either side; a fourth on the left, St. Bartholomew, presents the donor, who kneels in adoration before the Child, Who bends towards him bestowing a blessing. The signature: *"Luca da Peruxia : p."* is written on the seat of the throne while below, a long inscription tells us by whom the fresco was ordered : *"Bartholomeus de Mediolano Mercarius pro anima sua MCCCCXVII de mense Julii"*.

At Perugia there is mention of an artist called Luca d'Antonio di Mona between 1407 and 1416 (²) but we have nothing to justify our identifying him with the aforesaid painter, whose style moreover in no way resembles that in vogue in Perugia at that time. Nor does it betray the artist's adherence to the Bolognese school; the form of the throne and the appearance of the figures sooner recall certain of the frescoes in Padua, Verona and Lombardy. We should perhaps seek for the explanation of this little problem in the fact that the donor was of Milanese origin.

A polyptych in the museum of S. Stefano, representing the Coronation of the Virgin and four saints in the lateral panels, is

---

(¹) *F. Cavazza*, Rassegna d'Arte, 1905, p. 161. *W. Bombe*, Geschichte der Peruginer Malerei, Berlin, 1912, p. 76, believes that this artist was influenced by Nelli; I do not think that this is the case although Nelli, as also Luca, shows a certain connection with the art of Northern Italy. *U. Gnoli*, Rassegna d'Arte, 1914, p. 248.

(²) *A. Rossi* ,Giornale d'Erudizione artistica (Perugia), II, p. 311.

Fig. 239. Bolognese School, Detail of Hell, circa 1410. S. Petronio, Bologna.
Photo Minist. del. Pubbl. Istr.

of slightly earlier date. The signature at the foot of the central picture has been read in many different ways (¹) but seems to be: "*Giovanni di Canelo*". This artist is among the poorest members of the Bolognese school; his picture betrays a certain

---

(¹) *Moschetti*, Rassegna d'Arte, 1903, p. 33. *Testi*, op. cit., I, p. 296. *Baldani*, op. cit., p. 470. *Ricci*, Guida etc., p. 95. *Filippini*, Rassegna d'Arte, 1912, p. 103.

Fig. 240. Luca di Perugia, Madonna and saints, 1417. S. Petronio, Bologna.

knowledge of the works of Simone dei Crocifissi and Lippo Dalmasio. This, together with the slight element of Gothicism, dates the painting to about 1400 (¹).

Fig. 241. Detail of fig. 240.

Photo Poppi.

The history of Bolognese painting of the 14th century is varied but somewhat inconsistent. Summing it up in a few words we

(¹) *Filippini*, loc. cit., thinks that this master might be the son of "*Canellus pictor*", who was active between 1277 and 1280; the picture in this case would have to be placed at the beginning of the 14th century whereas it really dates from about a hundred years later.

480 THE SCHOOL OF BOLOGNA.

might say that having sprung from the art of miniature we note in the works of the first figure of any importance — Vitale — reminiscences of this origin together with Sienese elements.

The genuine style of Bolognese painting seems to have been created by the miniaturist, Niccolo di Giacomo, but such artists as the pseudo-Jacopo Avanzi and Andrea da Bologna introduced features foreign to the Bolognese school, the former being inspired by Riminese painting, the latter by the school of The Marches. In the second half of the 14th century, miniatures as well as painting deteriorated in quality on account of the enormous production, and although painters like Simone retain certain merits such as a vital and dramatic rendering, their vulgar technique is their great shortcoming.

Lippo Dalmasio seems to revive Vitale's types, but with Jacopo di Paolo Bolognese painting sinks very low. The master of the Bolognini chapel sooner belongs to the group of painters who, especially in Padua and Verona, created "scènes de genre", although his technique is thoroughly Bolognese ([1]).

([1]) Other Bolognese works of the 14th century are: *Bologna*, Pinacoteca, no. 169, the Last Supper; no. 589, the Madonna humbly seated holding the Child with six prophets in the predella; Gothic elements are evident in the contours of this picture which dates from about 1400; Museo Civico, no. 191, crucifix belonging to the Giottesque tradition with the pelican above and the Virgin and St. John in the lateral terminals; no. 196, crucifix with a sculptured central figure; the figures of the Virgin and St. John belong to the Giottesque current and date from the first half of the 14th century; no. 208, a half-length figure of the Saviour showing an influence of the school of The Marches; no. 202, a Madonna with the dead Christ between the Virgin and St. John on the predella; nos. 209—210, the Nativity and the Flight into Egypt, beautiful paintings of the early Bolognese school. In *the churches of Bologna*: Certosa delle Madonne, several figures representing the Virgin; S. Clemente (Collegio di Spagna), figures of Urban V, St. Catherine and an adorer; Crocifisso, on the wall to the right of the door, a repainted fresco of the Virgin between two saints of the end of the 14th century; in the crypt, an Ecce Homo and a restored Madonna; S. Domenico, 5th chapel on the right, a transferred and repainted fresco of the Madonna, called "della Febre", nursing the Child (Ricci, Guida etc., p. 52, ascribes it to the 15th century; I think it dates from about 1400 and belongs to Lippo Dalmasio's type of Madonna); S. Francesco, 5th chapel behind the choir, a crucifix after Simone's model but of slightly later date and executed in very clear colours; S. Giovanni a Monte, between the 5th and the 6th chapels, a Pietà with a sculptured central figure, the others painted; 6th chapel, a Madonna on the altar (the little crucifix on the left has been included with the works of Simone's school); between the choir and the first chapel to the left, a damaged fresco of the Madonna seated on an elaborate throne, probably of the beginning of the 15th century; S. Giuseppe, sacristy, a crucifix; S. Isaia, sacristy, a fresco of the Madonna; Sta. Maria della Purificazione, in a little room near the choir, we find, besides Lippo Dalmasio's Madonna, a fresco of the same subject; Sta. Maria dei Servi, 4'h chapel on the left behind the choir, Madonna and saints, a ruined canvas of the end of the 14th century; 8 h chapel, remains of a fresco; S. Martino, in the left aisle, some fragmentary frescoes executed under a Riminese influence, some of the figures belong to a representation of the Last Judgment; 2nd chapel on the right, a repainted figure of St. Onuphrius; S. Petronio, some figures of saints on the pillars, most of them however belong to the early 15th century; S. Stefano, in the courtyard, damaged or restored figures of saints of no importance except for the image of a holy warrior on one of the pillars; Museum of S. Stefano, four panels with scenes from the life of St. Benedict showing the pseudo-Jacopo Avanzi's influence; two fine triptychs and several insignificant works; Sala della Compagnia dei Lombardi, some unimportant panels; Casa Gualandi (via Farini no. 5), a fresco of the Madonna and some fragmentary paintings in the courtyard.

Outside Bologna we find: in *Boston*, Fine Arts Museum, no. 23, a Nativity attributed to Giotto's school which seems sooner to be an early Bolognese work; *Fiesole*, Bandini Museum, Nativity, the Arrival of the Magi, the Presentation in the Temple, the Massacre of the Innocents; four predella panels showing the vulgar dramatic realism of Simone dei Crocifissi's school; *Imola*, in the bell tower of S. Domenico, a series of frescoes with the Madonna and half-length figures of saints; *Fossignano* (near Imola), S. Michele, a Madonna (L. Orsini, Imola, Bergamo, 1907, pp. 99 and 45); *London*, Victoria and Albert Museum (143—1869), diptych with six scenes from the history of Christ; (351—1864), a little painted box with the Baptism and the birth of St. John on the lid and eighteen figures of saints on the four sides; two gilt glasses in the same museum seem to me Bolognese work. They were reproduced by P. Toesca in L'Arte, 1908, p. 52. who ascribes one of them to the school of the miniaturist, Niccolo di Giacomo. *Rome*, Vatican Gallery, no. 15, Crucifixion and other scenes from the history of Christ, probably early 15th century work (O. Sirén, L'Arte, 1912, p. 101, rightly states that it is reminiscent of Jacopo di Paolo); Capperoni coll., Crucifixion with several assistants and two adorers; the late Sterbini collection, a Calvary bearing some resemblance to the early works of Simone dei Crocifissi (A. Venturi, L'Arte, 1905, p. 427, attributes it to Simone Martini); for sale 1924, a half-length figure of the Madonna in the manner of Vitale; *Turin*, Museo Civico, gilt glass diptych with the Nativity and the Crucifixion (Toesca, op. cit., p. 252).

CHAPTER VII.

PAINTING IN FERRARA AND OTHER LITTLE CENTRES IN EMILIA.

In Emilia we find some other centres of painting besides those of Rimini, Modena and Bologna, but they are much less important and their productions are not always sufficiently characteristic for us to classify them.

We have some records of the existence of very early artistic activity in Ferrara (¹). Gelasio di Niccolo della Masnada di S. Giorgio (²) seems to have worked in 1242 and to have been the pupil of Theophanes, a Greek, living in Venice, but none of the works that are attributed to him looks of earlier date than the 15th century.

Among the 14th century painters active in Ferrara, Vasari mentions Giotto (³). Besides there is record of a Franciscan monk called Donato Brasavola who died in 1353 and to whom a St. Antony of Padua in the church of S. Francesco, Padua, has, for reasons unknown to me, been attributed; and a certain Laudadio Rambaldo who is mentioned as the author of a considerably restored Madonna that was found under the whitewash in the court of the Castle of Ferrara. This painter flourished about the year 1380 and is known to have worked at Castel Tedaldo, near Ferrara (⁴).

Lastly Vasari speaks of "Galasso ferrarese" who worked with Jacopo and Simone in the church of Mezzaratta in 1404. He informs us that their signatures were inscribed at the foot of the

---

(¹) *Barufaldi,* Vite de' pittori e scultori ferrarese, 2 vols, Ferrara, 1844. *Laderchi,* La pittura ferrarese, Ferrara, 1856. *The Same,* Catalogo istorico dei pittori ferraresi, Ferrara, 2 vols. *Cittadella,* Documenti riguardanti la storia artistica di Ferrara, 1866. *E. G. Gardner,* The Painters of the School of Ferrara, London, 1901.

(²) *Lanzi* dwells at some length on this painter, v. *Crowe and Cavalcaselle,* op. cit., p. 214, and the artist Gelasio in Thieme-Becker, Künstler Lexikon, XIII, p. 357.

(³) *Vasari-Milanesi,* I, p. 388.

(⁴) *Crowe and Cavalcaselle,* op. cit., p. 215.

frescoes which they executed and that Galasso painted the Passion scenes (¹).

The most important Ferrarese work is the series of frescoes in the church of the Abbey of Pomposa where previously we found some paintings of the Riminese school. Herr Brach (²) has already remarked that the mural decoration here does not all belong to the same school. The church is richly adorned with frescoes. On the entrance wall we see a large composition of the Last Judgment; high up on either side of the nave are three long rows of scenes while an image of the Saviour in majesty decorates the apse. The site of the representation of the Last Judgment is quite in accordance with the old Byzantine tradition and is found also on the entrance wall in S. Angelo in Formis near Capua, Sta. Maria in Vescovis, in the mosaic at Torcello and in Giotto's decoration in the Arena chapel, Padua.

The composition is divided into five rows (fig. 242) the four lowest of which do not display any unusual features: the Saviour within an aureole is seated in the middle; angelic trumpeters fly above at either side, below are the Twelve Apostles, six to the right and six to the left; below whom we see on the one side the Saved and on the other the Damned. The latter are being forced into Hell, while opposite, Paradise is depicted by three patriarchs carrying the souls of the Good, followed by a naked figure which is painted on the adjacent wall. An isolated picture close to these figures shows a holy monk apparently receiving a friar into his order. The highest tier, from an iconographical standpoint, is very unusual. Here we find an erect figure of the Saviour in an elliptical mandorla escorted by some angels; a row of figures is placed below at either side; over the one on the left is the city of Jerusalem while over that on the right a mandorla is borne to heaven by angels. This last representation is very damaged but the instruments of the Passion seem to be enclosed in the aureole. The whole of this upper part digresses from the

(¹) *Vasari-Milanesi*, II, p. 139 et seq. The biographer informs us that the belief existed that Galasso painted with oil colours. Perhaps he confounds with this artist, the Ferrarese painter, Galassi, of the following generation, an account of whose life he gives only in the first edition (*Vasari-Milanesi*, III, p. 89); in the others it is replaced by that of the older Galasso.

(²) *Brach*, op. cit, p. 52, v. also G. *Agnelli*, Ferrara e Pomposa, Bergamo, 1906, p. 102.

traditional iconography of the subject. As I said in the previous chapter, some of the figures in the fresco of Hell are possibly by Vitale to whom I attributed the apsidal decoration.

Contrary to all tradition also is the manner in which the scenes from the Old and New Testaments are placed in the church. Instead of painting the one opposite the other as was done during the 13th century (Upper Church, Assisi and Sta. Maria in Vescovis), we find here the Old Testament illustrated on the highest row of each of the walls, the Gospels on the second and the Apocalypse on the third. Beginning on the left, we see first Adam and Eve sitting on the ground eating the forbidden fruit, followed immediately by Cain's fratricidal act. We then find Noah's ark floating on the water, the three angels visiting Abraham, Abraham receiving them and serving them at table. Esau's discovery of his brother's deception is shown in two episodes; firstly Jacob bringing the dish to Isaac who is seated under a baldaquin, and then going out of the house in search of his brother. Then comes Jacob sleeping on the ground having a dream; the vision of the angels showing him a ladder is represented at the same time. Joseph's dream is depicted in the same way; following on this is Joseph sold by his brothers, together with the brothers telling the news to Jacob; the brothers before Joseph with Benjamin who is accused of the theft; and lastly Jacob with his sons kneeling at his feet.

The first two frescoes on the opposite wall have disappeared; the third, which is considerably damaged might represent, as Herr Brach believes, the exodus from Egypt: an angel guides a group of people who are led by two men, Moses and Aaron. Then come Moses kneeling with Aaron receiving the tables of the law, men carrying the Ark of the covenant (? Brach), Joshua ordering the sun to interrupt its course, Daniel praying in the lion's den, an angel flying towards him; Elijah borne to heaven in a fiery chariot and a scene from the history of the Maccabees. Some of these frescoes are in very poor condition.

The New Testament cycle is much better preserved. To the left we see the Annunciation together with the Visitation, the Nativity, Christ being bathed for the first time and, the Message to the Shepherds (fig. 243); the Adoration of the Magi in which the angel appearing to them in their sleep is represented; the

Fig. 242. Ferrarese School, Last Judgment, circa 1350—60 Abbey Church, Pomposa.

Photo Minist. del. Pubbl. Istr.

Massacre of the Innocents with the Flight into Egypt in the background (fig. 244); the Presentation in the Temple; the Baptism of Christ; (fig. 245), the Wedding at Cana; (fig. 246), the Saviour curing the woman suffering from gout; (fig. 247) and the Resur-

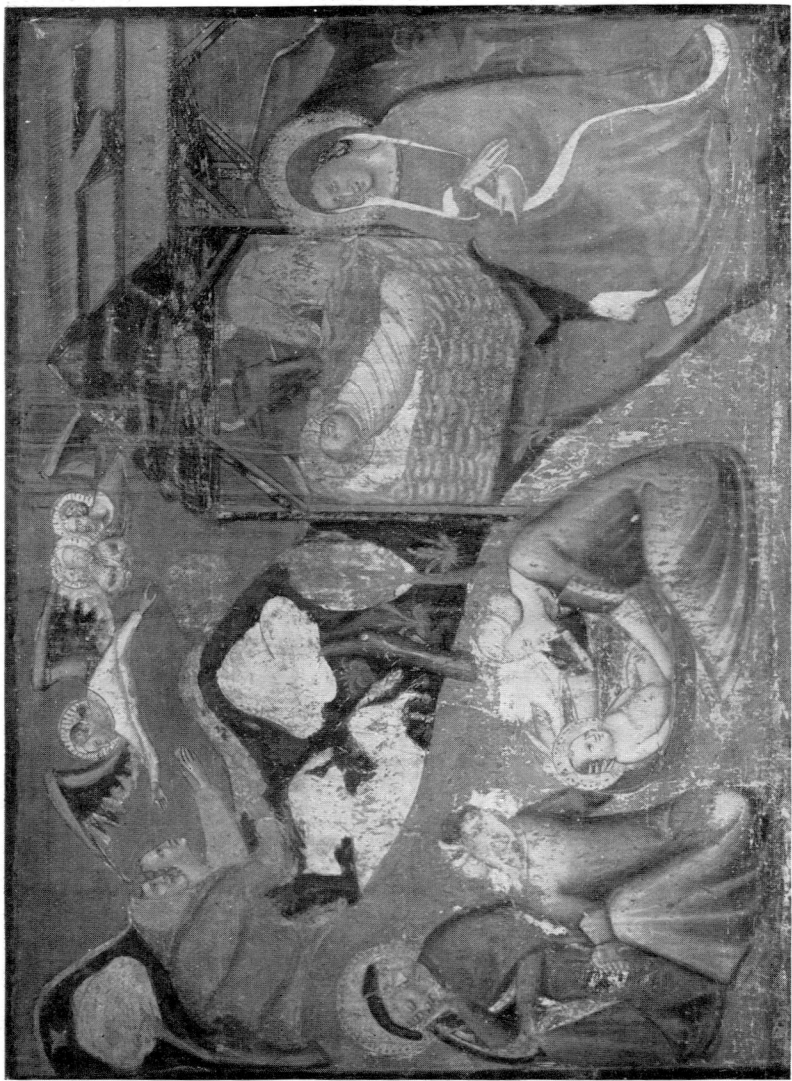

Fig. 243. Ferrarese School, the Nativity, circa 1350—60. Abbey Church, Pomposa. Photo Minist. del. Pubbl. Istr.

rection of the young man of Nain. On the other side are depicted the Resurrection of Lazarus, the Entry into Jerusalem (fig. 248), the Last Supper, the Prayer on the Mount of Olives with the moment when Christ asks the three disciples not to sleep but to

OTHER LITTLE CENTRES IN EMILIA. 487

Fig. 244. Ferrarese School, the Adoration of the Magi and the Massacre of the Innocents, circa 1350—60. Abbey Church, Pomposa.

Photo Minist. del. Pubbl. Istr.

watch, the Betrayal of Judas in which we see St. Peter cutting off Malchus' ear; the Crucifixion in an elaborate and dramatic composition (fig. 249); the Descent from the Cross with the Entombment (damaged); the Holy Women at the Empty Sepulchre; Noli me tangere; the Doubting Thomas (damaged); the Ascension and Pentecost.

Fig. 245. Ferrarese School, the Baptism, circa 1350—60. Abbey Church, Pomposa.

Photo Minist. del. Pubbl. Istr.

Fig. 246. Ferrarese School, the Marriage at Cana, circa 1350—60. Abbey Church, Pomposa.
Photo Minist. del. Pubbl. Istr.

Fig. 247. Ferrarese School, Christ cures the gouty person, circa 1350—60. Abbey Church, Pomposa.
Photo Minist. del. Pubbl. Istr.

On the third row there are sixteen scenes from the Apocalypse which I shall not detail. They have been interpreted by Herr Brach. The artist displays a great deal of fantasy and the frescoes of this row are among the finest in the church.

Besides the decoration of the apse which, as I have just said, is by Vitale da Bologna, except perhaps for the central figure of Christ which might be from the same hand as the frescoes in the nave, we find at the end of the left wall of the same church an

Fig. 248. Ferrarese School, the Entry into Jerusalem, circa 1350—60. Abbey Church, Pomposa.
Photo Minist. del. Pubbl. Istr.

enthroned Virgin with the Child between four saints, two erect and two kneeling, and a monk in adoration, and on the wall opposite some remains of fresco painting.

The Christological scenes that adorn the walls of the nave show certain iconographical peculiarities. I have already remarked on the unusual site that the Old and New Testament scenes occupy. Further the development of illustrations from the Apocalypse is very rare although Cimabue did also represent a good many scenes in the Upper Church of Assisi. The attitudes of Adam and Eve seated under a tree instead of standing, and of Isaac sitting on a chair instead of reclining on a couch are original and uncommon features; these are even more numerous in the New Testament representations.

The apparition of the angel to the Eastern Kings during their journey is rare, at least in 14th century iconography, while I do not know another painting of the Flight into Egypt without the ass, or one which takes, as it does here, a place of secondary importance in the background of the Massacre of the Innocents. In the scene of the Baptism, Christ is represented standing on a dragon, and in the portrayal of the Wedding at Cana the artist has invented an original means of filling the jars with water which, turned into wine, is drawn from a spout below. This procedure is presented in a manner that makes it look sooner like a sleight of hand than a holy miracle. The way in which the bearer supports himself with a stick as he bends under the weight of the curiously-shaped water barrel is very realistic. The Resurrection of Lazarus shows some resemblance to Giovanni da Milano's composition of this subject; the revived man is seen stepping from his coffin which has a curiously flat appearance. The Last Supper is taken at a round table but this is the persistence of a very old tradition rather than a new element. The Entombment is curiously presented; one person standing in the tomb pulls the body of Christ towards him by the arm.

From all these details it is evident that the artist followed an independent iconography and not the traditional one of the 13th century which the painters of Rimini, the Florentines, the Sienese and the Bolognese all observed. Nor is it Giottesque while there is only one detail in the Resurrection of Lazarus that links this master with Lombard art.

Fig. 249. Ferrarese School, the Crucifixion, circa 1350—60. Abbey Church, Pomposa.

Photo Minist. del. Pubbl. Istr.

This iconographical independence leads us to suppose that the artist who worked here did not belong to any of the more important centres but was a local minor master who profited from the productions that the two greater artists, Giuliano da Rimini and Vitale da Bologna, had left in this church (¹). His painting is an intermingling of elements borrowed from the works of these two artists and although rendered with but little grace, it is full of an exceptional force and vitality. It is in the very peculiar type of his figures that this mingling of styles is most evident. The general appearance of his figures reminds us of Vitale's; some of his female figures in particular possess a sweetness and regularity of feature which, together with a certain breadth of form, result in types very reminiscent of Vitale. The large, strongly marked shadows are also characteristic of the Bolognese school, although Vitale himself did not exaggerate this peculiarity.

On the other hand the elongated proportions and sharp features which we find side by side with the types borrowed from Vitale's art, seem to have found their origin in Giuliano da Rimini's manner; sometimes we even find the two distinct factors united in the same figure, as for example when he shows us the long necks of the Riminese painters on the large heavy bodies of the Bolognese.

In spite of the fact that our artist's figures are rather stiff and

---

(¹) Several critics have pronounced their opinion of this artist's manner. *Brach*, op. cit., pp. 52 and 106, is not very precise. He believes that two artists, both dependent on the Sienese tradition, worked here, one of them having executed the frescoes in the nave, the other the Last Judgment and the decoration of the choir. Later, when he says that the latter are by Vitale da Bologna, he apparently only alludes to the paintings in the choir and no longer includes the Last Judgment. This, in fact, as I remarked in the previous chapter, seems to be the correct opinion, for Vitale executed only the frescoes in the apse, while those in the nave and the Last Judgment are without any doubt from one hand. It will be recalled that *Filippini*, op. cit., gives this fresco as well as the apsidal decoration to Vitale. *Gardner*, op. cit., p. 2, doubts if the frescoes at Pomposa are Ferrarese. *Brach*, op. cit., p. 109, ascribes the scenes from the Old Testament and the Apocalypse on the right of the nave to Jacopo di Paolo da Bologna. Apart from the fact that there is no reason for attributing the frescoes in the nave to two different hands there is absolutely nothing in them that reminds us of this painter as *Bandani*, op. cit., p. 473, has already remarked. On the other hand this writer assigns to him the decoration of the apse.

Fig. 250. Ferrarese School, the Crucifixion. Pasini Collection, Rome

angular, not only in their movements but also in their drapery, they are much more imposing than those of Bolognese painting, and this is another quality that he has acquired from the school of Rimini. His types are very easily recognized and it is just this that enables us to affirm that the painter who worked in the nave is the same as the painter who decorated the entrance wall. The characteristic appearance of some of the old men especially, with their high foreheads, curved mouths and piercing looks, convinces us we are not led astray. In his love of minor details, as for instance in the scene of the Wedding at Cana, his works may be approximated to the "scènes de genre" of Northern Italian artists.

I know of only one other picture which may be grouped with the Pomposa frescoes and which may possibly be from the same hand. It is a little panel in the Pasini collection, Rome, representing the Crucifixion (fig. 250). Four little angels fly around the Crucified; the Virgin and St. John stand mourning below, Mary Magdalene embraces the foot of the Cross while more to the sides are the figures of SS. Catherine and Christopher. The large and somewhat coarse technique that the artist employed in the execution of his frescoes is not suited to a painting of small dimensions. The contrast of light and shade is even stronger than in the mural decoration.

There are two panels in the town gallery which for a long time were attributed to Cristoforo da Ferrara. It has, however, been well established that the painter of the name of Cristoforo was not a native of Ferrara but of Bologna. Furthermore, as one of Cristoforo's two signed works hangs in the same gallery, just alongside the two pictures in question, a glance suffices to prove that they are not from the same hand.

One of these panels (no. 22) shows the Virgin dreaming of the Crucifixion (fig. 251). Against a rocky landscape we see the Madonna lying asleep in bed near which a woman sits reading. From the body of the recumbent figure springs a tree on which the Saviour is crucified; six angels hover round the Redeemer while a pelican feeding its young is depicted at the top of the tree. This little picture is also the outcome of a mixture of Riminese and Bolognese elements. Not only is the form of the panel practically the same as that of the terminal of Baronzio's signed picture at Urbino and of another work of his school at Stras-

Fig. 251. Ferrarese School, the Virgin's Dream, 2nd half of the 14th century. Gallery, Ferrara.   Photo Minist. del. Pubbl. Istr.

bourg, but the beauty of line, the grace and the refined execution are all qualities borrowed from the Riminese school. On the other hand, the strong shadows remind us of the technique of the Bolognese artists, and although the master of this panel shows no connection with the painter who was active at Pomposa, his art derives from the same two sources.

The other little panel in the same Gallery (no. 21) is less pleasing but it bears more resemblance to the frescoes of the abbatial church. The subject of the painting is again the Crucifixion; two little angels fly under the arms of the Crucified, Mary Magdalene clasps His feet while the Virgin and St. John stand, one on either side (fig. 252). The artist has expressed his dramatic feeling in a very forcible manner; the light and shade effects are strongly contrasted.

The other 14th century paintings that we find at Ferrara do not belong to any well defined group. There is a certain number of detached frescoes in the different churches, especially in that of the Martiri, and in the town gallery; but for the greater part they are of little artistic value and only interesting because they reveal that not only the Bolognese manner, but also the Florentine and the Sienese schools, had adherents in Ferrara. A Madonna with the Child and a Coronation of the Virgin are executed by a descendant of the Giottesque tradition, while a group of saints (fig. 253) and some other fragments from the church of Sta. Caterina seem to have been inspired by Sienese art [1]. This is also evident in a beautiful picture of the Madonna nursing the Child which is preserved on the 5th altar in S. Domenico. In the Estense Palace, now the University, Cavalcaselle found some mural decoration representing battle scenes and disputes, which still exist, although others that he mentions in the churches of S. Polinare and S. Guglielmo have apparently disappeared [2].

A group of painters seems to have existed at Faenza [3] but few traces of their activity have survived. Vasari speaks of Ottaviano and Pace da Faenza as Giotto's pupils [4].

According to him, the former worked in the churches of S.

---

[1] *Agnelli*, op. cit., p. 34.
[2] *Crowe and Cavalcaselle*, op. cit., III, p. 215—16.
[3] *A. Messeri e A. Calzi*, Faenza nella storia e nell'arte Faenza, 1909, p. 381.
[4] *Vasari-Milanesi*, I p. 404.

Fig. 252. Ferrarese School, the Crucifixion, 2nd half of the 14th century. Gallery, Ferrara. Photo Minist. del. Pubbl. Istr.

Giorgio of Ferrara and S. Francesco of Faenza; he produced some other paintings in this town "where he lived and died", and was also active in Bologna(¹). Vasari affirms that Pace worked with Giotto for a long time. There were frescoes from his hand on the façade of S. Giovanni Decollato in Bologna, while a tree of the Cross and a panel with scenes from the lives of the Redeemer and the Virgin in the church of S. Francesco at Forli displayed his skill in depicting small figures. The same writer states with less certainty that Pace also adorned the chapel of S. Antonio at Assisi with scenes from the saint's legend for a Duke of Spoleto who, together with his son, is buried there. From the same source we learn that in an old register of the painters' corporation — the name of the town is not given — Francesco detto di Maestro Giotto is mentioned as being a pupil of Pace's. Lanzi speaks of a Madonna by Pace in the old Templar's church at Faenza while a picture in the town gallery representing the Virgin, many saints and four scenes from the Passion has, without any reason, been ascribed to him.

We possess one signed work by Bittino or Bitino da Faenza and another which may be attributed to him. This artist passed a considerable part of his life in Rimini (²).

He is mentioned there in 1398 when he married, while his picture in S. Giuliano dates probably from 1409. His family, then, must have settled in this town, for of his three sons, the eldest,

---

(¹) At one time there was a mediocre work of the Florentine school in the Villa Galletti at Torre del Gallo, near Florence. It represented the Virgin with four angels and for some quite unknown reason, was attributed to Ottaviano da Faenza and to the year 1390.

(²) *Tonini*, op. cit., IV, p. 394. *The Same*, Atti e Mem. della R. Dep. di Stor. Patr. per la Romagna, 1863, II², p. 159. *G. S. Battaglini*, Descrizione della tavola dipinta in 1409 del Maestro Bittino, Firenze, 1886. *The Same*, Di Bittino da Faenza e della scuola romagnola etc., Ravenna, 1890. *Brach*, op. cit., p. 114. *Thieme-Becker*, Künstler Lexikon, IV, p. 73. *F. Filippini*, Gli affreschi nell' abside di S. Agostino in Rimini. I have already remarked in the chapter on Riminese painters that this writer makes a great mistake in attributing to Bittino the frescoes in S. Agostino of Rimini which are about a hundred years older. His critical remarks on Bittino being based on this hypothesis, are consequently without any value. Thus, Bittino was not a member of the Riminese school as Signor Filippini affirms, while the frescoes in S. Agostino are certainly a production of this school.

Fig. 253. Ferrarese School, a group of saints, 2nd half of the 14th century. Gallery, Ferrara.

Ambrogio, worked there and *his* son, Lattanzio da Rimini, was a fairly good painter of the 15th century. Bittino died before 1427.

The signed picture shows, in the centre St. Julian with a little devotee, while around are eleven scenes from his legend, arranged in three rows. The spandrels are adorned with medallions containing busts of the four Doctors of the Church, the four Evangelists and two saints, (fig. 254). At the feet of the principal figure the following is inscribed on six lines: "*Bitinus fecit hoc opus fecit fieri die Sim . . . abbas M. Sci Juliani sub ano domini Mil. C . . . . . VIII . . . .*". The first line with the painter's name is written in characters a little different from the others but I do not think that for this reason we need doubt the authenticity of the inscription.

As for the date Tonini read it sixty years ago as: "*Miles . . . . CCCVIIII*". It is obviously a *C* that is missing and this is confirmed by the fact that there was a prior called Simon between 1401 and 1427 at the monastery of S. Giuliano.

Although the form of the principal figure and the drawing of it seem somewhat coarse, the surrounding small scenes are finely executed. In spite of the fact that Cavalcaselle's dictum that these paintings belong to Orcagna's school has been contradicted by many, I think his affirmation is not far from the truth. In the form of the figures, the architecture and the composition there are certainly more factors reminiscent of Florence than of Bologna, whence Lanzi and Brach believe Bittino's art is derived. The only Bolognese feature to be noted in this work is the colouring. The costumes and the slight Gothic line of certain of the figures herald the international Gothic style that flourished some years later.

The other work which I think may be ascribed to Bittino is much less pleasing, showing more resemblance to the central figure of the above panel. It is a little painting in the Faenza Gallery and represents SS. Vite the Martyr and John the Baptist. The supposition that it is a production of an earlier stage in the master's career is very likely true ([1]).

([1]) An hypothesis propounded by Herr *Brach* who hesitatingly attributes also to Bittino the panel of the Virgin with six saints below in the same Gallery, a work that I have already classified as a production of the Riminese school, v. p. 281.

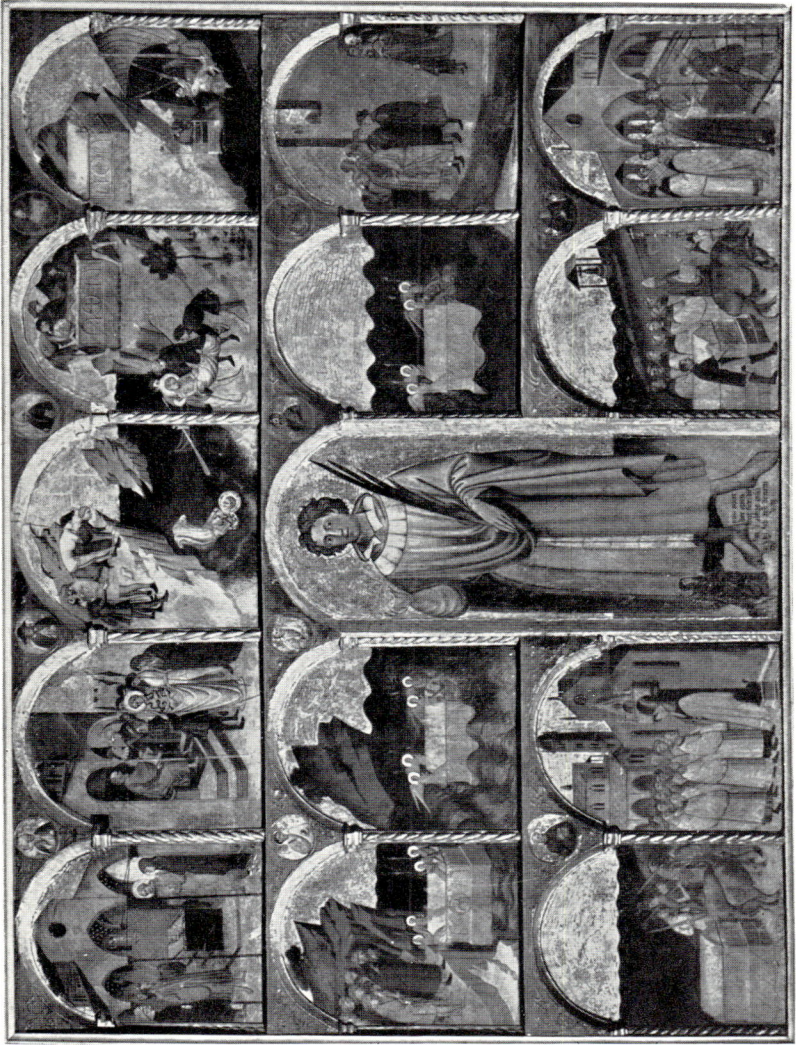

Fig. 254. Bittino da Faenza, St. Julian and scenes from his legend, 1409. S. Giuliano, Rimini.

Photo Brogi.

According to Vasari a certain painter called Guglielmo da Forli or degli Organi was a pupil of Giotto's and worked at Forli. Among other things, he decorated the walls of the choir of

S. Domenico (¹), while Lanzi speaks of his frescoes in S. Francesco but no trace of his works has survived. Some unimportant paintings in the sacristy of the Servi church, in the Chapter Room of the Cathedral and a Madonna delle grazie in the Cathedral itself have, however, been attributed to him without any reason (²). A painter, Bestello da Forli, is recorded in Ravenna between 1350 and 1360 and another, Baldassare, in 1354 at Forli. Cavalcaselle thought that it was possibly the latter painter who executed the only 14th century work of some importance in the town. It is a fresco that has been transported from the church "di Schiavonia" to the gallery, and represents the figures of SS. Peter, Jerome, Paul and Augustine, one of the adoring Kings and a servant holding the horses, the fragmentary remains of a scene of the Adoration of the Magi (³). It is a beautiful work in which the figures are imposing and the execution fine. Generally speaking it may be said that the artist was inspired chiefly by the Florentine school but was also slightly influenced by that of Rimini. No Bolognese elements are evident in his work.

Parma is the only other town in Emilia where we find a series of 14th century paintings of any importance. Here the niches of the Baptistery, the walls and cupola of which are covered with a magnificent cycle of 13th century frescoes, are adorned with 14th century paintings, probably concealing others of the original decoration which, moreover, are still seen in sixteen of the niches. They are by different artists and vary considerably in quality. Signor Testi has described them in detail (⁴). Following his description, I shall mention the subjects depicted. They are firstly the Crucifixion and a Madonna of the Misericordia, one below the other, beside each of these there are some standing figures of saints and above, the figures of the Annunciation. An inscription below tells us that this decoration was executed in 1398 (or 1399) for the confraternity of the Living and the Dead. It is a painting of little artistic merit, executed in a coarse manner with reminiscences of the Lombard style. In the next niche

---

(¹) *Vasari-Milanesi*, I, p. 405.
(²) *Crowe and Cavalcaselle*, ed. *E. Hutton*, I, p. 317 note.
(³) *Idem*, p. 317. *Brach*, op. cit., p. 117.
(⁴) *L. Testi*, Le Baptistère de Parme, Florence, 1916, p. 247 et seq

we find a representation of the Madonna seated on a Gothic throne between a holy pope and bishop, a painting which reveals through the restoration, a fairly refined execution, it dates probably from the second quarter of the 14th century.

Of an inferior quality and slightly later period is the decoration of the following niche where we see the Virgin adored by a holy monk followed by saints, while below others are depicted separately framed. The signature: "*Bartolinus De Placentia fecit*" is inscribed below the figures of SS. John the Baptist and Lucy ([1]). We shall presently find this painter in Piacenza.

Signor Testi has pointed out that as the other frescoes are painted on a different surface they are probably not by the same hand, as was stated by Lopez, in his description of the Baptistery. The appearance of the paintings, moreover, confirms this hypothesis. The Nativity in the adjacent recess shows two holy women, St. Joseph and a shepherd adoring the Child Christ. A fairly large number of angels above announce the glad tidings to the shepherds while below there are two rows of saints among whom we recognize St. Martin and St. Michael on horseback. Like the preceding fresco, this also is rather provincial in appearance; the Nativity, however, is depicted with a good deal of animation. Of little better quality are the frescoes in the following niche; they represent, above, a large erect figure of the Saviour and His Baptism and on two rows below a series of scenes, among which are the baptism and mystical marriage of St. Catherine. In style these works show a certain connection with the Bolognese school.

Then follows another representation of the enthroned Virgin, this time nursing the Child, and escorted by three saints; below, three of the five figures which were once probably represented, alone remain. Formerly the signature: "*Nicolaus De Reio (Reggio) fecit*" ([2]) could be read here. Signori Bertoni and Vicini have identified this painter with a Niccolo whose name they found recorded at Modena between 1363 and 1377([3]), but this

---

([1]) *Rosini,* Storia della pittura italiana, I, p. 206. *Thieme-Becker*, Künstler Lexikon, II, p. 557.

([2]) *Rosini,* op. cit., I, p. 206. *Testi,* op. cit., p. 253.

([3]) *G. Bertoni e E. P. Vicini*, Niccolo da Reggio, Rassegna d'Arte, 1903, p. 158.

decoration, which is rather crude, seems to be of earlier date.

Of the two painters who decorated the next niche one shows again a certain knowledge of Bolognese art. He has depicted, in two rows, the Prayer on the Mount of Olives, the Flagellation, the Mocking of Christ and the Calvary. Lower down another artist, working in a more Gothic manner and possessing a finer technique, executed the figure of St. Ursula accompanied by her virgins and a scene of the Circumcision in a style bearing a certain resemblance to Lombard painting. They date from the second half of the 14th century.

The following recess contains a somewhat heterogeneous ensemble of frescoes. Above we find a Pietà and the figures of SS. Wilgefort [1] and Catherine; lower down an image of St. Christopher with the date 1350, six little scenes of works of mercy and two figures of saints.

These paintings, which are of little importance, are by different artists and do not all belong to the same period. Then we see St. George killing the dragon and lower the Baptism of Christ, which in manner recalls the Nativity. In the next niche but one there are several frescoes, all very mediocre work, the most important being that of the Coronation of the Virgin dated 1361. The decoration of the second niche from here has preserved, in spite of the restoration, many of its original qualities. Here the Virgin, in an architectural frame, is enthroned between an angel and St. John the Baptist who presents a kneeling bishop who, according to the inscription, is Cardinal Gherardo Bianchi who died in 1302. In this case it must be a commemorative painting because the work can hardly have been executed before 1320 at the very earliest. The fineness of the technique recalls the Sienese school or certain productions of the Perugian miniaturists.

This collection of examples of the pictorial production during the 14th century proves that there was no school in Parma at this epoch. We can perceive the proximity of Bologna, the art of which town influenced — though only to a certain degree — the Parmesan painters.

Although the decoration in the different chapels of the Cathedral leads us to believe that there must have been a considerable

---

[1] *Testi*, op. cit., p. 256.

OTHER LITTLE CENTRES IN EMILIA. 507

artistic activity in Parma at the very beginning of the 15th century, there are no other works of any importance dating from the 14th century in the town (¹).

The town of Piacenza possessed the painter Bertolino whom we have found active in Parma. Rosini reproduces a fresco which adorns a lunette in the wall to the left of the entrance of the Cathedral as a certain work of Bertolino's, without however giving the reasons which have led him to this attribution. The painting, which shows a certain Gothicism in feeling and proportions, dates from about 1400.

It represents the Virgin enthroned in the midst of four saints, holding on her knee the naked Child Who bestows a blessing on an adoring bishop (²). Signor Toesca has already drawn our attention to the fact that it may have been the same painter who adorned a considerably repainted reliquary in the Museum of Piacenza with the figure of a saint seated on the ground on the upper part and St. Catherine on the lower part (³).

Elsewhere in Piacenza we find paintings of an earlier period. Above the door of the sacristy of the Cathedral, a lunette contains a half-length figure of the Virgin carrying the Child between two angels (⁴), a production probably of the beginning of the 14th century since, in looking at it, we feel that the Byzantine tradition is not far distant. A fresco in the lateral apse of the Cathedral representing the Resurrection of the Dead is of a less archaic style, while one of St. George carrying the delivered princess pillion on his horse is executed in a more Northern Gothic manner (⁵).

Rosini and, before him, Lanzi mention some representations — since lost — from the life of St. Antonino (and not of St. Antony

---

(¹) The names of several Parmesan painters of the 14th century are mentioned in Le Gallerie Nazionali Italiane, I, p. 21. L. *Testi*, Bolletino d'Arte, 1910, p. 57 note 3, informs us in a general manner that 14th century paintings are to be found in the churches and castles around Parma, but these are entirely unknown to me.

(²) *Rosini*, op. cit., II, p. 53. *Toesca*, La pittura lombarda, p. 392.
(³) *Toesca*, op. cit., p. 393.
(⁴) *Toesca*, op. cit., p. 144.
(⁵) *Toesca*, op. cit., p. 150.

as Lanzi says) in the church dedicated to this saint in Piacenza (¹).

Some beautiful frescoes have been discovered in the church of the Abbey of Chiaravalle della Colomba, near Alseno di Piacenza (²), they represent the Crucifixion, a mitred saint assisted by two acolytes celebrating mess, and a holy bishop in benediction. It is in the Crucifixion particularly that we note certain elements borrowed from the painting of the end of the 13th century; such, for example, as the proportions and form of the central figure, while the gestures of some of the assistants remind us of those in Cimabue's big fresco in the Upper Church of Assisi. The technique of the entire decoration, as well as the facial expressions and the general spirit of the work, points sooner to a Sienese influence.

The author of these paintings, which date from the first half of the 14th century, was a skilful painter and one familiar with the important artistic currents of Central Italy.

This rapid survey of Emilian painting outside Bologna, Rimini and Modena, suffices, I think, to prove that outside these three important centres, there were, with the exception perhaps of the little group at Ferrara, no other local schools. Further it may be stated that although we discover traces of the influence of the Riminese and Bolognese painters they did not entirely dominate the artistic activity in Emilia, where we find works inspired by Lombard, Florentine, Sienese and other artists, giving a heterogenous character to the native production.

(¹) *Rosini*, op. cit., II, p. 223.
(²) *G. Bertuzzi*, La badia di Chiaravalle della Colomba e gli affreschi recentemente scoperti, L'Arte, 1903, p. 306.

ADDITIONS AND CORRECTIONS.

p. 43 9th line from above: Giovanni di Paolo should read Jacopo di Paolo.

p. 57. To the works of Lorenzo Veneziano, I have been told, should still be added a panel in the collection of Prof. Mather of the University of Princetown (U.S.A.), representing the enthroned Madonna with the Crucifixion above and the Twelve Apostles in three rows below. The painting is unknown to me.

p. 382, note 1, 6th to 3nd line from below should read: *Supino*, Un dipinto di Barnaba d. M., Rivista d'Arte, 1905, p. 13, assigns to him a Crucifixion and Annunciation in the Gallery of Pisa which is a production of the Pisan school to which he had previously attributed it (Campo Santo, p. 68), while *Thode,* Repert. f. Kunstwiss., 1888, p. 21, ascribed it to the Master of the Triumph of Death.

INDICES

INDICES

An iconographical index, indicating New and Old Testament and hagiographical scenes and other important representations will be found at the end of volume V.

Compound names divided by di, de, del, etc., will be found under the letter of the first name, all the others under that of the second.

GEOGRAPHICAL INDEX

The ciphers in brackets are those of the museum catalogues. Illustrated descriptions are indicated by bold faced numbers.

Ajaccio.
Museum, *the Master of the Pirano altar-piece*, disappeared wings of a polyptych 23.
Alba (Piedmont).
S. Giovanni Battista, *Barnaba da Modena*, Madonna, from S. Francesco 379, 380.
Alessandria.
Cathedral, *Piedmontese school*, frescoes 276.
Alseno di Piacenza v. **Chiaravalle.**
Amsterdam.
Lanz coll., *Giovanni da Milano*, Crucifixion 238².
Ancona.
Gallery, *Andrea da Bologna*, Death of the Virgin **432**, 436.
S. Angelo in Formis (near Capua).
Benedictine fresco of the Last Judgment 483.
Angera (Lago Maggiore).
Castle, *Lombard school*, frescoes of battle scenes 210, 269.
Aquileia.
Baptistery, fresco fragments 98.
Basilica, fresco fragments 98.
Arbe (Dalmatia).
Cathedral, *Venetian school*, Madonna 95; polyptych **95**.
S. Arcangelo di Romagna.
Jacobello di Bonomo, polyptych, v. Venice, Accademia.
Arezzo.
Badia, *Segna di Bonaventura*, crucifix 338¹.

Gallery, *Giovanni da Milano, school of —*, Madonna (13) 238².
Ascoli Piceno.
Gallery, *Andrea da Bologna, school of —*, polyptych 432¹.
Assisi.
Giovanni da Milano, paintings 222.
Sta. Chiara, Madonna, crucifix and St. Clare, of the 13ᵗʰ cent., 222⁴.
S. Francesco, Upper Church, *Cavallini and helpers*, frescoes 304², 352, 353; *Cimabue*, apocalyptic scenes 493; Crucifixion 509; *Giotto and helpers*, St. Francis cycle 16, 298, 346, 352; *Roman school of the 13ᵗʰ cent.*, Old and New Testament scenes 484.
Lower Church, *Angelino di Corrado di Novarello, Giovanni di Maestro Nicola, Pace da Bologna*, active 428¹; *Pace da Faenza*, active 501; *Andrea da Bologna*, frescoes in the St. Catherine chapel 428, **428 – 430**, 434; *idem*, (wrongly attributed to), windows in that chapel 430; *Ceccolo di Giovanni (?)*, Madonna and saints 430²; *Giotto, school of —*, frescoes from the childhood of Christ 222⁴, 351; miracle of Mary Magdalene 226; *Maestro di S. Francesco*, St. Francis cycle 16.
Avigliano (Piedmont).
Castle, profane frescoes 273.
Avignon 277.

Bagnacavallo.
Pieve, *Giuliano da Rimini*, frescoes 310—312.

Baltimore.
Walters coll., *Caterino*, polyptych 62—64, 78, 80; *Veneziano, Lorenzo—, school of—*, triptych 58[1].

Bassano.
Martinello, active 100.
Cathedral, *Guariento, school of —*, Madonna and saints, crucifix 118.
S. Francesco, *Guariento, school of —*, Annunciation 118.
S. Francesco Monastery, *Guariento*, frescoes 116; *Guariento, school of —*, frescoes of St. Antony's legend 118.
Museum, *Guariento*, crucifix 119, **115**, 117; *Guariento, school of —*, marriage of St. Catherine 118.

Bellano.
S. Giorgio, *Simone da Corbetta, manner of —*, Madonna and two saints 258.

Bellinzona.
S. Biagio, *Lombard school*, frescoes 254

Belluno 100.
Cathedral, *Simone da Cusighe*, lost altar-piece 100.
S. Martino, *Simone da Cusighe*, lost altar-piece 100[3].
Pagani family, *Simone da Cusighe*, altar-piece from S Bartolommeo in Salce, v. Venice, Accademia.

Bergamo.
Sta. Maria Maggiore, *Giottesque-Lombard school*, tree S. Bonaventura **218**, 220; in the Campanile, frescoes, wrongly attrib. to Pierino de Nova 218[2].
Sta. Marta Convent, *Lombard school*, frescoes, v. Gallery.
Gallery, *Lombard school*, detached devotional frescoes **255—257**; frescoes from the Sta. Marta convent 266[4].

Berletta.
Metropolitana, *Serafini Paolo —*, Madonna and two pictures of the Lord **389**.

Berlin.
Kaiser Friedrich Museum, *Barnaba da Modena*, Madonna (1171) 370, **372**, 372; *Battista da Vicenza (?)*, figures of saints **108**; *Daddi, Bernardo —*, triptych (1064) 164; *Giovanni da Milano, school of —*, Mourning under the Cross 238[2]; *Veneziano Lorenzo —*, two saints 54; *Bohemian school*, Madonna (1624) 117[1]; *Florentine school of the 13th cent.*, Last Judgment and 5 other scenes 291[1].
Print Cabinet, *Giovanni da Milano, attrib. to —*, drawing of the Crucifixion 238. von Kaufmann coll.(dispersed), *Baronzio, manner of —*, Nativity 340. Japs coll., *Simone dei Crocifissi*, Coronation of the Virgin from the Gozzadini coll., Bologna 451[1].

Bohemia 356, 356[2], 363.

Bologna 109, 367, 387, 393, 394—481.
v. **Borgo Panicale, Credolo**. *Ottaviano da Faenza*, active 500.

Churches, Monasteries etc.
S. Andrea dei Padri Penitenziari, *Cristoforo*, lost detached fresco 414[1]; *Dalmasio, Lippo —*, lost Madonna, once near this church 455.
S. Apollonia, *Vitale*, Madonna, v. Davia Bargellini Gallery; two lost panels of saints 408.
S. Bartolommeo, *Dalmasio, Lippo —*, detached fresco from Sta. Maria di Porta 462[1].
Certosa della Madonna, *Bolognese school*, different representations of the Madonna 480[1].
S. Clemente (of the Spanish College) *Bolognese school*, frescoes of Pope Urban V, St. Catherine and adorer 480[1].
S. Cristoforo at Monte Maggiore, *Cristoforo*, lost picture 413.
Crocifisso church, *Dalmasio, Lippo —, school of —*, Madonna 462[1]; *Jacopo di Paolo*, (wrongly attrib. to), Calvary and Crucifixion 468; *Bolognese school*, two frescoes of the Madonna and one of the Ecce Homo 480[1].
S. Domenico, *Cristoforo*, lost frescoes in the sacristy 414[1]; *Dalmasio, Lippo —*, Madonna del Veluto 462; *Vitale*, lost panels 408; *Bolognese school*, Madonna delle Febre 480[1].
S. Domenico, cloister, *Dalmasio, Lippo —*, fresco fragments 462; *Veneziano, Lorenzo —*, active 403; *Pietro di Giovanni di Tovaglis (?)*,

GEOGRAPHICAL INDEX.

fragment of the Holy Trinity 451[1]; *Simone dei Crocifissi*, lost fresco 452; *Vitale*, lost fresco 40, 408.

S. Francesco, *Andrea da Bologna*, active 428; *Cristoforo*, active 412; *Dalmasio, Lippo* —, active (?) 456[1]; *Vitale*, active 399, 400, 408; *Bolognese school*, crucifix 480[1].

S. Francesco Monastery, *Francesco da Rimini*, lost frescoes 346, 352, 424; *Simone dei Crocifissi*, lost Coronation of the Virgin 440;

S. Giacomo Maggiore, *Jacopo di Paolo*, Coronation of the Virgin; Crucifixion and saint 43, 465; *Veneziano, Lorenzo* —, lost altarpiece 41—43; panels of a polyptych 42, 43; *Simone dei Crocifissi*, crucifix 440, 445.

S. Giovanni Decollato, *Pace da Faenza*, lost frescoes on façade 500.

S. Giovanni in Monte, *Simone dei Crocifissi, school of* —, crucifix, 451[1]. 480[1]; *Vitale*, Madonna 403; *Bolognese school*, panel and fresco of the Madonna, 480[1].

Guidalotti chapel, *Dalmasio, Lippo* —, lost painting 456.

S. Giuseppe, *Bolognese school*, crucifix 480[1].

S. Isaia, *Bolognese school*, fresco of the Madonna 480[1].

S. Marco, *Dalmasio, Lippo* —, Coronation of the Virgin, v. Gallery.

Sta. Margherita, *Simone dei Crocifissi*, lost Coronation of the Virgin 451[1].

Sta. Maria del Monte, *Vitale*, Madonna, v. Gallery.

Sta. Maria dell' Orazione, *Dalmasio, Lippo* —, Madonna 462.

Sta. Maria di Porta, *Dalmasio, Lippo* —, fresco, v. S. Bartolommeo.

Sta. Maria della Purificazione, *Dalmasio, Lippo* —, Madonna 462[1], 480[1]; *Bolognese school*, fresco of the Madonna 480[1].

Sta. Maria Maddalena agli Orfanelli, *Cristoforo*, lost Madonna and saints; *Simone dei Crocifissi*, lost Madonna; *Vitale*, lost Madonna 408.

S. Martino, *Simone dei Crocifissi*, lost Crucifixion 451[1]; *Simone dei Crocifissi, school of* —, fragments of a Crucifixion 451[1]; *Vitale*, Madonna 404, 406; *Bolognese school*, fresco fragments and figures of St. Onuphrius 480[1].

Mezzarata church, 404, 416, 420, 438; *Cristoforo*, active 412; frescoes, (wrongly attrib. to), 413, 414[1]; lost Madonna della Misericordia 413; *Gallasso*, active and frescoes, (wrongly attrib. to), 482; *Jacopo*, different signatures of that name 416; *Jacopo (pseudo-Jacopo Avanzi(?)*, frescoes 419, 420, 482; *Jacopo di Paolo*, frescoes 418, 464, 466, 468; *Veneziano, Lorenzo* —, active (?) 41; *Simone dei Crocifissi*, frescoes 418, 419, 450, 451, 482; *Bolognese school*, frescoes of the Nativity, the Ascension the Virgin and Old Testament scenes 408, 468, 469.

S. Michele in Bosco, *Simone dei Crocifissi*, lost Madonna 451[1].

Misericordia church, *Dalmasio, Lippo* —, Madonna 456, **458**.

Montalto College, church of — *Vitale*, lost St. Antony Abbot 408.

SS. Narborre e Felice, *Jacopo di Paolo*, lost Crucifixion and Annunciation 468.

S. Petronio, *Dalmasio, Lippo* —, Madonna (now in Museum of this church), lost Madonna and St. George 455; makes crucifix 456; *Giovanni da Modena*, active 476; *Jacopo di Paolo*, makes model of the church 463; designs statues for Maestro Paolo 464; wooden carved altar attrib. to him 464[1]; *Lola Francesco* —, active 476; *Luca da Perugia*, fresco of the Virgin and saints **476**; *Maestro Paolo, attrib. to* —, wooden carved altar 464[1]; *Simone dei Crocifissi*, lost Madonna 451[1]; *Bolognese school of the 14th and 15th cent.*, figures of saints on the pillars 480[1]; *Bolognese school of ab. 1410*, frescoes in the Bolognini chapel, 414[1] 468, **469**—**476**, 480.

S. Petronio, Museum of the church, *Dalmasio, Lippo* —, Madonna from a pillar of the church 456, 461.

S. Pietro, *Dalmasio, Lippo* —, lost painting 456; *Jacopo di Paolo*, active 463; *Simone dei Crocifissi*, lost Crucifixion 451[1].

S. Procolo, *Dalmasio, Lippo* —, Madonna 456, 462.

S. Salvatore, *Vitale*, Madonna 403, 404; polyptych 400, 403, **406**, 414¹.

S. Stefano, *Deodato Giovanello da Imola*, lost Madonna 398; *Simone dei Crocifissi*, Madonna 451¹; *Bolognese school,* figures of saints in the courtyard 480¹.

S. Stefano, Museum of the church, *Avanzi, pseudo-Jacopo—, school of* —, four scenes from the life of St. Benedict 480¹; *Dalmasio, Lippo* —, *school of* —, Madonna 462¹; *Giovanni di Canelo*, polyptych 82, 477; *Jacopo di Paolo,* St. John 466; *idem (?)*, triptych 466; *idem, school of* —, two saints 468¹; *Simone dei Crocifissi*, crucifix 446; *idem, manner of* —, three saints and two panels each with three saints 451¹; *idem, school of*—, crucifix 451¹; *Vitale, school of* —, Madonna 408; *Bolognese school,* two triptychs and some other panels 480¹.

Public and Private Collections.

Gallery, *Avanzi, pseudo-Jacopo* —, 426; polyptych (159) **422**, 424; Death of the Virgin (170) 422; Coronation of the Virgin 422; Coronation of the Virgin and Crucifixion (161) 422; Crucifixion (160) 422; Crucifixion (380) 422; *idem, school of* —, angel and two saints (363, 364) 422³; Last Judgment and Pietà (230) 422³; martyrdom of St. Cristina (167) 422³; St. Gregory (383) 422³; *Dalmasio, Lippo*—, Coronation of the Virgin (500), **456**, 456; Madonna (no number) 458; Madonna (752) 460; *idem, school of* —, Coronation of the Virgin, Crucifixion and saints from S. Marco (225) 462¹; Coronation of the Virgin, St. Ursula and other saints (232) 462¹; *Jacopo di Paolo*, Crucifixion (10) 464, **464**, 466, 468; Coronation of the Virgin (11) 464, **465**; two triptych wings (367, 368) 466; four saints (268, 269) 466; St. Romuald's vision (168) 466; *idem, school of* —, crucifix (191) 468¹; Coronation of the Virgin (270) 468¹; *Monaco, Lorenzo* —, Madonna (501) 406²; *Petrus*, crucifix 398;

Simone dei Crucifissi, portrait of Pope Urban V (340) 440, **443**; Crucifixion, Christ and the Virgin (162) 440, **446**; polyptych (474) **442** 448, 451¹; Coronation of the Virgin (164) **442**; polyptych (163) 448, 452¹; Madonna and ten angels (no number) 451¹; *idem, manner of* —, scenes from the life of the Virgin (601) 451¹; *idem, school of* —, St. Bernard dei Tolomei (166) 451¹; *Tommaso da Modena, school of* —, Lord's Supper, three Madonnas and four saints 367¹; *Veneziano, Lorenzo* —, two saints 42, **43**, 46; *Vitale*, Madonna from Sta. Maria del Monte (203) 398, **400**, 403, 406; triptych (351) 402, 403; St. Helen (328) 406; *idem, school of* —, Annunciation (384, 385) 408; scenes from the Lord's history (257, 258) 408; *Bolognese school,* Lord's Supper (169) 480¹; Madonna of Humility and prophets (589) 480¹; Paradise (229) 474; *Riminese school,* Crucifixion (231) 288, 292.

Museo Civico, *Jacopo di Paolo,* Annunciation from the notarial archives (221) 464; two *Giottesque* crucifixes (191, 196) 480¹; *Bolognese school,* the Saviour (208) 480¹; Madonna and Pietà (202) 480¹; Nativity and Flight in Egypt (209, 210) 480¹.

State Archives, *Niccolo di Giacomo,* miniatures in different ledgers 410.

Davia Bargellini Gallery, *Vitale,* Madonna from S. Apollonia 400, **404**, 406; *Simone dei Crocifissi,* Pietà 440, 444.

Ercolani coll. (dispersed), *Dalmasio, Lippo* —, Madonna, v. London, National Gallery; *Franco da Bologna,* (wrongly attrib. to), Madonna 397; *Veneziano, Lorenzo* —, signed picture 41, 42.

Gozzadini coll. (dispersed), *Avanzi, pseudo-Jacopo* —, five predella panels, v. Englewood, Platt coll.; *Jacobello di Bonomo, attrib. to* —, triptych 87¹; *Simone dei Crocefissi,* Coronation of the Virgin, Crucifixion and other representations 448; Coronation of the Virgin. v. London, Langton Douglas coll.; Coronation of the Virgin, v. Berlin, Japs coll.;

GEOGRAPHICAL INDEX.

idem, manner of —, two saints and the Annunciation 451[1]; *idem, school of* —, four saints 451[1].

Gualandi coll. (dispersed), *Giovanni da Bologna*, Coronation of the Virgin 82.

Malvezzi coll. (dispersed), *Franco da Bologna, attrib to* —, a painting 397; *Vitale*, two holy Benedictines 408.

Public and Private Buildings.

Town Hall, *Avanzi, Jacopo* —, paints a tile for the —, 416.

Notarial Archives, *Jacopo di Paolo*, Annunciation, v. Museo Civico.

Sta. Croce College, *Dalmasio, Lippo* —, triptych **462**.

Spanish College, *Dalmasio, Lippo* —, Madonna of Humility 460, v. S. Clemente.

Compagnia dei Lombardi, *Bolognese school*, some panels 480[1].

Palazzo Bolognetti, *Dalmasio, Lippo* —, lost painting 456.

Casa Gualandi, *Bolognese school*, fresco of the Madonna and some fresco fragments in the courtyard 480[1].

Borgo Panicale (near Bologna).
Parish church, *Dalmasio, Lippo* —, lost Madonna **455**.

Bormio.
Parish church and priest's house, *Lombard school*, frescoes 266[4].

Boston.
Fine Arts Museum, *Barnaba da Modena*, Madonna from the Langton Douglas coll., London (2) 368 **372**; *Bolognese school*, Nativity (23) 480[2].

Gardner coll., *Giuliano da Rimini*, Madonna and saints, from Urbania **300**, 306, 338[1].

Brescia.
Martinengo Gallery, *Veneziano, Lorenzo* —, four saints (12) 56.

Brianzale (near Lecco).

Budapest.
Castle, *Lombard school*, profane paintings 265, 269.

Gallery, *Master of St Cecily, school of* —, Madonna and saints (41) 350[3]; *Taddeo di Bartolo*, Madonna (29) 382[1].

Campione.
Sta. Maria de' Ghirli, *Lombard school*, scenes from the lives of the Lord and the Baptist 264, 265.

Capua v. S. Angelo-in-Formis.

Carpi.
Sagra church, different frescoes 393.

Carpineta (near Cesena).
Parish church, *Maestro Paolo*, Madonna 6, 12, 15.

Castel S. Pietro (near Como).
Parish church, *Giottesque-Lombard school*, frescoes 220.

Castel Tedaldo (near Ferrara).
Rambaldo, Laudadio —, active 482.

Castelbarco (near Verona).
Battle scenes 181, 210, 269.

Castelnuovo (near Recanati).
Sta. Maria, *Gulielmus*, Madonna **38**.

Caversago (near Como) 221.

Cazzano (near Verona).
S. Felice, *Maestro Cigogna*, frescoes 180; *Giottesque-Veronese school*, Crucifixion 200[1].

Cesena v. Carpineta.

Cesi (Umbria).
Town Hall, *Cavallini, school of* —, Madonna and saints 312[2].

Chantilly (France).
Musée Condé, Codex of the Canzone delle Virtu e delle Scienze 424, 432[1].

Chiaravalle della Colomba (near Alseno di Piacenza).
Abbey church, Crucifixion and saints 508.

Chioggia.
Oratory of S. Martino, *Master of the Pirano altar-piece*, polyptych **19 – 23**.

Cividale.
Tempietto, fresco 104.

Colalto.
Riminese school, frescoes 202, 342—344, 366, 367.

Cologne.
Schnützen Museum, *Cristoforo*, Crucifixion 414.

Wallraf-Richartz Museum, *Giuliano da Rimini, attrib to* —, Passion-scenes (disappeared) 350[3]; *Lorenzetti, school of* —, Madonna 382[1].

Como v. Carvesago, Castel S. Pietro.
S. Abondio, *Giottesque-Lombard school*, frescoes **216**.

Broletto, *Lombard school*, frescoes from **Sta. Margherita**, scenes from the legends of SS. Liberata e Faustina and another fresco 212, 216.
Compiègne (France).
Museum, *Simone dei Crocifissi*, two scenes from the legend of a saint, from the Campana coll. **450**.
Corrubio (near Verona).
S. Martino, *Maestro Cicogna*, frescoes 179.
Cortina d'Ampezzo.
Palazzo del Capitano della Giustizia, *Giotto, school of* —, sibyls 102.
Cracow.
Czatoryski Museum, *Giovanni da Milano, school of* —, Madonna and saints 238[2].
Credolo (near Bologna).
Parish church, *Dalmasio, Lippo* —, lost Madonna 456.
Cremona.
S. Agostino, *Giottesque-Lombard school*, Madonna 218.
Cathedral, *Lombard school*, scenes from the Old Testament 265, 269; *Casella,Polidoro* —, *attrib. to* —, Madonna and donor 218[4].
Crevola d'Ossola.
Sylva Castle, *Pietro, son of Pietro da Novarra*, active 273.
Curzola (Dalmatia).
Concezione, *Veneto-Byzantine school*, polyptych 95.
Ognissanti, *Veneto-Byzantine school*, crucifix **95**; polyptych 95.
Cusighe.
Parish church, *Simone da Cusighe*, lost frescoes 100.
Dalmatia 98.
Darmstadt.
Library, Petrarch codex 126[3], 208.
Dignano (Istria).
Cathedral, *Venetian school*, the Blessed Leo Bembo from S. Sebastiano, Venice 4.
Domodossola.
S. Quirico, *Lombard school*, Madonna and saints 266[4].
Dovera (near Lodi).
Oratorio, *Lombard school*, Annunciation 266[4].
Emilia 355—508.
Edinburgh.
Gallery, *Maestro Paolo, school of* —, St. Catherine (from the Earl of Southesk's coll) 29; *Riminese school*, Adoration and Annunciation (592), 350.
Englewood (U. S. A.)
Platt. coll., *Avanzi, pseudo-Jacopo* —, 5 panels from the Gozzadini coll., Bologna **421**, 424; *Semitecolo, manner of* —, Madonna 122[1].
Fabriano 392.
Gallery, *Marchegian school*, detached frescoes 351.
Faenza 498—504.
S. Francesco, *Ottaviano da Faenza*, active 498.
Old Templars' church, *Pace da Faenza*, lost Madonna 500.
Gallery, *Bittino da Faenza, attrib. to* —, two saints 502; *Pace da Faenza*, (wrongly attrib. to), Madonna, saints and Passion scenes 500; *Simone dei Crocifissi, manner of* —, dead Saviour 451; *Riminese school*, Madonna and saints **279**—**283**, 292, 502[1].
Fano.
S. Domenico, *Riminese school*, frescoes 350.
Fermo v. Torre di Palma.
S. Angelo, *Jacobello di Bonomo, school of* —, Coronation of the Virgin and saints 86, **87**, 432[1].
Gallery, *Venetian school*, Coronation of the Virgin 87; *Andrea da Bologna*, polyptych 428, **430**—**434**.
Ferrara 384, 386, 402, 412, 482—498.
v. Castel Tedaldo.
Gelasio di Niccolo della Masnada dé S. Giorgio, active 482.
Giotto, active 482.
St. Andrea, bell-tower, *Cristoforo* (?), fresco remains 414.
Sta. Caterina, frescoes, v. Gallery.
Cathedral, *Serafini, Serafino* —, active 384.
Corpus Domini monastery, *Ferrarese school*, SS. Francis and Dominic, v. Costabili coll.
S. Domenico, *Ferrarese school*, Madonna, 498.
S. Giorgio, *Ottaviano da Faenza*, active 500.
S Guglielmo, lost frescoes 498.
Martiri church, *Ferrarese school*, detached frescoes, 498.
S. Polinare, lost frescoes 498.

GEOGRAPHICAL INDEX. 519

Gallery, *Alberengo, Jacobello-*(?), sixteen saints (180—183), **84**; *Cristoforo*, Crucifixion and Entombment from the Costabili coll. (23) **413**, 414^1; *Ferrarese school,* Dream of the Virgin (22) 414^1, **496**; Crucifixion (21) 414^1, **498**, both from the Costabilli coll.; detached frescoes. Madonna and Child (5), Coronation of the Virgin (no number) and others (1—4) 498; group of saints, detached fresco from Sta. Caterina (6) **498**.

Costabili coll. (dispersed), *Cristoforo*, Crucifixion and Entombment, v. Gallery; *idem, attrib. to —,* SS. Francis and Dominic from the Corpus Domini monastery 414^1; *Simone dei Crocifissi,* triptych 451^1; *Ferrarese school,* Dream of the Virgin, Crucifixion, v. Gallery.

Castle, courtyard, *Rambaldo, Laudidio—, attrib. to —,* Madonna 482.

Estense Palace, v. University.

University, formerly the Estense Palace, *Ferrarese school,* battle scenes 498.

Fiesole.
Bandini Museum, *Bolognese school,* four panels with scenes from the Life of the Lord 480^1.

Florence 124, 128, 170.
Carmine, *Giovanni da Milano,* polyptych **234**; *idem* (?), fresco of the Madonna and saints in the cloister **234**.

Sta. Caterina convent, *Giovanni da Milano,* Pietà, v. S. Gerolamo, Accademia.

Cathedral, *Giotto,* active 215.

Sta. Croce, *Gaddi, Taddeo—,* frescoes in the Baroncelli chapel 116, 224, 225; *Giovanni da Milano,* lost panel 222; *idem and helpers,* frescoes in the Rinuccini chapel 221, **224—228**, 230, 234, 238^2, 242, 243; *Maso,* frescoes of the S. Silvestro legend 160;

S. Gerolamo, *Giovanni da Milano,* Pietà, v. Sta. Caterina convent and Accademia.

Ognissanti, *Giovanni da Milano,* altar-piece, v. Uffizi.

Accademia, *Giovanni da Milano,* Pietà, from S. Gerolamo and Sta. Caterina 221, **228**, 228^1, 230; triptych **234**, 235, 240.

Horne Museum, *Giovanni da Milano and Andrea da Firenze, follower of —,* SS. Paul and John the Baptist (75, 76) 238^2.

Pitti Palace, portraits of the Scala family, v. Vienna, coll. of the late Archduke Ferdinand of Austria.

Uffizi, *Giovanni da Milano,* altar-piece from the Ognissanti church (32) 222, **230**, 241; *idem, school of —,* two saints (storeroom 4696) 238^2; *Simone dei Crocifissi,* Nativity (disappeared, Old Cat. 260) 451^1.

Acton coll., *Avanzi, pseudo-Jacopo —,* Crucifixion 422; *Giovanni da Milano* (?), Madonna and saints 238^2.

Galletti coll., at Torre del Gallo, *Florentine school,* Madonna 500^1.

de Marquard coll., dispersed, *Giovanni da Milano,* Madonna, (since been for sale in Florence and Rome) 235, 235^1.

Pedulli coll., *Barnaba da Modena,* Madonna 382^1.

For sale in 1924 *Simone dei Crocifissi,* Coronation of the Virgin 450; in 1922 *idem, school of —,* Crucifixion (previously for sale in Rome).

Forli.
Guglielmo da Forli, active 503.

Cathedral, Madonna delle Grazie 504; frescoes in the Chapter Room 504.

S. Domenico, *Guglielmo da Forli,* active 504.

S. Francesco, *Guglielmo da Forli,* active 504; *Pace da Faenza,* lost tree of the Cross and scenes from the lives of the Redeemer and the Virgin 501.

Schiavonia church, *Baldassare, attrib. to —,* frescoes, v. Gallery.

Servi church, frescoes 504.

Gallery, *Baldassare, attrib. to —,* fresco from the Schiavonia church 504.

Fossignano (near Imola).
S. Michele, *Bolognese school,* Madonna 480^1.

Frankfort a. M.
Städelsche Kunstinstitut, *Barnaba da Modena,* Madonna (1)

370, 371, 372; *Lombard school,* seven panels with scenes from the life of St. Stephen (3 A—G) **259—262.**
Friule 100.
Galliano.
S. Vincenzo, crypt, *Lombard school of the 13th and 14th cent.*, frescoes 266[4].
Gemona (Friule).
Cathedral, *Nicolaus*, frescoes on the façade 102; *Venetian school*, miniatures 92.
Hospital, fresco of the Lord on the façade 102.
Genoa.
Barnaba da Modena, present 370.
SS. Cosme e Damiano, *Barnaba da Modena*, Madonna 380.
Palazzo Ducale, *Barnaba da Modena*, active 370
Loggia dei Banchi, *Barnaba da Modena*, active 370.
Germany 16.
Gloucester.
Parry coll., *Riminese school*, Adoration of the Magi **288**, 352.
Grado.
Cathedral, frescoes in the apse 104.
Grosetto.
Cathedral, *Sienese school of the 13th cent.*, Last Judgment 291[1].
Hohenfurth.
Bohemian school, Annunciation 117[1].
Imola v. Fossignano.
S. Domenico, bell-tower, *Bolognese school*, frescoes of the Madonna and saints 480[1].
Incino.
S. Eufemia, *Lombard school*, Madonna, saints and adorers 266[4].
Karlstein, 356, 356[3], 358.
Theodoric of Prague, Crucifixion 364; *Tommaso da Modena*, active 362; Madonna and two saints for a time in the Gallery of Vienna **362**; Madonna and dead Christ 364, 368; *idem and helpers*, panels of saints in the Holy Cross chapel 366; *idem, school of —*, SS. Ambrosius and Augustine 364; *Nicolas Wurmser*, active 364; *German school,* frescoes of St. Wenceslaus' legend and decoration of the Virgin Mary and St. Clare chapels 366.
Kremsmünster.
Library, *Niccolo di Giacomo*, miniatures 410.
Lavagnola (Liguria).
Parish church, *Barnaba da Modena*, polyptych 374.
Lecce.
Museum, *Master of the Pirano altar-piece*, polyptych 19, **23**, 109.
Lentate (Brianza).
Oratory, *Lombard school,* frescoes 220, 242, 248, **250**, 255, 264, 271, 274.
Lichtenberg (Tyrol).
Castle, frescoes 162.
Liguria 384.
Lodi v. Dovera.
S. Francesco, *Lombard school*, different frescoes 211,212,255,266[4]; *idem,* cycle of frescoes from the life of a holy bishop, 220.
Lodi Vecchio.
S. Bassiano, *Lombard school,* frescoes **211**, 264*a*, 269
Lombardy 209—272, 397, 476.
London.
National Gallery, *Barnaba da Modena*, Coronation of the Virgin and other scenes (2927) **375**, 378, 379; Descent of the Holy Ghost (1437) **378**; *Dalmasio, Lippo*—, Madonna of Humility (742) **458**; *Giovanni da Milano*, three panels (579*a*) **232**; *Giusto di Menabuoi*, triptych (701) 163, **164**, 174, 175; *Veneto-Byzantine school,* St. Jerome (3543) 39.
Victoria and Albert Museum, *Bolognese school*, diptych with scenes from the history of Christ (351—1864) 480[1]; painted box 479[2]; two gilt glasses 480[1].
Chillingworth coll. (dispersed), *Jacopo di Paolo*, Crucifixion 468.
R. Fry coll., *Giovanni da Milano,* part of an altar-piece 238[2].
R. Langton Douglas coll., *Barnaba da Modena*, Madonna, v. Boston, Fine Arts Museum; *Simone dei Crocifissi*, Coronation of the Madonna, from the Gozzadini coll., Bologna 451[1].
Lucerne.
Sale of Chillingworth coll., v. London, Chillingworth coll.

GEOGRAPHICAL INDEX.

Macerata.
S. Francesco Monastery, *Baronzio*, altar-piece, v. Gallery of Urbino.

Manchester.
Exhibition of 1857, *Barnaba da Modena*, Coronation of the Virgin, v. National Gallery.

Mantua.
S. Francesco, *Lombard school*, frescoes from the life of St. Francis 265; Gallery, detached frescoes 266[4]; Palazzo Ducale, *Lombard school*, saints (attrib. to *Tommaso da Modena*) 266[4], 367[1].

Marches, The — 109, 416, 428, 432, 434, 436, 458, 480.

Sta. Maria in Vescovis.
Roman school of the 13th. cent., Last Judgment 483, 484.

San Marino.
S. Francesco, *Riminese school*, Adoration of the Magi 350.

Mercatello.
S. Francesco, *Baronzio*, crucifix, 314, 328; *idem, school of* — polyptych 328.

Milan v. Vilboldone.
Giotto and Stefano, active 268.
Chiaravalle, Abbey church, *Lombard school*, frescoes 254.
S. Cristoforo on the Naviglio (near Milan), *Bassanolo de Magneris*, Madonna, saints and Crucifixion 258.
S. Eusturgio, crucifix of the end of the 13th cent. 214.
S. Giorgio in Palazzo, *Lombard school*, Crucifixion 266.
S. Lorenzo, *Lombard school*, Madonna and saints 266.
S. Marco, tower, *Lombard school*, frescoes 214, 217.
Sta. Maria delle Grazie, *Lombard school*, frescoes 266[4].
S. Maurilio, Missal, v. Vatican Library.
Monastero Maggiore, *Lombard school*, frescoes 214.
S. Pietro Celestino, *Lombard school*, fresco fragments 266[4].
Servi Monastery, *Simone da Corbetta*, fresco, v. Brera Gallery.
S. Siro, *Lombard school*, fresco 266[4].

Brera Gallery, *Giovanni da Bologna*, Madonna of Humility 80; *Maestro Paolo*, Coronation of the Virgin (227) **7**, 12, 68; *Simone da Corbetta*, fresco from the Servi Monastery (138) 255, **257**; *idem, attrib. to*—, fresco of the Madonna, St. Christopher and other figures (store-room) 258; *Veneto-Byzantine school*, head of St. Mark 35.
Archeological Museum. *Lombard school*, St. Helen (?) (34) 266[4]; miniature 272.
Ambrosiana Library, *Niccolo di Giacomo*, miniatures 424; *Lombard miniatures* in a Visconti Missal 270; *idem*, in a St. George Codex 270; *Lombard school*, drawings illustrating the Life of Christ 270.
Capitular Library, *Lombard school*, miniatures 270.
Archiepiscopal Palace, *Giottesque-Lombard school*, frescoes 216.
Visconti Palace, *Giotto*, active 214, 215; lost frescoes of the Punic wars and heroes 215.
Fasi coll. (dispersed) *Giusto di Menabuoi*, Madonna 163.

Mineapolis, U. S. A.
Museum, *Baronzio, school of* —, St. Francis receives the stigmata 350.

Mocchirolo (Brianza).
Oratory, *Lombard school*, frescoes 220, 242, **246—250**, 255, 261, 264, 271, 274.

Modena 355, 356, 370, 384, 386, 393, 412; *Niccolo*, active 505.
Cathedral, *Serafini, Serafino* —, polyptych **386**; fresco remains of the 13th and 14th cent. 392; *Modenese school*, two frescoes, v. Gallery.
Gallery, *Barnaba da Modena*, Madonna and Crucifixion from the Puccini coll., Pistoia **378**, 379; *Fra Paolo*, Madonna of Humility 391; *Simone dei Crocifissi*, Madonna and angels 451[1]; *Tommaso da Modena*, Madonna saints and Descent into Lymbo 366, 368; *Modenese school*, two detached frescoes from the cathedral 392; Madonna and Child, triptych 13. predella panel (44) 392[4].
Library, *Niccolo di Giacomo*, miniatures 410.
Bergolli coll. (dispersed), *Giovanni da Milano*, Madonna 238[2]

Monza.
S. Michele, *Giottesque-Lombard school*, praying saints 217.

Munich.
Ältere Pinakothek, *Riminese school*, diptych (979, 980) **284**.
Library, *Giovanni di Benedetto*, miniatures **270**; *Niccolo di Giacomo*, miniatures **412**; *Bolognese school*, miniatures **438**.

Murano.
S. Donato, *Maestro Paolo, school of* —, Death of the Virgin 29; *Venetian school*, relief of S. Donato **2**.

Nancy (France).
Museum, *Simone dei Crocifissi*, Crucifixion and scenes from the lives of holy martyrs **442**.

Naples.
Sta. Maria di Donna Regina, *Cavallini, school of* —, frescoes 298, 304[1], 352.

Newhaven (U. S. A.).
Yale University, Jarves coll., *Riminese school*, triptych **298**.

New York.
Metropolitan Museum, *Baronzio, school of* —, panel with scenes from the Life of the Lord **341**, 351; *Giovanni da Milano, school of* —, Madonna and adorers 238[2].
Historical Society, *Giovanni da Milano, school of* —, Crucifixion from the Artaud de Montor coll., Paris 238[2], 272[1]; *Venetian school*, Crucifixion 72[1].
Lehman coll., *Riminese school*, the Last Judgment and other scenes **288**; the beheading of the Baptist 298.

Novara.
Guerina coll., *Cristoforo*, Madonna 413.

Orez.
Simone da Cusighe, lost altarpiece 100[3].

Padua 110—178, 243, 368, 416, 426, 474, 476, 480.
Altichiero, active 126, 127; *Avanzo*, active 127; *Bertolino del quondam Jacopo di Brescia*, active 178[1].

S. Agostino, *Guariento*, active 112.
S. Antonio, *Altichiero*, frescoes in the S. Felice chapel 124, **128—149**, 128[1], 136, 160, 184[1]; *idem, follower of* —, Madonna and saints 152; fresco on the Lavelongo tomb 126, 152; frescoes on the Bolfaro and Bolzanello tomb in the cloister 152; *Giusto di Menabuoi(?)*, frescoes in the Bl. Luca Belludi chapel 163, 170, 174; *Paduan school*, Madonna 178; two damaged frescoes in the choir 178; five figures of saints in grisaille in a chapel in the cloister 178.
Arena chapel, *Giotto*, frescoes 16, 90, 110, 224, 342, 351, 352, 483. *Giusto di Menabuoi*, two Madonnas **172**.
Baptistery, *Antonio and Giovanni da Padua*, lost fresco 163; *Giusto di Menabuoi*, frescoes and altarpiece 163, 164, **166—170**, 172, 174, 175; lost frescoes outside 164.
Eremitani church, *Altichiero*, fresco on Dotto's tomb 150, 154; *idem, school of* —, fresco fragments 154; *Giusto di Menabuoi*, lost frescoes in the St. Augustine chapel 163, 166, 172, 178[1]; *Guariento and helpers*, frescoes in the choir **112**; *idem, school of* —, crucifix 117; Coronation of the Virgin and fresco-fragments 117; *Marino*, lost altar-piece in the St. Augustine chapel 178[1].
S. Francesco, *Brasavola, Donato* —, attrib. to —, St. Antony of Padua 482.
S. Giorgio chapel, *Altichiero and Avanzo*, frescoes 119, 124, 128[1], 135, **135—150**, 150, 161, 162, 176[1], 206.
Madonna di Lourdes, v. S. Michele.
S. Michele, *Jacopo da Verona*, frescoes 127, **176**.

Museum, *Altichiero, school of* —, Coronation of the Virgin **154**; head of a saint 154; *Giovanni da Bologna*, St. Christopher, from the Scuola dei Mercanti, Venice (348) 64, **78**; *Guariento*, ceiling decoration from the chapel of the Palazzo of the Capitano del Popolo **112**, 128; *Veneziano, Lorenzo* —, Madonna (383) 39, 51, 66[2]; *Paduan school*, drawn portraits in the "Liber de principibus Carrariensibus" 208.
Chapter House Library, *Semi-*

GEOGRAPHICAL INDEX.   523

tecolo, the Holy Trinity, Madonna and four scenes from the life of St. Sebastian, **120**.

University Library, *Altichiero(?),* Petrarch, from the Palazzo del Capitano del Popolo 152, 208.

Salone, *Guariento, school of* —, Coronation of the Virgin 117.

Palazzo del Capitano del Popolo, *Avanzo, Altichiero and Guariento,* active 111, 127, 128[1]; v. Museum, and University Library.

Carrara Palace, *Avanzo and Altichiero,* active 126, 152; *Guariento,* active 208.

Louvre, *Master of the Pirano altar-piece,* Madonna (1541) 19, **23**, 56[1], 66; *Veneziano, Lorenzo* —, Madonna (no number) 40, 56;

Bibliothèque Nationale, *Giovanni di Benedetto, manner of* —, miniatures 272; *Lombardian school,* miniatures 270.

Artaud de Montor coll. (dispersed), *Giovanni da Milano (?),* Madonna 238[2]; *idem, school of* —, Crucifixion, v. New York, Historical Society.

Lazzaroni coll., *Jacobello Alberenzo, attrib. to* —, Presentation in the Temple 85.

Martin Le Roy coll. (late), *Giovanni da Milano,* Pietà 238[2].

Parma 504—507.

Cathedral, frescoes of the early 15th cent. 506;

Baptistery, *Bertolino da Piacenza,* Virgin and saints 505; *Niccolo da Reggio,* Madonna and saints 505; frescoes of the 13th century 504; frescoes of the 14th century 504—506.

Gallery, *Giovanni da Milano, school of* —, two panels each with four saints (427, 428) 238[2]; *Veneto-Byzantine school,* triptych (458) 38.

Pasman, Isle of —. (**Dalmatia**).

Abbey of Teon, *Venetian school,* crucifix 94.

Pausola.

Town Hall, *Andrea da Bologna,* Madonna, from S. Agostino 428, **432**, 434, 436.

Pavia 418.

Perugia.

Gallery, *Riminese school,* Ascension of Mary Magdalene (68) **284—288**, 292, 294.

van Marle coll., *Maestro Paolo, school of* —, Coronation of the Virgin **29**; *Simone dei Crocifissi,* Crucifixion **448**.

Pesaro.

S Francesco, *Jacobello di Bonomo, school of* —, altar-piece from S. Ubaldo, v. Gallery.

Gallery *Jacobello di Bonomo, school of* —, altar-piece from S Francesco and S. Ubaldo 86, 87; *Jacopo di Paolo,* two saints 466; *Veneziano, Lorenzo* —, St. Ambrosius 54, 408[1]; *Simone dei Crocifissi,* Coronation of the Virgin **450**, 451; *Veneto-Byzantine school,* five scenes from the life of the Virgin 38.

Petrograd

Exhibition of Old Art, *Daddi, Bernardo*—, *school of* —, Madonna 367[1].

Philadelphia.

Johnson coll., *Andrea da Bologna, attrib. to* —, triptych (is it the same as the one that I attrib. later on to the school of Giovanni da Milano?) 432[1]; *Giovanni da Milano,* angel delivering St. Peter from prison 238[2]; *idem, school of* —, triptych (120) 238[2]; *Tommaso da Modena,* (wrongly attrib. to), diptych 367[1].

Piacenza 507.

S. Antonino, lost frescoes from the life of St. Antonino 507.

Cathedral, *Bartolino da Piacenza,* Madonna and saints 507 some other frescoes 507

Museum, *Bertolino da Piacenza (?),* two saints on a reliquary 507.

Piedmont 272—78, 384.

Piobese Torinese.

Piedmontese school, 274, 276, 277.

Piove di Sacco.

Parish church (previously Sta. Maria dei Penitenti), *Maestro Paolo, school of*—, polyptych 5, 17, 21, 23.

S. Niccolo, *Gulielmus,* Madonna 38.

Pirano Istria.

Cathedral, *Master of the Pirano altar-piece,* altar-piece 19, 23, 25.

Pisa 370. (**v. Ripoli**).

S. Francesco, *Barnaba da*

Modena, lost Coronation of the Virgin 380; Madonna, v. Gallery.
    S. Giovanni dei Fieri, *Barnaba da Modena,* Madonna, v. Campo Santo and Gallery.
    Campo Santo, *Barnaba da Modena,* Madonna from S. Giovanni dei Fieri, v. Gallery; *Master of the triumph of Death (Traini),* frescoes 382¹ and corrections.
    Gallery, *Barnaba da Modena,* Madonna from S. Francesco **380**; Madonna from S. Giovanni dei Fieri and the Campo Santo **380**; *Giovanni da Milano,* Annunciation 238; *Pisan school,* Crucifixion 382¹ and corrections.
    Schiff coll., *Barnaba da Modena,* Madonna 372.
Pistoia.
    Dalmasio and *Dalmasio, Lippo—,* active 453.
    Town Hall, *Dalmasio, Lippo —,* Madonna 463.
    Puccini coll., *Barnaba da Modena,* Madonna and Crucifixion, v. Modena, Gallery.
Poitiers.
    Museum, *Maestro Paolo, school of* —, Madonna and saints (186, 187) 29.
Pomposa.
    Abbey church 300, 344¹; *Giuliano da Rimini,* frescoes in the refectory 300—306, 308, 309, 310 312, 344¹, 494; *Vitale da Bologna,* frescoes on the entrance wall and in the apse 402, 484, 490; *Ferrarese school,* frescoes in the nave 468, **483**—**490**, 498; entrance wall **483**; apse 490; *Riminese school,* frescoes in the chapter-room 300, **344**, 483.
Pontasso (near Voghera).
    Oratory of Sta. Maria, *early Lombard school,* frescoes 214.
Prague.
    Cathedral, *Tommaso da Modena* and *Theodoric of Prague,* attrib. to —, frescoes 366.
    Museum, *Bohemian school,* Annunciation 117¹.
Prato.
    S. Domenico, *Giovanni da Milano, school of —,* Madonna and saints 238².
    Gallery, *Giovanni da Milano,* polyptych 222, **228**, 234, 241.

Princetown (U. S. A.).
    Mather coll., *Veneziano, Lorenzo —,* Madonna and Crucifixion, v. additions.
Ranoerso.
    S. Antonio, *Piedmontese school,* frescoes 276, 277.
Ravenno.
    Bestello da Forli, active 503.
    S. Agata, *Riminese school,* Madonna in the choir 349.
    Sta. Chiara, v. Poor-House chapel.
    S. Domenico, tower, *Riminese school,* fresco fragments 349.
    S. Francesco, *Baronzio,* Crucifixion **326**, 338; *Riminese school,* frescoes 348.
    S. Giovanni Evangelista, *Riminese school,* fresco 348.
    Sta. Maria in Porto fuori, *Baronzio and helpers,* frescoes 312², **316**—**324**, 325, 328, 330, 333, 338, 339; frescoes in the apse 320; *Byzantine* relief of the Madonna 316.
    Poor-House chapel, *Baronzio,* frescoes **324**.
    Gallery, *Dalmasio, Lippo —, school of —,* Annunciation 462¹; *Riminese school,* Madonna and saints 349; *Veneto-Byzantine school,* Crucifixion and Holy Trinity 35.
    Maestro Paolo, Coronation of the Virgin v. Sigmaringen.
Recanati v. Castelnuovo.
Rieti.
    Gallery, *Zanino di Pietro,* Crucifixion 70, 71.
    Potenziani coll., *Simone dei Crocifissi,* Madonna della Misericordia 450.
Rimini 279—354, 383, 402, 420. v. Veruchio, Villa.
    Ambrogio, son of Bittino, active 502; *Bittino da Faenza* active 501; *Giotto,* activity and influence 351, 353; *Lattanzio da Rimini,* active 502.
    S. Agostino, *Giuliano da Rimini,* frescoes **306**—**310**, 312; *Riminese school,* crucifix 348;
    S. Antonio 348.
    S. Francesco, *Riminese school,* Madonna, saints and adorer 348; tomb of *Francesco da Rimini* 346; epitaph of the sons of *Baronzio* 314¹.

GEOGRAPHICAL INDEX. 525

S. Giugliano, *Bittino da Faenza*, St. Julian panel 501, **502**.
Tempio Malatesta, *Riminese school*, crucifix 348.
Casa Romagnoli, *Riminese school*, lost fresco 348.
Hotel Aquila d'Oro, *Riminese school*, lost fresco 348.
Ripoli (near Pisa).
Barnaba da Modena, lost Madonna 380.
Rivoli.
S. Domenico, *Barnaba da Modena*, Madonna, v. Turin, Gallery.
Castle, profane paintings 273.
Romagna 397.
Rome 356, 397.
St. Peter's, Chapter Room Archives, Codex of St. George 397.
Vatican, *Giovanni da Milano*, active 222, *Guarnerius de Venitiis*, active 109¹.
National Gallery, v. Palazzo Venezia; *Giovanni da Milano*, Madonna and seven other representations **237**; *Nardo di Cione*, Coronation of the Virgin 238²; *Riminese school*, panel with six scenes from the Life of the Lord **279**, 342, 352; another similar panel from the Herz and Stroganoff colls. **283**, 292, 352; *Veneto-Byzantine school*, two saints **35**.
Print Cabinet, *Paduan school of the early 15th cent.*, sketches of Giusto di Menabuoi's frescoes in the Eremitani church, Padua 172, 208.
Museum in the Palazzo Venezia. The early pictures in the National Gallery (v. National Gallery) were all to have been transferred to the Museum in the Palazzo Venezia, where several of them were already exposed, when this museum, shortly after its opening, was closed.
Colonna Gallery, *Avanzi, Jacopo* —, Crucifixion **416**, 418, 420, 424, 426.
Vatican Gallery, *Andrea da Bologna, attrib. to* —, Nativity (172) 432¹; *Avanzi, pseudo-Jacopo* —, the Death of St. Francis (100) **420**, 424; *Giovanni da Milano*, triptych with the Crucifixion and Passion scenes (62), three scenes from the Life of Christ (93, 94, 95), Ascension (79), Nativity of the Virgin (67), Crucifixion (66) 238²; *Maestro Paolo, school of* —, two Evangelists (store-room 163, 164), polyptych (idem 122) 29²; *Simone dei Crocifissi*, two lost Coronations of the Virgin and a lost Madonna 451¹; *Vitale*, Madonna (103) **402**, 403, 406; *Bolognese school*, Crucifixion and other scenes from the Lord's history (15) 480¹; *Florentine school*, polyptych (6) 422³; *Riminese school*, Crucifixion and saints (54) **294**; Descent from the Cross (56) **294**; Crucifixion (52) **295**; four saints (44) **296**; Crucifixion and other scenes (42) **296**, 353; religious subject (store-room 132) 288.
Vatican Library, *Lombard* miniatures in a Missal from S. Maurilio, Milan 270.
Capperoni coll., *Bolognese school*, Crucifixion 480¹.
Herz coll. (dispersed), *Riminese school*, panel with six scenes from the Life of the Lord, from the Stroganoff coll., v. National Gallery.
Pasini coll., *Barnaba da Modena*, Ascension, from the Sterbini coll. **378**; *Ferrarese school*, Crucifixion **497**; *Riminese school*, Baptism of Christ, from the Sterbini coll. **288**.
Sterbini coll. (dispersed), *Barnaba da Modena*, Ascension, v. Pasini coll.; *Bolognese school*, Calvary 480¹; *Riminese school*, Baptism of the Lord, v. Pasini coll.
Stroganoff coll. (dispersed), *Riminese school*, panel with six scenes from the Life of the Lord, v. Herz. coll. and National Gallery.
Tavazzi coll. (for sale), *Vitale, attrib. to* —, Death of the Virgin 406².
For sale, in 1909, *Simone dei Crocifissi, manner of* —, triptych 451¹; *Dalmasio, Lippo* —, Madonna 462¹; in 1918 *Simone dei Crocifissi, school of* —, Crucifixion 451¹; in 1920 *Giovanni da Milano*, Madonna, v. Florence, de Marquard coll. 235¹; in 1923 *Maestro Paolo, school of* —, four half-length figures of saints 29²; in 1924 *Vitale, school of* —, Madonna 480¹; *Riminese school*, crucifix 350.
Rotterdam.
Booymans Museum, *Giovanni*

da Bologna, Pietà (179) 82, 83.
Rovigo.
Library, *Paduan school*, miniatures 206.
Runkelstein (Tyrol).
Castle, frescoes 162.
Sala.
Simone da Cusighe, lost altarpiece 100³.
Sandigliano (region of Biella).
S. Antonio, *Piedmontese school,* frescoes 276, 277.
Savona.
Gallery, *Niccolo da Voltri,* Madonna 382.
Sebenico (Dalmatia).
Polyptych of the 15th cent. 96;
S. Francesco Monastery, *Venetian school*, miniatures 92.
Sesto (Friule).
Abbey, *Giotto, school of* —, Crucifixion and other scenes, 102.
S. Severino (The Marches).
Gallery, *Veneziano, Lorenzo* —, polyptych panels (5) 42, 43, 46.
Siena 124, 160, 466².
Accademia, *Lorenzetti, Pietro* —, SS. Agnes and Catherine of Alexandria (578, 579), 50.
Sigmaringen.
Gallery, *Maestro Paolo,* Coronation of the Virgin, from Ravenna 7, 9, **12**.
Sirmioni.
S. Pietro in Movino, *Lombard school,* fresco 266⁴.
Solario.
Oratory, *Lombard school,* frescoes 246.
Susa.
S. Francesco (in the Valley of) *Piedmontese school,* frescoes 276, 277.
Castle, profane paintings 273.
Strasbourg.
Gallery, *Baronzio, school of* —, Crucifixion **340**, 497; *Giovanni da Milano,* Madonna, **234**; *Lombard school,* Nativity of the Virgin 262.
Stuttgart.
Gallery, *Maestro Paolo,* allegorical picture 7, 14.
Talamello.
Parish church, *Baronzio school of* —, crucifix 340.
Tiers (Tyrol).
Sta. Caterina, *Lombard school,* frescoes from the life of St. Catherine 262.
Tolentino.
St. Nicholas chapel, *Baronzio, follower of* —, frescoes **328—338**, 351, 352, 353.
Torcello.
Cathedral, mosaic of the Last Judgment 483.
Torre di Palma (near Fermo).
Sta Maria a Mare, *Venetian school,* Madonna and saints **90**.
Tortona (Piedmont).
S. Matteo, *Barnaba da Modena,* Madonna **372**.
Toulouse.
Museum, *Master of the Pirano altar-piece,* lost polyptych wings 23.
Tregnano (near Verona).
Pieve, *Veronese school,* frescoes 200¹.
Trento.
Cathedral, frescoes of the history of St. Julian **105**; some other frescoes 105.
Castle of Buon Consiglio, frescoes of the 15th century 104.
Treviso 110, 202—206, 368.
Cathedral, *Tommaso da Modena, school of* —, Crucifixion and two other frescoes 362.
S. Francesco, *Tommaso da Modena, attrib. to* —, Madonna and saints and St Marius 362.
Sta. Maria Maggiore, *Tommaso da Modena, school of* —, Madonna 362.
Sta. Margherita, frescoes of St. Ursula's legend, v. Museum.
S. Niccolo, *Tommaso da Modena and followers,* frescoes **360**, 368; frescoes in the Chapter Room 100, 198, 356, **358**, 368.
Museum, *Trevisan master,* frescoes from the legend of St. Ursula, from Sta. Margherita **202—206**, 269, 367.
Trezzo (Brianza).
Parish church, tower, *Lombard school,* fresco fragment 252.
Trieste 48, 109.
Cathedral, *Simone Martini, distant follower of* —, frescoes of the history of St. Justus 98.
Museum, *Maestro Paolo,* school of —, triptych **25**, 98.
Troyes (France).
Museum, *Simone dei Crocifissi,*

GEOGRAPHICAL INDEX.

Coronation of the Virgin, from the Campana coll. (269) **448**.
Turin.
Guido, active 273; *Jaquerio, Pietro* —, active 273.
S. Domenico, *Arconerio, Giacomo* —, active 273, *Piedmontese school*, frescoes 273, 274, 277.
S. Francesco di Chieri, *Jaquerio, Giovanni*—, lost painting 273.
Gallery, *Barnaba da Modena*, Madonna from S. Domenico, Rivoli 370, **374**.
Museo Civico, *Bolognese school*, gilt glass 480[1].
Town Hall, *Turineto*, active 273.
Castle, lost profane paintings 273.
Udine.
Nicolaus, mentioned 102[4].
Sta. Maria delle Grazie, frescoes 104.
Gallery, detached frescoes 104.
Umbria 396, 397, 400.
Urbania.
Confraternity of S. Giovanni Decollato, *Pietro da Rimini*, crucifix 338, 338[1].
Giuliano da Rimini, Madonna and saints, v. Boston, Gardner coll.
Urbino.
Gallery, *Baronzio*, altar-piece from the S. Francesco Monastery, Macerata **314**, 328, 340, 353[1], 496; *idem, attrib. to* —, crucifix 340, 348; *idem, school of* —, crucifix **340**, 340[1], 348; *Giuliano da Rimini*, Coronation of the Virgin and saints **300**, 306; *Pietro da Rimini, attrib. to* —, crucifix 340, 348; *Riminese school*, half of a diptych **284**.
Varese.
Albizzate Abbey (near Varese), *Lombard school*, frescoes 266.
Baptistery, *Giottesque-Lombard school*, Madonna and the Baptist 212; Madonna and two devotees 212; *Lombard school*, Madonna and saints 266[4].
Velo d'Astico.
S. Giorgio, *Battista da Vicenza*, polyptych 106; *idem*, (wrongly attrib. to), frescoes 108.
Venice 1—109, 119, 160, 364[3], 387.

Churches, Monasteries etc.
St. Agnese 66; *Donato and Caterino*, active 59, 60; painted box of the 13th cent. 2.
S. Alvise Monastery, *Stefano plebanus*, lost picture 66.
S. Antonio al Castello, *Veneziano, Lorenzo* —, polyptych, v. Accademia, Venice.
SS. Apostoli, frescoes 2.
Centurioni chapel, *Semitecolo*, lost panels 120.
Corpus Domini, *Caterino*, panel, v. Lichtenstein coll., Vienna.
Sta. Croce, *Francesco*, active 2.
S. Francesco alla Vigna, *Giovanni da Bologna, manner of* —, panel, v. Accademia, Venice; *Maestro Paolo, school of* —, Madonna 29.
Frari church 17[3]; *Maestro Paolo and his brother, Marco*, active 5.
S. Giorgio Maggiore, *Caterino*, lost polyptych 59, 60.
SS. Giovanni e Paolo, mosaic **72**.
S. Gregorio, *Giovanni da Bologna, manner of* —, Madonna, v. Accademia, Venice.
Lucchesi Oratory, *Semitecolo*, (wrongly attrib. to), frescoes 122[1].
S. Marco, *Maestro Paolo and his sons Luca and Giovanni*, Pala d'Oro 5, 9, **10**, 16, 123; Chapter Room, crucifix 2; S. Isidore chapel, mosaics 32—33.
San Marco, Baptistery, mosaics 2, **32**, 33.
Sta. Maria della Celestina Monastery, *Veneziano, Lorenzo* —, polyptych, v. Accademia, Venice.
Sta. Maria dei Miracoli, *Niccolo di Pietro*, fragment of a triptych 76.
Sta. Maria della Salute, *Maestro Paolo, school of* —, panel 5, **17**—**19**, 21.
Sta. Maria dei Servi 120.
S. Samuele, *Maestro Paolo, school of* —, Saviour 29.
S. Sebastiano, panel of the Blessed Leo Bembo, v. Cathedral, Dignano (Istria).
S. Silvestro, sacristy, *Maestro Paolo, school of* —, polyptych 29.
S. Trovaro, sacristy, *Maestro Paolo, school of* —, Madonna in prayer 29.
S. Zaccaria, *Veneziano, Lorenzo* —, *attrib. to* —, Madonna 56.

Public Collections.
Accademia, *Alberengo, Jacobello* —, Crucifixion (25) 84, 85; *Caterino*, Coronation of the Virgin (16) 59, 59[1], 62; triptych (702) **62**; *idem, manner of* —, Coronation of the Virgin (23) **64**; four scenes from the Life of the Saviour (4) **65—66**; *Jacobello di Bonomo*, polyptych from S. Arcangelo di Romagna (recent acquisition) 86, 87; *idem, school of* —, Adoration of the Magi (12) 89[1]; *Giovanni da Bologna*, Madonna of Humility, saints and members of a confraternity (17) 78, **80**; *idem, manner of* —, Madonna from S. Francesco alla Vigna or S. Gregorio (14) **82—84**, 90; *Niccolo di Pietro*, Madonna (19) **74**, 77; *idem*, (wrongly attrib. to), St. Lawrence (20) 77[1]; Maestro Paolo, panels belonging to the Coronation in the Brera, Milan (21) **9**, 16; *idem, school of* —, Madonna and saints (6) 29[1]; *Semitecolo*, false signature on panel of 1351 (23) 120; *Simone da Cusighe*, polyptych from the Pagani family and S. Bartolommeo in Salce, Belluno (18) **100**; *Stefanus plebanus*, Coronation of the Virgin (21) 67; *Veneziano, Lorenzo* —, SS. Pietro and Mark from the Ufficio della Zecca or della Seta (5 and 5a) 40, **53**; Annunciation and saints from the Scuola di S. Giovanni Evangelista (9) 40, **54**; Annunciation altar-piece (10), 39, 42, **46**, 50, 63; altar-piece from the Imperial Museum, Vienna, originally in the Sta. Maria della Celestina monastery (41) **50**, 52; mystical marriage of St. Catherine (650) 39, **50**, 52; *German school*, 15th cent., St. Catherine, with the false signature of Tommaso da Modena (not exhibited) 371[1]; *Giottesque-Venetian school*, altar-piece (2) 68, 85; *Riminese-school*, panel with scenes from the Life of the Lord (26), **284**, 352.
Correr Museum, *Caterino and Bartolomeo di M. Paolo*, wooden relief 60; *Cortese, Cristoforo* —, miniatures 91, 94; *Maestro Paolo, school of* —, 2 panels 29; *Stefano plebanus*, false signature on Madonna (XV, 21) 66; *Veneto, Niccolo* —, panel of 1371 120; *Veneziano, Lorenzo* —, the Saviour giving the keys to St. Peter 39, 52; *idem, school of* —, six saints (II, 6) 58[1]; St. Peter with a devotee and St. John the Baptist (II, 9) 58[1]; panel with four scenes (VII, 2) 58[1]; four saints (VII 15 and 22) 57[1], 58[1]; *Zanino di Pietro*, Crucifixion (3) **70**; *Venetian school*, dead Saviour between the Virgin and St. John 68; Coronation of the Virgin (VII, 16) 70; miniatures of 1311—1312 92; *Veneto-Byzantine school*, SS. John and Andrew (7 and 8) **34**; Crucifixion (10) 35; miniatures 91.

Querini-Stampalia Gallery, *Caterino and Donato*, Coronation of the Virgin, 59, **60**, 64.

Public Buildings.
Badoer Hospital, Virgin Orante, v. Scuola di S. Giovanni Evangelista Collegio dei Mercanti; *Giovanni da Bologna*, St. Christopher, v Museum, Padua.
Marciana Library, *Venetian school*, miniatures in antiphonary of Sta. Maria della Carita 92.
Palace of the Doges, *Guariento*, Coronation of the Virgin 110, 116, 120, 161; *Maestro Paolo*, active in the chapel of S. Niccolo 5.
Scuola di S. Giovanni Evangelista,*Veneziano, Lorenzo* —, polyptych, v. Accademia, Venice; in a room over the sacristy, Virgin Orante from the Badoer Hospital 2.
Scuola della Nunziata dei Servi, lost panel of the Saviour and the Virgin 4.
State Archives, *Venetian school*, miniatures 92.
Ufficio della Zecca or della Seta, *Veneziano, Lorenzo* —, SS. Peter and Mark, v. Accademia, Venice.
Ventimiglia.
Cathedral, *Barnaba da Modena*, Madonna 380.
Venzone.
S. Antonio Abbate 104[1].
Cathedral, fresco of the consecration **102**; other representations 104; lost frescoes 104[1].
Sta. Lucia, lost frescoes 104[1].
S. Giacomo, fresco 104, 109.

Vercelli.
S. Andrea, *Piedmontese school*, fresco 273, 277.

Verona 109, 110, 118, 124, 125, 127[5], 152, 160, 178—202, 243, 267, 368, 392, 474, 476, 480. v. **Castelbarco Cazzano, Corrubio, Tregnano.**
Altichiero, active 126, 127; *Avanzo*, active 126; *Giotto*, active 188; *Turone*, lost panel 184.

Churches, Monasteries etc.
St. Agnese, *Veronese school*, lost frescoes 194.
St. Anastasia, *Altichiero*, fresco in Cavalli chapel 127, **150**, 255; *idem, school of —*, St. Eligio in Cavalli chapel 158; *idem*, (late), fresco on the Bevilaqua tomb **158**, 200; *Boninsegna de Clocega*, effaced signature in Salerna chapel 179; *Veronese school*, frescoes 191—193, **198**; fresco in choir 200; fresco on outside wall 200; in Cavalli chapel 184, **191**, 198, 200; in Pellegrini chapel 200; in Rosario chapel 181; in Salerna chapel 179[3], 193.
Baptistery. *Veronese school*, frescoes 200[1].
Sta. Catherina, *Giottesque-Veronese school*, mystical marriage of St. Catherine, v. Gallery; panel with scenes from the Old Testament, v. Gallery.
St. Eufemia, *Veronese school*, fresco of a bishop 200[1]; other frescoes, v. Gallery.
Sta. Felicita, *Altichiero, school of —*, fresco fragments, v. Gallery.
S. Fermo, *Altichiero, school of —*, Crucifixion **155**; *Martino da Verona*, Crucifixion and other frescoes **198**; *Turone*, Crucifixion **185**; *Veronese school*, frescoes 180—181, 193—194, Madonna and other figures 200[1]; saints 200[1].
S. Francesco, *Giotto*, active 188.
S. Giovanni in Valle, *Veronese school*, frescoes in church and crypt 200[1].
Sta. Maria Antiqua, *Veronese school*, Madonna and devotees 181.
Sta. Maria della Scala, *Veronese school*, two Madonnas 200.
SS. Nazaro e Celso, *Giottesque-Veronese school*, repainted crucifix 197.
Padri del Oratorio, *Daniel*, lost altar-piece 179[1].
S. Pier di Castello, *Niccolo di Pietro*, lost panel 76, 179[2].
S. Pietro Martire, *Veronese school*, lost frescoes 194.
S. Silvestro, *Giottesque-Veronese school*, crucifix, v. Gallery.
SS. Siro e Libera, *Veronese school*, Saviour in benediction 200[1].
S. Stefano, *Altichiero, school of —*, fresco 156; *Giacomo da Riva*, Madonna 197; *idem, attrib. to —*, Madonna and saints 197.
Sta. Trinita, *Altichiero, school of —*, Crucifixion in the cloister, v. Gallery; *Turone*, altar-piece, v. Gallery.
S. Zeno, *Altichiero, school of —*, fresco 155; *Giacomo da Riva*, *attrib. to —*, Madonna 197; *Guariento, school of —*, crucifix **118**; *Giottesque-Veronese school*, Madonna della Misericordia **189**; Tobias and the angel **189**; St. Sigismund **189**; *Veronese school*, Crucifixion in the apse 188—189; votive Madonna **188**; St. George slaying the dragon, St George between two bishops and devotees and the Crucifixion **190**; profane paintings in the tower 190—191.

Public and Private Collections.
Gallery, *Altichiero, school of —*, Crucifixion from the cloister of Sta. Trinita (513) **154**; fresco fragments from Sta. Felicita (519—38) **154**; *Maestro Cigogna*, fresco from the Palazzo Comunale, Verona (1090) 180; *Martino da Verona, attrib. to —*, Madonna and saints 198[2]; *Turone*, altar-piece from Sta. Trinita (355) **181**; *Giottesque-Veronese school*, crucifix from S. Silvestro (857) 196; crucifix (257) 196; *Veronese school*, detached frescoes 194; frescoes from St. Eufemia (565, 567—570), 200[1]; panel from Sta. Caterina, the mystical marriage of St. Catherine (356) **194**, 312[2]; panel with scenes from the Old Testament from Sta. Caterina (362) 195; triptych (257) 196; St. Mamaso

GEOGRAPHICAL INDEX.

(124) 200; Madonna, saints and St. Wilgefortis crucified (545) 200[1].
Chapter House Library, *Veronese school,* miniatures **208**.
Maffei coll. (dispersed), *Veneziano, Lorenzo —,* panel 39.

Public Buildings.
Palazzo Comunale, *Maestro Cigogna,* frescoes, v. Gallery.
Scala Palace, *Altichiero and Avanzo,* active 126, 127, 127[5]; *Bressano, Ottaviano —,* active 127[5], *Guariento,* active 127[5].
Vertemate (near Como).
Abbey church, *Lombard school,* frescoes 254.
Verucchio.
S. Agostino, *Caterino and Niccolo di Pietro,* crucifix 60, 76; *Riminese school,* crucifix 348.
Vezzolano.
Abbey, *Piedmontese school of the 13th cent.,* frescoes 274; idem *middle 14th cent.* **273**, 276, 277.
Viboldone (near Milan).
Church, *Giovanni da Milano, school of —,* frescoes in the choir 220, 242, 243, 244; *Lombard school,* frescoes in the nave 244.
Vicenza 109.
S. Agostino, *Battista da Vicenza,* polyptych, v. Gallery, Vicenza.
Cathedral, *Veneziano, Lorenzo —,* polyptych 39, 43, 52, 53, 86.
Sta. Corona, frescoes on the tombs of the Thiene 108, 162.
S. Francesco, *Maestro Paolo,* Death of the Virgin, v. Gallery.
Gallery, *Battista da Vicenza,* polyptych from S. Agostino (17) **106**; Madonna (23) 108; four scenes from the legend of St. Sylvester (13—16) 108; saints (18—22) 108; *Maestro Paolo,* Death of the Virgin from S. Francesco (157) 5, **7**, 9, 15.
Vienna.
Imperial Museum, *Tommaso da Modena,* panels from Karlstein, v. Karlstein; *Veneziano, Lorenzo —,* polyptych, v. Accademia, Venice; *Milanese school,* miniatures 208[3].
Collection of the late Archduke Ferdinand of Austria, portraits of the Scala family from the Pitti Palace, Florence 126[1].
Lichtenstein coll., *Baronzio, school of —,* Adoration, Crucifixion and saints **341**; *Caterino,* lost panel of the Madonna and the Twelve Apostles from the Corpus Domini church, Venice 64.
Villa (near Rimini).
Riminese school, crucifix 348.
Vimercate (near Bergamo).
S. Francesco monastery, *Giottesque-Lombard school,* frescoes 218.
Viterbo.
Palazzo Gentile, *Baronzio,* Descent from the Cross **326**.
Voghera v. Potasso.
Worcester, (U. S. A.)
Museum, *Lombard school,* Madonna, saints and donor 258; *Veneto-Byzantine school,* Last Judgment 37.
Zara 98.
S. Crisogono, *Veneto-Byzantine school,* crucifix **94**.
S. Demetrio, *Clericopulo, Joannes —,* lost picture 98.
S. Francesco Monastery, *Venetian school,* polyptych 97; *Venetian school of the 13th cent.,* miniatures 91; idem, *14th cent.,* miniatures 91—92.
Sta. Maria, *Veneto-Byzantine school,* Madonna and St. Peter **94**.
Paravia Library, *Venetian school,* miniatures in the register of the Scuola S. Giovanni 92; *Bartolo di Fredi,* crucifix 94, 98; *Venetian school of the 15th cent.,* polyptych 96.
Zevio 124.

INDEX OF ARTISTS.

The more important passages are indicated by bold faced numbers.

Alberengo, Jacobello —, 58, **84**, 95.
Alberti di Ferrara, Antonio —, 470.
Altichiero, 110, 118, 119, **124—162**, 164, 174, 175, 176, 178, 181, 184[1], 195, 197, 198, 201, 202, 204, 205, 207, 243[1], 262, 268, 426.
Ambrogio, son of Bittino da Faenza, 502.
Andrea de' Bartoli, 418, 428.
Andrea da Bologna, 88, 414, 424[2], **427 - 436**, 458, 480.
Andrea da Firenze, 234, 238[2].
Angelino di Corrado di Novarello, 428[1].
Angelus, 68.
Anovelo da Imbonate, miniaturist, 266[1].
Antonio Giacomelli da Imola, 294.
Antonio da Mestre, sculptor, 197.
Antonio da Padova, 162, 163, 164.
Antonius pictor, 179.
Arconerio, Giacomo —, 273.
Aretino, Spinello —, 175.
Avanzi, Jacopo —, 127, 414, 416, **416**, 420, 424, 425, 426, 426[1], 450, 466[1].
Avanzi, pseudo-Jacopo —, (v. Jacopo), 414, 420, **420—427**, 480, 480[1].
Avanzo, Jacopo —, 110, 111, 118, **124—162**, 174, 175, 176, 176[1], 178, 202, 207, 262, 269, 426.
Baldassare, 503.
Barisino dei Barisini, 355.
Baronzio, Giovanni —, 292, 294, 294[3], 313, **314—328**, 328[1], 329, 329[1], 338, 340, 341, 350, 353, 424, 496.
Barnaba da Modena, 355, 358, 368, **368—384**, 384, 386, 392.
Bartolinus De Placentia, v. Bertolino da Piacenza.
Bartolo di Maestro Fredi, 29, 94, 98, 258[4].
Bartolomeo di Maestro Paolo, 60.
Bartolomeo di S. Stefano, 4.
Bartolomeus pictor quondam Magistri Nicolai, 179, 179[2].

Bassanolo de Magneris, **258**.
Battista, son of Jacopo da Verona, 176.
Battista da Vicenza, 7[1], 106, 109.
Beltranimo, 436[1].
Bertolino del quondam Jacopo di Brescia, 178[1].
Bertolino da Piacenza, 505, 507.
Bestello da Forli, 504.
Bindino da Faenza, 294.
Bittino da Faenza, 281[1], 306[3], **502**, 502.
Bonane, 355.
Bonifacio, 355.
Boninsegna de Clocego, 179, 188[1].
Bolognese, Franco —, miniaturist, 293, 293[1].
Botticelli, Sandro —, 238[2].
Brasavola, Donato —, 482.
Bressano, Ottaviano —, 127[5].
Buffalmacco, 470.
Canellus, 479[1].
Casella, Polidoro—, 218[4], 265[2].
Caterino, 15, 27, **59—64**, 68, 74, 78, 80, 87, 91.
Caterino di Maestro Andrea, sculptor, 59, 60.
Cavallini, Pietro —, 279, 284[3], 288[1], 292, 294, 298, 304, 312[2], 313, 328, 341, 351, 352, 353.
Ceccolo di Giovanni, 430[2].
Ciciolo, Paolino —, 294.
Cimabue, 184[1], 492.
Clericopulo, Joannes —, 98.
Cortese, Cristoforo —, 91, 94.
Cristoforo da Bologna, 406, 408, **412**, 469[2].
Cristoforo da Ferrara, v. Cristoforo da Bologna.
Crivelli, 119.
Daddi, Bernardo —, 164, 165, 166, 240, 436.
Dalmasio, Lippo —, 80, 397, 403, 404, 438, 451[1], **452—463**, 468, 474, 479, 480, 481[1].
Daniel, 179, 179[1].
Davanzo, Jacopo —, v. Avanzo.
Deodato Giovanello da Imola, 398.

Diana, Benedetto —, 48.
Diddo, Bartolommeo —, 355.
Diddo, Giovanni —, 355.
Donato, father of Niccolo Semitecolo, 120.
Donato di SanVitale, 15, 27, **59–64**.
Duccio, 39.
Francesco. 2,
Francesco detto il Maestro Giotto, 500.
Francesco da Rimini, 294, **346**, 352, 424.
Franco da Bologna, 396, 397, 398, 400.
Franco de Veris, 264.
Fusculus, Frater —. 294.
Gaddi, Agnolo —, 72, 175, 222, 254.
Gaddi, Taddeo —, 72¹, 163³, 166, 222, 222³, 224, 224², 225.
Galante da Bologna, 463.
Galassi, 483¹.
Galasso ferrarese, 482, 483, 483¹.
Gelasio di Niccolo della Masnada di S. Giorgio, 482.
Gentile da Fabriano, 474.
Georgi, M., v. Maestro Giuseppe.
Gerardo, 179.
Ghissi, Francescuccio —, 434, 458.
Giacomo da Riva, 179, **197**.
Giangolino, 294.
Giotto, 15, 16, 39, 66², 90, 102, 110, 122, 123, 158, 160, 161, 170, 175, 179², 181, 184, 184¹, 188, 189, 194, 195, 201, 206, 209, 212, 214, 215, 216, 218, 220, 224, 240, 244, 246, 268, 269, 279¹, 284, 284³, 292, 294³, 295, 298, 298², 304, 304², 313, 314, 318, 340, 342, 346, 349, 350, 351, 352, 353, 482, 498, 503.
Giottino, 238².
Giovanni, son of Gaddi, Taddeo —, 222.
Giovanni, son of Jaquerio, Pietro —, 273.
Giovanni, son of Maestro Paolo, v. Giovannino.
Giovanni di Alinerio. 294.
Giovanni di Benedetto, 238², **270**.
Giovanni del Biondo, 225¹.
Giovanni da Bologna, 64, **77–82**, 386.
Giovanni di Canelo, 82, 463, 477.
Giovanni de' Grassi, 209, 222, 264, 272.
Giovanni di Maestro Nicola, 428¹
Giovanni di Menabuoi, father of Giusto, 163.
Giovanni da Milano, 209, **220–243**, 243¹, 244, 255, 258, 261, 262, 264, 268, 269, 271, 274, 276, 470, 476, 492.
Giovanni da Padova, 163, 164.
Giovanni de Venetia, 35.
Giovanni quondam Ser Viano, 104.
Giovanni di Zanello, v. Giovanni di Canelo.
Giovannino, son of Maestro Paolo, 5, 6, 14.
Giuliano da Rimini, 297, 292, 294, 298¹, **300**, 315, 316, 328, 343, 350³, 353, 354, 494.
Giuliano da Urbino, 300².
Giusto di Menabuoi, 152, **162–175**, 176, 178, 178¹.
Giusto da Padova, v. Giusto di Menabuoi.
Gregorio, 294.
Guariento, 58, 66², 91, **110–120**, 122, 127, 127⁵, 128, 152¹, 161, 178, 196.
Guarnerius de Venitiis, 109¹.
Guglielmo da Forli, 503.
Guglielmo degli Organi, v. Guglielmo da Forli.
Guglielmus, 38.
Guido, 273
Gulielmus, **38**.
Jacobello di Bonomo, 58, **85**.
Jacobello del Fiore, 23³, 86, 87.
Jacobi da Como, Johannes —, v. Giovanni da Milano.
Jacopino de' Bavosi, 418, 419.
Jacopino de' Pappasoni, 418.
Jacopo, v. Jacopo Avanzi, pseudo-Jacopo —, 418, 419, 420, 420¹, **426**, 482.
Jacopo del Casentino, 222.
Jacopo di Guido, father of Giovanni da Milano, 221.
Jacopo di Paolo, 43, 288², 402, 416, 418, **463–469**, 470, 474, 480, 480¹, 494¹, corrections.
Jacopo da Verona, 127, 152, **176–178**, 179.
Jaquerio, Giovanni —, son of Jaquerio, Pietro —, **273**.
Jaquerio, Giovanni —, grandson of Jaquerio, Pietro —, 273
Jaquerio, Pietro —, 273.
Johannes pictor de Kaverzaio, v. Giovanni da Milano.
Lamberto, son of Jacopo da Verona, 176.
Lattanzio da Rimini, 502.
Lola, Francesco —, 470, 476.
Lorenzetti, Pietro —, 50, 52, 296, 340 ¹ and ².

INDEX OF ARTISTS.

Luca, son of Maestro Paolo, 5.
Luca d' Antonio di Mona, 476.
Luca da Perugia, **476**.
Maestro, v. Master.
Manno, 408.
Magister Johannes, 294.
Marco, brother of Maestro Paolo, 5.
Marco, son of Maestro Paolo, 7.
Marco de Lencisa, 294.
Marino, 178^1.
Martinello, 100.
Martini, Simone —, 82, 98, 149, 255, 397, 480^1.
Martino da Verona, 179, **197**.
Masaccio, 243.
Maso da Faenza, 294.
Maso-Giottino, 238^2,
Master of Chioggia, v. Master of the Pirano altar-piece.
Master Cicogna, **179**.
Master Cicogna, v. Master Cicogna.
Master Giuseppe, 266^4.
Master Paolo, 4, **5—17**, 19, 20, 21, 23, 26, 27, 35, 39, 42, 57, 58, 60, 68, 82^3, 90, 122, 123.
Master Paolo, Venetian sculptor, 464.
Master of the Pirano altar-piece, **19—25**, 35, 42, 46, 48, 56^1, 57, 64, 66, 90.
Master of the Triumph of Death (Traini?), 382
Memmi, Lippo —, 149, 264.
Michele di Ronco di Milano, 218^2.
Miginio, 294.
Monaco, Lorenzo —, 406^2.
Nanne da Ravenna, 294.
Nardo di Cione, 238^2.
Nason, Bartolomeo —, 4.
Naxon, Cà —, v. Nason, Bartolomeo —.
Nelli Ottaviano, 183^1, 476^1.
Nerio the Miniaturist, 294.
Niccolo, 505, 506.
Niccolo di Giacomo, 396, **410**, 424, 438, 440, 440^2, 480, 480^1.
Niccolo di Giacomo, pseudo —, 411.
Niccolo di Maestro Paolo, 463.
Niccolo di Pietro, 60, **72—77**, 91, 179^2.
Niccolo di Pietro, v. Semitecolo, Niccolo —.
Niccolo di Pietro Patecchi, 355.
Niccolo da Reggio, 355, 505.
Niccolo di Santi, grand-father of Niccolo di Pietro, 74.
Niccolo da Voltri, 382^1, 384.
Niccolo da Zara, 17.

Nicholas filius magistri Petri, v. Niccolo di Pietro.
Nicolas de Jadra, 98.
Nicolaus, 102.
Nicolo, 41.
Nuzi, Allegretto —, 43, 54, 238^2, 329^1, 434, 436. 458.
Oderisi da Gubbio, 292, 293^1, 396, 397, 398, 400.
Orcagna, 241, 502.
Orso, 463.
Otonello, Antonio —, 455.
Ottaviano da Faenza, 498.
Pace da Bologna, 428^1.
Pace da Faenza, 498, 500.
Paolo, 306.
Paolo da Modena, Fra —, 355, **390**
Paolo, pittore, 294.
Petecchi, v. Niccolo di Pietro Patecchi.
Paxino, v. Pierino de Nova.
Pecino, v. Pierino de Nova.
Petrus, 398.
Pierino de Nova, 218^2.
Pietro, son of Pietro di Novarra, 273.
Pietro di Giovanni (de Tovaglis?), 451^1.
Pietro di Niccolo, father of Niccolo di Pietro, 74.
Pietro da Rimini, 279^1, 294, 316, 324^1, **338**.
Pinsis, Franciscus —, 2.
Pisanello, 126^3, 208^2, 265.
Poja, 178.
Rambaldo, Laudadio —, 482.
Raniero da Porte, 355.
Rastello da Forli, 294.
Reni, Guido —, 456.
Semitecolo, Niccolo —, 58, 64, 77, 119, **120**, 124, 161, 178, 206.
Serafini, Paolo —, 355, **388**, 392.
Serafini, Serafino —, 355, **384 — 388**, 392
Simone da Corbetta. **257**.
Simone dei Crocifissi, 396, 406, 414, 418, 419, 420, 420^1, 422^3, **438—452**, 453, 456, 458, 463, 469, 479, 480, 480^1, 482.
Simone da Cusighe, 65, **100**.
Simone dal Peron, v. Simone da Cusighe.
Stefano, 268.
Stefano Pievan di S. Agnese, v. Stefano plebanus.
Stefano plebanus, 9, 58, **66**.
Stefano da Zevio, 124, 196, 198, 200, 200^1, 209.

Taddeo di Bartolo, 183^1, 195, 382^1, 384.
Theodoric of Prague, 356, 362, 364, 366.
Theophanes, 482.
Tommaso da Faenza, 294.
Tommaso da Modena, 100, 198, 202, 265, 266^4, 342, 355, **355 - 368**, 384, 386, 392.
Traini, v. Master of the Triumph of the Death.
Turineto, 273.
Turone, 155, 179, **181**.
Ugolino, 355, 355^2.
Veneto, Nicolo —, 120.
Veneziano, Antonio —, 162.

Veneziano, Lorenzo —, 7, 8, 9, 35, **39—58**, 62, 63, 64, 77, 78, 80, 81, 82, 84, 85, 86, 87, 91, 95, 104, 106.
Veneziano, Stefano —, 23.
Vitale da Bologna, 40, 80, 387, **398—410**, 412, 413, 438, 440, 442, 458, 463, 469, 470, 480, 480^1, 190, 494, 494^1.
Vivarini, Alvise —, 56, 70, 101.
Wurmser, Nicolas —, 358^1, 364.
Zagnonus, 294.
Zangolo, 294.
Zanino di Pietro, **70**.
Zeno pictor, son of Martino da Verone, 198.